*National Traditions of Opera*
General editor: John Warrack

# Czech Opera

*National Traditions of Opera*
General editor: John Warrack

*National Traditions of Opera* is a series which aims to study the development of
the genre in individual European countries. Volumes planned and in preparation cover France, Russia, Italy and Germany. Since each country has made a
very different contribution to operatic history, no systematic pattern of treatment has been imposed on authors; rather they have been asked to find the
method that will best provide an account of the manner in which each country's opera has reflected its character, history and culture. Considerations that
have been borne in mind are therefore not only musicological but literary,
historical, political, social and economic, in an attempt to determine what it is
that has shaped each particular tradition. Other matters discussed have been
language, in some cases folk music and folk traditions, national epic and
legend, the growth of national musical institutions, and much else that has
had a bearing on the expression of national character in opera. Naturally it
has also been necessary to view these matters in the context of the international development of opera. It is intended that the books should be of
value to the opera goer no less than to students and scholars.

A Czech bagpiper from the Strakonice area, a lithograph (1817–19) by Antonín
Machek included in the manuscript memoirs of J. Jeník z Bratřic, *Paměti-
hodno*, vi. Unlike the Scottish bagpipe, the Czech bagpipe is usually blown
entirely by an arm bellows, the animal origin of the 'bag' is all too evident.
Strakonice, in southern Bohemia, was well known for its bagpiping tradition; the
legend of Švanda the bagpiper arose from here in the eighteenth and early
nineteenth centuries and provided a powerful symbol of Czech musicianship
(see p. 163).

# Czech Opera

## JOHN TYRRELL

*Lecturer in music*
*University of Nottingham*

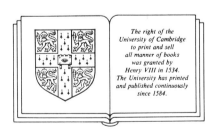

The right of the
University of Cambridge
to print and sell
all manner of books
was granted by
Henry VIII in 1534.
The University has printed
and published continuously
since 1584.

## CAMBRIDGE UNIVERSITY PRESS

*Cambridge*
*New York    New Rochelle    Melbourne    Sydney*

Published by the Press Syndicate of the University of Cambridge
The Pitt Building, Trumpington Street, Cambridge CB2 1RP
32 East 57th Street, New York, NY 10022, USA
10 Stamford Road, Oakleigh, Melbourne 3166, Australia

First published 1988

Printed in Great Britain at
the University Press, Cambridge

*British Library cataloguing in publication data*
Tyrrell, John
Czech opera. – (National traditions of opera).
1. Opera – Czechoslovakia – History and
criticism
I. Title II. Series
782.1'09437   ML1724

*Library of Congress cataloguing in publication data*
Tyrrell, John.
Czech opera.
(National traditions of opera)
Bibliography.
Includes index.
1. Opera – Czechoslovakia. I. Title. II. Series.
ML1724.T95   1988   782.1'09437   87–21825

ISBN 0 521 23531 6 hardcovers

ME

# Contents

# Illustrations

The illustrations appear by kind permission of the following: National Museum, Prague: Central Library (Frontispiece and no. 11); National Museum, Prague: Museum of Czech Music (nos. 1–4 and 7); National Museum, Prague: Theatre Division (nos. 5, 13b and 13c); Moravian Museum, Brno: Music History Division (no. 6); Mrs Zuzana Švabinská (no. 8).

# Preface

Czech opera, in a recent definition, is 'every work in this musical genre written by a composer of Czech origin' (Vysloužil 1980, 193). My book is conceived on a more modest scale: I take Czech opera simply to be opera composed to Czech texts. A more difficult question is where to start and where to end. Here I have been guided by the title of this series, 'National Traditions of Opera', and have taken as a significant beginning the opening of the Provisional Theatre in Prague in 1862. This, for the first time, allowed a continuous tradition of writing and performing opera in Czech to flourish. I have nevertheless sketched in the erratic developments in Czech opera before this date, though without the wholesale reappraisal that this early period needs.

It would be possible to argue that this study should end in 1918, when with the attainment of political self-determination by the Czechs the chief goal of the Czech national movement had been achieved. But such a date would leave one of Czech opera's greatest luminaries, Leoš Janáček, in mid-career and exclude the mature masterpieces of his old age. I have therefore pressed on until his death in 1928 and at the same time added for comparison the postwar operas of his contemporaries Foerster, Novák and Ostrčil. I have resisted the temptation to venture further into the century to take in another prominent twentieth-century Czech opera composer, Bohuslav Martinů. Despite the nostalgic Czechness of the music Martinů wrote during his long exile, many of his operas were composed in languages other than Czech and for audiences outside Czechoslovakia. Whether such works fall into the Czech national tradition is a fascinating question but one that I leave to others to pursue. My book is thus in essence a study of opera in Czech from Smetana to Janáček.

Of these two composers the better known outside Czechoslovakia today is Janáček, who, much more than his predecessors, was able to break through the language barrier into the international repertory. One of the purposes of this book is to examine his place in a Czech operatic tradition. This is a topic often ignored in discussions of Janáček, partly because after *Jenůfa* his choice of subject matter became so wide-ranging and eclectic that his Czechness apparently receded into the background: it is possible to come to emotional terms with a late Janáček opera with no knowledge at all of Czech nineteenth-century opera. Janáček, however, began as a committed nationalist composer and his first two operas fit into existing nationalist moulds. This book provides an opportunity to discuss these early works in context and to see what remained of the context in the later composer.

Though Janáček and Smetana, together with Dvořák and Fibich, naturally dominate the discussion, this does not mean that I have excluded their contemporaries. This book aims to be less a study of the operas of great composers than a study of a period of Czech cultural history in which opera is the grandest but by no means the only artistic manifestation. From this point of view the contributions of lesser figures are just as interesting and revealing as those of more substantial composers. Equally revealing is the interrelation of Czech opera with other forms of cultural expression. The period which saw the establishment of a Czech tradition in opera coincides with the final phase of the development of a Czech national awareness. Many of the operas of the period were written as a conscious expression of this nationalism, others reflect it unconsciously or had nationalist elements read into them by a community denied significant political expression and used to thinking in code. Any Czech opera of the period is inevitably full of extra-musical associations buttressing its claims as distinctively Czech, and any study of these works needs a broader approach than the purely musical. Accordingly, while a survey of the composers of Czech opera and the various genres and styles they cultivated is offered in Chapter 3, this is placed in its cultural context, preceded by a brief account of the Czech nationalist movement (Chapter 1) and of the history of Czech theatre (Chapter 2). The role of Czech librettists is discussed in Chapter 4 and the impact of the Czech language on Czech verse and on its musical setting is examined in Chapter 8. The remaining chapters are devoted to other areas in which Czech opera is particularly distinctive: its subject matter (Chapter 5), its characters and voice types (Chapter 6) and the role of folk music (Chapter 7).

# Acknowledgements

The initial research for this book was made possible by a grant from the British Academy and a sabbatical from my post at the University of Nottingham. My thanks are due to both institutions, and to my colleagues at Nottingham for their support. During the writing of the book I was stimulated by two conferences which I attended in 1984: the symposium 'Povědomí tradice v novodobé české kultuře' (the third of an annual series of interdisciplinary meetings organized in Plzeň jointly by the Prague National Gallery and the Czechoslovak Academy of Sciences: Institute of the Theory and History of Art) and the Smetana Centennial in San Diego, organized by Professor Jaroslav Mráček. The former greatly enlarged my knowledge of Czech nineteenth-century culture; the latter acquainted me at first hand with the work of American scholars of Czech music. I am much indebted to both Dr Milan Pospíšil and Professor Mráček for inviting me.

This book was commissioned twelve years ago and during that time it has seen out two heads of music books at Cambridge University Press. To all three – Claire Davies-Jones, Rosemary Dooley and Penny Souster – I am grateful for their good advice and above all for their patience. Even greater forbearance was shown by John Warrack, who, as series editor, has known the book from its earliest beginnings right through to completion and has been at all times a source of reassurance, wisdom and warm encouragement.

During such a long period an author runs up many debts. Not all can be mentioned here, but I would like in particular to record my thanks to the following institutions for library facilities and for supplying microfilms, xeroxes, photographs and other materials: in Brno: Moravian Museum, Music History Division; Music Information Centre; in Prague: Czechoslovak Academy of Sciences, Institute of the Theory and History of Art, Musicology Section; National Museum, Museum of Czech Music; National Museum, Theatre Division; National Theatre, Music Archive; Czechoslovak Radio; Theatre Institute; State Library, Music Division. I would like to thank Mrs Zuzana Švabinská for her kind permission to reproduce her father's sketch of Otakar Hostinský and the following libraries and firms for permission to reproduce photographs, music and other materials: Universal Edition, Vienna; Moravian Museum, Music History Division, Brno; British Library, London; National Museum, Prague.

I am particularly grateful to the following individuals for their help and advice: Dr Josef Bek, Mrs Dokoupilová, Dr Eva Drlíková, Mr Daniel Freeman, Dr Jana Fojtíková, Dr Eva Herrmannová, Mrs Hrubešová, Dr Michaela Kopecká, Dr Vojtěch Kyas, Dr Jitka Ludvová, Mr Nový, Dr Jitřenka Pešková, Dr Milan Poštolka CSc, Dr Svatava Přibáňová, Mrs Prokopcová, Dr Oldřich Pulkert, Dr Milada Rutová, Mr Josef Šeba, Dr Jiří Sehnal CSc, Dr Anna Šerých, Mrs Skládanková, Mr Jan Smaczny, Dr Miloš Štedroň, Mr Václav Štěpán CSc, Mrs Alena Valšubová, Mr Paul Wingfield, Dr Petr Vít, Dr Eva Vítová, Dr Tomislav Volek.

I need to give especial thanks to friends and colleagues, Jim Friedman, Ruth Thackeray, Audrey Twine, Michael Hall and Michael Beckerman, who have read parts or all of the manuscript and who made many valuable suggestions for improvements. Dr Marta Ottlová, Dr Milan Pospíšil and Dr Alena Němcová also read the manuscript, corrected many factual errors, and over a long period generously supplied me with information, books, xeroxes, records and many other materials. Without their help and interest this book could hardly have been written.

Twenty years ago, as a young research student, I spent my first Christmas in Czechoslovakia. One of the many kindnesses I received then was a present in the form of Nejedlý's two-volume history of the Prague National Theatre. The books had accompanied their former owner, JUDr Václav Křepelka, through many vicissitudes and have now done good service on my shelves. I could have had no better gift to demonstrate the central position of opera in Czech culture. To Dr Křepelka and all his compatriots who over twenty years have made me so welcome and my regular visits to their country such a pleasure this book is intended as a sincere gesture of my thanks.

JOHN TYRRELL

*Nottingham, May 1987*

# Note on music examples

Tempo and metre markings are shown in two ways:
  (1) without brackets: the composer's marking at that point in the score;
  (2) in brackets: the composer's marking at an earlier point in the score.

Orchestral accompaniments, when shown, are given in piano reduction. Indications of instrumentation are made only when this is important to the point of the example. All instruments are notated at pitch.

Consistency in showing the locations of music examples has been sacrificed in favour of helpfulness. Act and scene numbers are always given (e.g. 1, 2 = Act 1 Scene 2) but in the cases where critical editions exist (all of Smetana's operas, and some of Dvořák's), bar numbers have been added (e.g. 1, 2. 200 = Act 1 Scene 2, bar 200). In other cases where there is only one printed edition, and hence no ambiguity, page-number references are given (e.g. VS 15 = p. 15 of the vocal score concerned).

Music examples for works still in copyright appear by kind permission of the copyright owners, Universal Edition AG, Wien. Examples from Janáček's *Šárka* (pp. 293–7) appear by kind permission of the Moravian Museum, Brno: Music History Division.

# Note on terms, titles of works and currency

## Czech; Bohemian; Moravian; Czechoslovak

Bohemia and Moravia have for centuries been twin provinces, sharing a common language and culture, though differing in regional dialect and customs. Collectively, and rather clumsily, they are referred to in English as 'the Czech lands'. Together with Slovakia (whose inhabitants speak Slovak, a language closely related to Czech), they make up Czechoslovakia, which became an independent republic in 1918.

English uses two adjectives to refer to Bohemia and its people: 'Bohemian', deriving from what the Romans thought that the earlier Celtic inhabitants of the area called themselves, and 'Czech', deriving from what the present Slavonic inhabitants call themselves. In this book the two words are used in two different ways – 'Bohemian' as a geographical term, 'Czech' as an ethnic and linguistic one. 'Bohemian' refers to the inhabitants of Bohemia (irrespective of what language they speak); 'Czech' refers to the Czech-speaking inhabitants of both Bohemia and Moravia and to their common language. Bohemians, such as Smetana and Dvořák, and Moravians, such as Janáček, are all Czech composers. Of these three Janáček alone lived long enough to become also a Czechoslovak composer (after 1918).

## Solo ensemble; choral ensemble

By the term 'solo ensemble' I mean a texture made up of the combination of two or more solo voices. By 'choral ensemble' I mean a texture that includes solo voices and chorus.

## Titles of works

I refer to all Czech operas by English titles. Their full Czech titles, together with other details, are given in the List of Czech Operas on p. 321. All other Czech works are given both in English and Czech at their first appearance in the text, thereafter in English. Dates following titles of works are, unless stated otherwise, of their first performance.

# Currency

The currency referred to throughout the book is the Austrian Gulden or florin, known in Czech as a *zlatník* (abbreviation zl.). From 1811, when a new standard was established, until the First World War there were approximately ten Gulden to one pound sterling. It is difficult to give any realistic modern equivalent, but as a guide I offer a few figures.

In 1847 the average weekly wage for a working man in Bohemia was 5.22 zl., somewhat less than the average of 11s. a week in England. The writer Josef Štolba reported that his father, a clerk, earned 1000 zl. a year. Most musicians in Prague were rather worse off. When the Provisional Theatre opened in 1862, a member of the chorus was paid 120–80 zl. a year; the chorusmaster, soloists and second conductor 240 zl. a year and the chief conductor 600 zl. a year. At the end of the century a young soloist, Berta Lautererová (the wife of the composer J.B. Foerster) received 1800 zl. a year, though after pension deductions she received only 95 zl. a month and from that she had to pay for her own costumes.

Foerster was taken on as the critic of a daily newspaper in the 1890s at 25 zl. a month, and this was raised to 50 zl. after two years. Züngel received 60 zl. as an outright payment for his libretto for *The Two Widows*, Srb 50 zl. for each opera libretto translation he made and Rozkošný 100 zl. for the publication of the vocal score of his opera *St John's Rapids*. Bendl received 10 zl. as an outright payment for a single song. The same 10 zl. in 1886 bought the newly published vocal score of *Dimitrij*, a considerable increase on the 3 zl. at which the first published Czech vocal score, *The Bartered Bride*, was priced fourteen years earlier.

(Information drawn from: R.L. Bidwell: *Currency Conversion Tables* (London, 1970); Kimball 1966, 31, 44; Heller 1918, 44; Bartoš 1938, 27; Bráfová 1913, 37–8; Foerster 1929, 259, 309; Züngel 1962, 16, 22; Žižka 1939, 13, 18, 36, 44; Dolanský 1918, 220)

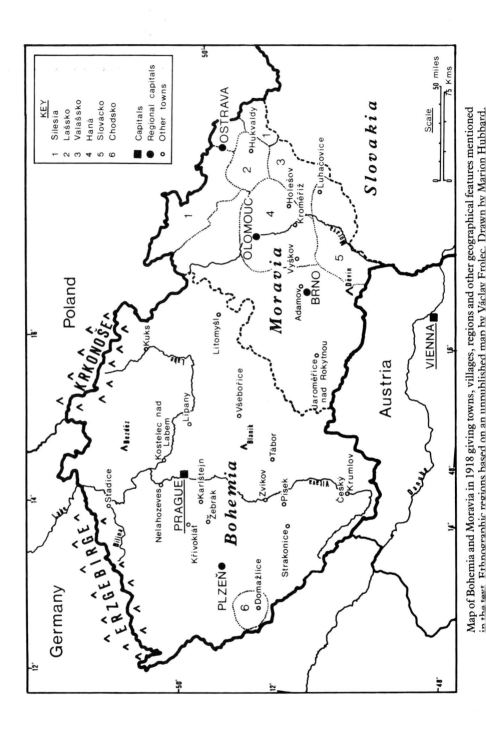

Map of Bohemia and Moravia in 1918 giving towns, villages, regions and other geographical features mentioned in the text. Ethnographic regions based on an unpublished map by Václav Frolec. Drawn by Marion Hubbard.

# 1. Czech nationalism

Já ale pravím: Nelze déle
tu trpěti cizácké sbory.
Už potřebí se chopit zbraně
a vyhnat z vlasti Branibory,
již hubí zem, náš jazyk tupí,
pod jejichž mečem národ úpí!

(But I say this: we can no longer tolerate foreign hordes here. We must now take up arms and drive the Brandenburgers from our homeland. They are destroying our country, blunting our language and under their sword the nation suffers!)

So begins Smetana's first opera, *The Brandenburgers in Bohemia*. The libretto provides a number of situations in thirteenth-century Bohemia (then occupied by the German Brandenburgers) that Smetana's nineteenth-century Czech contemporaries would easily be able to apply to their own times. Like the Brandenburgers, the Austrian Habsburgs were occupying Bohemia. But before the Habsburg domination the Czechs could look back to centuries of independence. By the fourteenth century the native Přemyslid dynasty had died out and new rulers from outside were elected. Under the Luxembourg dynasty, in particular the great king and Holy Roman Emperor Charles IV (1346–78), Bohemia developed into a European power. Its capital Prague, a Gothic city of great beauty, was the third largest in Europe with the first university (1348) to be established north of the Alps after Paris, Oxford and Cambridge. Later dynasties such as the Polish Jagellons proved less effective, while the Habsburgs, elected in 1526, soon showed themselves to have no interest in preserving the integrity and traditions of the historical crownlands of Bohemia, Moravia and Silesia. The last Habsburg monarch to have his seat in Prague was Rudolf II, and his reign (1576–1612) was a period of cultural and scientific flowering. But the anti-Habsburg rebellion, in essence a power struggle between Catholic absolutism and a Protestant oligarchy, came to a head under Rudolf's intolerant successor, and the political incompetence of the Czech aristocracy led to its defeat at the Battle of the White Mountain in 1620, as significant a date to the Czechs as 1066 is to the English. It marks the end of the Czechs' power to elect their own ruler and the end of their freedom in an independent kingdom.

During the next two centuries the Czech lands became increasingly integrated within the Habsburg Empire. The most tangible differences

1

between the Czechs and the Austrians – language and religion – were eroded. The enforced re-Catholicization of the Czechs began almost immediately after the Habsburg victory and was consolidated in 1624 through such measures as handing over Prague University to the Jesuits. As a result many Czechs fled the country, the first of many subsequent waves of Czech emigration. Over language the Austrians trod more cautiously. There had always been Germans in the area, particularly in the border lands settled by Germans (much later to become notorious as the Sudeten Germans), and in the second half of the thirteenth century a Přemyslid king, Přemysl Otakar II, had systematically encouraged skilled German craftsmen to settle in his kingdom. Unlike the Flemings and Huguenots in Britain, the Germans had resisted integration and after 1620 the German minority gained increasing power – in the towns in civil and governmental administration, and as landowners. But the Bohemian Diet continued to issue some patents in Czech into the eighteenth century and it was not until Joseph II's reforms towards the end of the century that Czech, as a language of educated people, was dealt a near death blow. In 1780 Czech was abolished in grammar schools; four years later German replaced Latin as the administrative language of the empire.

Public decree was reinforced by private ambition. The fluent command of German needed for professional and government posts meant that Czech parents began to use German in the home to better their children's chances. By the middle of the nineteenth century the Czech middle class was almost completely Germanized. German language and habits were accepted as those of a superior society, with Czech increasingly regarded as the primitive language of peasants and servants.

Some idea of the stranglehold of German on the Czech lands at this time can be gained by considering the linguistic background of the chief Czech opera composers of the nineteenth century. Smetana (1824–84), Dvořák (1841–1904), Fibich (1850–1900) and to some extent Janáček (1854–1928) were all educated in German. All wrote their early vocal works in German: in Fibich's case, three juvenile operas and over a hundred Schumannesque lieder; in Dvořák's case his first opera, *Alfred*. Smetana kept his diary in German into the 1860s. He wrote to his wife and her family in German whilst in one of his first surviving letters in Czech, to his friend Ludevít Procházka (11 March 1860; Löwenbach 1914, 5–6), he endearingly apologized to him for his mistakes in grammar and orthography. He continued to make such mistakes for the rest of his life. Two of his most overtly nationalist operas, *Dalibor* and *Libuše*, were written to texts translated from German. Even such a fervent nationalist as Janáček, later chauvinistically to boycott German trams and the German opera house in Brno, wrote all his love letters to his future wife in German.

Czech survived by its teaching at village schools and by the secret reading

2

of the Kralice Bible (1579–94), the humanistic culmination of two centuries of Czech bible translations and a codification of the language comparable to that achieved in English by the King James Bible. But if Czech were ever to become a means of expressing Czech nationalist ambitions it was necessary to re-establish its intellectual credibility and to revitalize as a medium of intellectual and literary discourse a language abandoned by most Czech writers in the eighteenth century. Ironically, it was in German that the first battles for the revival of the language were fought. The first Czech grammar (1809), by Josef Dobrovský, and the first volume (1836) of František Palacký's history of the Czech nation both appeared in German. These, together with Josef Jungmann's Czech–German dictionary (1834–9), represent the intellectual foundations of the Czech National Revival (Národní obrození) in the nineteenth century.

Writers followed. The first literary milestone of the new period is generally taken to be a Byronic narrative poem, *May (Máj)*, published in 1836, the year of the death of its author, Karel Hynek Mácha, at the age of twenty-six. Equally influential in shaping Czech sensibilities were Božena Němcová's *The Grandmother (Babička*, 1855), a novel of Czech country life, and Karel Jaromír Erben's elaboration of folk beliefs in his beautifully crafted ballads, published as a collection, *A Garland of National Tales (Kytice z pověstí národních)*, in 1853. These works have lost none of their popularity with Czech readers, nor their potency as an evocation of the Czech countryside, its people, its customs and its folk mythology.

The effect of a burgeoning Czech literature, together with the influential models of nationalist movements elsewhere, particularly among other Slav peoples such as the Poles, was to encourage or even create a Czech national consciousness. Previously inert material now became invested with a warm glow of nationalist sentiment that could be appealed to for patriotic purposes. Images of historical rulers and the past glory of the nation, of a civilization with a sophisticated literature stretching back into the distant past, or of a contented Czech countryside with its own distinct way of life, customs and music, were carefully fostered and imprinted on the minds of a susceptible Czech community.

An excellent example is the treatment of the Libuše legend. Up to the early nineteenth century this story, though purporting to relate to a Czech princess, the legendary founder of Prague (see pp. 135–41), was taken up by Italians, Germans and Czechs alike as suitable material for dramatic or operatic treatment, without any specific nationalist dimension. There is, as Petr Vít demonstrates (1982), little difference in approach between Kreutzer's *Libussa* composed to a German text and given in Vienna in 1822 and Škroup's *Libuše's Marriage*, composed to a text by a prominent poet of the Czech National Revival in 1835. The intensely patriotic effect of Smetana's opera half a century later was not achieved by the central legend alone, but by presenting it in the context of a whole number of nationalist symbols, deliberately inserted to trigger off a nationalist response. Thus Přemysl, seen alone in Act 2, addresses his invocation to the lime trees 'Ó, vy lípy'. As Macura argues (1983, 93–107), after the wide dissemination of the 'bible of Slavness', Kollár's epic poem *Sláva's Daughter* (*Slávy dcera*, second edition 1832), a Czech audience by the 1880s knew that a lime tree was 'Slavonic' (as opposed to the 'German' oak) and that by singing about lime trees Přemysl was both invoking a now well-established nationalist symbol, and at the same time reinforcing it.

With a nation that feared the demise of its language as a vehicle for cultured expression, it was inevitable that the written word would become particularly important. Indeed print nationalism, as Bernard Anderson has shown (1983, 41–9), is often a crucial factor in fostering national awareness, though an awareness inevitably restricted to those who could read. Consequently, until the 1848 Revolution the Czech National Revival remained a largely middle-class phenomenon. The only permanent gain of the Revolution was the clearing away of the last vestiges of serfdom – the abolition of *robota*, or forced labour (Joseph II's reforms of 1781 had begun the process by abolishing *nevolnictví*, which tied peasants and their descendants to the land). The effect of this, together with increasing mechanization, was to release the agricultural populace for industrial work in the towns, and thus to change the linguistic balance there. The middle-class patriots who had begun the National Revival in the first half of the nineteenth century were now joined by a flood of lower-class native Czech speakers from the country. During the nineteenth century Prague turned from a city with an overwhelmingly German culture to one whose culture increasingly reflected the fact that its population was predominantly Czech-speaking.

The linguistic tide was clearly turning in favour of the Czechs, but their prime political objective – autonomy – was not realized until the end of the First World War when the break-up of the Austro-Hungarian Empire brought about an independent Czechoslovakian state (rather than a federalization of the empire, which had been the aim of the historian Palacký and other farsighted reformers). During the nineteenth century, frustrated political energy was channelled elsewhere, into clubs and cultural organizations. Austria's defeat by France at Magenta and Solferino in June 1859, through which it lost most of its remaining Italian possessions, brought down the government. This included Count Alexander Bach, the notorious minister of the interior who from 1852 had presided over the most repressive period of Habsburg rule in the nineteenth century. Concerned that disaffection among other peoples in the empire might lead to further territorial losses, the new government adopted a more conciliatory stance and lifted restrictions on cultural and other activities. The 1860s saw the beginnings of many new Czech ventures. In 1862 the influential *Národní listy*, the first independent Czech newspaper for over a decade, began publication and the same year the gymnastic organization *Sokol* (falcon) was founded on the model of the earlier German Turnverein. The movement spread rapidly throughout the country, building *Sokol* halls (useful gathering places for other cultural–patriotic purposes), and inculcating an almost mystical patriotic sensibility whilst promoting physical education. The *Sokol* movement survived closures by the Austrians and the Nazis during two world wars and clung on until 1952, when it was incorporated into the new socialist republic's even more massive physical–cultural organization.

A similar nation-building role was supplied by the choral societies that proliferated in the 1860s. The most distinguished of these was the Prague Hlahol, founded in 1861 as a male-voice choir and directed in its earliest years by Smetana (1863–5) and Bendl (1865–77). In 1873 another composer, Janáček, took over the Brno male choral society Svatopluk (founded in 1868) and wrote some of his earliest pieces for it. Like the choral societies that sprang up during the political upheavals in London and Paris in the early 1830s, the Czech choral societies provided a type of group activity which could draw in members with little musical training. The better societies achieved a high standard and built up a solid, sober repertory but others were little more than a pretext for meeting and for singing texts in Czech, often with wildly inflated patriotic sentiments.

But by far the most important focus of national endeavour from the 1860s was the building of the National Theatre in Prague. Since theatre was almost the only way of reaching out to an often illiterate public and the one 'literary' activity that could operate as a popular community experience, it had played a most important part in the National Revival from the late eighteenth century onwards, despite the lack of a permanent home for Czech drama until the 1860s (see Chapter 2).

The National Theatre was opened with great pomp in June 1881. It replaced a more modest building, the Provisional Theatre, erected in 1862. The Provisional Theatre made possible a permanent Czech ensemble – drama, opera and ballet – to be created in preparation for the bigger theatre, and a repertory of new and translated works to be built up. For some twenty years, many more than originally envisaged, collections were needed to pay for the erection of the National Theatre, which soon became the most tangible expression of Czech nationhood. While the Provisional Theatre had been built with state funds, the National Theatre was the result of a huge exercise in private fund-raising by Czechs throughout Bohemia and Moravia and among scattered Czech communities and Pan-Slav sympathizers abroad. The building's origin was proudly recorded in the motto above the proscenium arch: 'Národ sobě' – 'The nation to itself'. The stops and starts in the thirty-year process bear witness to the inexperience of the organizers and the obstacles raised by the obstructive Austrian authorities;

similarly the ease with which the money was raised again in 1881, after a fire had destroyed much of the building a few weeks after its opening, reflected the growing wealth and national consciousness of the Czech community.

The Provisional Theatre opened in 1862 with a play by a young Czech writer, Vítězslav Hálek, followed the next evening by an opera, Cherubini's *Les deux journées*, sung in Czech. The opening of the National Theatre in 1881, and its rebuilt version in 1883, were celebrated not by a play but by an opera, Smetana's *Libuše*. Opening with an opera rather than with a play was an acknowledgement that the greatest achievement in Czech theatre in the previous two decades had been in opera, rather than in spoken drama. The ceremonial nature of opera was also felt to be more appropriate to such an occasion. And while spoken drama can provide a range of nationalist signals and references, from the use of the Czech language itself and the patriotic sentiments expressed in it to the enactment of Czech history and legends and the depiction of Czech locales through sets and costumes, opera was able to add its own even more powerful resources.

Gratifying though it was to hear Czech spoken from the stage of a lavishly decorated theatre, it was even more flattering to national pride to hear Czech sung, ennobled by music into the grandest style the theatre had at its command. The inbuilt emotional reference system of mid-nineteenth-century harmony was something that composers could draw on to exploit to the full the nationalist impact of a work. Music could fill out the emotional implications of a text and make absolutely clear where the audiences's sympathies should be. Thus the opening scene of Smetana's first opera, *The Brandenburgers in Bohemia*, begins with an exchange between two Prague citizens, Oldřich and Volfram, from whom we learn about the sad state of the country. To a disturbed, swirling accompaniment, Oldřich describes how 'from village to village the Brandenburger mercenaries rampage like wolves, looting churches, pillaging monasteries, murdering children, old men, women!' Then, with an abrupt shift up a semitone, he declares, *con summa forza*: 'our fields lie fallow, bespattered with innocent blood, and our lovely Czech land is turning into a barren desert' (Ex. 1). For the first time in the opera the voice settles into a songlike arioso, in contrast to the irregular parlando that has prevailed hitherto. Note-values lengthen and two sequential phrases lead to the heart of the matter: as Oldřich utters the first syllable of the first 'česká' (Czech) his part leaps up a fourth to the accompaniment of an 'affective' diminished seventh chord (a); a last drop of pathos is wrung out when the accompaniment shifts against the held voice part to create another emotionally loaded device, an appoggiatura of the ninth (b), resolved on to the second syllable of 'česká'. It is as if up to now all the words have been printed in small type while the reference to 'our lovely Czech land' appears in huge illuminated letters.

There is another example in the opening scene of Act 2, a hymn sung by

Ex. 1

[*The Brandenburgers in Bohemia*, 1.1.152–72]

a sorrowing village people cataloguing their woes and about to abandon their homes and flee to the safety of the woods. At first a solo voice – a village elder – and a four-part chorus alternate unaccompanied. As the music gathers momentum the orchestra creeps in and when the volume reaches *fortissimo* the elder finally reaches the crucial words, 'Through their cruel acts they have destroyed our lovely Czech land and enslaved the glorious Czech nation' ('Naši krásnou českou zem ukrutenstvím pohubili, a ten slavný česky národ zotročili'). The chorus repeats his words to a full orchestral accompaniment, now with a telling alteration: on the first syllable of 'českou' (Czech) there is a climactically placed dominant thirteenth – another emotionally loaded effect to clinch the patriotic argument.

Smetana was too sophisticated a composer to repeat such devices on every similar occasion, but many examples can be found in his works up to his final opera *The Devil's Wall*. As Jan Racek has demonstrated in his study of patriotism in Smetana's music, on key words like *vlast* (fatherland), *národ* (nation), and *sláva* (glory) there is often a noticeable musical underlining of the sentiment with affective harmony or with striking melodic leaps and melismas (Racek 1933, 92–134) – a musical parallel to the trembling of Smetana's voice (in Dolanský's much-quoted anecdote, 1918, 236) when he proclaimed the words 'my nation'. In those operas portraying Czech rulers such as *Dalibor* and *Libuše* Smetana wrote particularly stirring ceremonial music for entrances and exits, a special sort of Czech 'pomp and circumstance' music to dignify and monumentalize the ruler.

It was operas of this sort, rather than plays, that provided the ceremonial at the 'chrám umění', the 'shrine of art', as the catch phrase of the time put it. That music should form such a significant part of the expression of Czech nationalism is not surprising. Unlike the peoples of nationalist movements on the fringes of Europe, the Czechs, at the heart of Europe, had a well-established musical tradition. With their proximity to Vienna they were well placed to follow developments there, as it became an increasingly important and influential musical centre in the late eighteenth century. Solidly trained Czech musicians were sought after for musical posts throughout Europe and contributed significantly to the formation of the Classical style. With no gallant political folk heroes, and no writers or painters of international standing, the Czechs could at least boast of their musicians. 'What Czech does not love music?' asks the jailer Beneš in *Dalibor*. At a local level the humble musician–teacher, the village schoolmaster or kantor, inspired affection and gratitude for keeping Czech culture alive at the lowest ebb of the nation's fortunes. Playwrights, librettists and composers fondly contributed to depict Czech musicians at work, a recognition of their pre-eminence in national hagiography.

Once it had found a permanent home where it could be displayed and where it could prosper, opera became the chief vehicle of Czech cultural nationalism. Where other nations expressed their nationhood in the adulation of the monarchy or the military, or in the obeisance to a flag, a constitution or 'la gloire', the Czechs celebrated their nationhood in operatic rituals staged at the National Theatre. The building became endowed with a unique, almost sacred seriousness of purpose. In the words of Zdeněk Nejedlý, one of the most influential arbiters of Czech cultural and political tastes in the twentieth century, it was 'not a place of entertainment, but a hallowed place, a shrine, a school, where the nation had to speak with the highest form of its own language about its feelings and its dearest aims' (Nejedlý 1935, i, 114). Hence the disapproval of performing at the National Theatre anything thought to be light-weight. Nejedlý dismissed both operetta and ballet as not being 'art' at all, but merely social phenomena symptomatic of the frivolous and decadent societies in Paris and Vienna, and took comfort in their lack of success on the Czech stage (Nejedlý 1911, 228–34).

Czech nationalism differs from other nineteenth-century nationalisms in that its deepest roots go back to a much earlier epoch, to 1415, when Jan Hus was burnt for heresy at the Council of Constance. His martyrdom united the country, still more so when reinforced by the persistent and unsuccessful crusades waged against it by the whole of Catholic Europe. Hussitism became for the Czechs not just a faith but a form of patriotism. Four centuries before Napoleon's wars provoked the nationalist movements of the nineteenth century, the Czechs, in defence of their country and their faith, found a nationalism with strong ethical overtones which have persisted ever since. Although the Jesuits were able to re-Catholicize the Czech population in the seventeenth century and replace the cult figure of Jan Hus with their own candidate John of Nepomuk, whose effigy, in swaying Baroque drapes, still adorns many wayside shrines of the Czech countryside, no Habsburg or Jesuit was ever able to dissolve the moral residue of Hussitism in the Czech nation. Nationalism in the Czech lands was permanently intertwined with moral values. Jan Racek's book on Smetana (1933), revised in the heady postwar days of 1947, provides an apt example with its almost incantatory use of the epithet 'ethical' constantly applied to the actions of its heroic subject.

This approach is typical of much Czech writing about music. If music and in particular opera provided the most public focus of Czech cultural aspirations, they also formed the battleground for rival interpretations of these aspirations and how best they should be realized in music. Czech writers on music, much more than the composers, threw themselves into the fray with a ferocity and partisanship that often startles the outsider. That one composer is preferred to another is natural, but among the Czechs the choice was seldom a matter of mere personal taste or artistic excellence but rather one of political alignment. Because of the ideological burden that nationalist opera was forced to bear in nineteenth-century Bohemia, attitudes towards individual composers became charged with extramusical significance.

Thus the polemics between the Liszt–Wagner and Brahms camps, when translated into Czech terms – the 'progressive' Lisztian Smetana versus the 'conservative' Brahmsian Dvořák (confusingly also a Wagnerian) – locked into political debates of the late nineteenth century between the *staročech* (Old Czech) and *mladočech* (Young Czech) parties. In a letter explaining the Czech political scene to a pupil he had taught in Sweden (Kraus 1906, 411) Smetana characterized the *staročeši* as the 'feudal–clerical' party, the party of the propertied and monied classes, and the *mladočeši* as the free-thinking party, the party of artists, journalists and men of letters. Smetana, naturally, was a *mladočech*. Less is known about Dvořák's political affiliations, but his association with František Rieger, the prominent *staročech* politician whose daughter supplied Dvořák with two librettos, was proof enough for hostile commentators of his *staročech* inclinations. Since the *mladočech* party was, as Smetana wrote, the party of 'artists, journalists and men of letters' it is understandable that *mladočech* writers would find themselves better disposed towards Smetana than to Dvořák. Smetana did not lack committed propagandists from such quarters and they include some of the most important and influential Czech writers on music of their time, such as Otakar Hostinský and Zdeněk Nejedlý. For almost a century from the 1870s, when Hostinský began writing regular reviews and articles, until Nejedlý's death in 1962 these two scholars dominated their contemporaries and constituted a strongly pro-Smetana lobby, if necessary at the expense of other figures. Here is Nejedlý in his first book, published in 1901, when he was twenty-three.

Smetana's slogan was modernity and Czechness, so he sided enthusiastically with the progressive Weimar school, with Berlioz, Liszt and Wagner. He was the founder of Czech music by virtue of the fact that he based our national opera on modern Wagnerian music drama. . .and our symphonic literature with his first symphonic poems culminating in the cycle *Má vlast*.
[. . .]
Now let us turn to Dvořák. Smetana based Czech opera on modern soil, Dvořák on the soil of old French and Italian operas. His operas go in the opposite direction from those of Smetana. *Dimitrij* is Dvořák's best work; it is at the same time his most conservative – nay, his most regressive. Dvořák negates the development of Czech opera.
(Nejedlý 1901, 172)

Smetana's appeal was strengthened by two further factors. Unlike Dvořák, who was courted by foreign publishers, wrote freely for foreign commissions and was prepared to spend some of his mature years cultivating his reputation abroad, Smetana returned home as soon as conditions had relaxed sufficiently for Czech culture to flourish and devoted himself unsparingly to the advancement of opera aimed specifically at the Czechs.

Such a patriotic, 'ethical' gesture when he could easily – like Dvořák – have established a career abroad, has also weighed heavily in Smetana's favour. Nejedlý, writing in 1913–14, put the case with characteristic trenchancy: 'Smetana was a thousand times the more potent artist [of the two] since he never sold off his art, in which nationality was a basic element, in return for a little success abroad' (Nejedlý 1980, 114). The hostile, insensitive treatment Smetana received at the hands of *staročech* administrators while conductor at the Provisional Theatre, especially when deafness compelled him to give up his appointment, his heroic battle against deafness and ill health and the vindictive nature of some of his opponents have all solicited a strain of emotional protectiveness that has coloured much Czech and even foreign writing about him.

Writers such as Nejedlý devoted particular energy to the question of Smetana's spiritual successor. Dvořák clearly would not do, and Nejedlý's choice lighted on Zdeněk Fibich.

*Fibich continued in the progressive endeavours of Smetana.* Having taken over Smetana's watchword, he led Czech music to greater glory, ever higher. Thus the history of modern Czech music in the nineteenth century will be denoted by two chapters of which the first will bear Smetana's name, citing *Libuše*, *Má vlast* and the quartet 'From my Life'; the second will bear Fibich's name citing *The Bride of Messina*, *Hippodamia*, *The Fall of Arkona* and *Moods* [*Impressions and Reminiscences*].
[. . .]
. . .There is only one historical consequence. *Fibich is the true successor of Smetana while Dvořák represents the negation of the direction of both of these masters.* Therefore the famous Czech trinity should correctly read: *Smetana-Fibich contra Dvořák.*

(Nejedlý 1901, 172–3; Nejedlý's italics)

And since Fibich, dying in 1900, needed a successor himself, Nejedlý provided one in his book *Modern Czech Opera after Smetana* (*Česká moderní zpěvohra po Smetanovi*, 1911). The book ends with the motto: '*The Bride of Messina – Eva – The Bud*', in other words Fibich – Foerster – Ostrčil.

Today such a map of Czech opera seems a little odd. Despite the best efforts of Nejedlý and his followers, Fibich never quite captured the popular imagination. He, Foerster and Ostrčil account for no more than four operas that can still be occasionally heard in Czechoslovakia. What Nejedlý could not foresee is that Dvořák, for all his shortcomings as a natural operatic composer, would leave behind him several operas that seem to speak to the Czech heart more directly than anything by Fibich, Foerster or Ostrčil. Nor, when briskly writing off Janáček's *Jenůfa* after its Prague triumph, could Nejedlý have realized that its composer, a figure quite outside his golden succession, would do more to establish Czech opera as a vital force beyond the boundaries of Czechoslovakia. Today when a foreigner thinks of Czech opera he tends to think more of Janáček than any of his predecessors.

The map of Czech opera proposed in this book is inevitably a different one from that offered by Czech polemicists of the nineteenth and early twentieth conturies. It is different, too, from that offered by many of their successors, whose writings provide fascinating proof of the tenacity of nationalist attitudes. It would be naive to presume that it will be any more accurate; every historian writes within a context of his own geographical, historical and ideological assumptions, however he may strive for objectivity. But it may strike the reader that a foreigner with some sympathy for the achievements of the Czech nation may be able to write with fewer constraints than those whose outlook has been restricted by the emotional bonds of the Czech nationalist art they sought to describe. For a start there is no necessity to see Smetana as a hero figure. This means that it is not necessary to ignore and disparage his precedessors, contemporaries and successors so that he might appear all the greater; to play down the role of his librettists in order to present him as the only begetter of his operas; to assume that he wrote with a natural and instinctive Czechness that eschewed harmful foreign influences (apart from a few carefully sanctioned 'progressive' ones). Neither is it necessary to assume that although Smetana knew that his operas would be first performed in the tiny Provisional Theatre he wrote for the grander theatre of his imagination and that therefore the conditions at the Provisional Theatre and the voices available there had no effect on what and on how he wrote. To forego some of these assumptions is not to underrate Smetana's very considerable achievement; in fact to see him in the broader context that this book offers can only reinforce that achievement. Take away these assumptions and many new and productive areas of investigation open out, areas which Czech musicology only now, and with some caution, is at last beginning to examine.[1]

# 2. Theatres

## Before the Provisional Theatre[1]

### Italian opera in Bohemia and Moravia

The rise of opera coincided with the political decline of the Czech nation. The first recorded instance of an opera in Prague (a pastoral comedy performed by Mantuan singers) celebrated the coronation as King of Bohemia of the Habsburg Ferdinand II in 1627, seven years after the defeat of the Czech nobility at the Battle of the White Mountain. By the eighteenth century, when the popularity of Italian opera was at its height throughout Europe, Prague's status had sunk to that of a provincial capital. With the court permanently resident in Vienna, there was no focus in Prague for opera except for rare visits by the monarch, for instance Leopold I's removal there in 1679–80 to escape the plague. The only other opera performances came about through tours by enterprising opera companies, such as that of G.F. Sartorio in 1702–7, when among other works Bartolomeo Bernardi's *La Libussa* was given, the first opera on a Czech subject to be performed in Prague (see p. 140).

The coronation of Charles VI as King of Bohemia in 1723 was the occasion for one of the most elaborate opera performances in Europe in the eighteenth century – the production of Fux's coronation opera *Costanza e Fortezza* before 4000 guests in an open-air amphitheatre, built by the architect and stage designer Giuseppe Galli-Bibiena on a terrace beneath the Prague castle. Surviving prints (reproduced in *DČD*, i, 258–61) show the sets, also by Galli-Bibiena, to be on the most lavish scale and the performance under Caldara (Fux was suffering from gout) lasted five hours, until one in the morning. The event is, justly, mentioned in all accounts of opera in Bohemia, but it must be stressed that it was wholly exceptional. Charles, who had taken twelve years to get to Prague for his coronation, never returned during the remaining seventeen years of his reign and during her forty-year reign Charles's daughter and successor, Maria Theresa, came to Prague only twice – for her coronation as Queen of Bohemia in 1743, when less exalted fare of French and German comedies, Singspiels and French ballets was offered, and in 1754, when two buffo operas by Galuppi were staged by a local impresario.

As a city with an operatic tradition unsupported by any princely or imperial court, Prague is in some respects comparable to Hamburg (Volek 1986, 135). Hamburg's Theater auf dem Gänsemarkt (1678), the first independent public opera house in Germany, depended on the existence of a prosperous bourgeoisie. This was not the case in Prague until a half a century later; until then opera in Bohemia and Moravia was performed either under the aegis of the church (music and theatre were regarded by the Jesuits and other orders as important educational aids), or, in a more sophisticated form, at the homes of the aristocracy.

One of the most remarkable centres of opera in the Czech lands during the eighteenth century was the Questenberg estate at Jaroměřice nad Rokytnou, Moravia (Straková 1973). From 1723 Italian opera was produced there regularly several times a year in a specially constructed theatre, with librettos printed for the occasion. The company was largely domestic. There were no castratos (such parts were taken by women); local musicians made up an orchestra of about thirty, and the Kapellmeister was František Václav Míča (1694–1744), a prominent member of a Czech family of musicians in service with the Questenbergs. Míča wrote for court, chapel and stage. One Italian opera of his has survived, *L'origine di Jaromeriz in Moravia*, produced in December 1730. The insertion into the score of a Czech translation and the printing of the libretto in Czech led Vladimír Helfert to assume that a performance also took place in Czech (Helfert 1924, 279). Míča's opera, however, was a rarity. Count Johannes Adam Questenberg clearly preferred imported Italian opera, and works by Caldara, Leo, Hasse and many lesser composers made up the basic repertory plus a few German Singspiels (a concession to the local populace allowed to see the performances). Count Questenberg's musical establishment survived both the new artistic direction in Vienna with Maria Theresa's accession in 1740 and the death of Míča in 1744, and continued to his own death in 1752.

Elsewhere in Moravia opera was cultivated, chiefly in the 1730s, by Cardinal Schrattenbach, Bishop of Olomouc, on his estates at Kroměříž and Vyškov, and by the Rottal family in Holešov.[2] One of the most famous travelling opera companies of the period, that of the Mingotti brothers, took Brno into its regular circuit. At first Angelo Mingotti had to use the Estates Riding School, but from 1732 opera performances could take place in a newly erected theatre in the Vegetable Market Square (on the site of the present Reduta Theatre). Mingotti played in Brno three times a week for four successive winter seasons with a company of three men and five women singers. Other Italian companies followed in Brno at irregular intervals with increasingly varied and light-weight repertories, as for instance Vicenzo Nicolosi's company in 1767 with a collection of Italian comedies, German Singspiels, French pantomimes, operettas and plays.

Accounts of opera in Bohemia are less plentiful. At the southern Bohemian town of Český Krumlov, for instance, there still exists a superb eighteenth-century theatre together with its stage machinery – a Czech Drottningholm (both theatres were completed in 1766). From the nature of some of the sets and costumes, but in the absence of other documentary material, it is possible only to speculate that opera was performed there (several plates of sets and costumes are reproduced in *DČD*, i). Better records exist of the musical establishment run by Count Franz Anton Sporck (1662–1738), the Bohemian nobleman noted for his introduction of the french horn into Bohemian musical life and for his contacts with J.S. Bach (Fitzpatrick 1970, 11–25). From 1701 Sporck maintained a permanent theatre open to the public at his Prague residence, Na poříčí, and in 1724, under the impact of the Fux coronation opera, engaged a Venetian opera company to perform at his summer residence at Kuks, a spa town in north-east Bohemia. The company of twenty-three, including thirteen singers, opened in Kuks on 15 August 1724 with a setting (now believed to be by Vivaldi) of *Orlando furioso*. The opera was performed three times a week in Kuks and, from 23 October, for a further two months in Prague at Sporck's theatre there. This marked the beginnings of public opera in Prague. After another summer season in Kuks, the leading tenor of the company, Antonio Denzio, settled in Prague as an independent impresario. Over ten years he presented fifty-seven operas in Prague, including several Vivaldi premières, until debts overtook him in 1734 (Krupka 1923; Volek 1986).

Despite the War of the Austrian Succession, which broke out in 1742 following Maria Theresa's accession and which closed the theatres from time to time, opera flourished in Prague in the 1740s. The impresarios who followed Denzio included Santo Lapis (1737–40), Angelo Mingotti and his brother Pietro (1743–6), who brought Prague its first experience of opera buffa, and from 1748 Giovanni Battista Locatelli, who imported a more serious repertory, for instance the operas of Gluck, who himself directed the premières of his own *Ezio* (Carnival 1750) and *Issipile* (Carnival 1752). Opera buffa, however, soon got the upper hand and by Locatelli's departure in 1757 (which was hastened by the outbreak of the Seven Years War and the bombardment of Prague, during which he lost most of his sets and costumes), opera seria had disappeared from his repertory. After Locatelli, the most notable impresario was Giuseppe Bustelli, who during his seventeen years in Prague (1764–81) performed Italian operas by Czech composers such as Mysliveček and Koželuh.

*Prague theatres in the eighteenth century*

From 1739 the Italian companies were able to play at a new venue, the Nuovo teatro della communità della Reale Città Vecchia di Praga nel loco detto Kotzen, or more simply the Kotzen Opera und Comoedie-Haus. The 'Kotzen' were the booths of a medieval woollen-cloth market established in 1377; the theatre was created at a cost of 15,000 zl. by adapting the long narrow upper hall (while the booths continued to ply their trade beneath). It had a fairly deep stage, subdivided stalls, forty boxes in two tiers, and a gallery. It remained the chief public theatre in Prague until the opening of two new theatres in the 1780s; after 1783 it served as a theatrical store-house (*DP*, 10–14; Jareš 1984, 101–5). In 1781 Count Franz Anton von Nostitz–Rhineck (1725–94), president of the provincial administration (the chief state official in Bohemia) and the doyen of the Bohemian aristocracy, began the erection of a new theatre in the Staré Město (Old Town) opposite the Karolinum (part of Prague University). It was built at his own expense for 100,000 zl., a munificent and patriotic gesture to give Prague a theatre truly worthy of the city. With its two tiers of boxes, stalls divided into a 'parterre noble' and a second parterre, and a gallery with benches and standing room, it had a capacity of well over 1000 and was one of the finest theatres in central Europe in the eighteenth century. The 'Gräflich Nostitzsches Nationaltheater' opened on 21 April 1783 with a performance of Lessing's tragedy *Emilia Galotti* – the theatre was expected to provide a solid fare of German classics and so live up to a title in which the word 'national' meant German national, rather than Czech.

At first the German company, under Karel Wahr from the old Kotzen theatre, played three times a week and in the winter season five times: three days of German plays and two days of Singspiels. But the company had stiff competition from the excellent Italian opera company which Pasquale Bondini (?1737–89) had founded in Dresden in 1777 and which from 1781 had also begun performing in a new theatre built by Count Thun at his palace in the Malá Strana (Small Quarter). During manoeuvres in nearby Hloubětín in September 1783 that inveterate theatre-goer Joseph II spent most of his evenings in Count Thun's theatre and only half a performance at Count Nostitz's opulent new theatre. On his monarch's advice Nostitz dismissed Wahr in 1784 and let the theatre to Bondini (Branscombe 1980). Despite his commitments in Dresden and at the Leipzig summer fair, Bondini secured for the Nostitz theatre one of its most celebrated coups: the presentation in December 1786 of Mozart's *Le nozze di Figaro*. Its success greatly surpassed that of the Vienna première a few months earlier and led to Bondini's commissioning *Don Giovanni*, which opened in Prague under Mozart's direction on 29 October 1787. Domenico Guardasoni (*c* 1731–1806), Bondini's assistant and, after his death in 1789, his successor, similarly commissioned Mozart's *La clemenza di Tito* to celebrate the coronation of Leopold II in Prague in 1791.

The Nostitz Theatre was renamed the Royal Theatre of the Estates (Königliches Ständestheater/Královské stavovské divadlo) when Count Nostitz's son sold it to the Bohemian Estates in 1789, and in 1861 the Royal Provincial Theatre (Königliches Landestheater/Královské zemské divadlo). It remained the principal stage for German theatre and opera in Prague throughout the nineteenth century until 1888, when it was supplanted by a new theatre, the Neues Deutsches Theater (today the Smetana Theatre) and became the German community's second stage.

## The beginnings of Czech theatre

By about 1800 any linguistic contest in opera in the Czech lands was, as elsewhere in German-speaking Europe, a contest between Italian opera and German opera, between, on the one hand, an established, prestigious international style with international stars and impresarios and, on the other, a light-weight vernacular genre, usually of little artistic consequence and often nothing more than plays with a few songs thrown in. German opera nevertheless drew a wider public, as the impresarios discovered, but it was not until Karel Liebich, who leased the Estates Theatre from 1806 to 1816, that an impresario was able to get round the leasing condition of regular performances of operas in Italian. Until then it meant running two companies in the same theatre: a German company capable of mounting plays and simple Singspiels, and an Italian opera company. The Italian company was disbanded in 1807 (it sang its farewell to the public with a performance of Mozart's *La clemenza*, which since its cool reception in Prague during Leopold's coronation celebrations had become a great favourite), and the successor company sang only in German. It was now possible to engage German singers specifically for opera; under the musical directorship of Wenzel Müller (1803–13) and in particular that of Carl Maria von Weber (1813–16) standards were raised. Weber reorganized the entire theatre system, improved the orchestra, paid special attention to production, and expanded the hitherto mainly Singspiel repertory to include German versions of many French operas (he opened with Spontini's *Fernand Cortez*) as well as Beethoven's *Fidelio* and the première of Spohr's *Faust*.[3] Abandoning Italian and using a single language, German, considerably simplified the running of the theatre. But it also brought to the surface another, deeper-seated linguistic contest, that between German and Czech.

There had been isolated attempts in the eighteenth century to perform plays and operas in Czech. One of these, attested by reviews and a printed text, was a Czech translation of Johann Christian Krüger's play *Herzog Michel*, given at the Kotzen theatre in 1771, but even earlier is a one-act anonymous work, *The Lovelorn Nightwatchman* described as a 'Czech opera pantomime'. The printed libretto suggests that it was performed by an Italian company in Prague as early as 1763; a poster exists announcing a performance by a company from Baden (and apologizing for its unidiomatic

Czech) in Brno on 11 January 1767. Surviving vocal and instrumental parts reveal a considerable musical content: eight arias, one duet, a final quartet, and ten 'pantomimes'.[4] Evidence of the use of Czech on the stage before this date is more controversial. Trojan (1984) has expressed doubts about the performance in Czech of Míča's *L'origine di Jaromeriz in Moravia* in 1730 (see p. 14). As it is, the claim for Míča's opera as the first instance of Czech being sung on the operatic stage has been further undermined by Daniel Freeman's discovery of a Czech-language aria in the libretto of *Il confronto dell'amor coniugale*, performed in the Sporck theatre in Prague during the Carnival season of 1727.[5] The first systematic attempt to present Czech-language entertainment on the stage, however, began only in the late 1780s.

When Bondini took over the Nostitz Theatre in 1784 he hired a local company of German actors to complement his travelling Italian opera company. In January 1785 the German company, which included a number of bilingual Czech actors, presented a play in Czech, a translation of Gottlieb Stephanie's *Deserteur aus Kinderliebe*. Three more plays in Czech, all translated by Václav Thám (1765–?1816), were performed that year by the company to great acclaim, followed the next year by an original Czech drama by Thám on a Czech historical legend, *Břetislav and Jitka or the Abduction from the Convent* (*Břetislav a Jitka aneb Únos z kláštera*). The popularity with the public of the Czech performances had two results: Bondini's dismissal, on pressure from German chauvinists, of his Prague German company (thereafter his Dresden German company toured Prague); and the thought among members of the disbanded company that they might be able to survive independently, though it was only after the intervention of Joseph II that this was permitted by the local authorities. The new company, which opened in a hastily built wooden theatre (the *Bouda*, i.e. a 'hut', 'booth') on 8 July 1786, did not perform exclusively in Czech – there was neither sufficient repertory nor public for this – but nevertheless three or four Czech performances a week were given regularly by the bilingual company. Despite support from the Czech public and from Joseph II (who attended several performances), the company foundered after a couple of years, overcome by its debts, and the *Bouda* was pulled down. The name of the company, 'The Patriotic Theatre' (Vlastenské divadlo), continued to designate holders of the Czech franchise until 1804, when the Estates Theatre acquired it and with it the monopoly of all stage performances in Prague. For the next sixty years it was the trustees and intendants of the Estates Theatre who determined the language in which any professional performance took place in Prague.

At first Czech performances continued freely in the Estates Theatre largely because of the influential standing of the impresario Guardasoni, who fought off the Estates' opposition to this profitable enterprise, but when he died in June 1806 his successor had to submit to confining Czech performances to a smaller theatre in a part of town removed from the main centres of the Czech population. Attendances fell and regular Czech performances there ceased after the 1806–7 season, and the Czech professional company was disbanded.

### Music at the Patriotic Theatre

Music formed an important part of the Patriotic Theatre's presentations. Ballet (an excellent medium in a two-language city) was particularly favoured: in the 1786–7 season 40% of the evenings were made up of one-act plays or operas supplemented by a ballet, and a further 20% consisted of two-act plays with a short ballet. Even at the primitive *Bouda* the orchestra's expenses came to more than the actors' wages; and at the well-appointed Hibernian Theatre (Divadlo u Hybernů – housed in the library of a disbanded order of Irish Franciscans), to which the Patriotic Theatre moved at the end of 1789, there was room for a full Singspiel orchestra. The performance there of *Die Zauberflöte* in 1794 is sometimes cited as the 'first' performance of an opera in Czech, but in fact Czech versions of Singspiels such as Umlauf's *Die Bergknappen* and Dittersdorf's *Hieronymus Knicker* both preceded it in the early 1790s, and the Dittersdorf work, with its coloratura soprano parts and its extensive overture and finales, is hardly less demanding than the Mozart. In addition, plays with music could sometimes be as ambitious as *The Lutenists* (*Loutníci*, a Czech adaptation of Schikaneder's *Die Lyranten* with music by Franz Volkert, given for Joseph II's first visit in September 1786 and frequently revived), which contained twenty-one musical numbers, mostly entrance arias, couplets and final choruses. As a whole, Singspiels accounted for 40% of the total number of Czech performances from 1793, although fewer individual Singspiels were performed since they could take a larger number of repeated performances than plays. From 1793 to 1807, 57 operatic works are recorded as being performed in Czech by the Patriotic Theatre (about half of the total repertory is known). A third of these were by Mozart, Süssmayr, Dittersdorf and Umlauf, i.e. the foremost representatives of the Viennese Singspiel; 27 were by Viennese composers of Czech origin – Müller, Kauer, Schack (Žák) and Vincenc Tuček; and 13 were by local Prague composers. Compared with the faltering developments during the next half century, the achievement of the Patriotic Theatre in presenting operatic works and encouraging local talent was remarkable.

### Opera in Czech in the 1820s

After the demise of the Patriotic Theatre no Czech professional stage performances took place in Prague for fifteen years until 1824, though the impetus that its existence had given was now unstoppable. This can be seen in the emergence of a new generation of playwrights and translators. Two of these exerted considerable influence over the future development of the Czech theatre: Václav Kliment Klicpera (1793–1859), some of whose comedies survive on the Czech stage to this day (Martinů set his one-act *Comedy on the Bridge* as a radio opera in 1935), and Jan Nepomuk Štěpánek (1783–1844), whose plays were rather more popular with theatre audiences at the time, though they have now dropped out of the repertory. Štěpánek also translated over 120 plays, his thirteen opera translations include the first Czech versions of *Der Freischütz* and *Don Giovanni*. Štěpánek was above all an actor–manager, and as such the most important personality in the Czech theatre in the earlier part of the nineteenth century. Originally drawn into the Estates Theatre as a prompter, he began working with Czech amateurs when the professional Czech company at the Estates Theatre was disbanded and he became the focus of Czech amateur theatricals in Prague. His energy and enterprise were rewarded in 1824 when, at a point of crisis in the Estates Theatre, the Estates appointed a triumvirate of managers, including Štěpánek, who had the express task of reviving the Czech professional company there. That performers could be found for this is demonstrated by the very successful amateur production in Czech of Weigl's Singspiel *Die Schweizerfamilie* in 1823, a year before Štěpánek's appointment.

The newly formed Czech company was much the poor relation, allowed only a single weekly performance. This meant in effect 30 to 35 Czech performances a year and over the ten-year period up to 1834, when the Estates replaced the triumvirate with a single, German, manager with no commitment to Czech performances, only 320 performances in Czech had been given. But, coming at a time of growing national awareness, these performances were enough to take the Czech theatre into a new phase of its existence, and one which led ultimately to the establishment of the permanent and separate company at the Provisional Theatre in 1862.

The central position of opera among Czech performances at the Estates Theatre is a striking feature of this period. While Czech plays were performed by whatever actors Štěpánek could find – amateur Czechs or bilingual professionals – Czech operas were usually performed by professional singers, delighted to be able to sing occasionally in their mother tongue. (Most of the stars of the German opera company – for instance all the principals of the 1834 production of Spohr's *Jessonda* – were Czech; Emingerová 1924, 66–7). Opera accounted for over a third of the Czech performances, and Singspiels and plays with inserted songs formed a continuum into straight theatre so that Czech audiences regarded opera not so much as different in kind from straight theatre but simply a higher form of it. The respective repertories could only reinforce this notion. Plays given in Czech

tended to exclude foreign classics in favour of Viennese farces adapted to local conditions or the products of the fledgeling generation of Czech dramatists. The operatic repertory, however, was entirely foreign and much of it was the finest international fare available. *Der Freischütz* was one of the most frequently performed pieces in the Czech repertory during this period, edged into second place only by a popular play by Štěpánek. Mozart achieved an even higher number of performances. His *Don Giovanni*, introduced in Czech in the first season of the triumvirate (1824–5), reappeared frequently thereafter and was later joined by Czech versions of *Così fan tutte*, *Die Entführung* and an earlier favourite, *Die Zauberflöte*. Rossini's operas were also popular and included *Il barbiere di Siviglia*, *Tancredi* and *Otello* (with the part of Rodrigo linguistically simplified for the monoglot German tenor who had been coaxed into getting it up in Czech). French opera formed a large part of the repertory. Cherubini's *Les deux journées* and Méhul's *Joseph* were both given in Czech in the first season of the triumvirate and became mainstays of the repertory. Operas by Dalayrac, Grétry, Boieldieu, Auber and Isouard were introduced later. Altogether, 34 operas were given in Czech during this period (Srb 1891, 134). It should be stressed that the Czech opera company could perform only works already in the German repertory of the Estates Theatre. (The one exception was Škroup's *The Tinker*, see p. 60.) The sets, chorus and orchestra were all those of the German company, as were most of the opera soloists.[6]

Czech performances at this time were affected by a peculiar restraint that dated back to the absorption of the old Patriotic Theatre company by Guardasoni in 1804: they could take place only in the afternoons on Sundays or holidays from 4 p.m. (later 3.30) until 6 p.m. This was because of restrictions laid down by the Estates, which had acquired the Nostitz Theatre expressly to cultivate good German drama, not to encourage rival Czech-language performances, which anyway attracted a lower-class audience and thus lowered the tone of the establishment. The only way round this was for Czech-language performances to be presented as charitable ventures (the singers giving their services free), and for them to take place in the afternoons when the theatre was not in use. As it was, this time suited the Czech-speaking public, made up of small traders, craftsmen and servants, who were unable to attend later performances (at 7 p.m.) since work for such occupations continued well into the evenings. The matinée performances had to be squeezed into two hours, usually by extensive cuts and fast tempos. Sometimes the curtain had to be brought down before the performance had ended. Even with these restraints the Czech opera company achieved a reasonable standard comparable with that of the German company. The soloists were after all mostly the same (sometimes having to sing in Czech in the afternoon and in German in the evening; Plavec 1941, 104). Much of the bel canto repertory was actually easier to sing in the

21

Czech language, with its open, Italianate vowels. With the concentration of all sorts of theatrical activity into one building, the culturally unsophisticated Czech audiences came into contact with opera to a far greater extent than did corresponding audiences in Vienna, where separate theatres served separate needs. Czech historians point to the exceptional musical training in school and church that all Czechs, however humble, received at this time, an important factor in their enthusiastic reception of relatively demanding operatic works in the theatre (Volek 1973, 40).

## *Opera in Czech 1834–48*

After the triumvirate was dismissed, the Estates Theatre was let to the German theatrical impresario Johann August Stöger, who ran it from 1834 to 1846, when he was succeeded by the Viennese Jan Hoffmann. Both Stöger and Hoffmann were former opera singers, so that the existing, unwritten policy of favouring opera continued. Despite Štěpánek's dismissal as one of the three impresarios, Stöger kept him on to oversee Czech performances, which consequently suffered less under purely German management than might have been expected. In fact Stöger believed that Czech theatre could thrive as a commercial venture and in 1842 had a building adapted for this purpose: until his financial collapse in 1846, Czech theatrical performances took place more frequently than at any time since the height of the Patriotic Theatre. Like the Patriotic Theatre, Stöger's New Theatre in Rose Street (Nové divadlo v Růžové ulici) performed both in Czech and in German (presenting the lighter German repertory forbidden by the Estates in their own theatre). In the first season (1842–3) there were usually three Czech performances each week: on Tuesday and Thursday evenings works aimed mainly at the intelligentsia, and on Sunday and holiday afternoons pieces for a wider public. While Stöger undoubtedly stimulated Czech theatre by appointing a fully professional company and setting up a competition for an original Czech play, his venture nevertheless failed. His New Theatre was one of the biggest in central Europe and held more than 2000. Three Czech performances a week meant selling 6000 tickets a week to the Czech population of Prague – too steep an increase from the 1000 tickets hitherto taken up by the regular Sunday afternoon performances in Czech at the Estates Theatre.

Circumstances for Czech opera during this period at first appeared propitious. Performances could be more frequent and were moreover no longer restricted by the two-hour rule at the Estates Theatre, and there was an opera-loving impresario, who in 1837 had appointed a Czech, František Škroup, chief conductor at the Estates Theatre. Škroup's association with Czech opera at the Estates Theatre went back to 1823, when he sang in the historical performances of Weigl's *Die Schweizerfamilie*. As a singer, a high baritone who could manage tenor roles such as Max in *Der Freischütz* or even Iago in Rossini's *Otello*,[7] and from 1827 as assistant conductor at the Estates Theatre, Škroup had presided over the flowering of Czech opera under the triumvirate and might have been expected, now as chief conductor, to achieve even more. But Czech opera performances did not flourish. They were overshadowed by those of the increasingly fine German opera company (ironically, led by Škroup) and by the Czech drama company. Škroup seemed unable to solve pressing problems such as the lack of a good Czech tenor, which resulted in a narrowing of the repertory and sometimes the replacement of a complete opera by an evening of operatic excerpts. The percentage of operas in Czech dropped to a fifth of all Czech performances and only two original Czech operas were performed during this period, neither of them in full: Škroup's *Libuše's Marriage* (Act ?3 only, 1835) and an opera by his brother Jan Nepomuk Škroup, *The Swedes in Prague* (Act 1 only, 1845). Things improved under Hoffmann. Ten of the thirty-five Czech performances at the Estates Theatre in the 1846–7 season were of opera, and nine of the thirty-nine Czech performances of the following season. Hoffmann doubled the space for the orchestra, brought in new singers (including a Czech tenor, J.N. Maýr, see p. 33), and appointed a producer of Czech plays, a conductor of Czech operas, and a Czech dramaturg, Josef Kajetán Tyl.

Tyl (1808–56) is the most significant figure in Czech theatre in the middle of the century. Like Štěpánek he served the theatre in many capacities – as actor, manager, playwright and translator. He came to the fore in the 1830s as the author of several plays and from 1835 to 1837 directed the amateur theatre company which flourished in Prague at the demise of the Štěpánek triumvirate. In 1842 he quitted his post as an army clerk to become producer of Czech plays in Stöger's New Theatre, and in 1846 Hoffmann appointed him dramaturg at the Estates Theatre with a contract to arrange for five plays to be translated each year and to write two new plays himself. Many of his plays, particularly those exploiting a fairy-tale genre, are still in the repertory, for instance *The Bagpiper of Strakonice* (*Strakonický dudák*, 1847), *Jiřík's Dream* (*Jiříkovo vidění*, 1849), *The Obstinate Woman* (*Tvrdohlavá žena*, 1849), but he also wrote serious plays with historical and contemporary settings such as *Jan Hus* (1848) or *The Miners of Kutná Hora* (*Kutnohorští havíři*, 1848), that were able to take advantage of the abolition of Austrian censorship in March 1848 and so present material hitherto absent from the Czech stage.

Another effect of the 1848 Revolution was a general awareness that the ever-increasing Czech population was being inadequately served, especially after the demise of Stöger's New Theatre, by a single weekend performance in the Estates Theatre. A new theatre for the Czechs was actively discussed and a 'provisional intendant' for the Czech theatre, Antonín Pravoslav Trojan, was appointed in July 1849. Trojan succeeded for a brief period in obtaining an extra evening performance for Czechs (Thursday evenings from October 1849 to May 1850), and getting Hoffmann to build an outdoor summer theatre in the Pštroska Park, a venue outside the city walls and thus not subject to the city's theatre franchise restrictions.

The summer theatre was not exclusively for the Czechs, but it provided more opportunities for Czech performances and was particularly attractive to less sophisticated audiences. By the middle of the nineteenth century many of the larger European towns had open-air theatres outside the city walls, in gardens where the people went for recreation, particularly in the vicinity of summer restaurants. The Prague 'Arena v Pštrosce' was a large unroofed wooden building seating 2500 in a horseshoe auditorium. Although blinds could be raised against the sun, there was no covering against the rain, which inevitably washed out some performances. The Pštroska Theatre led to the erection of a similar open-air theatre in Hradec Králové (1851) and Písek (1852), and was the forerunner of several similar theatres in Prague in the second half of the nineteenth century (Javorin 1958, 31–52). It also gave rise to the idea of adapting a building in Prague for Czech performances during the winter months and the establishment of a fund-raising committee under the chairmanship of the historian František Palacký.

But the improvements of the late 1840s were followed by a period of repression far worse than anything the Czechs had previously experienced. Censorship was reimposed (25 November 1850), the extra Czech performances were clawed back, Tyl and most of the Czech actors were dismissed (1852), and the activities of the fund-raising committee obstructed. It was a full decade before Czech theatre and opera flourished again.

# The Provisional Theatre[8]

One of the first areas in which the more liberal atmosphere of the 1860s was apparent was the theatre. From December 1861 two extra Czech performances were allowed at the Estates Theatre in addition to the regular Sunday afternoon performances. Opera was now performed in Czech at least three times a month. This progress, however, was dwarfed by a more radical development – the building of a new theatre for the Czechs alone, the Royal Provincial Provisional Theatre in Prague (Královské zemské prozatímní divadlo v Praze), commonly known as the Provisional Theatre (Prozatímní divadlo).

The new theatre was provided by the state (through the Bohemian Provincial Council) and cost 106,626 zl. Building began at the end of May 1862 and progressed so rapidly that the theatre opened that same year, on 18 November. The theatre was 'provisional' since the Czechs considered it inadequate to their needs, and plans were already afoot for the building of the National Theatre, to be financed by the Czechs alone. No one imagined that this would take twenty years. For all the disparaging remarks at the time about the inadequacy of the theatre, and the arguments for waiting until a larger theatre could be built, the 'provisional' era was to prove the most crucial in the history of Czech opera. Small though it was, the theatre was at least an exclusively Czech home for drama and opera – the first ever; the company assembled to perform in it was the first permanent and exclusively Czech ensemble. Headed by Smetana, composers wrote expressly for the theatre and its company and took the attendant limitations of both into account. Twenty years later, when Czech drama and opera moved into more spacious accommodation at the National Theatre, and Czech theatres opened in Plzeň and Brno, the foundations for a Czech national style in opera had been laid.

At first Franz Thomé ran both the Provisional Theatre and the Estates Theatre, where he had held the lease since 1858, but with the third season (1864–5) the Provincial Council decided to separate the management of the two theatres and award the Provisional Theatre concession (with an annual subsidy of 10,500 zl.) to a businessman, František Liegert. During the year, Liegert went into debt and the more experienced Thomé returned the following season, though only for a year: the Austro-Prussian War in the summer of 1866 badly affected the theatres and Thomé withdrew. From September 1866, the fifth season, the Provincial Council agreed to a new method of running the Provisional Theatre, which continued into the National Theatre era right up to 1920. The administration of the theatre was entrusted to a specially formed company, which tendered for a fixed-term contract, generally of six years. (A familiar modern parallel in Britain is the allocation of commercial franchises to individual companies by the Independent Broadcasting Authority.) The first such company, known as the *družstvo* (consortium), was formed by a group of patriotic and wealthy Czechs headed by the politician František Rieger. The *družstvo* appointed an executive director to take charge of day-to-day administration; liaison between the *družstvo* and the Provisional Council was made by an intendant appointed by the Council. Political pressures led to the replacement of the largely *staročech* (Old Czech) *družstvo* by a *mladočech* (Young Czech) *družstvo* in 1876 and a year later by a group that represented both wings of Czech politics, the *Spojené družstvo* (United Consortium) (Nejedlý 1935, i, 14–21).

The Provisional Theatre was intended for three companies: drama, opera, and ballet. According to Thomé's contract, it was to play three or four times a week, with one evening reserved for opera, allowing for at least fifty opera performances a year. (The ballet company was at first merely an adjunct to the others and never provided full-evening entertainments in the Provisional Theatre.) From March 1864, performances in the Provisional

Theatre took place daily and opera was given two or three times a week. In 1865 Liegert opened a new summer theatre on the Žofín island on the Vltava, where a further fifty opera and operetta performances took place between 14 May and 31 August 1865. But in the 1865-6 season the total number of opera performances fell (see Table 1) since cultural life was dis-

Table 1. *Balance of musical genres at the Provisional Theatre under Smetana (1866-74); figures during the two previous years are given for comparison.*

| Under Maýr | Operas | Operettas | Musical farces |
| --- | --- | --- | --- |
| 1864-5 | 132 | 22 | 56 |
| 1865-6* | 104 | 28 | 43 |
| Under Smetana | | | |
| 1866-7 | 126 | 26 | 61 |
| 1867-8 | 143 | 28 | 59 |
| 1868-9 | 136 | 77 | 104 |
| 1869-70 | 121 | 50 | 108 |
| 1870-1 | 138 | 82 | 96 |
| 1871-2 | 120 | 56 | 94 |
| 1872-3 | 122 | 32 | 116 |
| 1873-4 | 102 | 72 | 78 |

figures from Bartoš 1938, 20-1, 120-1, quoting contemporary theatrical almanacs. Despite possible inaccuracies in the statistics I have given the figures which would have been available to the *Dalibor* obituarist (see p. 34) and later commentators. The year in each case is taken to run from 1 December to 30 November, i.e. the 1866-7 season began some months after Smetana's directorship and the 1873-4 season ended some months after he left.
* season curtailed by the Austro-Prussian war.

rupted by the Austro-Prussian War. From the next season (in which Smetana took over as chief conductor) opera performances settled down to an average of roughly 125 a year.

## Theatres

The Provisional Theatre was a tiny though handsome structure occupying what is now the rear of the present National Theatre building. Its front façade looked across the building site of the National Theatre on to Ferdinandova třída (now Národní třída), one of the main thoroughfares leading to the bank of the Vltava; the short side façade ran parallel to the river embankment. The neo-Renaissance styling, with heavy rustication, attempted to give the feeling of monumentality to a structure that was anything but monumental, and influenced the style of surrounding buildings and of the National Theatre itself, which incorporated the Provisional

Theatre's side façade into its structure (see illustrations 1–2) – this area was ultimately turned into green rooms and store rooms. While the architect Ignác Ullmann had done a remarkable job fitting a theatre on to a site only 32 metres by 18–20 metres, all accounts agree about the inevitably cramped conditions. The first difficulty, as Karel Šípek relates in his memoir of the building, was how to get in:

> Even the stalls were reached by a large number of stairs. The staircase was narrow and precipitous, the steps uncomfortably high, and the galleries on individual floors were narrow and virtually without cloakrooms. A visit to the new seat of the muses was achieved by a wearisome climb and an anxious return. Luckily the audiences of the time had good nerves . . .
> (Šípek 1918, 16)

According to a contemporary box-office plan, there were 362 individual seats, of which 159 were in the stalls, 44 boxes (seating four each) on three tiers, and standing room for 340 (about 140 of these in the stalls). As a photograph taken in the final season shows, a further two rows in the stalls were added to the existing nine, gaining another 23 seats and bringing the total capacity to 900, though this could be increased by requisitioning the orchestra pit (only slightly lower than the auditorium). Hostinský relates how Fibich's specially composed overture to J.J. Kolár's play *The Prague Jew* (*Pražský žid*) had to be sacrificed to box-office pressure on the first night (Hostinský 1909, 11).

There was some ostentation in the boxes and on the *parquet* (the standing area behind the stalls, in Šípek's words 'the élite place for male members of the public'), but otherwise the audience did not dress up. As Šípek reported,

> One went in scarves, caps and *vlňáky* [the blanket-like woollen shawls worn by women in the country]. Piles of outer clothing accumulated on the laps of older ladies. Between acts one remained in one's seat – there was nowhere else to go – and to while away the time in the intervals, music was played. [Alternatively, attractions such as the performances by the Spanish one-legged dancer Juliano Donato took place, even between the acts of serious operas.] Members of the audience would take refreshments in their pockets – sometimes a complete dinner from the pork-butcher.
> (Šípek 1918, 16, 20–1)

The stage was no less cramped. In one of the articles written in his capacity as music critic of the daily *Národní listy* Smetana complained about the size. There was not enough room for the chorus in the market scene or the revolutionary outburst in *La muette de Portici*, nor for the fight between Catholics and Protestants in *Les Huguenots*, nor for countless processions and victorious marches.

> How does one cope in our small theatre? The best effect is made when the chorus surges thickly forward to the front of the apron (each member taking good care not to do his neighbour an injury with his gestures). At other times the chorus usually stands in a semicircle or in a straight line along the wings, pressed tightly one to another in a solid

1 The Provisional Theatre, a photograph of 1864 by W. Rupp, two years after its opening. The single-storey building on the left was demolished a few years later to make way for the National Theatre. The Provisional Theatre was the first permanent and exclusive home for Czech opera and drama from 1862 until its replacement by the National Theatre in 1883, and saw the premières of most of the operas by Smetana and his generation. Its limited size and resources helped to determine the character of Czech opera in the 1860s and 1870s.

wall, each member declaring his eagerness to go off and fight, without being able to move hand or foot in case someone gets hurt. (Smetana 1948, 94)

If, when considering Smetana's words, one remembers that the chorus at first consisted of ten women and eight men, with another eight borrowed from the German theatre (the number was later brought up to sixteen men and sixteen women), one gets some idea of how small the stage was. It measured 9.5 metres across and 7.5 metres to the top of the proscenium arch, and had a depth from the apron to the back of 9.5 metres. It was with good reason that the theatre was known as the 'matchbox' (Krásnohorská 1897, 974).

There is ample evidence that the size of the theatre and its tiny budget, while not preventing the Czechs from staging the most scenically demand-

2   The National Theatre, a drawing by Würbs after Zítek's plan of 1867. The
National Theatre was financed almost entirely by public subscription and
became one of the most potent symbols of the Czech national movement. It
was completed in 1881 and rebuilt two years later after fire gutted the original
building. Its state-financed predecessor, the Provisional Theatre (Illustration
1, outlined in this illustration) was incorporated into the building.

ing works in the international repertory, had some impact on the nature of
Czech works especially written for it. It is possible to argue, as does Bořivoj
Srba (1985, 99), that the detrimental effect of so much reported (rather than
staged) action in *The Brandenburgers in Bohemia* can be traced to this. Similarly, Eliška Krásnohorská abandoned her promised revision of *Lumír* for
Smetana on the grounds that the theatre would not be able to afford the opulent sets which she considered necessary for the work (Očadlík 1940, 28).

As soon as the weather improved, use could be made of the various summer theatres – unheated, usually unroofed wooden buildings after the
model of the open air theatre in the Pštroska Park. More than ten were
erected in Prague during the second half of the century before the building
of the National Theatre. Czech opera made use of three: the summer
theatre on the Žofín island, a speculation by František Liegert (he adapted
an existing hall) used only during the 1865 season; the New Town Theatre
(Novoměstské divadlo; see Javorin 1958, 53–65) and, from 1876, the New

Czech Theatre (Nové české divadlo; see Javorin 1958, 189–200). As its name suggests, the New Czech Theatre was an exclusively Czech theatre; the New Town Theatre on the other hand, opened in 1859 as a second stage for the Estates Theatre. The Czechs were allowed to use it on Thursday evenings and Sunday afternoons, and from 1862 on Tuesday evenings as well. Apart from 1865, the Czechs used it regularly up to the end of July 1876, when their own summer theatre was available, by which time they had given 804 performances there. The Germans continued to use it until 1886, when it was demolished to make way for their new theatre. The New Czech Theatre was demolished in 1885, when the lease on the land ran out, but had been little used after the opening of the National Theatre in 1883.

During the months that the New Town Theatre was used for theatrical performances (in the winter it housed circuses, balls and bazaars) stickers on posters proclaimed that the performance would take place there 'if weather favourable'. As Jarka reports (Smetana 1948, 259), it often happened that the management, judging the weather to be inclement, decided that the Provisional Theatre should be used, while the audience thought the weather fine and set off on the long journey to the Nové město (New Town). To avoid this confusion, the practice later arose of hoisting a flag to indicate that the performance would take place at the New Town Theatre, though misunderstandings continued to occur.

The New Town Theatre was covered, though the roof had glass skylights which could be opened. The New Czech Theatre had a sliding glass roof. While this kept the rain off it was also very noisy. In a performance of Smetana's *The Brandenburgers in Bohemia* in 1877, the opening scene was rendered inaudible by the noise of hail stones against the glass roof during a sudden storm. Another problem was the size of the summer theatres, which were much larger than the Provisional Theatre (both the New Town Theatre and the New Czech Theatre held over 3000). The management was naturally glad of the increased capacity and box-office takings and the audience enjoyed the airiness (the Provisional Theatre could reach well over 90°F in the summer) and the less formal atmosphere, but the singers had problems in adjusting to a different acoustic and in making themselves heard. For important events orchestra and chorus were usually augmented – the orchestra by members of Jan Pavlis's school of military music, the chorus by members of the Prague Hlahol choral society. Even so Smetana complained in his reviews that if the full depth of the New Town Theatre stage were used, little sound reached the auditorium as it went straight up into the sky. The repertory of the summer theatres was mostly light – operettas and farces – but with its large stage, useful for ceremonial scenes, the New Town Theatre was also the venue of the ill-fated première of *Dalibor* in 1868. The New Czech Theatre saw the premières of several important Czech operas needing a larger stage, such as Smetana's *The Devil's Wall* and Dvořák's *Dimitrij* (both in 1882).

## Sets, producers

The Provisional Theatre lacked stage machinery and for a long time even a stage mechanic. The apparitions of the Wolf's Glen in Weber's *Der Freischütz*, let alone the shipwreck in Meyerbeer's *L'africaine*, created the gravest difficulties. Even such effects as the moon rising were fraught with problems, as an 1881 review of Smetana's *The Secret* makes clear:

> The poor moon, before appearing on the open stage, had first to make its laborious way up a rope into the heavenly regions from which, however, it seemed unwilling to appear on stage. Eventually, with one mighty bound, it soared above the clouds, appearing for a moment, only to retire at once to a well-earned rest.    (Bartoš 1938, 331)

As was common practice throughout Europe at the time, stage sets were drawn from a general stock serving many productions and the appearance of a new set was usually hailed as a particular attraction. According to the poster of the première of Smetana's *The Brandenburgers in Bohemia* (reproduced in Očadlík 1950, 13), the second act had 'a new set by the theatrical painter Mr Macourek'; the other acts presumably made do with what was around. Little money was spent on opera sets since it was assumed that audiences attended opera mainly for the singing. In other genres scenic display was taken to be the chief attraction and accordingly took up much of the budget for new sets.

During the early years of the Provisional Theatre the opera producer was little more than a props master, asserting himself against the singers only with the greatest difficulty. Many of the early opera producers were themselves singers – generally buffo basses, like the 'producers' in other European opera houses of the time. František Sák (1817–83), responsible for many of the productions up to 1872, was originally a buffo bass at the Estates Theatre and the Provisional Theatre. František Hynek (1837–1905), the first Kecal in *The Bartered Bride*, returned from fifteen years in Germany with 'a thick book full of good recipes for foreign operas' (Dolanský 1918, 151). He began producing operas at the Provisional Theatre in 1880 and continued with the company both as singer and producer until the end of the century.

In 1873 Smetana brought in Edmund Chvalovský (1843–1934), who combined a technical background with a love of music and painting (Novák 1944, 38–44). His productions were characterized by far greater attention to realistic detail. Some idea of the conditions that prevailed before his arrival (he stayed with the company to the end of the century, turning his hand later to directing plays) can be gleaned from a tribute by Bohumil Benoni, one of the singers who worked under him. Benoni described him as the first Czech opera producer apart from František Kolár [a theatre producer who also worked on operas] who knew how to harmonize sets, costumes and props appropriately with the time and place of the piece and the first, besides Kolár, who took care with singers' acting. Up to this time the assumption here still prevailed that any attempt at acting would disturb their singing. (quoted in Bartoš 1938, 186)

It was Chvalovský who produced all of Smetana's later operas.

## Singers

At first many of the solo singers were recruited from the German company at the Estates Theatre, and many of them continued to sing with both companies. Two years after the Provisional Theatre opened, five of its fourteen listed male singers still had shared contracts with the German theatre. The star female soloist, Eleonora z Ehrenbergů (the first Mařenka in *The Bartered Bride*), joined the Germany company in 1861 after experience in Stuttgart, Leipzig and Hamburg. She sang with the Provisional Theatre from its inception and two years later had an exclusive contract there. Although born and brought up as a Prague German (of noble birth), she spoke good Czech, unlike her chief rival Johanna Brenner, who was also a member of both companies. A Hungarian, Brenner managed to sing, in Smetana's words, only in 'easily intelligible Czech' (Smetana 1948, 175). Both singers were coloratura sopranos, and after the early departure of the Polish Helena Zawiszanka the Provisional Theatre had no dramatic soprano. The tendency towards coloratura rather than dramatic singing was indicative of the Italian school of voice training that prevailed in Prague. Singing teaching at the Prague Conservatory had for years been dominated by z Ehrenbergů's teacher, Giovanni Gordigiani (he taught there 1822–9, 1838–64), and even after his retirement this orientation continued. The most important private singing school, which was opened in 1869 by František Pivoda (1824–98) and which provided many of the soloists at the Provisional and the National theatres, also had strongly Italianate leanings – one reason why Smetana was determined to found an independent singing school at the Provisional Theatre.

Several singers at the Provisional Theatre started in the drama company. Arnošt Grund, a goldsmith by trade, joined the Provisional Theatre as an actor in 1863 at the age of nineteen. In one of his appearances in a farce he was required to sing, and did so with such success that he was immediately taken in hand with singing lessons. Eight months later he appeared as Max in *Der Freischütz*. Such desperate measures were sometimes needed to sustain a company thrown into disarray by illness (there were no understudies) and by the movement of singers (Grund replaced the star tenor Čeněk Vecko, who had absconded to the better-paid German theatre). There was a particular leakage of basses. František Hynek, the first Kecal, left in 1866, and Josef Paleček, the original Elder in *The Brandenburgers in Bohemia* and, after Hynek's departure, a highly successful Kecal, in 1870. A number of singers, however, remained faithful to the company and provided the inspiration for many of Smetana's later characters (see pp. 179–86).

## Mayr

The first conductor at the Provisional Theatre was Jan Nepomuk Mayr (1818–88). He had been principal tenor in Stöger's short-lived Czech company at the Rose Street Theatre (1842–4), at the Estates Theatre (1842–4, 1846–8), and abroad in Stuttgart and Darmstadt (1844–6), but in 1848 turned to conducting. He became second conductor at the Estates Theatre (by 1851), and from 1853 he served as choirmaster in several Prague churches; in 1854 he opened a singing school. With the increased provision for Czech performances at the Estates Theatre in the early 1860s, Mayr was given charge of Czech operas and was the logical choice for opera conductor when the Provisional Theatre opened in November 1862. By then František Škroup, the long-standing chief conductor of the Estates Theatre until 1857, had died in Rotterdam. Smetana, who had been hoping for the post, was not only six years younger than Mayr, but much less experienced and, after his exile in Sweden, much less known.

As the nucleus of his orchestra Mayr took over the band founded in 1854 by Karel Komzák. This eighteen-strong ensemble had been formed to play in taverns and places of amusement and continued to do so (with a maximum of four days a week in the theatre) until 1865, when Mayr wrested complete control from Komzák. Komzák's band was augmented by players from the Estates Theatre, who could play only when not required at the German Theatre and were allowed to attend only one rehearsal at the Provisional Theatre. The other players Mayr knocked into shape with a strenuous regime of rehearsals starting at eight in the morning. By the 1863–4 season Mayr had reduced the number of outside players to a mere two or three, and by 1864 the orchestra was standardized to thirty-four: four first violins, four seconds, two each of violas, cellos and double basses, double woodwind, four horns, two trumpets, three trombones, a harp and two percussionists. From 1868 the orchestra increased to forty when playing in the New Town Theatre, otherwise it remained at thirty-four throughout the Provisional Theatre era, occasionally enlarged on special occasions such as the première of *The Kiss*, when the *Národní listy* critic made a special point of praising the effect obtained by six rather than four first violins (Procházka 1958, 53). Shortly before the definitive opening of the National Theatre in 1883 the orchestra was brought up to fifty with extra string and percussion players.

Mayr was responsible for assembling the opera company. He was an excellent organizer and worked hard (he was not above writing out parts for his orchestra): in his four years as chief conductor he rehearsed and conducted fifty-seven new operatic productions. This has not prevented his becoming the target of much criticism, from press reproval when he took a bow at his début (his name, unlike that of the stage designer, did not appear on the poster), to his obituary in *Dalibor* (anon. 1888, 319), where 'the dark side of his activities' was energetically listed. Smetana, the chief of his critics and hardly an impartial one (in 1863, a year before he began reviewing in *Národní listy*, described Maýr in a private letter as his 'personal and irreconcilable enemy'; Kraus 1906, 358), criticized his lack of musical sensitivity, asserting that he made no stylistic differentiation in the music he conducted and subjected it to illogical and harmful cuts. These there certainly were – a hangover from the time-conscious afternoon performances at the Estates Theatre – but it was also Maýr who restored the recitatives in *Don Giovanni* and the final sextet (Smaczny 1987). The *Dalibor* obituary criticized Maýr's introduction of a lighter repertory; Smetana frequently commented on his fondness for 'old-fashioned' Italian opera. In this respect, however, it could be argued that Maýr was simply being realistic. The tiny chorus of the Provisional Theatre was not only too large for the stage but also for the theatre as a whole, its voices coming over unblended. The pit was also too small and could accommodate only a few strings, which were naturally swamped by the wind during any *forte*. With its smaller and less important orchestral resources and its emphasis on soloists rather than on the chorus, early nineteenth-century Italian opera was better suited to the building than most French and German operas of the same period.

### Smetana

In addition to his trenchant reviews in *Národní listy*, Smetana was beginning to draw attention to himself as a conductor. In 1863 he became choirmaster of the Hlahol choral society; in the 1864–5 season he organized and conducted a series of subscription orchestral concerts; early in 1866 he conducted the premières of his first two operas at the Provisional Theatre. When after the disruption of the Austro-Prussian War (summer 1866) the *družstvo* took over the running of the theatre, Smetana's adherents on its board of directors were in the majority and were able to get him appointed chief conductor instead of Maýr (Holzknecht 1979, 179–80). Maýr returned to directing church music and on 13 September Smetana took charge.

Smetana remained at the Provisional Theatre as conductor for eight years, though from 1870 he was subjected to increasingly unpleasant personal attacks in the press, largely originating from Pivoda (Clapham 1971). Smetana's personal kindness and his musicianship won him the lasting respect and affection of his orchestra and singers, but, as the attacks continued, he began to lose the confidence of the public and of the administration and was nearly unseated in 1872. What the anti-Smetana faction was unable to achieve itself, however, came about through natural causes. In 1874 Smetana became deaf and, unable to discharge his duties, he applied for indefinite leave. He was dismissed with a small pension and on 1 November Maýr, ousted for eight years, returned and remained until his retirement in 1881.

Whatever the ostensible grounds for Pivoda's attacks on Smetana (which ranged from incompetence to the neglect of Czech opera other than his own), his attitude seems to have been aggravated by personal hostility and by Smetana's unenthusiastic attitude to his singing school. Behind the anti-Smetana campaign also lies the political rift in Czech society mentioned in Chapter 1. Smetana was *mladočech*, Pivoda, Rieger and most of the theatre administration *staročech*. Smetana was certainly a different type of conductor from Maýr,[9] far less of a disciplinarian, more sensitive, and, unlike his rival, aware of Liszt's and Wagner's new conception of the orchestra and the conductor. He also had a greater sense of the mission of the Provisional Theatre and its opera. It was based on his knowledge of Wagner's writings, on Liszt's Weimar theatre, and on his own thoughts about the role of a Czech national opera. He had, however, much less control over opera at the Provisional Theatre than he would have needed to realize his plans.

### *Repertory*[10]

The repertory of the Provisional Theatre, though now independent of the German company's repertory at the Estates Theatre and officially drawn up by a committee headed by the intendant (Nejedlý 1935, i, 50) was still a haphazard affair. It came about mostly as the result of casting exigencies and management pressure for box-office draws (there was only a tiny state subsidy: 16,500 zl. in 1866 raised to 18,500 zl. ten years later – half of what the German theatre received; Nejedlý 1935, i, 96–7). Under Maýr, the *Dalibor* obituary claimed, 'The audience was not spared the most worn-out Offenbachiana, the most idiotic German farce'. But the pressure for this type of fare was something that Smetana was also little able to resist, as can be seen from Table 1. Under Maýr the number of farces and operettas together never exceeded the number of operas performed, and this is true also of Smetana's first two seasons. But in Smetana's third season the number of musical farces doubled and operettas almost trebled, while the number of opera performances fell slightly; this sort of balance, with a little fluctuation, continued into the National Theatre. Though he handed over much of the operetta conducting to his deputy Adolf Čech (also Maýr's deputy and in 1881 his successor), Smetana occasionally conducted

Offenbach himself, ten of whose operettas were introduced into the Provisional Theatre repertory during his term of office.

Equally important in the drawing up of repertory were the singers. Smetana and his colleagues were dependent on the singers at hand and whether they were well (it was a tiny company, without understudies); illness often meant the last-minute substitution of one opera for another. The Benefit system, whereby an artist's salary was augmented by an annual performance (in which he or she selected the piece and took the profits), flourished throughout the Provisional era. Though clearly incompatible with a well-considered dramaturgical plan, the system had some advantages. While many singers chose works that would draw a capacity house and thus capacity takings, others consciously chose rarely given though musically rewarding works. Smetana's *The Two Widows* remained in the repertory only by courtesy of Benefits (Smetana 1948, 402–3; Bartoš 1938, 60).

It is understandable that the German operatic repertory was poorly represented at the Provisional Theatre. The whole purpose of a specifically Czech theatre was to be different from the German theatre in Prague, where German repertory provided a central focus. Thus apart from Weber's *Der Freischütz* (49 performances at the Provisional Theatre), German operas were largely confined to the lighter ones; by Lortzing (notably his *Zar und Zimmermann*) and by those composers whose style was leavened by French or Italian influence, for instance Flotow, whose *Martha* and *Alessandro Stradella* became standard repertory pieces, and Nicolai, whose *Die lustigen Weiber von Windsor* achieved a respectable 44 performances.

Mozart and Gluck, though traditionally counted in Czech repertory lists as 'German', did not however suffer from the same anti-German tendency. Both *Orfeo ed Eurydice* and *Armide* (the Prague première) were introduced during Maýr's first term. *Orfeo* received 24 performances during the Provisional Theatre period, Maýr himself choosing it for one of his Benefits. Smetana, who had gone as Gluck to a fancy dress ball in 1848, introduced Wagner's revision of *Iphigénie en Aulide*.

Prague was proud of its connections with Mozart, and the frequent performances at the Provisional Theatre of *Figaro*, *Don Giovanni* and *Die Zauberflöte* were the continuation of a performance history in Czech that stretched back, in the case of *Die Zauberflöte*, to 1794. *La clemenza di Tito*, on the other hand, despite is première in Prague in 1791, was not given in Czech until a century later (at the National Theatre). *Così fan tutte*, performed four times in Czech under Škroup (in 1831) had to wait almost a century before it was revived at the National Theatre (1924). Smetana added *Die Entführung* to the Provisional Theatre repertory (it had been the second Mozart opera to be performed in Czech, in 1806), though it was not popular and was withdrawn when the Osmin left the company.

The chief difference in emphasis during Smetana's term of office was that he steered away as much as possible from the Italian repertory favoured by Maýr, and introduced more French pieces and a little Slavonic repertory. Smetana's attitude towards Italian opera emerges clearly from his reviews in *Národní listy*. He declared that he had heard too many *Normas*, while he found Bellini's *I Capuleti e i Montecchi* old-fashioned and deserving of a 'well-earned rest'. Altogether nine Donizetti operas were staged at the Provisional Theatre, seven of them premièred before Smetana's time, though only *Lucia di Lammermoor* (52 performances) and *Lucrezia Borgia* (37) achieved a lasting success.

About Rossini Smetana had mixed feelings. *Otello*, one of the earliest operas to be performed at the Provisional Theatre (and before that, under Škroup), he thought outdated and, with its three virtuoso tenors, impossible to cast, but *Il barbiere* he adored, finding it full of delightful numbers, and regretting the cuts made in it. Verdi was well established at the Provisional Theatre before Smetana took over: *Ernani* had received 35 performances and *Rigoletto* 28, while *Il trovatore*, with 106 performances at the Provisional Theatre, proved the third most popular opera to be given there. As with Rossini, Smetana was not wholly enthusiastic. He responded to Verdi's dramatic power but found many passages trivial. He nevertheless introduced *La traviata*, *Un ballo in maschera* and *Nabucco*, though the last, despite its stirring nationalist choruses, received only a handful of performances. One of the most popular Italian operas introduced by Smetana was the Ricci brothers' *Crispino e la comare*, whose folk flavour was felt to be particularly close to that of Czech opera.

Despite Smetana's attempts to enlarge the Slavonic repertory, for example with Polish operas, including Moniuszko's *Halka*, none caught on. Glinka's *Ruslan and Ludmila*, with 23 performances, proved to be by far the most popular foreign Slav opera, though this was undoubtedly due to its conductor – Balakirev, brought to Prague to conduct the première in January 1867 and four further performances. But even Balakirev's advocacy failed to generate much interest in *A Life for the Tsar*, introduced the previous year.

With German opera avoided and Italian opera frowned on by Smetana, it was inevitable that French opera would dominate the foreign repertory. Forty French operas were staged at the Provisional Theatre, nearly twice the number of Italian operas. Most of these were light – works, for instance, by Auber, Adam, Boieldieu, Delibes and Hérold. Auber, with no fewer than ten operas, two of them 'grand', emerges surprisingly as the best-represented foreign composer (apart from Offenbach). Despite the tiny stage and slender resources of the Provisional Theatre, French grand opera was enthusiastically cultivated. Rossini's *Guillaume Tell* (57 performances) and Auber's *La muette de Portici* (75) were together with Meyerbeer's *Les Huguenots* (77) and *Robert le diable* (56) two of the most frequently performed operas at the Provisional Theatre. Among later French operas

Gounod's *Faust* was the most popular of all; his *Roméo et Juliette*, first given in 1869, two years after its Paris première, also received 45 performances. Bizet's *Carmen* was never produced at the Provisional Theatre. It reached Prague (at the German theatre) in 1880 and was one of the first foreign novelties at the National Theatre in 1884.

The Czech repertory will be discussed in detail in Chapter 3; here it is considered statistically in relation to the other repertories. Particularly interesting are the anomalies that emerge when comparing the number of different operas produced during the Provisional era with the total number of performances (see Tables 2a–b). Although 41 different Czech operas were given, one more than the 40 French and many more than the 26 Italian operas, both the French and the Italian repertories separately achieved many more performances. In other words, while the management felt a duty to bring to performance most new Czech operas (surprisingly few were rejected), only a handful were popular with the public. Three-quarters of the Czech operas given at the Provisional Theatre were performed fewer than 20 times each, and of these operas a third were given a mere two or three times. These statistics are reinforced by Table 3a, a list of the fifteen most popular operas during the Provisional Theatre period. *The Bartered Bride* had just slightly fewer performances than the top favourite, *Faust* (introduced a year later), but it is the only Czech opera in the top ten. Smetana's *The Kiss*, as a latecomer in 1876, did well to receive 46 performances in seven years.

# The National Theatre[11]

## *The building*

By the time the Provisional Theatre opened in 1862 plans for the National Theatre had been in progress for over a decade. Applications for a separate Czech theatre had been made in the 1840s, but had been turned down by the Metternich government. The 1848 Revolution changed this situation. In 1849 the Bohemian Provincial Council appointed A.J. Trojan 'Provisional Intendant of the Czech Theatre' (though based at the Estates Theatre). After plans to adapt the old Kotzen theatre came to nothing it was on Trojan's initiative that the Committee for the Establishment of the Czech National Theatre (Sbor pro zřízení českého Národního divadla) under the chairmanship of František Palacký was formed on 7 September 1850. The committee, given official sanction in 1851, energetically set about raising funds through private collections but soon began to run into the active opposition of the new Governor of Bohemia, Baron Mecsery. Nevertheless the embankment site – at the time an old warehouse for storing salt stood

Table 2. Operas performed at the Provisional and National Theatres in Prague 1862–1920 arranged according to nationality of composer*

a. Analysed by number of performances

| | 1862–83 | % | 1883–92 | % | 1892–1900 | % | 1900–06 | % | 1906–12 | % | 1912–20 | % |
|---|---|---|---|---|---|---|---|---|---|---|---|---|
| Czech | 588 | 24.58 | 468 | 36.65 | 663 | 49.15 | 512 | 46.93 | 559 | 45.37 | 1060 | 53.97 |
| French | 722 | 30.18 | 322 | 25.21 | 204 | 15.12 | 219 | 19.76 | 235 | 19.08 | 271 | 13.80 |
| Italian | 611 | 25.54 | 314 | 24.59 | 297 | 22.01 | 168 | 15.16 | 146 | 11.85 | 218 | 11.10 |
| German | 397 | 16.60 | 111 | 8.69 | 87 | 6.45 | 158 | 14.25 | 235 | 19.08 | 324 | 16.50 |
| others** | 74 | 3.09 | 62 | 4.86 | 98 | 7.26 | 55 | 4.96 | 57 | 4.62 | 91 | 4.63 |
| Total | 2392 | | 1277 | | 1349 | | 1108 | | 1232 | | 1964 | |

b. Analysed by number of operas

| | 1862–83 | % | 1883–92 | % | 1892–1900 | % | 1900–06 | % | 1906–12 | % | 1912–20 | % |
|---|---|---|---|---|---|---|---|---|---|---|---|---|
| Czech | 41 | 29.93 | 33 | 28.95 | 40 | 35.71 | 32 | 39.02 | 34 | 37.36 | 38 | 38.00 |
| French | 40 | 29.19 | 30 | 26.32 | 23 | 20.54 | 17 | 20.73 | 20 | 21.98 | 18 | 18.00 |
| Italian | 26 | 18.98 | 20 | 17.54 | 28 | 25.00 | 13 | 15.85 | 12 | 13.19 | 16 | 16.00 |
| German | 21 | 15.32 | 24 | 21.05 | 13 | 11.61 | 16 | 19.51 | 21 | 23.08 | 24 | 24.00 |
| others** | 9 | 6.57 | 7 | 6.14 | 8 | 7.14 | 4 | 4.88 | 4 | 4.40 | 4 | 4.00 |
| Total | 137 | | 114 | | 112 | | 82 | | 91 | | 100 | |

statistics for 1862–83 derived from Smaczny 1987; the rest from Konečná 1983 and Němeček 1968

\* National origins follow those adopted in Czech lists (e.g. Konečná 1983 and Němeček 1968) whereby Gluck and Mozart are designated 'German' composers. Operetta is generally excluded though many of the French 'operas' included in these statistics are distinctly on the light side. In the Provisional period (1862–83) the Czech repertory generously includes composers born in Bohemia such as Abert, Kittl, Nápravník and Zavrtal, whose operas were written to non-Czech texts and were performed in Czech at the Provisional Theatre, usually after a staging abroad. While making up almost a quarter of the 'Czech' operas presented at the Provisional Theatre, they achieved only 40 performances, or 1.69% of the total.

\*\* 1862–83: English, Croatian, Polish and Russian; 1883–1900 Polish and Russian; 1900–1920 Russian

Table 3. *The operas most frequently performed at the Provisional and National Theatres in Prague, 1862–1920*

| (a) Provisional Theatre (1862–83) | | (b) National Theatre (1883–1900) | | (c) National Theatre (1900–1920) | |
|---|---|---|---|---|---|
| *No. of performances* | | *No. of performances* | | *No. of performances* | |
| 119 | Gounod, *Faust* | 241 | Smetana, *The Bartered Bride* | 399 | Smetana, *The Bartered Bride* |
| 114 | Smetana, *The Bartered Bride* | 105 | Bizet, *Carmen* | 169 | Smetana, *Dalibor* |
| 106 | Verdi, *Il trovatore* | 81 | Smetana, *Dalibor* | 142 | Smetana, *The Kiss* |
| 77 | Meyerbeer, *Les Huguenots* | 77 | Wagner, *Lohengrin* | 133 | Dvořák, *Rusalka* |
| 75 | Auber, *La muette de Portici* | 74 | Gounod, *Faust* | 126 | Kovařovic, *The Dogheads* |
| 58 | Rossini, *Il barbiere di Siviglia* | 70 | Mascagni, *Cavalleria rusticana* | 124 | Tchaikovsky, *Eugene Onegin* |
| 57 | Rossini, *Guillaume Tell* | 69 | Smetana, *The Kiss* | 109 | Bizet, *Carmen* |
| 56 | Meyerbeer, *Robert le diable* | 63 | Tchaikovsky, *Eugene Onegin* | 101 | Smetana, *Libuše* |
| 52 | Donizetti, *Lucia di Lammermoor* | 61 | Franchetti, *Asrael* | 101 | Smetana, *The Secret* |
| 49 | Weber, *Der Freischütz* | 61 | Verdi, *Aida* | 83 | Dvořák, *The Devil and Kate* |
| 47 | Halévy, *La juive* | 59 | Smetana, *Libuše* | 81 | Smetana, *The Two Widows* |
| 46 | Smetana, *The Kiss* | 57 | Dvořák, *Dimitrij* | 79 | Thomas, *Mignon* |
| 45 | Gounod, *Roméo et Juliette* | 56 | Mozart, *Die Zauberflöte* | 73 | Blodek, *In the Well* |
| 45 | Mozart, *Don Giovanni* | 55 | Verdi, *Otello* | 73 | Charpentier, *Louise* |
| 44 | Nicolai, *Die lustigen Weiber* | 54 | Blodek, *In the Well* | 69 | Offenbach, *Les contes d'Hoffmann* |

statistics for (a) from Smaczny 1987; for (b) and (c) from Konečná 1983 there – was purchased in 1852 for 45,000 zl. and in 1854 a competition for building plans produced seven entries, though lack of funds precluded any further progress. From 1855 the committee's activities, continually thwarted by the repressive atmosphere of the Bach era and its local representative Baron Mecsary, virtually ceased until 1860, when Bach's (and Mecsery's) departure allowed a fresh start.

In this new climate the Bohemian Provincial Council decided to appease the increasingly vociferous Czech nationalist aspirations by building, at its own expense, a small theatre for the Czech population of Prague – the Provisional Theatre. Its location at the rear of the embankment site meant that the 1854 plans for the National Theatre had to be scrapped. The frequently poor attendances at the Provisional Theatre, however, did not encourage an immediate start on the larger National Theatre, and it was not until 1865, when a new committee was elected, that much happened. A contract was signed with Josef Zítek (the winner of a new competition) in 1867, and 16 May 1868, the feast of St John of Nepomuk, was chosen for the laying of the foundation stone (see illustration 3). This became the central day of a three-day festival, now regarded as the Czechs' greatest national demonstration between the 1848 Revolution and their independence in 1918. Its timing was significant. It took place in the wave of disappointment in Bohemia that followed the creation of Austro-Hungary the previous year, a redistribution of political power in the empire that gave political equality to the Hungarians but not to the Czechs. The laying of the foundation stone of the National Theatre was 'at once a political demonstration, a cultural exhibition, a semireligious rite, a historical pageant and everything that the term "national celebration" has come to connote in Central European History' (Kimball 1966, 81). Special trains had to be chartered for the 60,000 visitors who descended on Prague; the huge procession, with guilds in medieval finery and students in fancy dress, included cultural representatives from the whole Czech-speaking world – for instance 148 choral societies and 1500 *Sokol* physical training groups – as well as guests from other Slav nations and high officials (Heller 1918, 14–40).

Sadly such national fervour had little impact on fund-raising attempts during the next decade: the building of the National Theatre proceeded as slowly as that of the Provisional Theatre had been fast. Work was temporarily halted in 1874 and again in 1877, though by 1875 the building had at least reached roof height. In 1881, as work neared completion, the opening had to be brought forward, to 11 June, to celebrate the marriage of Crown Prince Rudolf. Thus the première of Smetana's *Libuše*, reserved almost a decade for the opening of the National Theatre, had at the last moment to be coupled with a *tableau vivant* depicting the 'apotheosis' of the prince's marriage.[12] Eleven more performances (including four of *Libuše)* took place in the still incomplete theatre, the last on 23 July 1881, after which it was closed for further work and a hoped-for reopening on 28 September, the day of Bohemia's patron saint, St Václav.

On the evening of 12 August a fire broke out on the roof of the theatre. There is disagreement about its cause. Theories range from arson to carelessness by ironworkers when pouring out supposedly dead coals on the roof, but what is certain is that the fire-fighting arrangements proved inadequate (*DP*, 122–43) and by the end of the evening only the walls, the foyer, grand staircase and some of the anterooms were left standing. So shattering was the effect of this news that money began to pour in immediately, and by the end of the year 745,000 zl. had been raised through private donations. With 275,000 zl. insurance this amounted to over a million zl., enough to begin work again. If one takes into account that it had taken thirty years to raise 600,000 zl. towards the original building, the changes in attitude and in Czech prosperity are striking. The old building cost 1,800,000 zl., of which 200,000 zl. had come from a mortgage and another 200,000 zl. was a gift from the Bohemian parliament. The restoration cost

3 Laying the foundation stone of the National Theatre in 1868, engraving by Bohuslav Roubalík. The oration is being given by the Czech historian František Palacký (centre). Smetana (with beard and glasses) is prominent second from the right among the group of male dignitaries to the left of Palacký.

1,300,000 zl., making a total of 3,204,219 zl. – thirty times the cost of the Provisional Theatre.

Criticism had been made of details in Zítek's original plans and he was asked to take these into account in the new plans. His dilatoriness resulted in his former pupil, Josef Schulz, future architect of the National Museum in Prague, completing the work. The Provisional Theatre, which had survived the fire practically unscathed and had simply continued in use until 14 April 1883, was incorporated into the complex together with a newly purchased site at its rear. The plans were approved in May 1882 and work began immediately. Building was completed by the gala opening on 18 November 1883, again with *Libuše*, but without the Prince Rudolf apotheosis.

Like Ullmann's designs for the Provisional Theatre, Zítek's design for the National Theatre was conceived in the fashionable neo-Renaissance style. Ullmann's greatest problem had been to fit any sort of theatre into such a small space, Zítek's had been to give the impression of symmetry to an asymmetrical site (it tapered towards the rear and the front projected at an oblique angle). In this, as in so many other respects, the theatre was a triumphant success. Zítek was one of the finest Czech architects of the nineteenth century, and the site on the bank of the Vltava, with a panoramic view of the Hradčany castle complex on the opposite bank, is one of the most imposing of any opera house. As the project neared completion there was pressure to make the interior match the opulence of the outside. By 1881 Zítek's 1866 estimate of 472,400 zl. had been inflated to 1,824,800 zl. by items such as the interior decorations, for which the estimate of 50,000 zl. proved less than a quarter of the eventual cost. Leading Czech artists participated in providing the mythological and allegorical scenes such as the cycle 'Fatherland' ('Vlast') by Mikoláš Aleš in the foyer (happily untouched by the fire) and František Ženíšek's muses on the ceiling of the auditorium. The best-known of all these decorations, however, is Vojtěch Hynais's front curtain, symbolizing the sacrifices of the common people that made the theatre possible. One group, a widow with two small children offering two small coins, touched a special chord in Czech hearts. The theatre was after all unique in not being erected by a central authority – by royal or municipal decree – but by the immense effort of a small, politically repressed but culturally vibrant nation. At an early stage Zítek abandoned a 'golden horseshoe' plan for the auditorium and instead adopted a semicircle. Around this, as was noted by the Viennese press at the 1883 reopening, the boxes were 'open'. For all its magnificence the National Theatre was a democratic opera house. Hynais's curtain and the proscenium inscription are still reminders that it was a gift from 'the nation to itself' (Národ sobě). And the nation came in its thousands. In the year of its opening 114 special 'theatre trains' brought in countryfolk to Prague, eager to see their theatre.

After twenty years of the cramped conditions at the Provisional Theatre, the new theatre at last provided normal working conditions. The difference in size of the National Theatre and the Provisional Theatre is demonstrated by illustration 2 (p. 29): the Provisional Theatre (in box) occupies a small space at the rear of the National Theatre. Before the extensive overhaul in 1977–83 (which reduced the seating capacity) the National Theatre held 1188 seats in the stalls, two balconies, two galleries, and forty-four boxes. Standing room brought the total capacity to 1598, much more than that of the Provisional Theatre or even the old Estates Theatre.

The more spacious dimensions of the new building were appreciated even more in the orchestra pit and on stage. The pit, partly under the stage, could now take a full opera orchestra. By 1884 the orchestra, held at 34 for many years, had risen to 64. The stage itself, 22 metres across, 26 metres high and 19–20.5 metres deep (the corresponding dimensions at the Provisional Theatre were 9.5, 7.5 and 9.5 metres) could at last accommodate a full chorus. By 1883 the 32-strong chorus of the Provisional Theatre had become 57; by 1891, 69 (37 women and 32 men) and by 1900, 74 (41 and 33). Contracted opera soloists, originally 5 women and 7 men at the Provisional Theatre, rose to 27 in 1883, though this number declined to between 21 and 26 until the end of the century. By the mid-1960s the National Theatre had an orchestra of 117 (65 strings) and a chorus of 106.

*Administration*

The Committee for the Establishment of the Czech National Theatre handed over the complete theatre to the 'Czech nation', or rather its temporal representative, the Bohemian Provincial Council. This resulted in the same administrative system that had operated at the Provisional Theatre; the Provincial Council entrusted the running of the theatre on a six-year lease to a specially formed company. The *Spojené družstvo* (United Consortium), installed in 1877, gave way to a reconstituted *Družstvo Národního divadla* (Consortium of the National Theatre) in 1881 and with uncontested franchise renewals in 1888 and 1894 simply continued to run the theatre up to the end of the century, when the franchise was awarded instead to a newly formed competitor, *Společnost Národního divadla* (The Company of the National Theatre). From 1920, soon after the creation of the Czechoslovak Republic, the theatre was administered directly by the state without an intermediate franchise company.

From the opening of the National Theatre in 1883 to the change of franchise holder in 1900, the chief administrator of the company was the writer and dramatist František Adolf Šubert (1849–1915). Elected to this office at the age of thirty-four, Šubert, almost alone, determined the artistic policy of the National Theatre during the nineteenth century. On the drama side he had the advice of the house dramaturg (notably Ladislav Stroupežnický until his death in 1892) and of the chief producer František Kolár, but no comparable help was available to the non-musician Šubert in musical matters. He took informal advice from the critic Emanuel Chvála and in 1899 appointed Fibich music dramaturg, but the change of regime in the theatre and Fibich's death (both in 1900) meant that Fibich held this office for less than a year. Šubert's conductors, Adolf Čech (already a veteran from Smetana's day, he remained chief conductor until 1900) and Mořic Anger (taken on in 1881 and remaining with the company as an easy-going second conductor until his death in 1905) were able to make suggestions and give advice but they hardly asserted themselves against Šubert. They served as conductors rather than as musical directors, with little say in the choice of repertory, and in the engagement of solo singers.

The situation changed in 1900, when the franchise was awarded to the *Společnost Národního divadla*. Gustav Schmoranz, an architect teaching at an art college, replaced Šubert as administrative director, but, according to the new contract, the chief conductor now had charge of the artistic direction of the opera and ballet. Karel Kovařovic (1862–1920) had been harpist at the Provisional and National Theatres (1879–85) and by 1900 was an experienced symphonic and operatic conductor who had held posts in Brno and Plzeň and at the Pivoda singing school. His early operas and ballets had been regularly produced at the National Theatre and with *The Dogheads* (1898) he gave the National Theatre one of its most popular indigenous operas, one which was a staple of the repertory for many years to come. Kovařovic was the natural choice for the new post and in his twenty-year tenure as musical director he raised the company's performing standards to new heights. His death in 1920 and the nationalization of the theatre that year affected the company less than might have been expected. Kovařovic's successor Otakar Ostrčil (1879–1935; illustration 6) was a composer-conductor of even greater stature and the Kovařovic–Ostrčil era – the first third of the twentieth century – represents a golden age for the National Theatre and its opera company.

### The first decade

The first years of Šubert's administration were characterized by lavishly staged Czech premières of European operatic novelties such as *Carmen* (1884), *Aida* (1884), *Lohengrin* (1885 – hardly a 'novelty' but nevertheless the first Wagner opera to be presented in Czech) and Verdi's *Otello* (1888), and by guest appearances of star soloists such as Patti (1885) and the baritone Jean Lassalle (1886). *Aida* was given with an Italian Aida and Radamès singing in Italian against the Czech of the rest of the cast. The Radamès, Carlo Raverta, was house tenor at the National Theatre for three years

(1883–6). Although billed as 'Dalmatian' and thus acceptably 'Slav' (he was in fact born in Milan), he never mastered more than two roles in Czech, and both so poorly that further attempts were discouraged.

At the Provisional Theatre the small ballet company had merely provided the dances in operas, and even in the first National Theatre season no independent ballet was given. But, following the success in May 1885 of the elaborate ballet divertissement in Rozkošný's *Cinderella*, *Excelsior*, a full-length ballet with music by the Italian Romualdo Marenco, was given a few months later. In the next season an enlarged ballet repertory took up 64 performances, which reduced the total of drama and opera performances. (Opera accounted for 183 performances in the first season and by the third only 159, although the total number of performances given at the National Theatre that season had risen by 20.) Under Šubert the ballet repertory at the National Theatre included such works as *Giselle*, *Sylvia* and *Swan Lake*, but by far the greatest success remained its first ballet, *Excelsior*. Its panoramic view of human history and civilization was aided by sets of 'The Ruins of a Spanish Town', 'An African Landscape', 'A Telegraph Building', 'The Seat of the Genii of Light and Science' etc. It was performed 170 times at the National Theatre during Šubert's regime – many more than *Carmen* (with 105 performances, the most popular foreign opera during Šubert's time), though not as many as *The Bartered Bride* (241 performances during Šubert's time).

Lavishly staged plays such as Verne's *Around the World in Eighty Days* provided another mainstay during this period. In the late 1870s Prague had followed European fashion by presenting Verne-based spectacles at the New Czech Theatre. Like *Excelsior*, such pieces catered for wider audiences in a way that looked towards twentieth-century 'revues' by providing a dazzling succession of exotic, contrasting scenes (though here with the added attraction of stage simulations of the latest advances in travel technology). With sets from Paris, and a dromedary and a young elephant from a local circus, *Round the World in Eighty Days* had proved particularly popular. A decade later Šubert presented a new version making full use of the ballet troupe (with music by Suppé); in the month it opened it crowded out almost everything else.

Šubert has been heavily criticized for allowing such things in the hallowed precincts of the National Theatre, especially at the expense of the repertory for which the theatre had been built – Czech opera and Czech drama. But he was an astute and energetic administrator with the means and the will to dictate his own artistic policy. By outlawing the previous system of personal Benefit performances and by insisting, where possible, on double casting, he had minimized the influence of singers' whims and singers' illnesses on the repertory. He dominated his executive committee (which however eventually wore him down with its demands to introduce operetta). But while it was on Šubert's initiative that new works were added to the repertory, he had no influence on how long they would stay there. Subsidies from the Provincial Council, though steadily rising throughout the century, accounted for only a small part of the income; the bulk had to come from the box-office takings. A new work could be guaranteed four performances if it were given within the subscription system – four performances for the four groups of subscribers. Thereafter it had to fend for itself, and if it proved unpopular it had to be taken off (Foerster 1929, 261). Jan Němeček's study of the first years of the twentieth century at the National Theatre shows clearly how even with a strong musical director such as Kovařovic, the fate of any work depended ultimately on its box-office success and not on the favour of the management. Once takings sank below a certain minimum the work was withdrawn (Němeček 1968, i, 3, 123, 176).

In order to keep finances healthy the National Theatre clearly needed a few stable box-office favourites, even if they were ballets, operettas or spectacles. At least, it was argued, the audience drawn to such events might return to the theatre for more artistically rewarding ones. It was evident that Šubert had a more difficult task filling the 1600 seats of the National Theatre than his predecessors had had filling the Provisional Theatre's 900, and in paying for the larger chorus, orchestra and administrative staff. Furthermore, the magnificence of the new surroundings meant that products had to be on a scale to match. The National Theatre was in a new league and it was felt proper, for the most important productions, to acquire sets from the international scenic studios that supplied stage sets to other leading opera houses. Thus the 1884 *Carmen*, the first production of a foreign opera in the National Theatre, had sets ordered from Angelo Quaglio of Munich. Even *Libuše*, that most sacred of Czech operas, had at its 1881 gala première sets supplied by the Viennese firm of Brioschi, Burghardt and Kautsky. After the fire the same firm supplied sets again, with the exception of the mountainous landscape in Act 2 Scene 1, which came from the Brückner brothers in Coburg (Srba 1983). This procedure was typical. Costumes, properties and sets usually came from different sources (soloists provided their own costumes into the 1890s; Foerster 1929, 309), while the sets themselves were often a combination of house sets and sets from one or more outside firms, for example the 1884 *L'africaine*, which had sets by Quaglio for Acts 1 and 4, by the Brückner brothers for Act 2, and house sets for Acts 3 and 5.

Opera productions, however, continued in much the same way, with Kolár, Chvalovský and Hynek joined in the late 1890s by another singer, the buffo tenor Adolf Krössing, who like Hynek had little other than theatrical routine to offer. The most interesting development in opera production during Šubert's term of office was the occasional use of the actor and drama producer Josef Šmaha. Šmaha, who was alive to the new realism of the times, was responsible for the greater naturalism and the more credible acting that contributed to the success of the Czech premières, both in 1888, of Verdi's *Otello* and Tchaikovsky's *Eugene Onegin*.

The success of *Onegin* was one of the unexpected triumphs of the Šubert era. In accordance with his *staročech* philosophy, Šubert believed in strengthening the Slavonic repertory, which he attempted to do with not very popular productions of Dargomyzhsky's *Rusalka* (1889), Moniuszko's *The Haunted Manor* (1891) and the first production outside Russia of Borodin's *Prince Igor* (1899). The more westernized Tchaikovsky was another matter. His *Maid of Orleans*, staged at the Provisional Theatre in 1882, was the first Tchaikovsky opera to be produced outside Russia though its four performances then hardly attested to any great public enthusiasm. Six years later, however, *Onegin* found a Czech public which saw it sixty-three times up to 1900, making it one of the most popular operas of the Šubert era, and encouraging the similarly successful production, again the first outside Russia, of *The Queen of Spades*, in 1894. The many performances of the two works helped Russian opera maintain a proportion of just under five per cent of all opera performances during the Kovařovic era. Pan-Slav considerations were no longer paramount with the new management and Kovařovic himself was keen to keep abreast of new developments in France and Germany. The only Russian opera of significance that he introduced was *Boris Godunov*, one of only six Russian operas in the repertory between 1900 and 1920 (no other foreign Slav nations were represented), as opposed to the eleven Polish and Russian operas of the Šubert era.

## Wagner[13]

Šubert, who had been zealous in securing early productions of Verdi's *Otello* and *Falstaff*, was responsible for at last bringing Wagner to the Czech stage. Although it was under the Czech conductor František Škroup that early and successful productions of Wagner's pre-*Ring* operas had been mounted at the Estates Theatre, no Wagner opera was performed in Czech until 1885, when a fine *Lohengrin* was daringly given in Šubert's second season. In the same year that the Czechs felt confident to allow in their opera house a work by the composer often seen as the greatest threat to their fledgeling opera tradition, Angelo Neumann was installed as director of the rival German theatre in Prague. With his 132-member company, the 'Richard Wagner Theatre', he had toured Europe, winning from an approving Wagner family the exclusive rights to all Wagner's operas (except *Parsifal*) in whatever town his company visited. Now permanently in Prague, Neumann insisted on his monopoly, reluctantly conceding only

*Lohengrin*. By artful diplomacy Šubert managed to stage a Czech *Tannhäuser* in 1891. By then a sensible agreement had been worked out between the two rival theatres to regulate rights to new theatrical works and the movement of singers between the two houses, putting an end to the poaching of singers that had occurred previously. Under the new agreement the German opera house had first option on all new German works and the Czech opera house on all new French and Italian works. This meant that Šubert had first pick of the profitable *verismo* operas now coming out of Italy, and this advantage allowed him to trade a German production of *Pagliacci* (a month after the Czech première) in return for permission to stage *Die Meistersinger* in 1894 (it seemed a bargain, though Czech audiences never took to *Die Meistersinger* as they had done to *Lohengrin* and *Tannhäuser*).

The agreement survived the change of management at the National Theatre in 1900 so that the new opera director Kovařovic, who had never been enthusiastic about Italian opera, gladly relinquished *Madama Butterfly* to the Germans in return for Czech rights to *Der fliegende Holländer* (Czech première 1906). It was not until Neumann's death in 1910 that any of the later Wagner works were able to be given in Czech. *Tristan und Isolde* was staged in 1913 and *Parsifal*, when the Bayreuth monopoly expired, was given simultaneously by both Prague opera houses on 1 January 1914 (the Czech performance under Kovařovic began at 4 p.m., while the German performance under Zemlinsky began at 5). Kovařovic's plan for a *Ring* cycle was thwarted by the war. It was impossible to find extra players for the orchestra (much depleted by conscription) and Kovařovic got no further than a *Rheingold* in 1915 and a *Walküre* in 1916; *Siegfried* followed only in 1932 under Otakar Ostrčil. No Czech company has yet attempted *Die Götterdämmerung*.

In addition to Wagner, Kovařovic was also anxious to cultivate Richard Strauss, the rights to whose operas again fell to the German theatre in Prague rather than to the National Theatre. *Salome* was not performed in Czech until 1923, under Ostrčil, but the German theatre showed less interest in *Elektra*, which Kovařovic was able to stage in 1910 with unexpected popular success. Strauss himself conducted one of the performances and was so pleased with the company that rights were allowed for *Der Rosenkavalier* (on condition that the National Theatre also stage *Feuersnot*) with a première on 4 March 1911, just a few weeks after the Dresden première. With forty performances over the next five seasons it became almost a repertory piece.

## Czech opera

Only Czech works (including eight Czech operas) were given at the National Theatre between 11 November 1883, when it opened with *Libuše*, and the end of that year. This gesture made, Šubert looked to more profitable ventures to fill his house. By the third season Czech opera accounted for only 13% of all works played in the theatre. Smetana was represented mostly by *Libuše*, which continued to receive a few ceremonial performances each year, and by his two popular operas, *The Bartered Bride* and *The Kiss*. None of his other operas had become repertory pieces. A committed production of *Dalibor* in 1886, however, began to change this. Except for three performances in 1879, *Dalibor* had not been played since 1871. The 1886 production established the opera's present reputation as one of Smetana's finest works, and even one of his most popular. During Šubert's time it was performed eighty-one times and has remained a repertory opera in Prague ever since.

What seems to have had the greatest impact in changing the balance of the repertory was the series of exhibitions held in the 1890s. The Provincial Jubilee Exhibition (Zemská jubilejní výstava), was held in Prague in 1891, one hundred years after the Prague coronation of Leopold II. Intended to commemorate Bohemian advances in industry in the past hundred years, it was boycotted by the Germans and became instead a manifestation of cultural solidarity by the Czechs. To entertain the many visitors that flocked in from the country the theatre played without interruption between mid-May and the end of August. A more specifically Czech repertory was clearly desirable for the occasion and, somewhat to the management's surprise, turned out to be popular. An atmosphere reminiscent of the opening of the National Theatre was re-created with ceremonial evenings that began with an overture, continued with a speech and then a patriotic *tableau vivant* (twenty-three different *tableaux vivants* were devised that year) leading up to the main work. In all, over half of the 222 afternoon and evening performances during 156 days of the exhibition were devoted to Czech works. These included six of Smetana's operas, Dvořák's *Dimitrij* and *The Jacobin*, two parts of Fibich's melodrama trilogy, and Bendl's *Lejla*, revived for the first time at the National Theatre and performed nine times that season. The Czecho-Slavonic Ethnographic Exhibition (Národopisná výstava česko-slovanská) held in Prague from mid-April to the end of August 1895 and planned expressly as a celebration of the national and spiritual progress of the Czechs had a similar effect in promoting Czech operatic repertory. By then, however, Šubert had achieved the crowning act of his career – the visit by the Prague National Theatre to the Vienna Music and Theatre Exhibition in June 1892.

The opening of the National Theatre was a visible symbol of the success of Czech efforts to establish the nation's own cultural identity in the face of Austrian political and cultural oppression. With their triumphant appearance at the Viennese Exhibition a decade later the Czechs took their hard-won culture to the Austro-Hungarian capital, where they were acknowledged, at least culturally, as equals and were received with much more enthusiasm than the Deutsches Theater of Berlin or the Comédie française had been in the previous weeks. From the moment the curtain went up on yet another *tableau*, this time revealing the National Theatre company respectfully grouped round busts of the Emperor and the Empress and singing the Austrian national anthem, the Czechs could do no wrong. The ensemble was recognized as one of the major opera companies of the world, and some of its singers were lured away to more profitable engagements in Hamburg and Vienna. This hurt the company less than might be supposed for Šubert was particularly successful in seeking out and engaging new talent. It was in Šubert's era and in the first two decades of the next century that the National Theatre could boast such fine native singers as Emmy Destinn (Ema Destinnová), Otakar Mařák, and Carl Burrian (Karel Burian), all of whom made international careers but often returned to Prague for guest appearances.

The Vienna shop window had another effect in gaining recognition for Smetana both at home and abroad. His *The Bartered Bride* had failed when presented in St Petersburg in 1871 (apart from the production in Zagreb, 1873, its only foreign showing); but the success of the opera in Vienna, where it was given four times together with three plays, as well as Dvořák's *Dimitrij*, Fibich's scenic melodrama *The Courtship of Pelops* and two performances of *Dalibor*, led to its presentation in German at the Theater an der Wien the next season and so to its rapid acceptance in the international repertory. This also gave the Czechs, having laboriously built up their National Theatre only to fill it with countless performances of Verne epics and Marenco's *Excelsior*, greater self-confidence in their home product. The next year the first complete cycle of Smetana operas was given in Prague, and though this was repeated only once more under Šubert (1899), Kovařovic made Smetana cycles a regular feature of his programme planning after his first complete cycle in 1904. His successor Ostrčil went even further with Smetana cycles (1924, 1927, 1934), Dvořák cycles (1929, 1934) and Fibich cycles (1925, 1932) as well as cycles of the operas of his contemporaries Foerster (1929) and Novák (1930). From *The Excursions of Mr Brouček* (1920) onwards Ostrčil introduced to Prague audiences all of Janáček's later operas as fast as they were written.

### Repertory trends

The change of balance in the repertory is clear from Tables 2 and 3. Throughout the Provisional Theatre period (during which Smetana's operas were being written) Czech operas made up less than 25% of all opera performances. Only two Czech operas were among the fifteen most frequently performed operas in the repertory. There was a steady increase to the end of the century in the proportion of Czech operas performed in Prague, from under a quarter to almost half. The figure remained static (few durable Czech operas were added to the repertory) in the first decade of the new century but in the final term of the *Společnost* (1912–20) it rose almost to 54%. By then nine of the eleven most frequently performed operas at the National Theatre, including the top five, were Czech. The higher proportion in the second half of the Šubert era (1892–1900; see Table 2) is accounted for by the nationalist fervour generated by the various exhibitions during that decade. The higher proportion in the final term of the *Společnost* can be linked to the excitement at the end of the First World War with the creation of a new Czechoslovak state. In the 1918–19 season forty-two performances of *The Bartered Bride* were given, double that of the previous season.

There was a corresponding slump in the French and Italian repertories. The decline in popularity of French opera, from its high point of 30% in the Provisional Theatre period to 15% a decade later in the second half of the Šubert era, coincides with the decline in popularity in Prague of the grand opera repertory. Auber's *La muette de Portici*, Rossini's *Guillaume Tell* and Meyerbeer's *Robert le diable* and *Les Huguenots* were among the most popular operas at the Provisional Theatre. None of these figure among the fifteen most frequently performed operas at the National Theatre (see Table 3) and their loss was only partly compensated by such works as Gounod's *Faust*, whose popularity was already on the decline (it had sunk from first place at the Provisional Theatre to fifth during Šubert's time), and *Carmen*. Even with Kovařovic's special interest in French music and the success of Thomas's *Mignon* (put on occasionally from 1878 onwards but only really popular after its 1909 revival), Charpentier's *Louise* and Offenbach's *Les contes d'Hoffmann* (see Table 3c) French opera performances never rose above 20% under Kovařovic and sank to under 14% in his final eight-year term.

Italian opera did increasingly better than French under Šubert, boosted by such popular successes as *Aida*, *Otello*, Franchetti's *Asrael*, and the new *verismo* wave (see Table 3b). This advance was checked under Kovařovic. While Leoncavallo and Mascagni continued to do well, Puccini did not achieve the same success at the National Theatre as he did elsewhere, and no Italian opera was among the National Theatre's most frequently performed operas of the period (see Table 3c). There is no doubt that this was a dramaturgical decision on Kovařovic's part. Whereas twenty-eight different Italian operas were in the National Theatre repertory in the last eight years of Šubert's regime, Kovařovic allowed only sixteen Italian operas to be performed during his twenty years.

## Prague, Vienna and Dresden

In 1908, two years into the second term of the *Společnost*, the assistant conductor František Picka published a defence of Kovařovic's artistic policy, then coming increasingly under attack in the press. His details of the 1906–7 season repertory in Prague, Vienna and Dresden (Picka 1908) provide an excellent profile of the National Theatre as a Czech company compared with two leading German-speaking companies. The differences are summarized in Table 4. In considering these figures it should be borne in mind that while all three houses included a ballet company, only Vienna's gave a substantial number of independent performances (96 against Dresden's 8 and Prague's 23). The Prague house, furthermore, was the only one also to include drama, giving 214 drama performances that season and consequently fewer opera performances.

About 40% of the individual operas presented at the three houses were French or Italian. This represented about 30% of all performances in both Dresden and Prague. With more repeats of individual operas, 30% of all opera performances in Vienna were of Italian opera; French opera performances in Vienna brought this total to over 50%. Where the houses differed most noticeably was in their attitude towards German opera. Half of the operas presented that season by the two German-speaking companies were German (Dresden staged 34 different German operas, Vienna 29) while only 9 operas at the Prague National Theatre (18.75% of the total) were German. In terms of actual performances the differences are even more acute: four of every six performances in Dresden that season were of German operas, one in every six in Prague. Dresden's devotion to German operas was thus even more intense than Prague's devotion to Czech opera: 50% of opera performances in Prague that season were of Czech operas, under 40% of the repertory. The figures for German opera in Dresden were 67% and 58% respectively. Vienna occupied an intermediate position with over 46% of all its performances made up of German operas, the rest of foreign works, including one Czech opera. What is clear from these statistics is that by the early twentieth century, less than forty years after Smetana's operas were first heard, the Czech repertory had achieved the stable and unassailable position at the National Theatre that it has enjoyed ever since, and the company was strong enough to stand up to new competition.

## Other opera houses in Prague

One form of competition was a second Czech theatre in Prague, also presenting opera. The Town Theatre in the Royal Vineyards (Městské divadlo na Královských Vinohradech), which opened in 1907 in the Vinohrady suburb of Prague, included opera and operetta in its repertory

Table 4. *Operas performed in the 1906–7 season at the Court Opera, Dresden, at the Court Opera, Vienna and the National Theatre, Prague, arranged according to nationality of composer*

*a. Analysed by number of performances*

| | Dresden | | Vienna | | Prague | |
|---|---|---|---|---|---|---|
| | | % | | % | | % |
| German | 208 | 66.88 | 135 | 46.55 | 35 | 16.83 |
| French | 62 | 19.94 | 66 | 22.76 | 30 | 14.42 |
| Italian | 40 | 12.86 | 86 | 29.66 | 28 | 13.46 |
| Russian | 1 | 0.32 | 1 | 0.34 | 11 | 5.29 |
| Czech | 0 | 0.00 | 2 | 0.69 | 104 | 50.00 |
| Total | 311 | | 290 | | 208 | |

*b. Analysed by number of operas*

| | Dresden | | Vienna | | Prague | |
|---|---|---|---|---|---|---|
| | | % | | % | | % |
| German | 34 | 57.62 | 29 | 50.88 | 9 | 18.75 |
| French | 14 | 23.72 | 14 | 24.56 | 10 | 20.83 |
| Italian | 10 | 16.94 | 12 | 21.05 | 8 | 16.67 |
| Russian | 1 | 1.69 | 1 | 1.75 | 2 | 4.17 |
| Czech | 0 | 0.00 | 1 | 1.75 | 19 | 39.58 |
| Total | 59 | | 57 | | 48 | |

statistics derived from Picka 1908

for the first twelve years of its existence. Its musical directors included the composer Ludvík Čelanský and from 1914 to 1919 Otakar Ostrčil, the future musical director of the National Theatre. But while the theatre managed to present a few foreign operatic novelties (works by d'Albert, Massenet, Kienzl and others) that had escaped the interest of the two major opera houses, it was generally in no position to challenge them. None of the new Czech operas it staged was of lasting importance (Janáček's *Fate* was accepted but never performed), and its musical repertory tended more and more to the operettas looked on askance by the National Theatre.

The German opera house in Prague thus remained the National Theatre's chief rival. So long the senior house in Prague, it had been forced on to the defensive by the building of the National Theatre. But the arrival in 1885 of an enterprising intendant, Angelo Neumann, and the opening in 1888 of a handsome new opera house (the Neues Deutsches Theater) to replace the almost century-old Estates Theatre ushered in a new era for the German opera house. Neumann was responsible for the appointment of conductors of the calibre of Gustav Mahler, Karl Muck, Franz Schalk,

Leo Blech, Otto Klemperer and Erich Kleiber. After his death the high musical standards were maintained during the musical directorships of Alexander Zemlinsky (1911–26) and Georg Szell (1929–37).

Political and demographic changes, however, were now on the Czechs' side. By the time of Neumann's intendancy Germans no longer formed the majority in Prague. After the First World War (in which opera continued unabated in both houses, with Kovařovic initiating a *Ring* cycle and other important premières), the Germans found themselves a minority nation within the Czechoslovak state rather than part of the dominant nation in the Austro-Hungarian Empire. The Estates Theatre, which since the building of the new German opera house had served the Germans as a second stage, was now shared between the two companies. After the Second World War and the expulsion of the Germans, the National Theatre took over the Estates Theatre completely, renaming it the Tyl Theatre (Tylovo divadlo). The German theatre, now in Czech hands, operated for a few years as an independent experimental theatre, the Grand Opera of the Fifth of May (Velká opera 5. května). In 1948 it too became absorbed in the National Theatre complex and was renamed the Smetana Theatre (Smetanovo divadlo). In 1983 the National Theatre complex was expanded by a fourth, experimental modern theatre, the New Stage (Nová scéna), erected beside the National Theatre, itself newly refurbished to celebrate its first centenary.

## *Outside Prague*[14]

A handsome stone theatre had been erected by the town of Plzeň in 1830–2, but this was reserved mostly for German plays until the changing political circumstances in the 1860s allowed the Czech community regular access to it. In 1865, three years after the opening of the Provisional Theatre in Prague, Pavel Švanda ze Semčic established in Plzeň a permanent Czech drama company which, three years later, was expanded to include opera; a milestone was the first performance outside Prague of *The Bartered Bride* in 1869. In 1902 a new, exclusively Czech, opera house was opened holding 1100. From 1955 it was officially designated the J.K. Tyl Theatre in Plzeň (Divadlo J.K. Tyla v Plzni) though generally known as the Large Theatre (Velké divadlo, renovated 1986). The old German theatre, which the Czechs took over after the expulsion of the Germans in 1945 and which is today generally used for drama and smaller musical forms, is by comparison known as the Small Theatre (Malé divadlo). Although the Plzeň operatic repertory has sometimes included works by composers with local connections, much of the town's operatic history reflected developments in Prague and its stage offered a useful training ground for soloists and conductors. Mořic Anger, later assistant conductor at the National Theatre in Prague, was the first conductor in Plzeň and many other conductors such as

Kovařovic, Čelanský, Talich and Vogel obtained their first experience here. The pattern of development in Brno was rather different, both because of Brno's proximity to Vienna, which meant that Viennese trends, rather than those from Prague, often served as models and because of the somewhat belated appearance in Moravia of the National Revival movement. Whereas by the second half of the nineteenth century several Bohemian towns had specially built Czech theatres, Moravian Czech communities made do with adapted buildings and other improvisations. In the eighteenth century, however, Brno anticipated Prague in several theatrical trends. For instance it built a permanent theatre (the Theater in der Taffern) in 1732, five years before the Kotzen theatre in Prague. This wooden theatre, erected in the old Vegetable Market, survived for fifty years before being destroyed by fire in 1785. Its successor, too, was similarly destroyed a year later and was replaced in 1786 by a new theatre holding about 1200 on three floors with forty-eight boxes. The intervention of Joseph II, who decreed that the town should pay for and should run the theatre, was reflected in its official title, the Königlich-Städtisches Nationaltheater, though it was popularly known as the Redoutensaale. It was partly destroyed by fire in 1870 and restored as a theatre only after the First World War. It still exists (with a capacity of 414) as the Reduta. Brno also anticipated Prague as far as repertory was concerned, reacting rather more quickly to the changes of taste in the Austrian capital. While Italian opera continued to be performed in Prague until 1806, the last Italian impresario in Brno, Vicenzo Nicolosi, departed in 1768 and his successors were Germans who brought to the stage mainly German plays and Singspiels. Occasionally more musically demanding repertory was given, such as works by Piccinni, Paisiello, Grétry and Monsigny. From 1792 there was an orchestra of about twenty-four, and the repertory for a brief spell included works by Mozart and Gluck.

In fostering a Czech national awareness however, Brno lagged far behind Prague, and this is particularly evident in the history of its theatre. Even if irregular, Prague's record of performing plays in Czech stretches back to the 1780s (see p. 18). Apart from the performance by a visiting company of *The Lovelorn Nightwatchman* in 1767 the earliest report of a complete theatrical performance in Czech in Brno is of the Singspiel *The Ghost in the Mill* (*Strašidlo ve mlejně*, probably an adaptation of Paul Weidmann's *Der Bettelstudent oder Das Donnerwetter*) in 1814. Around this time several plays based on local Moravian subjects (e.g. *Die Schweden vor Brünn* and *Swatopluk, König von Grossmähren oder Der Verrath in der Adamshöhle*) were given in Brno but these were in German; the first plays in Czech were staged in 1822. These were isolated performances, dependent on the presence in the German theatre company of Czech-speaking actors and on the good will of the German company director. Similar conditions prevailed again only after 1835, when for a few years (until 1842) Czech performances were put on with increasing frequency. In 1838 excerpts from operas such as Rossini's *Il barbiere* and *Die Zauberflöte* were given in Czech leading early in 1839 to the first performance in Brno of a complete opera in Czech, Méhul's *Joseph*. Further notable Brno premières were of Škroup's *The Tinker* (1840) and of a new opera by a Brno composer, Kott's *Žižka's Oak* (1841; see pp. 64–5). Thereafter, apart from occasional performances by travelling companies in the Czech Besední dům (Meeting House, built in 1874), the history of opera in Czech at Brno hardly exists until the opening of the Provisional Czech National Theatre (Prozatímní české národní divadlo) in 1884, some twenty years after the Prague model.

The Provisional Theatre was set up in an adapted building acquired for 60,000 zl. in 1883 by the *Družstvo Národního divadla v Brně* (Consortium of the National Theatre in Brno, formed in 1881). It was originally a dance hall. The new stage measured 11.5 metres across and 7.5 metres deep (cf the Provisional Theatre measurements on p. 28); the auditorium, with eight boxes, 310 stalls seats (and further room for standing) and forty-eight seats in the gallery was sanctioned to take an audience of 771. Any hope of a custom-built theatre soon evaporated and after further adaptations in 1894 (which added a second gallery at a cost of 33,000 zl. and took the capacity up to 1000) it was retitled the National Theatre (Národní divadlo) though generally known as the Old Theatre (Staré divadlo) or the Theatre on Veveří Street (Divadlo na Veveří). Czech opera and drama played in this theatre up to 1918. At first there was no subsidy (for the first four years the Czech company had to pay a fee for their franchise, the money going to the subsidized German company, which with fewer financial restrictions could offer a more adventurous fare in its custom-built theatre). In 1898 a subsidy was conceded: 8000 zl. as opposed to the Prague National Theatre's existing annual subsidy of 300,000 zl. at that time, or the Brno German theatre's subsidy of 115,000 zl.

The *družstvo* could not afford to run its own company but instead let out the theatre to touring companies. Brno became an autumn-to-winter asylum for combined drama and opera companies which performed in the Prague open-air theatres in the summer and toured smaller towns in the spring once Brno audiences began dropping off. The system meant that in the first thirty-four years (until the end of the First World War) there was a constant change of companies: fourteen general directors and twenty-two musical directors and thus little chance of building up any sort of permanent and artistic relationship with the town. A more stable ensemble began to be formed only at the beginning of the twentieth century when new conductors were required to take on some of the singers used by their predecessors, though the orchestra continued to be disbanded at the end of each annual season.

The effect of such a system on repertory is predictable. The director determined the repertory mostly on the basis of profitability coupled with the vagaries of the Benefit system, which, abolished in Prague in 1883, persisted in Brno until the 1903–4 season. Although new works were added to augment the popular summer fare, repertory, especially early in the season, tended towards farces, operettas or well-known operas (especially those for which no royalties were paid, for instance Boieldieu's *La dame blanche* or Flotow's *Martha*). French opera predominated, though from 1894 more Czech works began to be introduced. Under such circumstances there was no question of the high artistic standards that could now be achieved in Prague. Until 1918 Brno was lucky to assemble a core of reasonably competent solo singers, but the untrained chorus was restricted to 20–4 and the orchestra incomplete. For the first two decades it rose to no more than 24 players; even in 1908 there were only 6 violins (4 firsts, 2 seconds) and in 1913 had at its disposal only one horn. The première of Janáček's *Jenůfa*, an exceptional event very carefully prepared with more than fifty rehearsals, was performed with an orchestra of twenty-nine (lacking harp, bass clarinet and english horn); later performances made do with even smaller forces. No wonder Janáček offered his operas to Prague first, and that Dvořák vetoed the productions of his larger operas in Brno, despite his friendly attitude to Moravia. Janáček's *Jenůfa* and the earlier *The Beginning of a Romance* represented some of the very few Moravian operas produced at the theatre; otherwise the 132 operas given in Brno up to 1918 generally mirrored Prague trends, even to the extent of attempting French grand operas such as *Les Huguenots*. Virtually every opera had to be given in a shortened and reorchestrated form to accommodate the tiny orchestra, and ballets, even the dances in *The Bartered Bride*, were routinely omitted.

After Czechoslovak independence in 1918 circumstances changed much for the better. For the first time the Czechs had access to the well-equipped theatre built by the Germans in 1881–2 to replace the old Redoutensaale, the City Theatre (Stadttheater; capacity 1185 reduced at its centenary restoration to 621), the first with electric lighting in central Europe. For the next twenty years Czechs shared the City Theatre and the Reduta Theatre with the Germans, while continuing to use the Old Theatre for drama and operetta (the Old Theatre came into its own again during the Second World War when it once again became the only venue in Brno open to Czech performances; it was demolished in 1952). From 1919 until his death in 1929 František Neumann was head of opera, inaugurating (with Janáček's *Jenůfa*) the most exciting period of Brno's operatic history. The orchestra was brought up to 56, the chorus to 53, a ballet company of 23 was formed and some outstanding soloists engaged. In the first ten years 101 operas were given of which half were new to the repertory (26 Czech operas and 20 foreign works). From *Káťa Kabanová* all Janáček's premières were now first given in Brno. After Neumann's death the première of *From the House of the*

*Dead* took place in 1930 under Janáček's pupil Břetislav Bakala, who from 1929 to 1931 formed one of a young triumvirate of conductors, succeeded after Bakala's departure to the radio orchestra by Milan Sachs in 1932. Altogether the interwar period set a remarkable standard allowing the presentation of many important premières. Apart from the Janáček premières, Ostrčil, as director of the National Theatre in Prague, scrupulously entrusted all his later operas to Brno. Among foreign works the Czech première of *Pelléas et Mélisande* took place in Brno, while the ballet company achieved particular distinction, giving the world première of Prokofiev's *Romeo and Juliet* and of Martinů's earliest ballets.

After the war and the expulsion of the German population, the German City Theatre came fully into Czech ownership, and was renamed the Janáček Theatre (Janáčkovo divadlo), until in 1965 a new opera house (capacity 1400) was opened which took this name. The old German City Theatre, now used exclusively for drama, was renamed the Mahen Theatre (Mahenovo divadlo), with the oldest theatre of all, the Reduta, used for operettas.

# 3. Composers

## Before the Provisional Theatre

Czech composers had been writing operas since the eighteenth century but apart from a tradition, chiefly in Moravia, of local amateur opera, it was not until the nineteenth century that they began to write them in Czech. The reasons will be clear from the previous chapters. During the eighteenth century Czech was dying out as a cultural language, there was no permanent Czech theatre or opera house, and the majority of Czech musicians lived and worked abroad, where they wrote their operas in the chief operatic languages of the time. Mysliveček, Gassmann and J.A. Kozeluch (Koželuh) composed in Italian, the Benda family, Gyrowetz (Jírovec) and Paul Wranitzky (Pavel Vranický) mostly in German, Kohaut (Kohout) and Reicha (Rejcha) mostly in French. The Viennese Singspiel tradition engaged the energies of prolific composers of Czech origin such as Kauer and Müller. Even those who remained at home, for instance Tomášek and Jan Josef Rösler, served the German community rather than the Czech and wrote to German or Italian texts. Although two of Rösler's operas were later given in Czech (*Elisene, Princessin von Bulgarien* 1807, Czech 1827; *Die Rache, oder Das Raubschloss in Sardinien* 1808, Czech 1832), there is no question of his operas or others of this kind constituting part of a Czech tradition. They merely contributed to the Italian, French, German or Viennese traditions within which they were written.

Thus it is that historians assign to František Škroup (1801–62) the status of the first Czech opera composer, and to his Singspiel *The Tinker* (1826) that of the first Czech opera. This, however, is to ignore the amateur tradition of Czech opera which flourished from about the 1740s to the end of the century. None of the works it produced was published at the time and most were rediscovered at the beginning of the twentieth century, long after Smetana had established his own tradition of Czech opera. But from the wide distribution of copies of some of the more important works, from the graphic representation (e.g. on porcelain) of some of the characters from them, and from the absorption of some of their music into the folksong culture of the nineteenth century, it is possible to speculate that their influence was more widespread and persistent than is usually acknowledged. Even the doyen of Prague composers in the first half of the nineteenth century, Václav Jan Tomášek (1774–1850), the composer of a German opera *Seraphine* (1811) and a large number of operatic fragments on Schiller texts (*Die Braut von Messina, Maria Stuart, Die Piccolomini* and others; see Emingerová 1925, 111), recounts in his autobiography that in his youth he took part in performances of two of these amateur operas (Němec 1942, 17–18). Whatever their quality, the Czech eighteenth-century amateur operas were the first to be written in Czech, often with more convincing solutions to its setting than later attempts in the next century. In dealing with local history and local characters they anticipate Czech nationalist opera. Their music suggests an interesting two-way relationship with Czech folksong.

### Eighteenth-century operas

At their most unpretentious the Czech eighteenth-century operas[1] take the form of short scenes for two characters: a few songs and duets interspersed with spoken dialogue and accompanied by an ensemble of two violins and basso continuo. The best known are the 'Haná Singspiels', *Jora and Manda* and *Maréna and Kedrota*, written in the distinctive dialect of the Moravian farming district of Haná. The works were aimed at a wide, uncultured audience and their modest forces enabled them to be played virtually anywhere. The more ambitious ones might run to two acts and many numbers, involving a small classical orchestra and a cast of five or six singers. Jan Antoš's *Opera about the Peasant Rebellion* (1775–7) has both remarkable subject matter (an account of the reasons for the 1775 revolt) and an ambitious musical setting. While restricted to a three-part instrumental accompaniment and four characters, it has a total of seventeen numbers with recitative, arias and a final chorus, and is preceded by an overture in three sections. The earlier *Landebork* (1757–8?) has an overture, two choruses, and eight arias connected by recitative; its five singers (soprano, alto, tenor and two basses) are accompanied by a string orchestra. *Pargamotéka* (1747), another opera in the same tradition and by the same composer, now thought to be the Cistercian monk Father Alanus Plumlovský, expands into two acts and several individual scenes. Its music has disappeared, but from indications in the text it is evident that its orchestral forces included several wind instruments.

Like Antoš's *Opera about the Peasant Rebellion*, *Landebork* and *Pargamotéka* deal with local reaction to political events. *Pargamotéka* is a comic dialect corruption of 'Pragmatická [sankce]' (Pragmatic Sanction), Charles VI's edict which allowed a woman, his daughter Maria Theresa, to ascend the Habsburg throne. Maria Theresa's accession was contested by neighbouring states, notably Prussia, whose invasion of Moravia was the subject of *Landebork* (Brandenburg). Both works, like others in this genre, were written as a loyal defence of the monarch (who visited the monastery near Olomouc where they were staged, and attended a performance), and both took the form of operatic disputations, in the tradition of the Latin didactic plays cultivated by the Catholic teaching orders. The public in mind was thus a select monastery audience of clerics who would be educated enough to grasp the political implications of the text, while relishing its occasional vulgarities and its good-natured parody of the local populace and its dialect. According to the monastery annals, Plumlovský seems to have had considerable success with his local operas and fulfilled commissions for further ones.

The composers of many of the other amateur operas such as Jan Antoš and Josef Pekárek (who wrote the music for the Haná Singspiels) were kantors – village schoolmaster–musicians (see p. 166). In most cases little is known about them. They were all purely local figures, writing for local needs, adapting what they had picked up of Italian opera (usually of a generation earlier) as seen through the prism of Catholic church music. The most distinguished and professional of the kantor composers, Jan Jakub Ryba (1765–1815), is known to have written six 'operas' and pantomimes in the 1790s, but only the texts of two survive (Poštolka 1980).

One family that could have offered a transition from a regional to a town-based opera tradition were the Tučeks.[2] Jan Tuček (c 1743–83) is usually credited with the music to the early Czech play *The Lovelorn Night-watchman* (?1763, see pp. 17–18). His *Recruiting at the Horse Fair* (c 1770) belongs among the amateur tradition of operas about the crafts and occupations such as Karel Loos's little opera about a chimney sweep and a bricklayer (*Opera bohemica de camino. . .*). *The Drunken Man*, a play for which Tuček composed an overture, seven arias, six duets, a trio and five recitatives, was with Antoš's opera the other amateur work that Tomášek mentions in his autobiography. Tuček's son Vincenc (1773–1821), the first Czech Tamino, composed the music for several works at the Patriotic Theatre (notably *The Prague Brewers*, 1795, and *The Butchers' Shops*, 1796, both plays with songs dealing with local trades and conditions) and from his later career as a successful composer of Singspiels in Vienna it is possible to speculate how the country tradition might have become permanently absorbed into the professional tradition had the Patriotic Theatre survived and the younger Tuček remained at home. But, as Tomislav Volek explains in his survey of eighteenth-century Czech operas (*DČD*, i, 334–5), this did not happen. Unlike German vernacular opera at the time, Czech professional opera was denied propitious conditions in which to thrive. The middle classes, which might have supported it, were rapidly becoming Germanized, and it was a German rather than a Czech company that replaced the Italian company in 1807. By the 1820s, when the Estates Theatre management was better disposed towards Czech vernacular theatre, and had a Czech patriot conductor on its staff in the person of František Škroup, international opera had moved on. The Czech regional operas of the eighteenth century had nothing to offer an audience familiar with Rossini and Weber, and Czech opera had to start again from scratch.

## Škroup's The Tinker

The starting point was Škroup's Singspiel *The Tinker*. Its first performance in 1826 came two years after the memorable Czech première of *Der Freischütz* at the Estates Theatre (1824), but the work is so devoid of Romantic colour in its harmony, orchestration and plot that Weber could not have been the model. A much more likely model was the first opera given in Czech in the 1820s, Weigl's *Die Schweizerfamilie*. Based on *The Swiss Family Robinson*, Weigl's Singspiel (1809) is a lyrical German folk opera, modest in its orchestral and vocal demands (only a small male chorus and half a dozen soloists with little coloratura). Its vein of tuneful, nostalgic sentimentality struck such a responsive chord among Czech patriots in the 1820s that it was sometimes mistaken for a native work (Očadlík 1940a, 20). Škroup's *The Tinker* is even less demanding. He dispensed with the chorus altogether. Half of the fifteen numbers are solos and only one of these is anything more than a simple strophic or ternary song. Růžena's solo at the beginning of Act 2 has some of the trappings of an Italian aria (*Il barbiere di Siviglia* was another early and influential addition to the Czech repertory), with a slow orchestral introduction and recitative leading into a 6/8 Andante grazioso, but its final Allegro con fuoco lacks the structure of a true cabaletta. If there is any Rossinian influence in the work apart from the plot (the hero, like Almaviva, gains admittance to his sweetheart by adopting a disguise – in this case the clothes of a friendly tinker), then it is in the orchestral bustle that accompanies some of the more conversational numbers and in the occasional comic patter, rather than in any elaborate vocal display; only the leading lady has a little coloratura. The other parts all seem to have been deliberately restricted in view of the amateur forces involved.

Much of the action takes place through spoken dialogue, though the end of Act 2 consists of a cumulative series of ensembles (trio, quintet, sextet and septet-finale), which take in the successive dénouements and the reactions of the participants. Recitative is used only sparingly. The overture is a surprisingly substantial sonata form with a slow introduction. It makes use of thematic material from the opera more as a pot-pourri than to presage characters or events in the manner of *Der Freischütz*.

## Kott

*The Tinker* was a success and was revived annually for several years in Prague, and was taken up by amateurs in the provinces from the mid-1830s (list in *DČD*, ii, 308). It was first seen in Brno on 22 November 1840; perhaps this performance of 'the first Czech opera' encouraged the Brno composer František Kott (1808–84) to try his hand at an opera. As his libretto he used Klicpera's *Žižka's Oak*. Klicpera's text (which was designated by the author as 'a Romantic opera in two acts') was written in 1823, a date which suggests that it may have been inspired by the Czech performances that year of Weigl's *Die Schweizerfamilie*. It was published in 1826. Of the several operatic settings made from 1838 onwards (Bezdíčková–Ingerlová 1975, 122) the only one to survive was Kott's and a later reworking by Adolf Albert Pozděna (interestingly, both Kott and Pozděna also composed operas based on the Dalibor legend). Kott's *Žižka's Oak* was premièred in Brno on 28 November 1841 and revived the next year (despite earlier accounts, both performances were in Czech; see *DČD*, ii, 377, fn. 233). It makes an instructive comparison with *The Tinker*.

The text itself, as Klicpera's designation suggests, is more Romantically orientated than that of *The Tinker*. Act 2 takes place outside, which allows for its Schilleresque robbers (*Die Räuber*, translated into Czech as early as 1786, was a great favourite with Czech audiences), an underground chorus and the Romantic trappings of a haunted oak tree. (The hero, like Max in *Der Freischütz*, is required to go there at midnight in order to win his bride.) By contrast, it looks at first as though the composer has taken his inspiration from Italian rather than from German opera.[3] Klicpera's homely Czech nomenclature for solo (*zpěv*) and duet (*dvojzpěv*) – used also in *The Tinker* – was replaced in the score by more Italianate terms: 'cantabile', 'duetto', and 'duettino'. The finale of Act 1 has a central slow concertato for three soloists entering successively with the same tune before being joined by the chorus; an elaborate cadenza leads into a vigorous allegro and homophonic final stretta: all the hallmarks of a Rossinian finale. These aspects, however, are misleading. The vocal cadenza in the finale is almost the only one in the opera. The heroine's entrance cantabile is preceded by nothing more elaborate than a two-bar orchestral introduction and turns out to be a simple ternary form with chorus in the middle; the duet is a Mendelssohnian Allegro scherzo. *Žižka's Oak* is thus still a Singspiel, with much more spoken than sung text and virtually no recitative, but unlike *The Tinker* it has a chorus and makes extensive use of it not just in the genre numbers which open each act (blacksmiths in Act 1, robbers in Act 2) but as contrast and support to several of the solos. Its musical language, too, is considerably different. This is no better demonstrated than in Darovín's '*řečení*' – Klicpera's made-up word for recitative, which Kott suggestively retitled

'melodrama'. Kott's 'melodrama', however, has no spoken text against the
orchestra but is instead a dramatic declamation – a well-graduated baritone
solo leading to a climactic top F above a diminished seventh chord for its
punch-line revelation at the end. The soft *sul ponticello* tremolo strings of its
orchestral introduction could have come straight out of Weber's Wolf's Glen
introduction, as indeed could the woodwind gestures against it.

### Škroup's serious operas

By the time of Kott's *Žižka's Oak*, Škroup had written several more operas,
all of them, like Kott's work, responding to contemporary operatic trends.
Nothing demonstrates better the bilingual atmosphere that prevailed in
Prague in the 1820s and 1830s than the direction of Škroup's career.
Immediately after finishing a successful Czech Singspiel, widely celebrated
as the 'first Czech opera', he wrote a German fairy-tale opera *Der Nachtschat-
ten* (composed 1827) with many suggestive parallels to Weber's *Euryanthe*
(described in Plavec 1941, 146–7). He followed this with a Czech historical
opera, *Oldřich and Božena* with a text by J.K. Chmelenský, the librettist of
*The Tinker*. Its première, on 14 December 1828, was received so coldly that
only one further performance took place and Škroup later had the producer
Ferdinand Ernst rework the opera in German, to which he wrote a completely new score which allegedly retained only one of the old numbers
(Hostinský 1885, 154–5; the original Czech score has disappeared). *Udalrich und Božena* received its première in 1833, although it achieved no more
popularity among the German population, or indeed among the Czechs in
1847, when the German version was translated into Czech by Tyl and the
opera presented three times (Plavec 1941, 165–6). Thereafter Škroup's
operatic career became exclusively German-orientated with the exception of
*Libuše's Marriage*, composed in 1835 again to a text by Chmelenský, and his
incidental music to plays – his music to Tyl's play *Fidlovačka* (the name of a
traditional spring fair; 1834) is extensive and elaborate and hardly less
'operatic' than that of *The Tinker*.

Škroup seems to have had so little faith in the public's acceptance of
*Libuše's Marriage* that he performed only extracts, although his position on
the staff of the Estates Theatre (assistant conductor from 1827, music director 1837–57) provided him with the opportunity to promote his own work.
The opera, slightly revised, was heard complete as late as 11 April 1850.
It was, nevertheless, Škroup's most mature and ambitious Czech opera,
a large-scale, three-act work, this time with an extensive chorus part and
with orchestrally accompanied recitative in place of the spoken dialogue of
*The Tinker*. The only concession to local conditions was the absence of a
proper tenor part (Prague lacked a Czech-speaking tenor at the time). If the
ladies' hunting chorus of Act 2 suggests a German Romantic world, then

the coloratura of the leading role suggests an Italian heroine – a Norma without the pathos and intensity of Bellini (Škroup conducted the Prague première of *Norma* in February 1835). Despite the local subject matter (see pp. 137–42), a genuine Czech voice is hard to find: all Josef Plavec, in his extensive analysis of the work (1941, 174–88), came up with was the occasional polka-like rhythm, or melodic reminiscence of the song 'Where is my homeland?' ('Kde domov můj') from Škroup's incidental music to *Fidlovačka*. From its first performance this simple strophic song, the quintessence of Czech Biedermeier culture, captured the patriotic imagination and it has long served as the unofficial, and from 1918 official, Czech national anthem – the only piece by Škroup still regularly heard today.

The most successful aspects of *Libuše's Marriage* were in fact its least ambitious ones. Přemysl's strophic song from Act 3, 'I am finishing ploughing' ('Doorávám'), was the best received number at its infrequent hearings (Plavec 1941, 183–5) and achieved wider popularity through its publication in the periodical *Věnec* (i, 1835). While able to touch the Czech heart with a simple song, Skroup seems to have lacked the artistic personality to rise above his European operatic models and create a personal, let alone a national style. *The Tinker*, the only native Czech opera to be given in the first Provisional Theatre season, was revived more out of piety than with the intention of providing the seed for future development. It was published as late as 1913. It could in fact be argued that Škroup's chief contribution to the Czech operatic tradition was as a conductor at the Estates Theatre helping to keep alive opera performances in Czech in the 1820s and 1830s. While his musical style advanced no further in his later German operas, *Drahomíra* (1848), *Der Meergeuse* (1851) and *Columbus* (composed 1855, performed in 1942), Škroup earned considerable credit for his early performances of Wagner to German audiences at the Estates Theatre. He introduced *Tannhäuser* in 1854 and *Lohengrin* and *Der fliegende Holländer* in 1856, before his dismissal in 1857. He later took up a conducting post at the Rotterdam opera and died there in 1862, nine months before the Provisional Theatre was opened.

Altogether the forty-year period of the first Czech 'professional' opera from Škroup's *The Tinker* to the first operas of Smetana and Šebor in 1866 is remarkable for the paucity of works and for their mediocre quality. Škroup himself, the best-placed and most experienced Czech stage musician of his time, wrote only three.

## Škroup's successors

Outside Prague a performance of *The Brewers* took place in 1837, in the central Bohemian town of Žebrák where its composer, Josef Vorel (1801–74), was then curate. Although the work falls outside the group of professional operas under discussion – a late survivor of the amateur kantor tradition, it is more of a play with songs – its libretto by the distinguished writer and folklorist K.J. Erben has several points of contact with that of *The Bartered Bride*. The Brno 1841 première of Kott's *Žižka's Oak* has already been mentioned. Kott's German opera on the Dalibor story may not have been performed (no reliable record survives) and a third opera *The Treasure* is now known to be a version of *Žižka's Oak* (Bezdíčková–Ingerlová 1975, 115–16; see also Vejdělek 1982, 267). Even including the 1874 concert performance of a one-act opera *The Chapel in the Woods* by Josef Leopold Zvonař (1824–65) and two excerpts performed at a concert in 1863 of Zvonař's *Záboj* (canvassed unsuccessfully as a work to open the Provisional Theatre), new Czech operas written and performed between 1826 and 1866 amount to fewer than ten, and apart from the first and by far the least ambitious, Škroup's *The Tinker*, none of these achieved more than a couple of performances nor any popularity.

Rather more German operas were written in Bohemia during this period. Škroup himself wrote seven, of which six were performed. His brother, Jan Nepomuk Škroup (1811–92), who also held conducting posts at the Estates Theatre and later at the Provisional Theatre, wrote, in addition to *The Swedes in Prague* (his only Czech opera, given complete in 1867), three German operas, though none was performed publicly, if at all (accounts differ). The German operas by semi-amateur figures such as Leopold Eugen Měchura (1804–70) and Ludvík Ritter z Rittersberku (1809–58) received only private performances, though two operas by the little known Josef August Heller (*c* 1800–55) were staged at the Estates Theatre in the 1840s. But the greatest success of any Czech composer writing operas in German at this time was had by Jan Bedřich Kittl (1806–68), whose *Bianca und Giuseppe oder Die Franzozen vor Nizza* was given at the Estates Theatre on 19 February 1848. The fact that its libretto is by Wagner (Kittl had warm relations not only with Spohr and Mendelssohn, but also with more full-blown Romantics such as Berlioz, Liszt and Wagner) contributes to its interest, but so does its subject matter. It deals with stormy events in Savoy-ruled Nice in 1793 during the French Revolution, and contemporary Prague audiences read into it parallels with the revolution which broke out in Prague eleven days after its première. The military march from Act 2 (based on the French revolutionary song 'Ça ira') was taken up by the National Guard during the revolutionary period in Prague (Hostinský 1901, 95). Even after the excitement died down Kittl's opera had a respectable career on the European stage, with performances in several German towns (performances took place in Hamburg and at Prague's German Theatre as late as 1886). A vocal score was issued by Breitkopf. Kittl wrote two more operas in the 1850s, though neither was performed.

## *Skuherský*

When Kittl retired from the directorship of the Prague Conservatory, where since 1843 he had been one of its most successful and innovative incumbents, his place was sought not only by Smetana but by the theoretician and composer František Skuherský (1830–92). Trained in Prague (chiefly under Kittl), Skuherský had settled in Innsbruck in 1854, where he worked as a conductor, first in the theatre and later in the music society and university church. He failed in his bid for the Conservatory directorship but instead became director (1866–89) of the Prague Organ School, a Czech-orientated rival to the Prague Conservatory with which it was amalgamated on Skuherský's retirement. His two most distinguished pupils there were J.B. Foerster and Janáček.[4]

That Skuherský was drawn to the theatre is evidenced by his seeking a theatre appointment in Innsbruck and by his six operas, but his lack of dramatic flair is also apparent from his failure in both activities. He completed none of his three Czech operas. In Innsbruck he wrote three German operas, one of which, *Der Liebesring*, was performed there in 1861. Retitled *Lóra*, it was staged in a Czech translation at the Provisional Theatre in 1868, but by then Skuherský's *Der Apostat*, revised as *Vladimír, God's Chosen One*, had been given in 1863 at the Provisional Theatre as the first new Czech opera.

Reviewing its 1865 revival in *Národní listy*, Smetana was cautious, praising the chorus and ballet though also criticizing the mixture of styles whereby Wagner's principles mingled uneasily with old-fashioned recitative and old forms (Smetana 1948, 147–8). Despite Smetana's attempt to argue that in its new form *Vladimír* was a 'Czech' work, the score provides little support for this view. The sober handling of the voices (Smetana singled out the female parts as 'unsingable and unpleasant'), avoiding coloratura and even melisma, and a solid, almost continuous four-in-a-bar rhythm reflects, instead, German provincial routine (though there are aberrations such as a short 5/4 chorus in Act 4). Skuherský's last performed opera, *Rector and General* (1873), was in fact a Czech version of *Der Rekrut* from his Innsbruck days. Contemporary critical opinion judged *Lóra* to be 'very melodic' with the occasional trace of 'national tone' and *Rector and General*, with its unusual musical sermon, an enrichment of the repertory (Bartoš 1938, 253) but neither opera achieved more than three performances. The fact was that with the opening of the Provisional Theatre and the advent of a new generation of composers writing directly in Czech a new phase of Czech opera, its most important phase, had begun.

# The Provisional Theatre period

## Smetana

On 10 February 1861, the year before the Provisional Theatre was opened, the Czech patriot Count Jan Harrach announced a competition in which he would give prizes for the best Czech historical and comic operas. Since by the closing date, 30 September 1862, no entries had been received, the competition had to be extended by a further twelve months, thereby dashing Harrach's hopes of opening the Provisional Theatre with the winning work. The panel of six adjudicators, which included Erben (for librettos) and Kittl (for music), deliberated over three years, during which time the most dilatory member of the panel had to be replaced. (It was thought at the time to be Kittl, by then in alcoholic decline; it turned out to have been Ambros, no doubt more anxious to work on his vast *Geschichte der Musik*, which had begun to appear in 1862.) When, on 25 March 1866, the panel awarded first prize to Smetana's *The Brandenburgers in Bohemia*, the decision had been pre-empted – perhaps forced – by the opera's successful première on 5 January that year.[5]

By 1866 Smetana (see illustration 4) then 42, was prominent in Prague musical circles as a critic, conductor, piano virtuoso and teacher. As a composer he would have been known for his many piano works, chiefly dances and other miniatures, though he had composed a fine piano trio and three Lisztian tone poems, *Richard III*, *Wallenstein's Camp*, and *Hakon Jarl*, written during his years abroad in Sweden (1856–61), when he was unable to secure a suitable post at home.

The influence of Liszt, to whom Smetana dedicated his op.1, his *Six morceaux caractéristiques pour piano* (1847–8), quickly shifted the earlier Schumann–Mendelssohn orientation of his music, and was to be felt both in the harmonic and orchestral colour of his tone poems and in his ingenious thematic transformations. Back in Prague, Smetana now began to concentrate on the composition of operas in a variety of genres. His historical opera *The Brandenburgers in Bohemia* (composed 1862–3) was quickly followed by a village comedy *The Bartered Bride* (composed 1863–6). Revised several times up to 1870, *The Bartered Bride* became the most popular Czech opera of all time, but Smetana's next opera, the heroic tragedy *Dalibor* (composed 1865–7), was denounced by critics after its première in 1868 as German and Wagnerian and was taken off after six performances. A long gap followed before his next première. Czech audiences of the time did not realize that Smetana spent several years during this period composing a festival opera, *Libuše*, based on Czech mythology, destined to inaugurate the National Theatre, no more than Smetana realized that his opera would have to be set aside for a decade until sufficient money had been collected to build the

4 Bedřich Smetana in 1863, photograph by S. Kohn. Smetana's eight completed operas inaugurated a fruitful tradition of Czech opera and ranged over
a variety of genres. Smetana was also chief conductor at the Provisional
Theatre at a formative time, from 1866 until he was incapacitated by deafness in 1874.

theatre. It was not until 1874 that Czech audiences heard a new opera by Smetana, *The Two Widows*. Its light, conversational style was a deliberate attempt to give Czech opera something to match the elegance of its French model (see Smetana's letter to Procházka, 21 February 1882; Teige 1896, 124).

In 1874 Smetana went deaf. He had to leave his post at the Provisional Theatre (which he had held since September 1866, a few months after the premières of *The Brandenburgers* and *The Bartered Bride*) and from this moment until his death in 1884 he was hounded by the difficulties of supporting his family and by the attacks made on him in Prague musical circles. Working against total deafness, increasing ill health caused by his syphilitic condition and, in the end, madness, he nevertheless managed to complete the epic series of six tone poems *My Fatherland* (*Má vlast*, 1872–9) and to write his autobiographical string quartet *From my Life* (*Z mého života*, 1876), in which the onslaught of deafness and the maddening tinnitus which accompanied it are vividly depicted. Even more surprising is that in this condition he was still able to write three more operas, *The Kiss* (1876), *The Secret* (1878) and *The Devil's Wall* (1882), all to librettos by Eliška Krásnohorská. In 1881, the year before the première of *The Devil's Wall*, the National Theatre was opened and Smetana's *Libuše* was heard at last. In his final years Smetana returned to *Viola*, begun in 1874, but he left only 365 bars – three and a half scenes.

The canon of Smetana's eight completed operas constitutes the most important body of Czech nineteenth-century opera. It is remarkable for its consistent quality, for its personal voice that became virtually synonymous with a 'Czech' style, and for the models it provided for Smetana's contemporaries and successors. Smetana's operas fall into three groups: three serious operas based on Czech history or myths, *The Brandenburgers in Bohemia*, *Dalibor*, and *Libuše*; two comic operas, *The Bartered Bride* and *The Two Widows*, both originally conceived and performed as *opéras comiques* with spoken dialogue; and the three last operas which, however designated – *The Kiss* is called a 'folk' opera, *The Secret* a 'comic' opera, *The Devil's Wall* a 'comic-romantic' opera – inhabit the same mixed genre in which comedy and potential tragedy combine in equal proportions. Later provided with linking recitatives and other additions, Smetana's two *opéras comiques* have many elements in common with these three last operas.

The variations in scale and pacing within these works are striking. The most sparkling and high-spirited, *The Bartered Bride*, was immediately followed by Smetana's most consistently tragic opera, *Dalibor*. After the monumental, appropriately ceremonial *Libuše*, Smetana wrote the virtually chamber opera *The Two Widows* and then *The Kiss*, so short that it was not regarded in the nineteenth century as a full evening's entertainment and was usually given with a one-act play or orchestral work (Nejedlý 1935, i, 247).

Despite these contrasts it is possible to discern a consistent attitude towards operatic convention running through the eight operas.

For all the later charges of Wagnerianism levelled against him, Smetana relies in his first opera more obviously on French and even Italian tradition. *The Brandenburgers in Bohemia* begins, after a short prelude, with a declamatory dialogue exchange, but it is not long before Smetana's attitudes towards solo and choral ensemble conventions show a less Wagnerian orientation. This first scene ends with a vigorous ensemble for male chorus and three male soloists. It is followed by the entrance of the heroine Ludiše, who is allowed a short aria, and whose subsequent duet with the villain Tausendmark has elements of a cabaletta ending (her duet in Act 2 with her lover Junoš has an even more clear-cut cabaletta). The fact that Ludiše has two sisters usefully provides enough solo female voices for the finale ensembles, but it also saddles the score with ubiquitous female trios, as for instance the Andante religioso that follows the duet, in effect a 'prière' for female soloists and chorus. The revolutionary scene, like the preceding prayer, seems to point to the influence of Auber's *La muette de Portici* and to French grand opera in general, especially since the scene includes a lively though non-essential ballet. The ensuing finale follows the standard Italianate formula. After the unexpected arrival of Tausendmark, a slow concertato begins, in which a broad tune is taken up successively and cumulatively by all the soloists and finally the chorus. Recitative exchanges and the arrival of Ludiše's father and Junoš separate the concertato from the Allegro con fuoco with which the act ends. Exactly the same plan is used for the Act 3 finale except that it follows the Rossinian model more clearly, with less extraneous matter between the two sections and a more homophonic stretta.

Though this type of finale disappeared from Smetana's next operas, the concept of a visual finale, incorporating elements of the popular *tableaux vivants* of the time, remained in Smetana's operas until the end, most obviously in the staged *tableaux* depicting Libuše's visions, but equally in the visual spectacle with which *The Devil's Wall* culminates (Srba 1985, 79). Nor in fact did Smetana's attitude towards choral and solo ensembles change substantially. The most restricted in this respect is his third opera, *Dalibor*, which has nothing more elaborate than duets and choruses, and seldom combines the two. But in his last three operas Smetana seemed happy to follow his librettist Eliška Krásnohorská, who liked ensembles (see pp. 110, 111–12) and supplied them in large quantities, though placing them within the dynamic plan of the whole work with more flexibility than in traditional models. *The Secret* contains some of Smetana's most substantial ensembles. Act 2, for instance has a scherzando ensemble for six soloists and chorus and then a slow 'ensemble of perplexity' for eight soloists and chorus. Here the usual slow–fast pattern is reversed, and instead of acting as a musical culmination of the act, the ensembles are followed by solo scenes. The same is true of Act 1 of *The Kiss*, where a substantial choral reaction is provoked by Vendulka's public refusal of a kiss from her husband-to-be. A more traditional plan would have ended the act there, but instead this musical climax marks the halfway point and leads into a painful scene between Vendulka and Lukáš, where the attempt to patch up their differences breaks up in recriminations. A forthright choral conclusion to an opera is still Smetana's rule, but it is usually short and even perfunctory.

While the trios, quartets and larger solo ensembles that can be found in virtually all the rest of Smetana's operas are absent from *Dalibor*, Smetana seems to have had no inhibitions in this opera about the use of simultaneous duet. Duets are used to conclude both Acts 1 and 2 (the Act 1 duet for Milada and Jitka even has a cabaletta). Also typical of Smetana is the equal-voice duet for soprano and tenor near the beginning of *Dalibor* Act 2. Examples can be found in most of his operas where the voices blend in thirds and sixths, or, as in the *Dalibor* duet, in a constant fluctuation between the two. Some duets, with their submergence of the individuality of the two characters in a show of amorous togetherness, usually suit the subsidiary couple best, as here, but 'We belong to one another' ('Jsme svojí') in *The Kiss* takes on a particular poignancy as it is sung by a more experienced couple and because its tenderness is a deceptive prelude to Vendulka's abrupt refusal of Lukáš's kiss. Perhaps stressing the almost fatal mutual independence of the main couple in *The Bartered Bride*, Smetana makes use of more contrapuntal interplay in the 'Faithful love' ('Věrné milování') duet in Act 1 and naturally even more so in the couple's angry duet exchange in Act 3. As a whole this opera provides a sparkling demonstration of Smetana's range and ingenuity in duet writing. Apart from the lovers' duets, it includes two outstanding comic duets (Kecal and Jeník's bargaining duet in Act 2 and the delightful duet in Act 3 in which Esmeralda and the Circusmaster persuade Vašek to become a bear) and, most accomplished of all, a duet between Smetana's lyric heroine Mařenka and her stuttering comic suitor Vašek.

Though *The Brandenburgers in Bohemia* was Smetana's only opera to have a full-blooded responsorial chorus in the French tradition (the 'Choral' which opens Act 2), a sturdy choral element runs through all of his operas. It is least strong in *The Two Widows*, essentially a solo opera, but even here Smetana increased the chorus's contribution in his revision by adding a choral finale to conclude Act 1. The conventional framing chorus that opens Act 1 of *The Two Widows* is not however an obligatory feature of his operas. While *The Bartered Bride* and *Dalibor* begin with choruses, in both cases beautifully calculated to conjure up the entirely different atmosphere of these two works, half his operas open with dialogue between two or more soloists, and then increase forces. Except in *The Brandenburgers in Bohemia* and *Dalibor*, where the concept of the people takes on a political dimension,

Smetana's choruses, however plentiful, have a limited dramatic role. Their function rather is to provide musical weight and to paint genre scenes, from the happy villagers of *The Bartered Bride* to the smugglers in *The Kiss* and the medieval court of *The Devil's Wall*.

Formal arias, let alone applause-winning entrance or exit arias, are rare in Smetana's operas since individual characters are generally shown in the context of others, reacting to them and on them. Musically this is usually conducted in dialogue or duet (Smetana's favourite mode of writing, as he told Krásnohorská; Očadlík 1940, 102). There are nevertheless some important soliloquy solos. *Dalibor,* lacking ensembles, has extended solos for its hero and heroine, and even the lesser characters have their share of arias. The fine declamatory writing for Milada in her appeal to King Vladislav was a useful model for the even more heroic language of Libuše's vision of the future. In the later operas, monologues are associated with personal development at moments of spiritual crisis, as for instance the reluctant widow Anežka's realization of her situation, Lukáš's flight to the forest in *The Kiss,* or Kalina's humiliation at his poverty at the beginning of Act 2 of *The Secret.* These are all depicted in substantial arias whose sectional, multi-tempo nature gives them a somewhat Italianate feel, but at the same time invests them with an appropriate seriousness. Smetana's extension of Mařenka's Act 3 solo in his revision of *The Bartered Bride* has exactly the same effect. It is one of only five arias in the opera: two for Mařenka, one for her lover Jeník, and two short solos for Vašek. *The Brandenburgers in Bohemia* is even more sparing: its only substantial aria in Act 3 was a later addition for a favoured singer, the baritone Josef Lev, as were many of the lyrical baritone solos in the later operas (see p. 110).

Ludiše's solo in Act 2 of *The Brandenburgers in Bohemia* – it becomes a duet only when her lover, concealed, surprises her with a second verse – provides another model for the later operas: the folklike, usually strophic, song (see pp. 223–5). The most famous examples are Vendulka's two lullabies in *The Kiss,* but there are others, such as Ladislav's two songs in *The Two Widows* (the first stylized as a 'ballad' – see Pospíšil 1979, 23, the second as a 'romance') or the 'professional' songs of the ballad singer Skřivánek in *The Secret.* All of Smetana's later operas also have comic arias. Sometimes their humour is a little forced, as for example in the comic solos for Mumlal in *The Two Widows* or for Bonifác in *The Secret.* In other cases, for instance Vašek in *The Bartered Bride* or Father Paloucký in *The Kiss,* Smetana's music was capable of supplying a depth of characterization absent from the libretto.

Smetana's contribution to Czech opera dominates the twenty-year period of the Provisional Theatre and inevitably overshadows the achievements of his contemporaries, but this period also saw the operatic careers of Šebor,

Hřímalý and Blodek and the beginnings of those of Bendl, Rozkošný, Dvořák and Fibich. Many of these composers had connections with the Provisional Theatre. Šebor, after a brief period in Erfurt as theatre conductor, joined as chorus master in 1864, becoming second conductor (1865–70) after the success of his first opera. Hřímalý worked with Škroup in Rotterdam (1861) and then followed in Smetana's footsteps to Göteborg before becoming Konzertmeister at the Provisional Theatre (1868–73). Fibich was chorusmaster at the Provisional Theatre (1875–8) and, at the very end of his life, dramaturg at the National Theatre (1899–1900). Dvořák was already a violist in Komzák's café orchestra before it became the orchestra of the Provisional Theatre. He continued playing at the Provisional Theatre, latterly under Smetana, until 1871, when he became known as a composer.

It is striking that no composer survived long at the Provisional Theatre. An exposed and politicized focus of cultural life, the theatre seemed to arouse destructive tensions among its employees, and tenure of its posts often reflected changes in the political complexion of its management. It was only Smetana's strong will and sense of purpose that sustained him during his eight years in the theatre. Fibich, less robust, left after only three years, with the change of *družstvo*. Bendl spent less than a year there (1874–5). Šebor, who had been contracted by the theatre to write an opera each year, left in 1870 when his fourth opera *Blanka* failed. He worked briefly in the theatre in Lwów, then became bandmaster in a number of towns, and returned to Prague only in 1894. After disagreements with the management Hřímalý actually joined the opposition, the German theatre, as second conductor (1873–4) before similarly going into exile, in his case in Bukovina, a largely Romanian-speaking province of the Austro-Hungarian Empire.

## Šebor

At the time it was Karel Šebor (1843–1903) who seemed to offer Smetana the most competition. A child prodigy, Šebor had studied at the Prague Conservatory from the age of eleven (he was a composition pupil of Kittl) and his *The Templars in Moravia* (1865), produced when he was twenty-two, was followed in close succession by *Drahomíra* (1867), *The Hussite Bride* (1868) and *Blanka* (1870). Up to the *The Hussite Bride* his operas were increasingly popular: the eight complete performances of *The Templars* was followed by nineteen of *Drahomíra*; *The Hussite Bride* was constantly revived and remained in the repertory until the mid-1890s.

Šebor's first opera, *The Templars in Moravia*,[6] was staged a couple of months before Smetana's *The Brandenburgers in Bohemia* and thus occupies the interesting historical position of the first newly written Czech opera to be performed at the Provisional Theatre. Some of the responsibility for its construction and orientation must go to Sabina the librettist, who clearly had Meyerbeer in mind. The opening scene, for instance, with its double male chorus of court knights and templars, its duel challenges, and its isolated male hero, retraces similar situations in *Robert le diable* and *Les Huguenots*, though with none of the theatrical deftness of Scribe. In this short scene all the main characters of the opera are introduced with little chance to establish themselves. In the face of this, Šebor's attempt to differentiate the characters musically is done skilfully and resourcefully. The scene itself is given some shape by the use of recurrent material and by effective ensemble climaxing. It is, however, the next two scenes that best display Šebor's particular operatic instincts and talents.

Here an aria (in essence a cantabile–cabaletta structure) for the heroine's rival is followed by a duet for her with the villain and an end-of-act ensemble stretta with the chorus. The scheme is Italianate, as is the effective handling of the voices (and the elaborate cadenzas), as well as the Verdian accompanimental patterns, but beneath these formulas lurks a real feeling for atmosphere (for instance in the evocative orchestral introduction), an acute ear for orchestral and vocal colour, and a gift for writing memorable tunes. The most famous scene of the opera, for the Templars in Act 2, may owe something musically to Bertram's invocation in *Robert le diable* (for the opening brass prelude which recurs to unite the first part of the scene) and to the coronation march from *Le prophète* (for the Templars' march at the end), but it is still an effective piece of theatrical writing in its own right and with a rather catchier march than in Meyerbeer.

Although all of Šebor's operas have different librettists, most of them conform to the same plan. Their historical-romantic plots, with plenty of opportunities for showy set pieces, suggest a Scribian model for the librettos, but the solo and duet scenes owe more to Verdi, and the fine handling of the orchestra, with its brightly scored details and sudden gestures, anticipates Tchaikovsky. In its mixture of French and Italian models *The Templars* is in fact close in type to Smetana's *The Brandenburgers in Bohemia* – not altogether surprisingly since they were written at the same time and have the same librettist. But while Smetana moved away to explore new solutions and develop a more individual style, Šebor continued with the same formulas. The strong theatrical instincts he displayed, notably the feeling for dramatic pace, an ability to handle long musical spans and his melodic gifts, make it a matter for regret that he worked so fast and so superficially and denied himself the chance of building on these promising beginnings.

After the failure of *Blanka*, Šebor left Prague. He returned to opera almost a decade later with his only comedy, *The Frustrated Wedding* (1879), to a libretto by Marie Červinková-Riegrová. This 'folk opera' (see pp. 234–6) was not the success he had hoped for and, disappointed and dilatory, Šebor never began work on the next libretto that Červinková-Riegrová wrote for him, *Dimitrij*. Šebor's eclipse was total. No vocal scores of any of his operas were published (only a few individual numbers were issued). The National Theatre has not staged a Šebor opera for ninety years. By the 1970s Šebor would seem to have been effectively buried. *The New Grove* did not notice him. But a revival of interest in the 1980s brought about concert perform- ances of *The Templars*[7] and uncovered music of remarkable dramatic power.

5   Czech composers in 1885. Left to right: Karel Bendl, Antonín Dvořák, Josef Bohuslav Foerster, Jindřich z Albestů Kàan, Karel Kovařovic and Zdeněk Fibich. Kàan (1852–1926) was a teacher and pianist and a future director of the Prague Conservatory. His two operas remained unperformed. Foerster was privileged to be included in this group since at the time he had not made his name as a composer and was known only as Dvořák's successor as organist at St Vojtěch's church and as a young music critic on *Národní listy*. The more precocious Kovařovic had already seen the première of his first opera at the National Theatre. Bendl is the oldest figure in the group with a career as an opera composer stretching back almost two decades, though by this time his friend Dvořák similarly had five operatic premières behind him. Fibich, seen by some as the true successor of Smetana (who died the previous year), still had all his major operas except *The Bride of Messina* before him.

## *Bendl*

Though Šebor's senior by several years, Karel Bendl (1838–97; see illustration 5) sustained an operatic career into the 1890s and during his thirty-year span of composing revealed himself as the most versatile, if not eclectic, Czech opera composer of his day. His first opera *Lejla* (1868) was, according to its Scribian libretto, a 'grand romantic opera' based on Bulwer-Lytton's novel of the downfall of the last Moorish king in Spain. He then attempted a Czech historical opera, *Břetislav* (1870 – a failure, performed only four times), a comic village opera, *The Elderly Suitor* (written 1871–4, performed in Prague in 1883), and the first Czech operetta, *The Indian Princess* (1877). Bendl also turned his hand to an Italian opera, *Gina* (composed 1884, not produced), while his opera *Karel Škreta* (1883) about the famous Czech Baroque painter is set partly in Italy and includes several Italian pastiches – carnival choruses, a song in Italian, etc. On the other hand an earlier direction of his music is evident from the fairy-tale opera *Die Wunderblume* he wrote to a German text (in ?1876, not produced) and from his nickname 'Bendlssohn'. When *verismo* hit the Czech stage he obligingly composed *Mother Míla* (1895), a study of hot-blooded peasant passion in Cyprus. Bendl also wrote enthusiastically and prolifically in other genres, particularly songs and choruses (he was one of the most successful of Czech choral conductors of his day and directed the choral society Hlahol from Smetana's resignation in 1865 until 1877). His cantata *Švanda the Bagpiper* (1880) was later revised as a ballet-opera in 1895–6 and produced at the National Theatre in 1907.

Bendl's first opera, *Lejla*, was a popular success and like *The Brandenburgers in Bohemia* and *The Templars* is particularly interesting as an example of the type of opera thought appropriate to the Czech theatre before Smetana established his ascendancy (it was staged in January 1868, after the initial success of *The Templars* and *The Brandenburgers* had worn off and a few months before the première of *Dalibor*). Unlike *The Templars*, *Lejla* remained in the repertory, with a run of fourteen performances at the National Theatre as late as the 1890s; it was the first Czech opera to be published after *The Bartered Bride*.

*Lejla* was also Eliška Krásnohorská's début as a librettist and by far her most elaborate libretto. It is one of the few Czech operas to emulate the French five-act plan, with the usual trappings of a ballet, real historical personages (King Ferdinand of Spain, the Inquisitor General Tomás de Torquemada, and Boabdil el Chico, the last Moorish King of Granada), multiple choruses (the Moorish and Spanish armies, monks, nuns, slaves and the Ethiopian guard), and several well-distributed *coups de théâtre* – for instance Almamen's Houdini-like escape in a blaze of fire at the end of Act 4. The opera has too many characters, and Bendl's limited powers of characterization fail to differentiate even the most clear-cut of them, making, for instance, an out-and-out villain of the far from straightforward Jewish adviser Almamen, with nothing left in reserve for the more sinister Inquisitor. Bendl responded to the exotic locale only fitfully. He wrote striking Muezzin music, and some attractive numbers based on a mock Arab scale for his Moorish soubrette Zorajda, but he had trouble differentiating the military choruses for the Spanish and Moorish armies. Bendl was more at ease with the short set pieces – for instance the Act 3 Romance for Zorajda and the charming duet for her and Boabdil (the lighter of the two main tenor parts) – than in the larger ensembles and concertatos. The cut of the libretto may be Scribian, but Bendl was more of a Gounod than a Meyerbeer and his attractive lyrical gifts were ill-suited to the large-scale serious works that he attempted.

Nevertheless it was Bendl's serious historical operas that attracted the greatest attention. *The Montenegrins* (1881) received thirteen performances at the Provisional Theatre and was revived at the National Theatre (for which it was intended) in 1886. *The Child of Tábor* (1892), again to a libretto by Krásnohorská, was revived at the National Theatre as late as 1927. Most of Bendl's music is well crafted and the lighter works in particular retain some charm, for instance his *Elderly Suitor* (written in the shadow of *The Bartered Bride)*, which was published in vocal score in 1883 and has been heard occasionally this century on provincial and amateur stages, and his operetta *The Indian Princess*, which, kitted out with a new text, was revived by the National Theatre in 1906. But as a whole no distinctive personality emerges to unify Bendl's diverse oeuvre in the way that clearly links, for instance, Smetana's *Libuše* and *The Two Widows*.


## Rozkošný

Richard Rozkošný (1833–1913) was the only prominent Czech opera composer of this period not to earn his living through music. Though he conducted an amateur choir in Prague for several years, he worked all his life as a clerk in a savings bank. He had an even longer span of opera composition than Bendl, from his one-act *Ave Maria*, written several years before the opening of the Provisional Theatre and produced privately in 1855 or 1856, to his *The Black Lake*, premièred at the National Theatre in 1906, long after the deaths of all his immediate contemporaries. In between he completed eight operas, seven of which were staged by the Provisional or the National Theatres. His first opera to be professionally produced was *Mikuláš* (1870), another village comedy to a Sabina libretto, and its moderate success paved the way for his *St John's Rapids* (1871), one of the most popular Czech operas of the 1870s. It was his only opera to be published. Smetana is said to have admired it,[8] and caught something of the opening of its overture in the opening of his 'Vltava'; Janáček published an extended analysis of it in his review of the Brno première in 1887 (reprinted in Firkušný 1935, 69–70). A contemporary critic, Emanuel Chvála (1886, 38), found echoes of Gounod in it, but in most respects it inclines more to the world of German Romantic opera. Its libretto was originally written in German (and was translated into Czech by Šubert), its subject matter drawn from the world of Weber and his successors – for instance its hunters' and bridesmaids' choruses, and its attitude to the supernatural. Other German traits include its four-square phrase structure, and generally unambitious approach to ensemble. It is an effective work of its kind, and was still playing at the National Theatre in the 1890s.

By then, however, Rozkošný had won an even greater success with his *Cinderella* (1885), one of the few new Czech operas to achieve popular success in the early years of the National Theatre, where it played seventy times up to 1912. It is a continuously written piece with few set numbers (only two duets, two quartets and hardly any ensembles),[9] but these bulk large within the work, especially the four-seasons ballet, which occupies a central position in Act 2 and, together with the familiar fairy-story and the opulent staging, seem to have accounted for the opera's appeal. The folklike language of Cinderella's Act 1 aria (see pp. 232–4) is one of the few Czech touches in what is otherwise a conventional piece with little psychological depth. None of Rozkošný's later operas had anything like the same success. Like Bendl, he also attempted a one-act *verismo* opera, *Stoja* (1894). Whereas Bendl seems to have tried out almost everything, Rozkošný's *Stoja* stands significantly apart from the line of fairy-tale or supernatural operas that he cultivated after his less successful attempts at other genres, whether comic village (*Mikuláš*) or serious historical (*Záviš z Falkenštejna*, 1877).

### Hřímalý; Blodek

Like *Cinderella*, Hřímalý's *Enchanted Prince* (1872), based on a tale from *The 1001 Nights*, won considerable popularity as a fairy-tale opera and was revived at the National Theatre as recently as 1933. Vojtěch Hřímalý (1842–1908), however, transferred to the German theatre soon afterwards and this, together with his exile abroad, put an end to any future career in Prague as an opera composer. His later opera *Švanda the Bagpiper* was turned down by Prague and received its première in his native Plzeň (1896).

One of the most promising composers of the period was Vilém Blodek (1834–74). His one-act opera *In the Well* belongs to the group of comic village operas with Sabina librettos and it has remained a repertory opera in Czechoslovakia ever since its first performance in 1867 (there were forty-seven performances at the National Theatre in the 1960s alone). Amateur performances were facilitated by the score's modest demands and dimensions – a sequence of four solos, two duets, one quartet, an overture and an intermezzo, and three short numbers involving a chorus and soloists. It was the first Czech comic opera to dispense with spoken dialogue, replacing it with short recitatives. Blodek's opera is often considered to be one of the most 'Czech' operas after those of Smetana (it was written shortly after the première of *The Bartered Bride*), but in fact its pleasant melodic style and rather four-square craftsmanship owe as much to composers such as Nicolai and Lortzing. This is even more true of his next opera, *Zítek* (composed 1869), again to a Sabina libretto, this time a historical comedy set in the fourteenth century. It is a much more ambitious work than *In the Well*, in three acts, with a large cast, and some attempt to break down the divisions between the closed numbers of its predecessor. The music has a vitality and charm that at times rivals that of Smetana's music. A nervous breakdown followed by a complete mental collapse put an end to Blodek's career and he completed only Act 1 and part of Act 2. This torso was given nine performances at the National Theatre in 1934; a recording issued in 1984 gives some idea of its qualities.

### Dvořák I

Dvořák's early operas also fall into this period. His first opera, *Alfred*, composed to a German text in 1870, was never staged until rediscovered this century, nor was the first version of his *King and Charcoal Burner*, put into rehearsal by Smetana in 1872, but withdrawn by Dvořák when its difficulties, caused chiefly by his inexperience in vocal and dramatic writing, became apparent. To the same text he then composed a completely new opera, which was premièred in 1874 and was later joined by his other early comic opera *The Stubborn Lovers* (composed 1874, première 1881) and *The Cunning Peasant* (composed 1877; première 1878), both of which overtook *King and Charcoal Burner* in popularity and remained repertory operas well into this century. There are also two serious historical operas from this period, *Vanda* (1876), set in Poland, and *Dimitrij* (1882), set in Russia. It has been argued that *Vanda* was Dvořák's response to Smetana's still unperformed *Libuše* (Houtchens 1984), but it was *Dimitrij*, begun a month before the first opening of the National Theatre, that represented a more serious rival. It was Dvořák's greatest operatic achievement to date and his last opera for several years, before he immersed himself in the composition of his Seventh Symphony in D minor and the oratorios *The Spectre's Bride* (*Svatební košile*) and *St Ludmilla*. *Dimitrij* had considerable popular success, and was Dvořák's only stage work from this period to measure up to his later operas.

It is difficult to form a clear picture of Dvořák's early operatic career not only because of the inaccessibility of some of the material (*Alfred*, *Vanda* and the first version of *King and Charcoal Burner* remain unpublished), but also because of Dvořák's confusing changes in style and approach. Broadly speaking, however, a grand opera aesthetic informs the three serious operas, while the second version of *King and Charcoal Burner* and the two comic operas are closer to Lortzing and to the Smetana of *The Bartered Bride*. This division, however, is complicated by the shadow that Wagner casts, particularly over *Alfred* (for instance in its chromaticized melody and harmony, its leitmotivic system and the importance of the orchestra – see Šourek 1916, i, 62–3) and the first version of *King and Charcoal Burner*. These Wagnerian traits co-exist with full-scale ensembles, concerted finales and other trappings of grand opera such as the 'Gebet' in Act 3 of *Alfred* or the 'Romance' in Act 2 – in other words this is the Wagner of *Tannhäuser* rather than that of *Tristan*. By the next decade Dvořák had moved nearer to Meyerbeer than to mature Wagner. *Dimitrij* has a Scribian libretto with a carefully controlled build-up of characters and scenes in Act 1, opposing choruses to represent two hostile nationalities and a charismatic imposter as its central character that bears more than a passing resemblance to John of Leyden. It was Dvořák himself who insisted on more ensembles and wrote formal concertatos of the grandest scale in all four acts.

The comic operas are not so clear-cut in their aesthetic. Their simple act-structure (*The Cunning Peasant* is in two acts, *The Stubborn Lovers* in one) and their casts of mainly humble characters set them apart from Dvořák's grander operas, but like these, both *King and Charcoal Burner* (all versions) and *The Cunning Peasant*, have ballets and elaborate concerted sections. The second act of *King and Charcoal Burner* (all versions) ends with a multi-movement concertato finale; the finale of *The Cunning Peasant* concludes in a series of accumulative ensembles which include more and more singers until all eight soloists are singing. *The Stubborn Lovers* is rather different in being more conversational, with more solos, fewer ensembles and virtually no chorus until the end. All three operas, however, share an involved scheme of recurring themes and thematic manipulation – one characteristic that runs through all of Dvořák's operas.

# The National Theatre period

The opening of the National Theatre, it was thought, would act as a stimulus to the composition of new Czech operas. Smetana's *Libuše* was at last unveiled; operas such as Dvořák's *Dimitrij* had been written with the new theatre in mind. But competitions held in 1880 and 1883 failed to produce many new works. Neither Bendl's *Montenegrins* nor Fibich's *Blaník* were considered worthy of the 1880 prize and the winner of the 1883 competition, Bendl's *Karel Škreta*, failed to stay in the repertory after its initial ten performances. Bendl's next première, *The Child of Tábor*, came only in 1892.

Šubert's policy for the theatre in the 1880s may have been a factor in ensuring that the two most prominent and talented opera composers after Smetana – Dvořák and Fibich – produced very little for the theatre during this period. Although Dvořák's comic opera *The Cunning Peasant* was given in the season of eight Czech operas which opened the theatre, it was an older work, composed in 1877. Apart from *Dimitrij* (1882), his next operatic première came only in 1889.

### Fibich

Something of the atmosphere prevailing in these years can be seen from the fact that one of the most frequently performed operas was Rozkošný's fairy-tale *Cinderella* (1885), with its lavish sets and attractive but light-weight music, whereas Fibich's *Bride of Messina* (1884), regarded by some as one of the finest Czech tragic operas, received only eight performances during the composer's lifetime.

It was not Fibich's first opera. While still in his teens he had written several operas and one of them, a one-act comedy, *Der Kapellmeister in Venedig*, composed to his own text, had received an informal performance at his parents' home in 1868. Fibich (see illustration 5) was the most cultured and cosmopolitan Czech composer of his generation. His musical education took him to the Leipzig Conservatory (which reinforced his early 'Schuman-nesque' affiliation), to Paris, where he acquired a lifelong interest in art, and to Mannheim as a pupil of the local Kapellmeister. Though his year in Mannheim coincided with the preparations for an early performance, in 1869, of *Die Meistersinger*, the opera that he wrote soon after this experience was essentially in the Weberian mould. This was *Bukovín*, written when the composer was only twenty-one, and given three performances at the Provisional Theatre in 1874. At the age of sixteen Fibich had solicited a libretto from Smetana's librettist Sabina, who indulged his request for 'another *Freischütz*' (Hostinský 1909, 8; Nejedlý 1911, 16) by throwing off a libretto so encumbered with Romantic nonsense that the work was never heard again after its initial run, nor published.

The canon of Fibich's operas thus really begins with *Blaník* (1881), by which time the influence of both Wagner and Smetana had had time to make itself felt in Fibich's music, and Fibich's spell of conducting at the Provisional Theatre (1875–8) had given him some practical experience of the stage. He had also had his fill of tragedy when, during a year abroad in Vilnius, Lithuania, the birth of his twins was followed immediately by the death of one of them and by that of his wife's sister attending the birth.

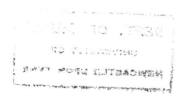

Within two years both his wife and the other twin had died. One might see a link between Fibich's domestic tragedy and the succession of doom-laden operas, wracked by gloomy forebodings of Fate (and appropriate leitmotifs) that became Fibich's speciality. But, as Nejedlý has argued (1911, 26–7), Fibich always had a penchant for the gloomier manifestations of Romanticism, which Nejedlý attributed to his upbringing, as the son of a forestry official, in the depths of dark Bohemian forests. Only two of Fibich's mature operas have specifically Czech settings – the early *Blaník* and his penultimate opera *Šárka*. The rest bear witness to his own cosmopolitan leanings and to those of highly cultured literary friends such as the aesthetician Otakar Hostinský, the poet and dramatist Jaroslav Vrchlický, and the writer Anežka Schulzová, all of whom supplied him with librettos.

After the cool reception of the public to *The Bride of Messina* (after Schiller, 1884), Fibich waited a few years before writing again for the theatre, and when he did so, he produced a work unique in musical literature, a trilogy of stage melodramas based on Vrchlický's *Hippodamia* (after Sophocles and Euripides). Melodrama – the union of spoken words with instrumental music – is a medium with a long Czech pedigree. It was the 'duodramas' of Georg (Jiří) Benda, *Medea* and *Ariadne auf Naxos*, that had so excited Mozart in 1778. Fibich had conducted both these works in 1875 during his spell at the Provisional Theatre, and before tackling a complex stage work had already explored the possibilities of the medium in his highly successful concert melodrama settings of some of Erben's ballads such as *Christmas Eve* (*Štědrý večer*) and *The Water Gnome* (*Vodník*). His *Hippodamia* (*Hippodamie*) trilogy, when given at the National Theatre (*The Courtship of Pelops* (*Námluvy Pelopovy*, 1890); *The Atonement of Tantalus* (*Smír Tantalův*, 1891); *Hippodamia's Death* (*Smrt Hippodamie*, 1891)) proved surprisingly successful. *The Courtship of Pelops* was performed eighteen times in three years and was one of the four Czech works presented in Vienna in 1892. This paved the way for his return to opera.

Fibich's four last operas are all imbued with proof of his new-found happiness with his former pupil Anežka Schulzová. *The Tempest* (1895), Fibich's only mature opera with comic elements, changed Shakespeare's centre of gravity from Prospero and his enchanted island to the lovers; *Hedy* (1896, based on an episode in Byron's *Don Juan*), with its second act consisting mostly of love duet, and a heroine who expires in a closing *Liebestod*, was described by its librettist as a 'Czech *Tristan und Isolde*' (Richter 1900, 172). By his next opera, Fibich had left his second wife and installed Anežka as the house librettist (she had already supplied him with the libretto to *Hedy*), and with her he wrote his most successful and popular opera, *Šárka* (1897), based on one of the few Czech legends that deals with the conflict of erotic passion and duty. The rather more sober *Fall of Arkona* (1900) has a central passionate father–daughter relationship, which seems to reflect the nature of Fibich's relationship with Anežka, eighteen years his junior.

*The Bride of Messina* is a music drama rather than an opera and is organized orchestrally into acts through a complex web of leitmotifs above which a generally declamatory vocal part is superimposed – it made little difference, as Nejedlý has pointed out (1911, 67), when in Fibich's next stage work, *Hippodamia*, the declamatory voice part became a spoken one. Arias in *The Bride of Messina* are replaced by monologues, there are no duets and, apart from twenty-two bars of a trio and an impressive funeral march, there are few concessions to operatic conventions. The chief exception lies in the extensive use of a double chorus to represent the supporters of the rival brothers and to which Fibich added solo voice parts to create large-scale mixed ensembles. The chorus element can be found already in Schiller's play – an attempt to re-create the ancient Greek chorus in its dual role as actor and commentator. Fibich's chorus is almost all male (Don César's supporters include altos to give a slight colour differentiation) and this combines with the dominance of males among the principals, the sombre colours of Fibich's orchestra, and the relentlessly tragic dénouement of Schiller's plot to give an effect of unrelieved gloom.

But by the time of Fibich's operas a decade later, Anežka had come into his life, and his adherence to such severe models was strained. *Hedy* and *Šárka* have memorable love duets; *The Tempest* has several strophic songs; *Hedy* has a ballet and a full-blown multi-tempo concertato finale. As in Fibich's earlier operas, there are robust choruses and choral ensembles. All these works break quite easily into set numbers, not surprisingly since many of them are based not on leitmotif-fuelled symphonic development (Fibich was an accomplished composer of symphonies and tone poems), as in *The Bride of Messina*, *Hippodamia* and even *Blaník*, but instead on some of the 376 short piano pieces entitled *Moods, Impressions and Reminiscences* (*Nálady, dojmy a upomínky*) – a musical 'diary' in which Fibich charted his affair with Anežka. The tuneful ABA conclusion of Ferdinand's aria at the beginning of Act 2 of *The Tempest* is none other than a reworking of piece no.44, written to depict Anežka wearing a purple dress (the last of eight studies of Anežka in different clothes).

Fibich's final opera, *The Fall of Arkona*, retains the choruses but the solo writing is more declamatory. The text is again by Schulzová but it sits above a symphonic texture that seems to have grown more out of its own motives than out of a patchwork of coded love messages to Anežka. The self-contained prologue (*Helga*) is of chamber music proportions with only four characters. One of Fibich's projects for the future was a setting of an Ibsen play; it is fascinating to speculate in what direction he might have moved had he lived longer.

## Dvořák II

While Fibich in the 1890s was moving away from Wagnerian music drama, Dvořák seemed to be going in the opposite direction. *The Jacobin* (1889), like its predecessor, *Dimitrij*, had full-scale ensemble finales, and, like the even earlier *King and Charcoal Burner*, an elaborate succession of *divertissement* dances at the end. However, he had replaced the grand manner of *Dimitrij* with more homely duets and songs better suited to its humble protagonists – a trend further emphasized in Dvořák's 1897 revisions: more than Smetana's last opera, let alone Fibich's *Bride of Messina*, *The Jacobin* is an unashamedly set-number opera. But when *Dimitrij*, at its showing during the National Theatre's Vienna tour of 1892, failed to win the same success as Smetana's operas – despite Dvořák's much greater familiarity as an international figure – he embarked on a radical revision of his 'old-fashioned' work to bring it more in touch with Wagnerian practices.

About a third of the opera remained the same,[10] including much of the chorus work, though the striking double-chorus opening to the work was jettisoned in favour of a much duller single-chorus version. Heeding criticism of his word-setting, Dvořák reset and shortened many of the solo voice parts, omitting repeated words and coloratura. Otherwise the most striking changes were in the large choral ensembles, for instance in Act 3 or at the end of Act 1, which are cut, shortened, or recomposed for smaller forces. Saddest of all was the sacrifice of the ensemble for quintet and chorus near the end of Act 4, dramatically static (the action freezes for a moment of contemplation before Marfa's crucial decision) but musically quite magnificent and, within its chosen aesthetic, essential to provide emphasis at the most important moment of the drama. Dvořák was clearly sorry to lose such fine music and rewrote the Act 4 Dimitrij–Xenie duet using this material – itself another sad sacrifice. The new version was not much liked when presented at the opera's 1894 revival, and rightly so, since the changes that Dvořák made went against the nature of the work and left it as an unsatisfactory amalgam of conventions. Dvořák himself is said to have regretted his changes,[11] and when Kovařovic revived the opera in 1906 he produced a new version (subsequently printed – the form in which the opera is generally known today) which incorporated some of Dvořák's later word-setting but few other changes.

Nevertheless the new 'Wagnerian' direction was evident in Dvořák's next opera *The Devil and Kate* (1899). Though there are still some evident set numbers showing through (e.g. strophic songs such as Jirka's shepherd song or Marbuel's description of his 'Red Castle' in Act 1 and of the people's afflictions in Act 2), Dvořák built up larger musical structures by means of recurring themes. But Dvořák treated these themes more in the manner of a symphonist attempting to unify a long, complex work than like a true leit-motivist intent on exploring their musico-dramatic tensions. The voice parts are melodically less important and much of the burden of musical continuity is taken up by the orchestra, perhaps in the new confidence that Dvořák acquired in his powers of programmatic expression after the composition, in 1896, of the series of tone poems based on Erben ballads. In addition to an overture, there are substantial preludes to each act (Act 2 even includes a Nibelheim-like descent into Hell), and dance music is provided abundantly both on earth and in Hell. Not surprisingly in an opera that lacks any love interest, there are no duets, and, most striking of all, the large-scale ensembles that can be found in all of Dvořák's previous operas have disappeared.

The result is not an unqualified success. The symphonic weight goes against the grain of the light-hearted folktale on which the opera is based. But in Dvořák's next opera tale and musical language were matched in one of the most magical blends in the Czech operatic repertory and gave birth to Dvořák's richest and most heartfelt opera score, *Rusalka*. Most of the conventions resemble those of *The Devil and Kate*: no choral ensemble, duets limited to just two between the Prince and the Foreign Princess in Act 2. With its ballet and formal choruses this is the most openly 'old-fashioned' of the three acts, despite Dvořák's ingenuous justification of the duets to his librettist on the grounds of Wagner's 'exception' in Act 2 in *Tristan* (Šourek 1911, 431). Where *Rusalka* scores over its predecessor is in the strength and profusion of the solo numbers. These vary from light or mock-serious numbers for Ježibaba the Witch and for the wholly comic characters such as the Gamekeeper and the Kitchen Boy, baleful laments for the gloomy Water Goblin, to full-blooded Heldentenor arias for the Prince. Rusalka herself has a part that can match the Prince's in vocal fervour but whose characteristic utterance is the aching poignancy of the opera's most famous number, Rusalka's Hymn to the Moon.

*Rusalka* was instantly successful from its première in 1901 and has remained Dvořák's most popular opera ever since. His next opera, *Armida* (1904), which turned out to be his last, had few of *Rusalka*'s natural advantages. Dvořák is reported to have wanted 'a nice role for Maturová' (the singer who had created the part of Rusalka; Kvapil 1911, 430) and indeed the poignancy of a couple of her arias – for instance her entrance arias in the first and second acts – have in them little of the pagan sorceress of Tasso's poem (his Czech adapter obligingly 'humanized' the part) and much of Dvořák's fragile water nymph. *Parsifal*, with its rather similar cast of Christian knights pitted against a pagan magician in his enchanted castle, may have been in Dvořák's mind when he took on his first non-Slavonic opera subject since *Alfred*. But while Wagner's juxtaposition of an intense Christian mysticism and a world of sensuous temptation exploited already well-developed gifts and a musical language almost expressly developed for this purpose, Dvořák responded to Armida's enchanted garden with little more than pretty orientalisms, and to the Christian soldiers with four-square martial music of a particularly undistinguished cut. Unlike those in *Rusalka*, none of the subsidiary characters comes alive. The music has much of the earnest motivicism of *The Devil and Kate* and *Rusalka* but with so little truly memorable music that the effect is of a long and repetitious work.

## Kovařovic

Even had Dvořák possessed more of a gift for stage dramaturgy it is by no means certain that he would have been able to make a successful opera of *Armida*. It is significant that Karel Kovařovic (1862–1920; see p. 45) worked on the same libretto for several years, but completed only a single act (Šourek 1943, 38–9). Kovařovic's strong theatrical instincts were given more scope in his best-known work, *The Dogheads* (1898), a vigorous historical drama dealing with the 1695 rebellion of the Czechs of the western border region, the Chods (whose emblem was a dog's head), against Habsburg attempts to deny them their ancient privileges. To Nejedlý (1911, 251–3) it seemed like an old-fashioned nationalist–historical opera twenty years after its time, based on equally old-fashioned operatic conventions: folk merry-making, a ballroom scene *à la* Tchaikovsky, an unaccompanied sextet in Act 2 in the vein of the *Bartered Bride* sextet, and so on. Nevertheless, Kovařovic's opera won the *družstvo*'s 1897 opera competition (ahead of Fibich's *Šárka*) and proved one of the most popular Czech operas of its time – evidence that black-hearted villains, defiant folk heroes, grieving womenfolk, and lively, if unauthentic, folk scenes were still a powerful mix in the hands of a deft technician, and that sentimental Czech nationalism was still very much alive. With virtually no plot and no scope at all for melodramatic tragedy, Kovařovic's next opera *At the Old Bleachery* (1901), a series of gentle genre scenes based on Němcová's classic novel *The Grandmother*, had less impact. Although Kovařovic was only thirty-nine and lived another nineteen years, it was his last completed opera – his duties as musical director at the National Theatre from 1900 to his death in 1920 proved too onerous to admit any more large-scale creative work.

If Kovařovic's later career as a composer provoked Nejedlý's hostility for its vein of sentimental patriotism, his earlier career fared no better with Nejedlý because of its espousal of foreign texts and foreign genres (Nejedlý 1911, 239–48). A pupil of Fibich, Kovařovic shared his teacher's cosmopolitan outlook and in his earliest operas looked outside Bohemia for his subject matter. His first opera, *The Bridegrooms* (1884), was admittedly based on an early nineteenth-century Czech play, a light-hearted comedy from the 'chivalric era', but his second opera, *The Way through the Window* (1886), was a reworking of a comedy by Scribe and his third, *The Night of St Simon and*

*St Jude* (1892), was an operatic version of Alarcón's *Three-cornered Hat*. None achieved more than a handful of performances at the National Theatre. *The Bridegrooms*, whose music was described by Foerster (1942, 354) as 'witty and full of French grace and charm', had the longest initial run – nine performances. It was also given in Brno, where it aroused Janáček's critical fury (his notice in *Hudební listy* (15 January 1887, reprinted in Firkušný 1935, 68-9) led to the cool relations between the two composers and to Kovařovic's consequent reluctance to stage *Jenůfa* at the National Theatre). Kovařovic's ballets – in Nejedlý's eyes (1911, 231-3) another sign of pernicious foreign influence – did little better and instead he achieved the greatest popular success before *The Dogheads* with the incidental music that he wrote for *The Excursion of Mr Brouček from the Moon to the Exhibition* (1894; see p. 119). Kovařovic's light-weight music proved popular (a couple of items can still occasionally be heard today) and the next year, 1895, Kovařovic was asked to form and conduct the large orchestra that played at the Czech Ethnographical Exhibition in Prague. Together with his conducting of some of the first concerts (1896-8) of the newly formed Czech Philharmonic and the success in 1898 of his first serious opera *The Dogheads*, Kovařovic's appointment as musical director at the National Theatre in 1900 became almost a foregone conclusion.

## Ostrčil

His successor, Otakar Ostrčil (1879-1935), proved rather more adept at keeping a composition career alive during his period as musical director at the National Theatre (1920-35). Ostrčil's finest orchestral compositions were written in the 1920s, his most successful and most substantial opera, *Johnny's Kingdom* (1934), between 1928 and 1933. Like his predecessor Kovařovic, Ostrčil had been a pupil of Fibich – Fibich's 'famulus' as the master liked to describe him – receiving lessons from the age of sixteen, by which time he had already begun his first opera. He made such good progress that he was allowed to help out as amanuensis with the orchestration of Fibich's last opera (Nejedlý 1935a, 44-5). Ostrčil's first completed opera, *Jan Zhořelecký*, with a libretto drawn from fourteenth-century Czech history, was written when he was eighteen and a student of Czech and German at the Charles University of Prague. Although he held several distinguished conducting posts, including that of musical director at the Vinohrady Theatre 1914-18, it was not until he was appointed dramaturg at the National Theatre in 1919 that he gave up his post as a language teacher. On Kovařovic's death the following year Ostrčil succeeded him as musical director of the National Theatre and until his own death in 1935 consolidated the most fruitful period of opera production at the theatre.

Apart from the early *Jan Zhořelecký* and several uncompleted projects (including a *Cymbeline*, 1900), Ostrčil wrote five operas, spanning his entire mature creative life. The first, *The Death of Vlasta* (1904), continues the tradition of Czech mythological opera (see pp. 142–3). Its conventions are similarly restrospective. Although a little inhibited in its use of solo ensemble (Act 1 has a trio and quartet, and there is a short duet in Act 2), all three acts have a large number of choruses and Act 2 ends with a concertato finale. With several long preludes and interludes, the orchestra plays an important part in providing the musical continuity. Ostrčil's espousal of the mythological world of Vlasta was, however, less of a pious nationalist gesture than a response to a creative need that was to reassert itself in his later works. His next opera, *Kunála's Eyes* (1908), and the later *The Legend of Erin* (1921) are both based on material by the Czech symbolist Julius Zeyer, set respectively in mythical India and in mythical Ireland. In neither case did the exotic provenances of the action affect the music, which continued to explore a late Romantic idiom that owed less to the world of Debussy than Ostrčil's penchant for symbolist librettos might have suggested, and rather more to Richard Strauss.

This was particularly evident in his third opera, *The Bud* (1911 – the title is a metaphor for a young girl's awakening into womanhood), both from its ripe harmonic style (with many Straussian juxtapositions of unrelated dominant sevenths/ninths) and from Ostrčil's decision to set a one-act stage play without substantial libretto changes. This was the first Czech prose opera after Janáček's *Jenůfa*. The gentle subject, however, could not have been further from Strauss's *Salome* or *Elektra*. With just four characters whose subtle interaction provides the chief dramatic interest, the work is in fact much more in the spirit of Smetana's late 'comic' operas – short on humour but long on spiritual growth. The chamber dimensions recall *The Two Widows* but the tenderness suggests *The Kiss*. There are no set numbers, no simultaneous singing, and, as in *The Death of Vlasta*, musical continuity is provided chiefly by the orchestra. It was Ostrčil's first opera to be published and, especially after the First World War, won a modest public following. Ostrčil's most popular opera, however, was his last, *Johnny's Kingdom*, which was able to build on the theme of spiritual development that runs most obviously through *The Bud* and *Kunála's Eyes*. (In the latter opera Kunála is blinded at the instructions of his wicked mother-in-law but attains a saintlike inner vision and in a final miraculous apotheosis has his sight restored when he forgives his tormentors.)

*Johnny's Kingdom* is the story of a man who through his simple goodness of heart wins out against all manner of adversity – evil-minded and rapacious brothers, wars and rebellions, even the active animosity of the devil. Though based on a tale by Tolstoy, the popularity of the work owed much to the apparent 'Czechness' of its characters, in particular its hero, Tolstoy's Ivan now transformed into 'hloupý Honza' (simple Johnny), the hero of many Czech folk legends. Another factor in its success was Ostrčil's conscious simplification of his style. The harmony is simpler, perhaps to accommodate the folksongs and sections based on Czech dance rhythms. While the orchestra continues to play an important part, for instance in the preludes and interludes that mark the scene changes, there is considerable retrenchment from the strict declamatory style of *The Bud*. The many large-scale choruses form an essential element and there is a much greater reliance on the power of the voice in the building of emotional climaxes, whether in solo passages (now, in effect, 'arias') or in ensemble, as for instance the concertato end to Act 1. With its anti-militarist message the opera scored something of a sensation at its first performances in the 1930s in a Europe over which war clouds were gathering.

## Novák

If Ostrčil has affiliations with Richard Strauss, his contemporary Vítězslav Novák (1870–1949) was sometimes considered the country's representative of Impressionism. Both comparisons are misleading, as was the stress laid by Nejedlý and his school on the fruitful line of succession from Smetana through Fibich to Ostrčil as compared with the less fruitful succession from Dvořák to his pupil Novák. But as far as opera is concerned, there is clearly a connection between Dvořák's chequered relationship with opera and the attitudes towards opera of his two most prominent direct pupils, Josef Suk and Vítězslav Novák. Suk wrote no operas at all, while Novák turned to it only in his early forties, once he had established his reputation in other fields.

Over the next sixteen years, from 1913 to 1929, Novák wrote four operas and two ballets. The first three operas were all based on classic Czech plays: *The Imp of Zvíkov* (1915) on Stroupežnický's one-act comedy of the same name, *Karlštejn* (1916) on Vrchlický's three-act *A Night at Karlštejn*, and *The Lantern* (1923) on Jirásek's well-loved four-act play. Only his final opera, *The Grandfather's Legacy* (1926), had a different origin, being adapted from a poem by the Czech poet Adolf Heyduk. The verbal structures of his librettos played a large part in determining the type of opera that Novák created from them. *The Imp of Zvíkov*, set to an unchanged prose text, consists mostly of rapid declamation over an orchestral background made up of involved motivic commentary, much in the spirit of Ostrčil's *The Bud*. On the other hand, his next two operas were both set only after considerable modification by librettists of the original plays. Both *Karlštejn* and *The Lantern* were composed to rhymed verse, which Novák did little to override rhythmically. His setting of *The Lantern*, for instance, falls into regular, almost singsong rhythmic periods that, especially in dialogue, can give a very formal, mannered impression. Despite this apparent concession to operatic convention, there is no ensemble singing: only for the depiction of supernatural events in the final act does Novák bring in an offstage chorus. The same attitude is true of *The Lantern*'s predecessors. The virtual absence of choral writing from *Karlštejn*, apart from very short sections at the ends of the first two acts, is particularly surprising considering the possibilities that its subject (a portrait of Bohemia's greatest king, Charles IV) offered and the fact that the opera was written during the First World War as a consciously patriotic vehicle.

In his final opera Novák returned to what he regarded as surer ground: symphonic writing. *The Grandfather's Legacy* has great swathes of symphonic interludes, postludes and dances. There is also an abrupt turnabout as regards choral writing, with the chorus constituting a particularly important element. The voice parts themselves became less realistic, with extensive melismatic and coloratura passages. This opera, however, had the least success of any of Novák's, and after the ill-fated cycle of his operas initiated by Ostrčil at the National Theatre in 1930, which Novák publicly denounced in a bruising pamphlet that did his reputation nothing but harm, he abandoned the medium. He continued his compositional career, however, until an advanced age.

In fact Novák's star was waning almost before he began his operas. His oratorio *The Wedding Shift* (*Svatebni košile*) (1913) was castigated as presumptuous after Dvořák's famous setting of Erben's text. By this time, his contemporaries such as Suk were gaining ground with the public in the symphonic field, and in opera Novák had to compete with already established figures such as Ostrčil and Foerster (who returned to Prague in 1918), while in the same year as the première of *Karlštejn*, the Prague première of Janáček's *Jenůfa* drew attention to an unexpected late arrival on the Prague operatic scene.

### Foerster

Unlike Novák, for whom opera was not an especially congenial medium, his older contemporary Josef Bohuslav Foerster (1859–1951; see illustration 5) was passionately interested in opera from an early age. He had been drawn to the theatre as a youth (he had even considered acting as a career; Foerster 1929, 150), attended theatre and opera frequently at the National Theatre, especially from 1884, when he became music critic for the Prague daily *Národní listy*, and was married to an opera singer, Berta Lautererová, one of the National Theatre soloists. None of this, however, prevented an end to his operatic career rather similar to that of Novák's. Foerster's last three operas, *The Invincible Ones* (1918), *The Heart* (1923) and *The Fool* (1936), were received with embarrassment as the ageing composer explored an increasingly personal vein of opera in which the psychological depiction of the main characters and their spiritual development were paramount. It is also not surprising that a composer, writing on the eve of his sixtieth birthday and on into his seventies, was using a harmonic and musical language little changed from that of his youth. Foerster's late operas were felt to be out of touch with their times and seemed to have little to say to the newer, postwar generation.

This was a sad end to a career that had begun so promisingly, and in the vanguard of Czech opera. Foerster's first two operas, *Debora* (1893) and *Eva* (1899), both explored what was then new territory: serious village opera. The first was based on a relatively well-known play, *Deborah* (1849), by the German dramatist Salomon von Mosenthal, and only the names of the characters in its Czech libretto adaptation suggest a Czech location. The second, however, was set specifically in a Moravian village and had as one of its chief aims the realistic depiction of village life. By giving an unsentimental, brutal and (to contemporary audiences) thoroughly immoral view of village life, Gabriela Preissová's first play, *The Farm Mistress*, had created a sensation when it was presented at the National Theatre in 1889. It was bold of Foerster to see in it the potential for an opera, especially in the light of the idealized picture of the village that the nationalist public had from its favourite village opera, *The Bartered Bride*. Nevertheless Preissová's text served Foerster as the basis for his second and by far his most successful opera, *Eva*.

*Debora* had little impact on the Czech public at the time (it was performed only four times until its revival during the Foerster cycle in 1930) and its chief virtue was as a dry run for *Eva*. It shared not only the village milieu but also the same type of long-suffering heroine, rejected, after parental interference, by her better-class suitor. The experience gained in *Debora* ensured that *Eva*, written at the height of Foerster's powers and based on a subject that allowed him to exploit his most individual asset – a strong line in melancholy lyricism – achieved both popular and critical success at its première, and survived almost to this day as a repertory piece. Foerster's third opera, *Jessica* (1905), was based on a Czech adaptation of *The Merchant of Venice* (see p. 115).

### Foerster and Janáček

It was against the background of the later operas of Dvořák and Fibich, and the outputs of the younger generation, Kovařovic, Ostrčil and Foerster, that Janáček began his operatic career. The differences that set Janáček apart from his Prague contemporaries are strikingly demonstrated by comparing Foerster's *Eva* and Janáček's *Jenůfa*. Both are based on plays by Gabriela Preissová, both set in the same ethnographic region of Moravia. The two operas were begun at much the same time, Foerster's in 1893,

Janáček's in 1894, though it took him a full decade to bring his work to the stage, in 1904, while Foerster's *Eva* was premièred five years earlier, in 1899. Both composers made their own librettos from the plays. Here, however, the similarities end. Preissová's *The Farm Mistress* has a cast of twenty which Foerster reduced to six. Janáček, on the other hand, retained all the individual characters of Preissová's *Her Foster-daughter* and in a series of skilful vignettes brought alive even the smallest of them. No doubt Janáček considered the peripheral characters an essential ingredient of the folk element of the play, a major reason for his selecting it in the first place. He made the return of the recruits in Act 1 a major folkloristic climax. Foerster, however, avoided folk-music references even in the choruses (as in Janáček's opera, confined to the outer acts). But perhaps the most salient difference between the two works was Janáček's bold decision to set Preissová's play in its original prose, while Foerster first turned *The Farm Mistress* into rhymed verse before he began composition. It is this single difference that emphasizes that Foerster's work belongs essentially to the nineteenth century, in its harmonic language and above all in its construction. Although the transitions are skilful enough, the work falls into obvious numbers, reinforced by the regularity of the verse lines and metres. There are arias and duets and even a trio. It is not quite true to say that such elements are lacking in Janáček's *Jenůfa*. The first act in particular, written rather earlier than the later acts, has a substantial 'ensemble of perplexity' for four soloists and chorus (which Janáček carved out of a single line of Preissová's text) and several other vestiges of a number opera (Tyrrell 1987, 333–4, 341–4). But even though Janáček restructured some of the prose text into symmetrical lines (see pp. 283–7), he was still forced to forge a new relationship between voice part and orchestra, and to undertake a radical remodelling of his operatic style. This, rather than the pressure of his teaching commitments, stretched out the composition of the opera over almost a decade.

The differences in approach between *Eva* and *Jenůfa* highlight differences between two Czech-speaking composers who in many other ways had much in common. Only five years separated their births. Both had grown up in the kantor tradition that had such a profound impact on the formation of a Czech consciousness. The Foersters had converted from full-time schoolteaching to music at an earlier generation: Josef Bohuslav's father was a composer and from 1866 to 1904 taught music theory at the Prague Conservatory. Whereas it was natural that his talented son would follow this career, Janáček's musical training had to be carved out of his spare time while he qualified, like generations of Janáčeks before him, as a schoolteacher. Both Janáček and Foerster studied at the Prague Organ School, but while Foerster could undertake the full three-year course, Janáček had leave to attend only for a year, during which time he completed two years of the course. It was only when he was twenty-five, and had been teaching for several years, that he was able to supplement his musical studies with a further year away, this time at the Leipzig and Vienna conservatories. Both composers went on to become influential teachers; Janáček himself founded the Brno Organ School, and was director until 1918, when it became the Brno Conservatory.

A further parallel between the two composers was their strong literary talents. Both were responsible for their own librettos for their later operas. Both wrote with considerable flair on both musical and non-musical topics, and had distinguished careers as music critics. Janáček founded his own musical journal, *Hudební listy*, which ran for four years, with himself as chief contributor, writing articles on music theory and reviews of operas at the recently opened Brno theatre. After Foerster's nine years as musical critic of the *Národní listy* he continued to serve as critic for German-language papers when his wife's career as a singer took the couple to Hamburg and Vienna (1893–1918). Nevertheless these many similarities between the two composers were dwarfed by even greater differences, of which perhaps the most profound was that Janáček was Moravian and Foerster was Bohemian. While Foerster made a trip to Moravia to absorb 'atmosphere' in preparation for the composition of *Eva* (Štědroň 1947, 54–5), Janáček had it in his blood. This difference, however, was not immediately apparent.

## *Janáček*

Like Ostrčil, Janáček launched his operatic career with a work that fell unambiguously into the tradition of Czech mythological opera, his *Šárka*, written in 1887–8. The opera was submitted to Dvořák for his approval and considerably altered in the light of his comments. Were it not for the fact that the author of the text, still hoping that Dvořák might set it, withheld his permission for Janáček to use it and thus prevented a production at this time, the Czech public's image of Janáček as an opera composer might well have been a far more traditional one. In the event, *Šárka* lay unperformed for thirty years until resurrected after the composer's seventieth birthday, and Janáček put Czech mythological opera behind him and turned instead to Moravian folksong. 1888, the date of Janáček's first trip as an adult to his native Lašsko to collect folksongs, marks a turning point in his life.

At first sight Janáček's second opera, *The Beginning of a Romance* (composed 1891), might appear to be a one-act comic village opera in the tradition of Blodek's *In the Well* or Dvořák's *The Stubborn Lovers*. The difference from these works was Janáček's enthusiastic espousal of folksong to such a degree that much of the work originated in the recycling of folksongs and dances rather than in newly written material (see p. 247). By the time he came to write *Jenůfa*, set in the same region, and based on a work by the same author (in the case of *The Beginning of a Romance* a short story), folksong had infected Janáček's musical language at a far more profound and creatively stimulating level.

Both *The Beginning of a Romance* and *Jenůfa* were staged in Brno (in 1894 and 1904 respectively), and both with considerable popular success. But *Jenůfa*, revolutionary in so many aspects, in particular as the first Czech opera set to a prose text, had no impact on the development of Czech opera in Prague. It was not until 1916 that the opera was finally accepted at the National Theatre. However belated, the Prague performances made a huge impression. They led directly to the opera's publication by Universal Edition and productions in Vienna and Berlin, and to the work's speedy acceptance as a repertory piece throughout the German-speaking world.

It should be remembered, however, that Janáček was now sixty-two. A natural opera composer, he had had his enthusiasm and confidence sapped by the long years of neglect between the two premières of *Jenůfa*. His fourth opera, *Fate* (composed 1903–5), had been accepted for production both at the Vinohrady theatre in Prague and by Brno, but was never produced, and his fifth opera, *The Excursions of Mr Brouček*, was quietly abandoned in 1912, partly because of problems with librettists, but mostly because he saw no hope of its production. These two works, however, are crucial in an understanding of Janáček's development as an operatic composer. In the year that *Jenůfa* was produced in Brno, Janáček turned fifty and was able to retire from his school post (he continued to run the Organ School). With more spare time, he was able to travel to Prague much more frequently than before to see new works given at the opera houses there. He was drawn in particular to Puccini, and to Charpentier's *Louise*, then much in vogue in Prague. *Fate*, to his own scenario, was his response to *Louise*, with many parallels, especially in the depiction of an artistic milieu, and the naturalism of the crowd scenes. The influence of Puccini was even more far-reaching, and can be discerned even in his later works such as *Káťa Kabanová*. The result was that by the time Janáček eventually found his audience, he was a very different composer from the man who had written *Jenůfa*. The numerous rewritings of both *Fate* and *The Excursions of Mr Brouček* (originally designed as a single excursion, rewritten several times) bear witness to Janáček's struggle to absorb new techniques and to forge a new style.

The paradox was that Janáček, born in the middle of the nineteenth century, communicated to a postwar audience in a fresh and absorbing way that was eventually to find just as much favour beyond the borders of the new republic, while his younger contemporaries, Novák and Foerster, continued to write their operas in idioms that were rooted in the previous century. One has only to compare Janáček's *The Cunning Little Vixen* and Novák's *The Lantern*, produced within a year of one another, to appreciate the difference. Novák wrote his most popular opera on a well-loved national play, peopled with the traditional characters of folk mythology, and in a backward-looking musical idiom. Janáček's opera had much the same audience in mind, but by setting a seemingly non-operatic subject – a novel based on a cartoon strip giving a light-hearted account of a resourceful vixen and her relationship to a gamekeeper who rears her – created his own mythologies, and ones that could appeal to a wider audience than the water goblins beloved by Czech folk mythology (see p. 212).

And much the same is true of Janáček's next opera, *The Makropulos Affair* (1926), the last première during his lifetime (see illustration 6), in which Karel Čapek's fantasy of a 300-year-old woman flourishing in modern times allowed Janáček a contemporary setting, with telephones, lawyer's offices, hotel rooms, and deserted theatres. If one compares Novák's and Foerster's later experiments in 'modern' settings (in *The Grandfather's Legacy*, or

6  Curtain call at the Prague première of *The Makropulos Affair* in March 1928: Leoš Janáček takes a bow with the producer (Josef Munclingr, left) and conductor (Otakar Ostrčil, right). This was Janáček's last operatic première; within a few months he was dead, his final opera *From the House of the Dead* still unheard. Ostrčil's career, too, was nearing its end: in the following summer he began work on his final opera, *Johnny's Kingdom*.

Foerster's *The Invincible Ones*) Janáček's surer touch is strikingly evident. His operatic reach went unimaginably further than that of his Czech contemporaries, whose works seem amateurish in comparison.

In the last decade of his life, between the ages of sixty-four and seventy-four, Janáček enjoyed a remarkable Indian summer of creativity in which he wrote most of his best-known non-operatic works (such as the Sinfonietta, the *Glagolitic Mass*, the song cycle *The Diary of One who Disappeared* (*Zápisník zmizelého*), and the two strings quartets) and also the four last operas on which, together with *Jenůfa*, his reputation now rests. Only one of them, *Kát'a Kabanová*, has a conventionally operatic libretto (adultery on the banks of the Volga); its successors have some of the oddest librettos in operatic history. All inhabit quite different dramatic and musical worlds and yet are all firmly imprinted with Janáček's forceful and energetic musical personality. His final opera, *From the House of the Dead* (composed 1927–8 and produced posthumously in 1930), is the most remarkable. Janáček adapted the text himself from Dostoyevsky's memoirs (lightly disguised as fiction) of his two years in a Siberian prison. There is no 'story', no plot. The lack of narrative thrust in this remarkably modern-sounding reportage meant that Janáček was forced to create an opera whose pacing seems quite unlike that of any other. Long confessional monologues – little operas in themselves – provide the central focus of each of the three acts. Their narrators are not main characters in a conventional sense; their narrations over, they merge back into the anonymity of the chorus of prisoners. The work's succession of tiny scenes is cinematic in its impact and is held together only tenuously by the orchestral continuum. The range of colour is extraordinary: almost entirely male voices, against an often precarious orchestral background that concentrates on extreme registers with little in between.

Though contemporary audiences and even Janáček's pupils found it baffling at its prewar performances (in a heavily revised and reorchestrated version), the work was a logical culmination of several aspects of Janáček's operatic style. The central narrations, appropriately enough the prisoners' accounts of how they had come to be in prison, were merely longer versions of the confessional monologues that had attracted Janáček to all his operas from *Jenůfa* onwards – an important source of solo singing within a naturalistic convention of opera. Similarly the 'folksongs' of the middle act have their origins in the light, generally strophic songs that can be found in all Janáček's later works as a means of genre painting, from Dr Suda's satirical urban song in *Fate* to Hauk's 'Spanish' song in *The Makropulos Affair*. The chorus, virtually banished from the operas Foerster and Novák were writing at this time, is the culmination both of the stirring male-voice chorales in *The Excursion of Mr Brouček to the Fifteenth Century*, and of the offstage symbolic choruses that run through all of Janáček's last operas (see further, p. 250). The cinematic succession of scenes in *From the House of the Dead* is a continuation of the type of episodic structure that Janáček worked out particularly in those of his operas not based on plays (*Fate, Brouček, The Vixen*). Musically this construction is reinforced by a disarmingly simple-seeming technique based on rondos and sets of variations. The relatively loose construction allows a constant fluctuation of importance between voice and orchestra – one of the keys to Janáček's success. While there is no doubt that in the later operas the orchestra supplies musical continuity, the voice part is no mere reciting adjunct above it. From *Jenůfa* onwards Janáček had stressed the importance for him of the study of what he called 'speech melody' – the emotional world that he believed was revealed through the rhythmic and melodic fluctuations of casual speech (see pp. 292–7). His notations of this served not as raw thematic material for his works but instead as a means of sharpening his own dramatic awareness, and he regarded such training as essential preparation for an opera composer. The voice parts in the central narrations of *From the House of the Dead* constitute, with their effortless suggestion of multiple characters, a virtuoso display of what Janáček was able to achieve in this way.

The one respect in which *From the House of the Dead* differs noticeably from its predecessors is its all-male cast. While Janáček's transitional operas, *Fate* and *The Excursions of Mr Brouček*, both have male heroes, *Kát'a Kabanová*, *The Cunning Little Vixen* and *The Makropulos Affair* are all dominated by a central female portrait. In all of these the heroine dies at the end (and if she did not die in the original – the case in both *Makropulos* and the *Vixen* – then Janáček introduced the death himself). Part of the reason for this can no doubt be found in Janáček's practical instincts as a musical dramatist who, like Puccini, believed in powerful and effective act endings. But equally pertinent is Janáček's humanistic philosophy which shines through and unites this odd bunch of operas. In them Janáček dealt with death and other serious events of life, but within a framework that was able to comprehend and come to terms with them.

# 4. Librettists

Although a continuous tradition of Czech-language opera began only with Smetana, Czech composers could look back to centuries of music-making, and those composers who made their way in opera in the second half of the nineteenth century were all professionals, well-trained in Prague's long-established teaching institutions. Their librettists, in comparison, appear much inferior – either unpaid amateurs, or overworked literary hacks. It seems reasonable to conclude that in Czech opera the composers would be the driving force, determining the subject matter, the dramatic structure and operatic conventions of their operas. And in this they would differ from the composers of French grand opera or Italian *opera seria*, where most of these crucial decisions had already been taken by the librettist or the impresario. Smetana above all, with impressive artistic and patriotic credentials as the leading Czech opera composer of the nineteenth century, is generally held responsible for the dramaturgical planning of his operas, a view that seems all the more persuasive in the light of his somewhat mixed bag of literary collaborators. Where the evidence is missing, it has not seemed unreasonable to credit Smetana with most of the decision making, and blame any shortcomings on the librettists. Because documentation is indeed limited, except for Smetana's dealings with his last librettist, the literature on this topic from Nejedlý onwards has always taken this view, buttressed by a comforting store of expressions such as 'Smetana surely must have. . .', 'it is most probable that Smetana. . .'. Jaroslav Jiránek, the author of the most detailed examination of Smetana's operas (1984), offers as one justification for such an approach the comment that only in Smetana's hands did librettos by his librettists prosper (Jiránek 1981, 81). True, it needed Smetana's genius to bring the librettos alive, but this does not necessarily rule out a substantial share in the dramaturgical planning by some or all of his librettists. At the start of his stimulating discussion of the influence of contemporary theatrical conventions on Smetana's operas, Bořivoj Srba dismisses any discussion of the librettists' part in this by saying how impractical this would be and points to the one opera where Smetana is known to have made substantial changes (Srba 1985, 72f).

However, Smetana's relationship with his last librettist, Eliška Krásno-horská, is well documented, and it suggests a different pattern. Is it possible that this pattern could also apply to Smetana's earlier operas? Several things point to this. With the exception of the unfinished *Viola*, there is no evidence that Smetana personally chose the subject matter of any of his operas. He seems to have accepted the verse structures of the librettos with equanimity, whether it was Krásnohorská's predominant iambs, or Züngel's predominant trochees. The operatic conventions of Smetana's operas vary from work to work in accordance with who wrote the librettos. Perhaps most revealing of all is a chance remark of Smetana's in a letter to the conductor Adolf Čech. He mentions a couple of librettos that he is considering, but fears that they would require music 'according to the old, standard forms' (Teige 1896, 146). There is no question of his overriding this, or sending the libretto back for changes. Smetana was evidently no Verdi insisting on the addition or elimination of a set number, or on a different metrical scheme.

Smetana composed to librettos by four writers: Karel Sabina for his first two operas, *The Brandenburgers in Bohemia* and *The Bartered Bride*; Josef Wenzig for *Dalibor* and *Libuše*; Emanuel Züngel for *The Two Widows*, and Eliška Krásnohorská for his final operas, *The Kiss*, *The Secret*, *The Devil's Wall* and *Viola*. Two of these writers, Sabina and Züngel, were the nearest that could be found at the time in Bohemia to professional librettists. Emanuel Züngel (1840–94) made a living for himself through journalism and translations. He had a fine talent for versification and from 1864 to the early 1880s was constantly in demand at the Provisional Theatre as a translator of plays and operas. He translated quickly, but nevertheless carefully; his words fitted the music well and were found by singers to be memorable and singable (Žižka 1939, 117–18). Očadlík estimated (Züngel 1962, 14, 27) that by the time of his collaboration with Smetana he had some fifty theatre works to his credit. Altogether he seems to have translated or adapted some seventy-five plays into Czech and about sixty operas and operettas. Züngel also wrote half a dozen original plays himself and a couple of opera librettos, though the best-known, *The Two Widows* and *The Way through the Window* (for Kovařovic), were both adaptations of French sources.

Karel Sabina (1813–77) was another professional writer who in the midst of his vast literary and journalistic activities also wrote opera librettos. Unlike Züngel, he made no theatre translations and came to the field with little experience: his earliest librettos (for Smetana and Šebor) antedate his four plays. However there seemed to be no other Czech writer at the time prepared to take on such work and deliver it so quickly, and his name soon got around. Between the 1860s and the early 1870s every Czech opera composer of note set Sabina librettos. Apart from Smetana's two operas, Sabina wrote the librettos for Šebor's *The Templars in Moravia* (1865), Blodek's *In the Well* (1867) and his unfinished *Zítek*, Rozkošný's *Mikuláš* (1870), Bendl's *The Elderly Suitor* (composed 1871-4) and Fibich's

*Bukovín* (composed 1870–1). Sabina never established a particular artistic rapport with a single composer but instead wrote for all comers; he was never asked more than twice. There was no evidence that he considered his librettos anything more than a financial transaction and the roughness of his verse bears witness to his haste. Erben was deadly accurate when in his report for the Harrach competition he described Sabina's libretto to *The Brandenburgers in Bohemia* as 'a hurriedly cobbled-up job' ('slátanina na kvap') (Daněk 1983, 154).

In the cases of these two professional writers Smetana paid a lump sum for the copyright of the librettos, which then became his property. Züngel received 60 zl. for *The Two Widows* (Züngel 1962, 22); Sabina, according to Heller (1917, 33) earned only 10 zl. for *The Bartered Bride*. Even if this is an exaggeration, there is little doubt that Sabina was poorly paid for his work and one can reasonably argue that he would consequently have had no further interest in the libretto, especially in view of his other work and his many worries at the time. Once the libretto was out of his hands any changes would automatically have been undertaken by the composer (Jiránek 1981, 81). This is of course sheer speculation. Sabina's original libretto for *The Brandenburgers in Bohemia* has not survived. Changes were certainly made, as can be charted by comparing Smetana's pencil sketch (originally in two acts with a different order of scenes) with the final score, but we do not know for certain who was responsible for such changes. In Sabina's second Smetana libretto, *The Bartered Bride*, where the original libretto has survived and shows some differences from Smetana's pencil sketch of the vocal score, Nejedlý argued that 'the forms are almost entirely the work of Smetana. . . For Smetana could not possibly have needed the librettist to prescribe for him in the libretto, as was the custom, where there was to be an aria, a duet, an ensemble etc. It was up to Smetana to decide what form was required at what point by the course of the music' (Sabina 1930, 23–4). But the examples that Nejedlý cites – the displacement by one line of the beginning of Jeník's Act 2 aria, the replacement of a rhyming three-syllable word ('nevěsta') by a non-rhyming two-syllable word ('hanba') at the end of Act 2, the addition of one line to Jeník and Mařenka's Act 1 love duet – hardly change the 'forms'. The most crucial changes to the work came about purely through outside pressure. The additional numbers, in particular the three dances that can be found in the two 1869 revisions of the work, were written as a response to a possible Paris production (Bartoš 1955, 17–20), and the fourth and final version of the score, with the transformation of the original spoken dialogue into sung recitative, was made in 1870 for the production in St Petersburg, where, as Smetana was told, spoken dialogue might create difficulties (Bartoš 1955, 20–1).

The view that Smetana was responsible for the choice of subject matter is no better founded. Nejedlý argues in his introduction to the critical edition of the libretto of *The Brandenburgers in Bohemia* (Sabina 1918, viii) that the choice of subject was 'surely' unanimous on the part of both librettist and composer. All we know, however, is that Smetana was found a librettist and a libretto through his friend Ludevít Procházka, as he mentions in his diary, and that Karel Sabina delivered the requested libretto within a few weeks (Sabina 1918, vi). One could indeed argue that Sabina, as a literary man, would be more likely than Smetana to be acquainted with the two main literary sources for the libretto and with the period of Czech history in which it is set. While there is no more information about the origins of *The Bartered Bride*, there is a good case for assuming that the idea for the plot of the opera came from Sabina rather than Smetana since some of the characters were drawn from a novel he had completed shortly before (Sabina 1930, 12-14), and which Sabina continued to use as a source for the comic librettos he wrote for Bendl, Rozkošný and Blodek. Smetana's diary entry for 5 July 1863 'I have bought from Sabina a text for a comic opera, as yet unnamed' (Bartoš 1939, 65) sounds as though he bought the libretto ready made. His later remark in a speech 'I ran to Sabina for a libretto' (Bartoš 1939, 210) rather implies that he ran there with nothing particular in mind about its content.

With *The Two Widows* we similarly lack any information about Smetana's negotiations with Züngel (Züngel 1962, 15) but even if it was Smetana's idea, he clearly did not need to look very far since it was Züngel's translation from the French of Mallefille's play *Les deux veuves* that had played at the Provisional Theatre in 1868. The two men already had contacts over Züngel's translations of opera librettos at the Provisional Theatre and in 1869 Smetana paid Züngel for making a German translation of *The Bartered Bride* (Bartoš 1955, 17). In 1877, three years after the première of *The Two Widows*, it was decided that the opera should be revised. Again we do not know who instigated this, though the major change – the replacement of the spoken dialogue by continuously composed passages – was suggested by several of the first reviews. Züngel, however, was still sufficiently involved with the project to send Smetana twenty-eight pages of additional text, and for this, Očadlík speculates, he would have received no more than 20 zl., perhaps no payment at all, now that Smetana's financial straits were even more dire than his own (Züngel 1962, 25).

If it was Züngel and Sabina who were mostly responsible for the subject matter and for the conventions of these three operas, on what models would they have drawn? Züngel, having translated some twenty-five operas and operettas before *The Two Widows*, could call on an extensive knowledge, especially of the operetta repertory. His libretto went a long way towards suggesting the type of opera that Smetana was to write to this text, adding words such as 'recit', 'arioso', 'melodrama', and even making indications for melodic reminiscence and for folksong models for the choral scenes (Züngel

1962, 18). Sabina's knowledge of opera, however, was much more limited. His libretto for *The Brandenburgers in Bohemia* was written soon after the opening of the Provisional Theatre and he was probably too poor and too busy to attend much opera. Ottlová and Pospíšil argue that the most likely model for the first Czech historical operas of this period, both with Sabina librettos – Smetana's *The Brandenburgers in Bohemia* and Šebor's *The Templars in Moravia* – would have been grand opera. However they also argue that the allegedly 'progressive' features in Smetana's first opera – the lack of closed numbers and the large amount of quasi-Wagnerian arioso – were less the result of Sabina's attempt ('under Smetana's influence') to provide an ultra-modern dramaturgical framework, than the reflection of Sabina's incompetence in arranging for suitable aria or duet situations, and his inability to write metrically identical lines as a basis for ensembles (Ottlová 1981, 169–72).

The case for Smetana's involvement in libretto-making with his 'professional' librettists is at best unproven. With the two 'amateur' librettists, both of whom gave their services free, there is even more reason to assume that the responsibility for the subject matter, the type of opera and its conventions, and for the verse schemes, stemmed from the librettist, not the composer.

The librettos to Smetana's next two operas were both written by Josef Wenzig (1807–76). A teacher of German and geography, and later, after 1848, the instigator and director of the first Czech *Realschule* (technical grammar school), Wenzig played an important part in the establishment of Czech-language schooling. He also had ambitions as a dramatist. Several of his plays were performed both in German at the Estates Theatre and in Czech at the Provisional Theatre. In 1872 he published a volume of six of them ranging from a one-act farce to five-act histories (Wenzig 1944, 57). Though sympathizing with the Czechs and their history (six of his plays were based on Czech historical subjects – Wenzig 1944, 9–10), Wenzig was more fluent in German, and wrote his plays and his opera librettos in that language. Smetana made his acquaintance at the Umělecká Beseda (an important Czech cultural society founded in 1863, with Wenzig as chairman) and learnt that he had written a couple of opera librettos. His interest, however, diminished somewhat when he discovered that *Dalibor* (1865) and *Libušas Urtheilsspruch und Vermählung* (1866) were both in German. Wenzig therefore asked a former pupil of his, the young Ervín Špindler (1843–1919), to make Czech translations.

It is from Špindler that we have some knowledge of how Smetana set to work. From time to time he asked for certain changes to the text, but, as Špindler relates, with the chief aim that high notes should be set to open vowels; in general only a simple change of word order was involved (Špindler 1909, 251). In fact, most of the important changes that were made to the librettos took place either before or after Špindler's involvement. As is clear from Wenzig's German libretto (Wenzig 1944, 138-40), Act 2 of *Dalibor* was to have ended with a scene between the young couple, Jitka and Vítek. This scene was not translated into Czech; its omission resulted in making the previous love duet for Milada and Dalibor the climactic conclusion to the act. There were further omissions and changes to the end of this act and the next both before and after the première (Wenzig 1944, 28-34). In *Libuše* Act 2 the scene at the tomb between Chrudoš and Krasava was an afterthought, the only section of the libretto written in Czech by Wenzig himself (Wenzig 1951, 108-12).

Commentators from Šilhan (1909) to Jiránek (1984) agree that Smetana was behind these changes, which were much more substantial than anything he may have done in the Sabina librettos,[1] and with a clearly beneficial effect on the dramatic pacing of the two operas. But in other respects Smetana was more passive. The two librettos were not commissioned by him but existed before he had heard of them (see Fischer 1915, 206-7). Thus the patriotic conception in them of figures such as Dalibor and Libuše, however quintessentially Smetana-like it may seem, is something that goes back to Wenzig's original German librettos. One of Špindler's achievements in his translation was to provide a Czech imitation of the metrical and rhyme schemes of the original German. The implications of this, and of Smetana's acceptance of these schemes, is discussed in Chapter 8. All that need be noted here is that much of the difference in character between the musical language of Smetana's next opera *The Two Widows*, with its predominantly trochaic metre (leading to the frequency of polka-like musical settings), and that of the two preceding Wenzig operas, with their longer, predominantly iambic lines (leading to a style with more upbeats and strong endings), is a direct result of metrical differences in the librettos.

Furthermore, although Wenzig designated *Dalibor* an opera libretto, and accordingly included a few chorus items and numbers whose identical or similar stanzas for two different characters were clearly intended as duets, he made no provision for larger solo ensembles or for choral ensembles and Smetana, accordingly, did not write any. Much the same can be said of Wenzig's libretto for *Libuše* though, perhaps in view of the ceremonial nature of the work, Smetana was more active in combining solo lines to form end-of-scene ensembles. On the other hand, Smetana's next two librettists, Züngel and Krásnohorská, were much more ensemble-conscious and provided more evident scope for trios, quartets and choral ensembles. Smetana happily fell in with that too.

Alžběta Pechová (1847-1926; see illustration 7), better known under her *nom de plume* Eliška Krásnohorská, was born into a cultured Prague family (one brother was a painter, another a musician). Though musically gifted

7  Eliška Krásnohorská, photograph by H. Fiedler. A poet and writer, Krásnohorská was one of the chief librettists of Czech opera, supplying librettos for
Bendl, Fibich and for Smetana's last four operas. Her enthusiasm for ensembles was largely responsible for their proliferation in these works and her
forthright article on the setting of Czech influenced Smetana's own practice
from the 1870s onwards.

herself, she devoted her life to her writing, chiefly poetry and books for
children, and translations of Pushkin, Byron and Mickiewicz. She was
active in the women's movement, edited a women's periodical *Ženské listy*,
and in 1890 helped found Minerva, the first Czech Gymnasium for girls.
Today she is mostly remembered as the librettist of Smetana's last decade.
It was through her brother's friendship with the young Karel Bendl that she
found herself, at the age of twenty, writing the libretto for his five-act opera
*Lejla* (Krásnohorská 1897, 974). Its successful première in 1868 led her to
write at least twelve more librettos, of which eight (including *Lejla*) were set
and performed.

Four of these were for Bendl, but Smetana, who had conducted the
première of *Lejla*, himself soon approached the young librettist. From a
letter Krásnohorská wrote to her mentor Karolina Světlá on 5 July 1869 it is
clear that negotiations had already taken place (Suchá 1974, 108). She
offered Smetana *Lumír*, based on Czech mythic history and thus from the

same world as *Libuše*, the opera on which he was currently working. Their proposed collaboration did not however inhibit her, during this period, from publishing an article on Czech declamation in which she pointed out examples of poor word-setting in Smetana's *Bartered Bride* (Krásnohorská 1871). Smetana duly took her criticism to heart. He made a careful revision of the word-setting in *Libuše* (demonstrated in Jiránek 1976, 62–4) and thereafter took considerable pains over it in his later operas. This incident was characteristic of the future relationship. While Krásnohorská had great respect and sympathy for Smetana (and it was to her that he poured out many of the sorrows of his final years), this never prevented her from standing up for what she regarded as her rights. When her libretto to Bendl's next opera, *Břetislav*, was attacked, she wrote a spirited reply in which she attributed much of the failure of the work to the cuts which Bendl had made. Why should a composer be allowed to cut the text when he would certainly not allow a librettist to cut his music (Krásnohorská 1870, 299)?

Krásnohorská nevertheless withdrew *Lumír*, partly as a response to the criticisms of *Břetislav* and partly because, as she wrote in her letter to Smetana of 26 April 1871, the work would demand more elaborate sets than would be possible on the restricted stage of the Provisional Theatre.[2] Instead, she offered to undertake Smetana's earlier request of an opera based on Shakespeare's *Twelfth Night*, initially entitled *Sebastian and Viola*. Even at this early stage she seems to have had very clear ideas about the work:

I have also taken the liberty of indicating what voice types are blended in my imagination with the characters concerned, and I beg you to let me know if you want any other distribution of voices, as this is important to me for the composition of ensembles. Further, I have drawn up a table of numbers [*přehled formálný*] and similarly ask if you could kindly add your remarks and your wishes to it. If, for instance, you want somewhere an aria or a song etc inserted or if any type of formal requirement seems apt to you.

From her next extant letter (11 May 1871) it is clear that Smetana accepted her conditions and suggestions:

If every composer would answer my questions as willingly, and as concretely, without prejudging the issue, as you, esteemed Sir, I would count myself happy and it would be sheer pleasure to write librettos; composers however usually deal extremely arbitrarily with the poet and are usually offended by every objection.

By her next letter (20 June 1871), Krásnohorská had worked up her scenario for *Viola* into a full libretto, but since Smetana was still working on *Libuše*, he did not start the composition of *Viola* immediately. It seems odd, however, that with the libretto in hand *Viola* was not his next opera. Instead it was *The Two Widows* that Smetana composed next (1873–4), and had hardly got down to sketching *Viola*, in 1874, when deafness overtook him. For the moment he avoided opera and concentrated instead on instrumental works, for instance 'From Bohemian Fields and Groves'. By 1875, when Smetana felt able to resume the composition of opera, he now had a fresh libretto to work on, Krásnohorská's *The Kiss*, and *Viola* was once more set aside. Krásnohorská herself had second thoughts about her earlier libretto and asked for it back for changes. But even when he had finished *The Kiss* Smetana found himself setting Krásnohorská's latest libretto, *The Secret*. The combination of Krásnohorská's reluctance to work on *Viola* (her only libretto whose subject she did not choose herself) and her eagerness for Smetana to set the Czech subjects with which she supplied him, meant that it was not until Smetana had written three operas to her librettos, *The Kiss* (1876), *The Secret* (1878) and *The Devil's Wall* (1882), that he returned to *Viola*, and by then his illness had advanced so far that he was capable of little more than orchestrating some of the fragment he had written almost a decade earlier.

Considerable criticism was levelled at Krásnohorská's librettos by her contemporaries, usually by writers jealous of her collaboration with Smetana. The more polite, like Hostinský, praised the quality of the verse, but found them 'undramatic' (Hostinský 1901, 336), a criticism which persists to this day. Whatever their shortcomings, her librettos had two undeniable advantages for Smetana. The first was that he found 'music' in them that he did not find elsewhere.

So that I can compose better, they want to tear me away from what I have grown close to. And I have grown together with your lines and with that music which I always feel in them and which I no longer hear in any other lines.

(Očadlík 1940, 119–20, quoting Krásnohorská's memoirs)

The second attraction for Smetana was that Krásnohorská's librettos all contained situations and relationships which, whatever their lack of 'drama', touched a deep vein in him and brought to the surface some of his most personal utterances. In one of his letters to Krásnohorská (16 February 1880) Smetana described Vok's aria in Act 1 of *The Devil's Wall*, 'Jen jediná mě ženy krásná tvář tak dojala' ('Only one woman's pretty face has so moved me'), and how it always moved him to tears, 'nearly fitting [his] own unhappy state'. The greater part of Smetana's collaboration with Krásnohorská took place after he became deaf. It was due to her tact, her kindness and the infinite trouble that she took that Smetana was encouraged to struggle against his deafness, and his worsening health.

Krásnohorská's correspondence with Smetana and her autographs of three librettos written for him (the original libretto to *The Secret* has disappeared), together with her extensive memoirs, constitute the most complete material charting the relationship between Smetana and any of his librettists. All his previous contacts with librettists were generally made by word of mouth. But Smetana's deafness and his withdrawal from Prague meant that most of his transactions with Krásnohorská were written down. She destroyed some of his more bitter letters (though passages found their way into her memoirs – see Očadlík 1940, 15–16), but Smetana kept all hers and they provide a fascinating picture of the two at work.

What is abundantly clear from this material is how many of the compositional decisions implicit in the librettos stem from Krásnohorská, not from Smetana. For a start, she chose all the subjects (apart from *Viola*). It was for instance her idea to make an opera out of the short story *The Kiss* by her mentor, Karolina Světlá. Smetana read the book, and concluded that it 'wasn't musical enough'. To change his mind Krásnohorská drafted some dialogue between Lukáš and Tomeš. Smetana was at once convinced of the viability of the subject and encouraged Krásnohorská to carry on writing. For this incident we have only Krásnohorská's testimony from her memoirs (Očadlík 1940, 44), but the subjects of both the next operas, *The Secret* and *The Devil's Wall*, emerge as her suggestions during the course of the correspondence. Naturally, Smetana could have turned these down, as he did one or two other suggestions from her (for example, *The Child of Tábor*, later set by Bendl – see Očadlík 1940, 119), but the fact remains that it was Krásnohorská who was the active partner who suggested and shaped these plots. All Smetana did was to use an occasional veto. The only positive suggestion he made, apart from insisting that *The Devil's Wall* should be 'comic', was that she should finish her much-delayed revisions of *Viola*, which he was anxious to get back to since he liked the subject and had some of the first act drafted. But Krásnohorská instead urged 'Czech' material. *Viola*, she wrote, had gone cold on her, and she would much rather get on with these other projects. In the wake of such firmness Smetana capitulated: she must send him whatever she wants (Očadlík 1940, 98–102).

It is clear, too, that the dramatic structure of the operas, and their employment of operatic conventions, were also Krásnohorská's responsibility and that Smetana made few changes in these respects once he had received the completed librettos. In her librettos Krásnohorská indicated ensembles not by words such as 'duet', 'trio' etc (though they were occasionally pencilled into the libretto of *The Kiss*), but by writing the same words for two or more characters, or by bracketing together two or more stanzas. Arias were shown by the indentation of the stanzas concerned and by different rhyme or metrical schemes.[3] Although the libretto to *The Secret* has disappeared, we know from Smetana's letter of 20 October 1877 that he set the first act in its entirety, omitting only four lines, which Krásnohorská had marked as a possible cut. When he may have suggested cuts in the long Act 2, he received a prompt letter from her (23 October 1877), advising against this. What requests he did make for changes in the conventions were received with little enthusiasm. It seems that Smetana would have liked more ensembles in *The Kiss*. In response (her letter of 11 December 1875)

Krásnohorská went through possible places, and concluded that she had as many ensembles as was possible. Conversely, during the composition of *The Secret*, Smetana's concentration began to falter and he mentioned that he was finding the long ensembles in Act 2 particularly tiring (2 October and 20 October 1877). Krásnohorská expressed her sympathy, but would not take the hint:

> Those wretched ensembles! I think I know what trouble they must be giving you!. . .But it can't be helped; you will just have to put up with the bother of the odd ensemble if you are not to deprive opera of one of its most individual means of musical effect.
>
> (23 October 1877)

It was only towards the end of their relationship, soured through Smetana's handling of *The Devil's Wall*, that Krásnohorská suggested that the ensembles in *Viola* need not have everyone singing (23 February 1882).

As for Smetana's own requests, these seem to have arisen not out of his own musico-dramatic judgements, but mostly from special requests from favoured singers for insertion arias. The baritone Josef Lev was allowed an extra section in Kalina's aria at the beginning of Act 2 of *The Secret* (Očadlík 1940, 119, 122). In the same opera Smetana felt that the part of Bonifác, with no independent aria, would not be sufficiently attractive to a singer of the first rank like Karel Čech; he suggested making Skřivánek's Act 3 song into a duet to include Bonifác. This was realized – a rare instance of Smetana's making an ensemble piece out of a solo – but Krásnohorská also supplied words for a new aria for him in Act 2. Though other changes were made to the libretto of *The Secret* once Smetana began work on composition, it is clear from the correspondence that these derived from Krásnohorská's own second thoughts rather than from Smetana's (Očadlík 1940, 97, 104, 109). According to Očadlík's summary (Krásnohorská 1942, 22-3), Smetana's changes to the libretto of *The Kiss* consisted of the new genre description of the opera (see pp. 302-3 n.1), the insertion of a scene change and related additions such as the insertion of Barče's 'lark song' (for Laušmannová), the transference of a short scene, and the addition here and there of about twenty-four new lines.

The only opera that Smetana substantially modified was *The Devil's Wall*. He asked for a broadly comic opera, which Krásnohorská did her best to supply, much against her talent and inclination. She was understandably put out when he cut the work drastically (by as much as a third – Očadlík 1940, 169), omitting many of the comic aspects. By the time Smetana got to Act 3 he was not up to the ensemble demands of the libretto and had to make simplifications (Očadlík 1940, 175). Smetana's distortions of her original conception of the opera were the reason for the cooling of relations, after a collaboration which had flourished happily and profitably for over a decade. Krásnohorská did not of course know the extent of Smetana's illness and the fact that his changes were made not because he preferred his own musico-dramatic designs and conventions, but because he was physically no longer capable of carrying out hers.

It may have been that Smetana's lack of active participation in many aspects of the librettos of his operas was due to temperament – to the fact that he was essentially a musicianly opera composer, content to leave most aspects of the libretto to his librettists, rather than a composer like Wagner, or even Verdi, who needed to engage with the words at the earliest possible stage. It may be of interest to consider the interaction between librettist and a more literary-minded Czech opera composer, namely Zdeněk Fibich.

Fibich's knowledge of literature is well documented. In their memoirs of him, both his pupils Zdeněk Nejedlý and Anežka Schulzová (1902, 22) stressed his wide-ranging interests in European literature (particularly German and English) and his discriminating taste. Nejedlý (1911, 7) mentions that Fibich wrote several novels in his youth; three of his youthful operas have librettos which he wrote or adapted himself. His conversation was said to show great verbal dexterity, for instance in his impromptu poems (Schulzová 1902, 17–18) and his love for punning and verbal play. Most of the instances of this that Boleška cites in his memoir (1903, 315) need a knowledge of Czech to make their point, but an 'Italian' one is fairly typical: 'Se non è Verdi, è ben Trovatore'.

In this context it is perhaps unfair to consider *Bukovín*, Fibich's first opera to be performed at the Provisional Theatre. The composer was only sixteen when he approached Sabina for a libretto, hardly at an age to object if the now well-established librettist did not give him what he wanted, or treated the commission even more cavalierly than usual. Hostinský reports that Sabina later confessed to him that he had not taken the 'Wunderkind''s request at all seriously. Several years after Fibich had completed the opera, Hostinský tried to improve the text for him, but he could do little more then than tidy up a few of its linguistic crudities (Hostinský 1909, 8–9). But by the time he began composing his next opera, *Blaník*, Fibich was twenty-seven, with an established reputation. For the libretto he turned to Krásnohorská. Like Sabina before her, she chose the subject, and before she agreed to work, she made sure of Fibich's acceptance of her views on ensemble. Fibich's reputation as an admirer of Wagner may have worried her, but she was merely repeating an approach that she adopted with Smetana when she sent him her scenario of *Viola*.

I am decidedly against taking dramatic purity in opera to the extreme of denying sung ensemble; to the contrary, I consider this a most powerful means of dramatic effect and an overwhelming advantage which opera will always have over drama.

I don't mean to broadcast my own views, I'm asking only that you should kindly let me know your own view on this matter. On it depends the whole form of the opera and – in all honesty! – I *would not know* how to write a musical drama if I could not, in the scenes where conflicts of passion come to a head, think of employing the stirring expression of the polyphony of human voices.

(Krásnohorská to Fibich 12 September 1873, reprinted in Rektorys 1951, ii, 692)

Krásnohorská got her way and *Blaník*, like Smetana's *The Secret*, contains many solo and choral ensembles. Fibich's next opera, *The Bride of Messina*, has even more choral ensemble but little solo ensemble. His friend and biographer Otakar Hostinský explained this with the bland statement that Fibich wanted to write 'a musical tragedy, true, pure, stylistic *without the usual concessions to operatic tradition*' (Hostinský 1909, 80–1; my emphases). Hostinský, however, was also Fibich's librettist in this work and his role needs investigating in more detail.

Otakar Hostinský (1847–1910; see illustration 8) is one of the most remarkable and influential cultural figures of this period. By the time of *The*

8  Otakar Hostinský, sketched in benevolent pose towards the end of his life by Max Švabinský. Historian, aesthetician and writer, Hostinský was one of Smetana's first champions, and the friend and biographer of Fibich.

*Bride of Messina* he had established himself in Prague both as a university professor and as a well-known cultural journalist and polemicist. His range of interests was enormous. His training was in aesthetics, and much of his output reflects this. But he also left behind him important writings in the fields of history, literary theory, theatre studies and art history. In musicology alone he wrote seminal articles on word-setting in Czech music, on Czech folk music, and on nationalism and Wagnerianism – all topics concerned with the problem of nationality in music and ones relevant to the present study. He was a doughty defender of Smetana and was the author of some of the earliest biographies of Smetana and Fibich, based on his own reminiscences of the composers. Smetana was a generation older than him, but Fibich was three years younger than Hostinský and he enjoyed a close personal friendship with him for many years.

Though most of his talents lay in more scholarly pursuits, Hostinský had creative ambitions. He drew well enough to design the title page of the first edition of *Dalibor* (Jůzl 1980, 161) and the maquette for the cave for the 1894 revival of *Blaník* (Hostinský 1909, 68–9; Hepner 1955, 101). In his youth he composed songs and an orchestral overture and even began to write an opera on Mickiewicz's *Konrad Wallenrod*, a subject he later offered to both Smetana and Fibich as a libretto (Nejedlý 1910, 339). In 1881, a few months before the première of *Blaník*, Fibich turned to Hostinský for a libretto. Hostinský offered to adapt Schiller's *Die Braut von Messina*, a suggestion that coincided with Fibich's literary tastes, but also meant, as Hostinský frankly relates (1909, 79–83) that his task would 'be little more than a translation of Schiller's tragedy, naturally fairly free and considerably shortened'. Schiller's play employed a quasi-Greek chorus. This, with solo parts superimposed, became the basis for the opera's choral ensemble, built from the chorus up, so to speak. But Hostinský made no provision for solo ensemble any more than Fibich combined individual lines to create it, so much of the opera was conducted in declamatory dialogue.

Hostinský's Czech libretto, unlike Schiller's play, came mostly unrhymed. In his memoir of Fibich Hostinský gave the reason:

I had not mastered the technique of verse to such an extent that I could happily subscribe to the usual method of our librettists and continually use rhyme. Indeed I was convinced that for anyone who is not a virtuoso with words rhyme must be the stumbling block and subsequent experience has only confirmed this opinion. How many empty, futile lines have been written because of the tyrannical pressure of the inevitable rhyme and how many serious errors in prosody have crept into Czech translations of foreign operas for the same reason! It was therefore agreed between us that the dramatic dialogue would remain generally unrhymed, while rhyme would be confined mainly to the more lyrical parts. (Hostinský 1909, 80)

Even when Hostinský wrote a libretto for a very different type of opera, Rozkošný's *Cinderella*, he was similarly sparing in his use of rhymes.

Hostinský's adaptation of an existing play as an opera libretto was one of the first of its time in Czech, and it set the pattern for Fibich's next stage works. If it seems curious that no more use had been made of this method then it must be borne in mind that there was considerable pressure, both internal and external, on Czech opera composers to set domestic material (see pp. 122–3). The use of foreign classics was frowned on and Hostinský felt it necessary to justify it in his preface to the printed libretto of *The Bride of Messina* (1884, vii–viii). On the other hand the level of Czech indigenous drama had slumped noticeably after 1848, a decline which the rise of opera in the 1860s had only served to accentuate, and Czech librettists like Krásnohorská understandably preferred to be regarded as 'poets' in their own right rather than mere adapters.[4] This situation changed only towards the end of the nineteenth century, by which time a new and distinguished generation of Czech writers had emerged. This included Julius Zeyer (1841–1901), Svatopluk Čech (1846–1908), Ladislav Stroupežnický (1850–92), Alois Jirásek (1851–1930), Jaroslav Vrchlický (1853–1912) and Gabriela Preissová (1862–1945), all authors of plays, novels or poems which from the 1890s onwards formed the basis for operas.

Julius Zeyer's home background – a father of French Alsatian descent, a German Jewish mother – and extensive foreign travels led to an openness to contemporary foreign literature and to his association with the 'Lumír' school of Czech writers grouped round the periodical *Lumír* (founded in 1873 and known for its outward-looking assimilation of foreign trends). The Zeyer texts which provided librettos for two of Ostrčil's operas, his play *The Legend of Erin* (1886) and his tale *Kunála's Eyes* (which appeared in *Lumír* in 1892), are typical in their exploration of foreign legendary worlds (Ireland and India) and also in the melancholic, deeply pessimistic passivity that pervades them. The Czech material that attracted Zeyer was of a similar nature: mythical and generally tragic, as for example his five-part poetic cycle *Vyšehrad*, an elegiac recounting of the early Czech heroic myths. Many of the blank-verse lines of the fourth part, 'Ctirad', went straight into *Šárka*, the libretto that he wrote in about 1879, possibly at Dvořák's request (Mazlová 1968, 71–2). Dvořák never got further than a few sketches (he used them in *The Devil and Kate* – see Šourek 1916, ii, 12) and in the end the libretto was set, soon after its publication in 1887, by a composer even less temperamentally attuned to Zeyer's world – Leoš Janáček.

The opening of the National Theatre in 1881 encouraged Jaroslav Vrchlický, another 'Lumírovec' and one of the most prolific and important Czech poets and translators of his time, to begin writing plays. His antique trilogy *Hippodamia* (originally a five-act tragedy written 1883–5, and then expanded into three plays 1887–90; Hudec 1971, 96) was set by Fibich as a cycle of scenic melodramas. Since Vrchlický wrote the second part of the trilogy and revised the third after Fibich had set the first as a melodrama (in 1888–9), both Hostinský (1909, 146) and Nejedlý (1911, 63–4) have speculated that Vrchlický's approach to the rest of the cycle was inevitably affected by this knowledge. Little is known about the extent of any collaboration apart from a charming though probably unreliable anecdote about Vrchlický turning out Tantalus' opening monologue in the second part of the cycle on demand on the bank of the Vltava (Hudec 1971, 109, fn. 19). However it may be significant that when Fibich returned to opera writing in 1893, it was Vrchlický, rather than his old friend Hostinský, that he asked to adapt Shakespeare's *The Tempest* for him as an opera libretto. Vrchlický, it is reported, found Fibich a model collaborator, who did not allow himself the slightest departure from the poet's text, or ask for changes, unlike Dvořák, whose constant demands for short lines with monosyllabic endings caused Vrchlický no end of trouble in *Armida* (Kundera 1933, 288-9).

*Armida* was Vrchlický's dramatization of Tasso's *Gerusalemme liberata* (which he had published in his own Czech translation in 1887), and had been commissioned as an opera libretto by Kovařovic in 1888 at the cost of 100 zl. (Šourek 1943, 38). When nine years later Kovařovic had written no more than one act and seemed unable to write more, Vrchlický retrieved his text (paying back the 100 zl.) and *Armida*, after being considered by Bendl and Fibich, ended up with Dvořák, who had previously collaborated with Vrchlický over his oratorio *St Ludmilla*. Vrchlický seems to have been better suited to writing oratorio texts than opera librettos. Bendl's *Švanda the Bagpiper* (1880), Fibich's *Spring Romance* (*Jarní romance*) (1881), Dvořák's *St Ludmilla* (1886) and Janáček's cantata *Amarus* (1898), all to Vrchlický's texts, are some of the most successful and popular Czech works of their type and exemplify the poet's lyrical and evocative talents at their best. His opera librettos, by comparison, show signs of haste and, despite his idolization of Wagner, little interest in the genre. They tend towards lyricism at the expense of drama, as exemplified by his version of *The Merchant of Venice* in which the anti-semitism was toned down and the trial scene omitted (it was reluctantly added after the first run of performances), to make way for the romantic comedy suggested by its retitling to *Jessica*. Like *Armida*, Vrchlický's *Jessica* ended up, many years later, being set by a different composer (Foerster) from the one for whom it had been intended (Bendl). Vrchlický's popular comedy *A Night at Karlštejn* (*Noc na Karlštejně*) (1884) became the basis for Novák's opera *Karlštejn* (1916), while his poetic epic *Satanella* (1874) provided the inspiration for Rozkošný's penultimate opera (1898).

Hostinský, who as late as 1892 was contemplating the possibility of writing further opera librettos, was somewhat taken aback by Fibich's commission from Vrchlický for *The Tempest* (Hudec 1971, 124). But then he was not to know of the erotic identification Fibich and his young pupil Anežka Schulzová made with the Ferdinand and Miranda of Shakespeare's play, especially since Vrchlický had transformed the work, in Nejedlý's words (1935, i, 427), into 'a tale after Shakespeare, but more than a tale: an intimate song of love, full of passion, fire and tenderness'. Anežka Schulzová (1868–1905), who was to provide Fibich with the librettos for his three last operas, *Hedy* (1896), *Šárka* (1897) and *The Fall of Arkona* (1900), was the well-educated daughter of a literary critic and historian, and from her early twenties she wrote theatre reviews and made translations from German, French and Danish. In addition to her literary education (under Vrchlický among others) she received a thorough musical grounding from Fibich. She was his piano pupil from 1886 and composition pupil from 1892 and was herself responsible for several published piano reductions of his orchestral and instrumental works.

Schulzová's librettos for Fibich were clearly the result of very close collaboration. How much their dramatic conception and organization owed to Fibich's own considerable experience as an opera composer is hard to say in view of the paucity of materials and the special nature of the relationship. What is interesting, however, is that with these three operas there is a perceptible shift both in the type of conventions adopted and in their subject matter. *Hedy*, with its love duet and concertato finale, is closer to the much earlier *Blaník* than its immediate predecessors, and Hostinský, normally the most tactful of commentators, openly speculated that Fibich's alleged later hostility to *The Bride of Messina* and its very different conventions was a result of Anežka's views (Hostinský 1909, 127 fn; see also Jůzl 1980, 167–8). Similarly, in *Šárka* Fibich treated a Czech subject, which he had not done for the twenty years since *Blaník*. Anežka's particular attraction to northern literature is evident in the Baltic setting of *The Fall of Arkona*.

Anežka Schulzová wrote librettos for no other composer. Her intense involvement with Fibich, clear from the biography of him she published in 1900, the year of his death, under the male pseudonym of Carl Ludwig Richter, and the more personal memoir of 1902, was no doubt strengthened by the social opprobrium she risked in a less permissive age (Fibich left his wife for Anežka in 1897). Her life disintegrated after his death, and she committed suicide a few years later at the age of thirty-seven.

Schulzová's mother came from the Grégr family (her brothers were well-known *mladočech* politicians and publicists) and she was the force behind the family's acceptance of Anežka's 'advanced' views. Marie Červinková-Riegrová (1854–95), librettist for two of Dvořák's finest operas, was the daughter of the most prominent *staročech* politician of the latter half of the century, František Rieger. Father and daughter were close and Rieger took a pride and a virtually participatory interest in her work. He saw early drafts of her librettos and made observations which influenced their future development. (This is beautifully charted by Kuna (1982, 1984) in the case of *The Jacobin*.) Her first opera libretto, *The Frustrated Wedding* (1879), was written for her composer husband Václav Červinka (who did not care for it) and on Rieger's suggestion it was then offered to Šebor, now virtually in exile as a military bandmaster in Slovakia, to coax him back to composition. This achieved, Červinková-Riegrová wrote her next libretto directly for Šebor. From his four suggestions for a serious opera (Schiller's *Turandot* and historical plays by Czech writers, Josef Jiří Kolár and Ferdinand Břetislav Mikovec; see Bráfová 1913, 55-6) Červinková-Riegrová chose Mikovec's *Dimitr Ivanovič*, itself an adaptation of Schiller's unfinished *Demetrius*, but Šebor's dilatory attitude led her to withdraw her text and offer it, again at her father's suggestion, to Dvořák. Červinková-Riegrová's final libretto, *The Jacobin*, was written directly for Dvořák.

It could perhaps be argued that Červinková-Riegrová's choice of the Russian *Dimitrij* as an opera libretto reflected the *staročech* admiration for Russia and the pan-Slavonic world, or that the generally approving picture she paints in *The Jacobin* of a feudal society was typical of the Riegers' conservative views, but it is hard to see Schulzová's librettos to *Hedy* or *Šárka*, weighed down with the paraphernalia of nineteenth-century operatic conventions, as being any more 'progressive'. Similarly the cluster of village operas written by the radical Sabina (e.g. *The Bartered Bride, In the Well, The Elderly Suitor*) seem little different from the conservative Červinková-Riegrová's imitation of them in *The Frustrated Wedding*.

As it was, Sabina's radicalism masked a more ominous side. At the same time as he was writing opera librettos apparently to further the Czech nationalist cause, Sabina was undermining any effect this good work might have had by helping the Austrians to bring other Czech patriots to heel. His role as police informer has understandably been a source of embarrassment to the Czechs ever since. When his contacts with the police were discovered, his name was left off theatre posters; later just his initials were given, finally his whole name crept back (Heller 1918, 97). Only Sabina's initials were given in the first edition of the vocal score (see the title page shown in illustration 15). Even as late as 1962 the German-Czech writer, Max Brod, friend of Kafka and Janáček, and translator of many of Janáček's operas, devoted his final novel to elaborating the theory that the libretto to *The Bartered Bride* encoded a secret message to the Czech people and a defence of Sabina's actions (Brod 1962). Just as Jeník appeared to sell his bride purely for gain while in fact hoodwinking the village authorities (thus having his cake and eating it), Sabina was doing the same: his 'contract' with the Austrian authorities brought him an income but gave them nothing of significance in return, while at the same time he bequeathed to the nation an infinitely more powerful vehicle of pro-Czech propaganda in the form of his libretto to *The Bartered Bride*. Brod's compassionate hypothesis (Sabina had a wretched life after his imprisonment for his part in the 1848 Revolution) rests on shaky foundations. All the evidence suggests that Sabina churned out the libretto hastily as just another piece of journalism, and research in Austrian state archives in Vienna has established that Sabina was the most important police informer in Prague from the late 1850s to the early 1870s, and was responsible for implicating several of his compatriots as well as members of other nationalist movements within the Habsburg Empire (Purš 1959).

Fervent though Sabina's first Smetana libretto *The Brandenburgers* may be, it is no less so than those of *Dalibor* and *Libuše*, both of them written not by a Czech radical, but by an elderly German with Czech sympathies; in 1848, the year of Sabina's involvement with revolutionary forces, Wenzig was writing hymns with titles like 'Noch ist Oesterreich nicht verloren' (Wenzig, Josef', *ČSHS*). Wenzig's later espousal of the Czech cause was sincere but led to the curious fact that Smetana's two most patriotic operas had librettos written originally in German (a fact that Smetana and Wenzig did their best to disguise by leaving out any mention of Špindler's name – see Jiránek 1984, 233, fn. 11), while Smetana's most popular opera had a libretto written by a traitor.

Vrchlický and Zeyer, both poets and playwrights, had more impact than Czech novelists on opera. It was not until the twentieth century that composers made operatic versions of Němcová's classic novel *The Grandmother* (1855) such as A.V. Horák's *The Grandmother* (1900) and Kovařovic's better known *At the Old Bleachery* (1901). It was Kovařovic, too, who with his *The Dogheads* was one of the few Czech composers to base an opera on one of the historical novels of Alois Jirásek, the Walter Scott of Czech literature. Though Šourek noted connections between the milieu and characters of Jirásek's *At the Duke's Court* (*Na dvoře vévodském*, 1877) and Dvořák's *The Jacobin*, Dvořák's librettist Marie Červinková-Riegrová nowhere mentions this as a source and, as Kuna (1982, 246) demonstrates, other sources are more important. But Jirásek's fairy-tale play *The Lantern* (1905) was made into an opera libretto for Novák's opera of the same name (1923).

The most popular Czech novels for operatic treatment were by Svatopluk Čech. During his life Čech was known chiefly as a poet, a slightly old-fashioned figure, 'the last of the National Revival poets', though a well-developed social awareness led him to explore more proletarian subject matter such as his verse novel *The Blacksmith of Lešetín* (*Lešetínský kovář*, 1883), which attracted two twentieth-century settings, by Stanislav Suda (1903) and Karel Weis (1920). (Dvořák also considered it in 1901, after *Rusalka*). Today much of Čech's work is forgotten, though not the satirical novels about the Prague rentier, Mr Brouček, transported into unlikely milieus. His *True Excursion of Mr Brouček to the Moon* (*Pravý výlet pana Broučka do měsíce*, 1888), inhabited by caricatures of the Art-for-Art's sake poets of the time – a barb directed at the *Lumír* school – was set by Janáček (1908–17; produced 1920) and as an operetta with spoken dialogue by Karel

Moor (1910). The pantomimic and dance elements stressed in Moor's setting (the final act is mimed) was something that appealed to Janáček from his first jottings in his copy of the novel (Tyrrell 1968, 106) and which found ultimate expression in the lively succession of waltzes and polkas in the opera. As late as 1942 J.E. Zelinka wrote a *Journey of Mr Brouček to the Moon* (*Cesta pana Broučka na měsíc*), described by the composer, as a 'dance and pantomime burlesque'.

Mr Brouček's second excursion – *The New Epoch-making Excursion of Mr Brouček, this time to the Fifteenth Century* (*Nový epochální výlet pana Broučka, tentokráte do XV. století*, 1888) – displayed the more serious, patriotic side of Čech and was set only by Janáček, and this as an afterthought suggested by the prospect of an independent Czech state while Janáček was finishing his much protracted earlier excursion. The light-weight *Matěj Brouček at the Exhibition* (*Matěj Brouček na výstavě*, 1892), a topical piece capitalizing on the popularity of the 1891 Jubilee Exhibition, became the subject of a play with incidental music by Kovařovic (1894).

The wave of Czech realist drama towards the end of the century inspired several operas. Surprisingly, the most famous play from this movement, Ladislav Stroupežnický's iconoclastic comedy of village life *Our Swaggerers* (*Naši furianti*, 1887), did not attract operatic settings until much later in the twentieth century although his earlier historical plays such as *The Imp of Zvíkov* (*Zvíkovský rarášek*, 1883) and *The Mintmaster's Wife* (*Paní mincmistrová*, 1885) were later set, respectively by Novák (1915) and Janáček (1906–7 – only sketches). So it was in the end a much less prominent and experienced figure, Gabriela Preissová, who provided the chief literary material in this genre. Her two dramas of Moravian village life, *The Farm Mistress* (*Gazdina roba*, 1889) and *Her Foster-daughter* (*Její pastorkyňa*, 1890) were turned into librettos, respectively, for *Eva* (1899), Foerster's most popular opera, and *Jenůfa* (1904), Janáček's first mature opera.

As discussed in Chapter 3, Foerster's verse libretto tended to mute the naturalistic impact of the original play. Janáček's earliest work on *Jenůfa* (modified as he went along, and in subsequent revisions) bears witness to the need that he also seems to have felt for metrical lines and even duet-like set numbers. Nevertheless the use of Preissová's prose without a consistently applied metrical scheme meant that he was writing something different in kind from any Czech opera before it, with profound implications for the sort of music which would thereby result. Furthermore the fact that no outside librettist was involved meant that Janáček in *Jenůfa*, like Foerster in *Eva*, had an undisputed control over aspects of his opera which in earlier Czech operas had been often the responsibility of the librettists.

It is thus all the more interesting that Janáček's next two operas both drew on outside librettists. One reason for this was that neither was based on an existing play. Another, at least in *Fate*, was that Janáček had still not completely come to terms with setting prose rather than metrical lines of verse. It is significant that in this opera he took on a very young, inexperienced collaborator who simply carried out his instructions and versified his scenario (Straková 1956, 213-15). In other words there is no question here that Janáček had anything less than complete control over subject, dramatic plan and operatic conventions of his opera. The story of the composition of *The Excursions of Mr Brouček* is too complex to unravel here. Briefly, one could say that despite the large number of 'librettists' involved in the first *Excursion*, Janáček not only chose the subject, but also wrote the scenario and, in the end, did most of the work. The most substantial outside contributions were songs written to his specification (see Tyrrell 1968). Only with the second *Excursion*, where Janáček received a full libretto from one of his more helpful collaborators on the first, the poet F.S. Procházka (1861-1939), can a case be made for a greater involvement of the librettist in some of the compositional choices.

Procházka was to be Janáček's last librettist. After his work on *Brouček*, he found himself odd-jobbing on the revision of *Šárka*, filling in lines according to Janáček's metrical needs (Rektorys 1949, 88-9). There is evidence that Janáček continued to call in such occasional help for the songs in *Kát'a Kabanová* and *The Cunning Little Vixen* (Tyrrell 1982, 58-60). By the time of the latter opera Janáček felt confident enough to adapt a novel himself, and in his final opera, *From the House of the Dead*, he did so again, this time managing even without a formal libretto written out in advance. All he had was a scenario which contained little more than references to annotated pages of his Russian edition of the Dostoyevsky novel, which he translated into Czech as he went along (Tyrrell 1980, 4).

Janáček chose the subjects of all his operas. His first opera, *Šárka*, written to an existing libretto, might be considered an exception. Others, like *Kát'a Kabanová*, may have been drawn to his attention (Tyrrell 1982, 91), but he considered these along with many other subjects before finally settling on his own unlikely choices. While naturally the structure of the literary antecedents, especially of the stage plays, influenced that of the operas Janáček made from them – *Jenůfa* has the same three acts as that of Preissová's play with emotional climaxes at the same points – in his later operas Janáček made radical changes to the material. Where he needed a different dramatic shape he changed it. Ostrovsky's play in five acts (one in two scenes) was rearranged into an opera in three acts of two scenes each, an adaptation more radical than it sounds since Janáček made an exciting end-of-act climax from the middle of one of Ostrovsky's scenes (Tyrrell 1982, 49-52). Similarly the death of Emilia Marty that Janáček introduced at the end of *The Makropulos Affair* gave the opera quite a different emotional shape to that of Čapek's play. The two adapted novels differ even more from their literary antecedents, with incidents placed often in quite a different order and then subjected to Janáček's own emotional climaxing.

Janáček's personal control of the libretto and the compositional decisions implicit in it is one of the features that most distinguishes his operas from the nineteenth-century Czech tradition. His contemporaries such as Novák and Ostrčil continued to make use of outside librettists, and when Ostrčil did not, as in *The Bud* or *The Legend of Erin*, this was because he was content to take over the conventions and emotional structure of existing plays. Janáček's only fellow among his Czech contemporaries in this respect was Foerster, who in *Eva* and in his last three operas was responsible for his own librettos. But Foerster made far less use of this freedom than did Janáček. In fact with the exception of *Eva*, adapted from a play, it might be argued that Foerster would have been better off had he continued to use librettists, unlike Janáček, all of whose operas from librettists have problems. Janáček's dismissal of the librettist seems to have been one of the preconditions for the realization of his full potential as an operatic composer.

# 5. Subjects

## Non-Czech and Slavonic subjects

For much of the nineteenth century Czech librettists and composers chose Czech subject matter because they thought it their patriotic duty to do so. All but one of Smetana's operas were drawn from Czech history or Czech town or village life. The exception, *The Two Widows*, consciously modified its French origins by the introduction of 'typically' Czech characters and a Czech chorus. Late in life Smetana turned down a libretto entitled 'Ahasaver' because 'the choruses of the Jews or the Romans could not be composed in any Czechoslavonic style'. The Czech 'national style had not yet been firmly implanted' and until this time Smetana 'would give preference to librettos drawn from Czech history over cosmopolitan librettos' (Bartoš 1939, 168).

Another reason for composers preferring librettos from Czech history was that Czech audiences also seemed to prefer them. Fibich's operas provide an instructive example. Their subject matter, whether chosen by him or his librettists, marks him out as an 'internationalist' composer, little concerned by local pressures, and, perhaps consequently, Fibich was also the least popular of the major Czech opera composers of his time, with fewer performances in the nineteenth century than lesser figures such as Bendl and Rozkošný. The one opera of his that has held the stage, *Šárka*, is his only mature opera with a Czech setting (*Blaník*, which is also based on Czech legends, was complete in vocal score by the time he was twenty-five). His other late operas, written during the same creative period as *Šárka*, two of them with the same librettist, achieved nothing like *Šárka*'s lasting success, despite the initially promising first runs of *The Tempest* and *Hedy*.

Few Czech composers in the nineteenth century followed Fibich's example and composed operas to 'cosmopolitan' librettos. Even his pupil Karel Kovařovic found, after the disappointing reception of his operas based on Scribe or Alarcón, that he was much better off with operas based on Czech history, such as *The Dogheads*, or on Němcová's classic novel *The Grandmother* (*At the Old Bleachery*). *The Dogheads* was one of the most frequently performed Czech operas of its time, much more than any of Fibich's.

While Czech connections could not of course guarantee an opera's success with the public, there was a fair chance that they would help it along. Conversely, an opera without Czech connections seemed at a disadvantage. Šebor's least performed opera, *Blanka*, was also his least nationalist opera. Similarly Dvořák's least popular mature opera was *Armida*, his only opera without a Czech or at least a Slavonic libretto. (His first opera, *Alfred*, was never staged during his lifetime.) The few nineteenth-century Czech operas to win favour with the public despite a lack of Czech connections tended to do so because of other, somewhat meretricious factors such as novelty, or elaborate sets. Thus Bendl's *Lejla* made a great impact on its audiences by being the first Czech 'grand opera', its exotic subject perhaps a response to that of *L'africaine*, recently given at Prague's German Theatre, just as Rozkošný's *Cinderella* was one of the few early successes in Czech opera in the National Theatre by virtue of its spectacular ballet scenes.

The new wave of verist operas, however, gave a fresh burst of life to foreign and exotic locales. Beginning with *Cavalleria rusticana* in January 1891, Šubert mounted three Mascagni operas in two years at the National Theatre, as well as works by the German verist school, such as Ferdinand Hummel's *Mara*, which had already been performed in January 1894 at Prague's German Theatre, a few months after its Berlin première. Its Czech translator was Otakar Kučera, who wrote the libretto for the first Czech verist opera, Rozkošný's *Stoja* (June 1894). And it was the librettist of *Mara*, Axel Delmar, who provided the libretto (when translated into Czech) for the second Czech verist opera, Bendl's *Mother Míla* (June 1895).

Following their models *Mara* and *Cavalleria rusticana*, both *Stoja* and *Mother Míla* were one-act pieces, and placed their actions in peasant communities. *Stoja* is set in Bosnia, *Mother Míla* in Cyprus – both somewhat exotic for Czech audiences, though the first had an agreeably Slavonic resonance. And, like their models, both works tell tales of violent passions and violent crimes. Stoja contrives both to stab her lover and betray her husband (ranged on opposite sides in the civil war) before being stabbed herself. Míla intervenes in the brawl between the husband and returned lover of her daughter. By shooting the husband herself, she sacrifices his life and her own to her daughter's future happiness.

Neither work had many performances (*Stoja*, perhaps because of its novelty value, did better), and the verist experiment was roundly denounced by critics such as Nejedlý (1911, 324) and by composers such as Foerster (1897, 25–7, 42–3) and Čelanský (1897, 50). Čelanský's views were put into practice in his opera *Kamilla* (1897), where, instead of the violence which he deplored in verist opera, he sought a gentler path. A one-act conversation piece – its wordy libretto is longer than many full-evening librettos – *Kamilla* is set in *fin-de-siècle* salon society. The beautiful heroine is wooed by a poet, who recites poems to her, and by a wealthy philistine neighbour, who encourages her to smoke and flirts with her chambermaid when her back is turned. Kamilla chooses the neighbour and then regrets her decision, but too late – the sensitive poet goes off in a huff.

*Kamilla* is remembered today only as the shadowy precursor of Janáček's *Fate*. Kamilla Urválková, who claimed to be the real-life Kamilla in the opera and resented her depiction there as a shallow flirt, met Janáček in the spa town of Luhačovice in the summer of 1903 and suggested that he write another *Kamilla* opera to clear her name. Janáček's *Fate*, however, was no more chivalrous to its heroine (contracted to Míla Válková) than its predecessor. There is no evidence that Janáček ever heard Čelanský's *Kamilla*, which was given ten performances in Prague 1897–9, or saw a score (the opera remained unpublished, though a printed libretto was available), but he probably gathered something about the work from Mrs Urválková and indeed there are several parallels between his opera and Čelanský's. Both have contemporary bourgeois settings. Čelanský's opera 'from modern salon life' takes place in the 'English park' of a suburban villa, from which the strains of a piano can be heard from time to time. The first act of Janáček's opera is similarly set outside, in a fashionable spa; the piano is heard in Act 2 in the more intimate surroundings of Živný's studio. The poet's love song recited to Kamilla is reflected in the composer's love song addressed to Míla in Act 2 of *Fate*; the red roses with which Čelanský's poet initiated his advances became the roses Mrs Urválková sent to Janáček, and one of the tentative titles for his opera.[1]

Janáček's chance meeting with Mrs Urválková in Luhačovice may seem an unlikely beginning for an important new phase of his operatic development, but it clearly came at the right time, coinciding with his growing interest in foreign composers such as Charpentier, whose *Louise* he greatly admired, or Puccini, whose direct influence can be charted in Janáček's operas as late as *Kát'a Kabanová*. But in breaking out of the nationalist straitjacket after *Jenůfa* and seeking to emulate fashionable European composers, Janáček nevertheless kept firmly to Czech soil. His spa scene in *Fate* may have all the gaiety and variety of the Café Momus, but it is nevertheless a Moravian spa. Even at the height of his fame and with a spreading European reputation, Janáček persisted with Czech or Slavonic settings for all his last operas. *The Cunning Little Vixen* takes place in the forests outside Brno, *The Makropulos Affair* in Prague; the remaining operas, *Kát'a Kabanová* and *From the House of the Dead*, are set in Russia.

Janáček's Russophilism, which led to the inspiration of many of his works and even the naming of his children, Vladimír and Olga, was an important part of his personality. But it was an attitude shared by many Czechs of his time, partly as an anti-German gesture, but partly also a manifestation of Pan-Slav ideals. Pan-Slavism came into prominence in the revolutionary year of 1848, when a Slavonic Congress took place in Prague, and was favoured by some conservative politicians who saw the salvation of the

Czechs in a Russian-centred, Pan-Slav confederation. Perceptive political commentators such as Havlíček pointed out that although the Russians were Slavonic, they were more autocratic and repressive than the Czechs' present masters, the Austrians; Pan-Slavists should not forget Russia's cynical treatment of another Slav people, the Poles, whose state she had helped dismember.

Dvořák was the most prominent Pan-Slav Czech composer.[2] His 'Slavonic' (rather than merely Bohemian) orientation is apparent from his Slavonic Dances, from the 'dumka' movements of his instrumental works (a typical Pan-Slav genre, with strong Ukrainian and Polish traditions before Dvořák took it over), and from his two operas with Polish or Russian subject matter: *Vanda* (set in Poland) and *Dimitrij* (set in Russia). These were not the only Czech nationalist operas that depict other Slavonic peoples. One of the first Czech operas to be performed at the Provisional Theatre was Skuherský's *Vladimír* (1863), set in Bulgaria.

In view of Austrian theatre censorship, which restricted the portrayal of racial conflict – a sensible precaution in a multi-national state such as the Austrian Empire (*DČD* ii, 210) – it is not surprising that few Czech operas depicted the oppression of Slav peoples. The subject of the Turks' treatment of the Montenegrins was considered too provocative for the Czech stage in 1877 and performances of Bendl's opera *The Montenegrins* did not take place until 1881, after the opera had won an honourable mention in the competition to mark the opening of the National Theatre (Hostinský 1974, 469). Its popularity (it was performed nine times in the first season and continually revived up to 1894) owed much to the domestic parallels that could be drawn by a Czech audience. And the lack of such parallels may explain the indifference of the public to Fibich's last opera, *The Fall of Arkona*. Though this work deals with the defeat of the Baltic Slavs on the island of Rujan (now Rügen) by the Danes in 1168, and was thus potentially a vehicle for attracting inter-Slav sympathy, much of this sympathy was alienated by the unsympathetic portrayal of the Slavs, and in particular their leader, the head priest Dargun. Furthermore the whole emphasis of the work is personal rather than collective – a fate-infested psychological drama whose roots are explained in its prologue, set twenty years before the main action.

Other Slav subjects had even less to offer in terms of useful nationalist parallels. Although Poles fight against Germans in Dvořák's *Vanda* much more stress is laid on Vanda's personal decision to sacrifice love for duty by leaping to her death in the Elbe, while in his *Dimitrij* the conflict between two Slav peoples seems positively counterproductive.

The non-Czech settings described above, however, were in the minority. Most Czech operas in the nineteenth century and early twentieth were set on home soil, many of them based on events from Czech history.

# Czech history

Count Harrach's opera competition of 1861 stipulated two genres: a comic opera based on Czech folk life, and a historical opera based on 'the history of the Czech crownlands'. It was the second category that attracted all the entries, three operas and one unset libretto. One of these four entries, Pozděna's *Dearest Treasure*, was an adaptation of Kott's *Žižka's Oak*, and thus used as its libretto Klicpera's play written forty years earlier. The other three, newly written librettos were all based on incidents from Czech history: Sabina's *The Brandenburgers in Bohemia* (written for Smetana); Emilie Ujková's *Jaromír, Duke of Bohemia* (written for her husband, the Provisional Theatre conductor J.N. Maýr) and František Šír's *Drahomíra* (submitted independently, and later set by Šebor) (Vejdělek 1982, 267). These three librettos provide a convenient starting point for an examination of the treatment of history as source material in Czech opera.

### Drahomíra and her sons

Šír's libretto *Drahomíra* covers the earliest period of Czech history of the three. Drahomíra was the mother of St Václav, the St Wenceslas of the English carol. The first local account of him and his equally saintly grandmother Ludmilla (the subject of Dvořák's oratorio) was written by the chronicler Christianus, who relied on several older Latin legends and perhaps some personal involvement: some scholars have identified him as Strachkvas, Václav's nephew (see Table 5), though his most recent editor

Table 5. *Early Přemyslid rulers (family tree extracted from Hrdina 1947, between pp. 248–9). The succession is complicated further by the brief intrusions of two Polish rulers, Vladivoj (1002–3) and Boleslav the Brave (1003–4).*

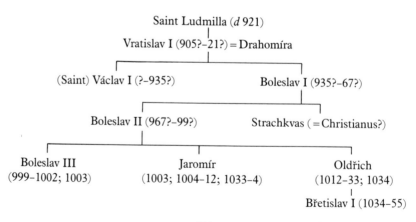

(Ludvíkovský 1978, 127–33) concludes that he was a member of a leading rival family. 'Good King Wenceslas' was not in fact a 'king' but a duke or prince (Bohemian rulers were granted the hereditary title of king only in 1198), and he was 'good' mostly in the sense of pious. He was soon supplanted by his brother Boleslav I, who murdered him in 935(?), a much abler ruler who successfully enlarged and consolidated the country.

Even during the lifetime of his successor, Václav became the object of a sacred cult which venerated him as the first Czech saint, a useful Slavonic recruit to the Latin hagiarchy. A later secular cult promoted him as father-figure of the nation – the largest and most famous square in Prague, the Václavské náměstí, was renamed after him. In the nineteenth century the Václav cult excited the visual arts rather more than the dramatic ones, which preferred his formidable mother Drahomíra. She is the 'Jezebel' (Christianus's term) who gave her name to Škroup's German opera *Drahomíra*, first performed in 1848, and, a year later, to Tyl's play *Drahomíra and her Sons* (*Drahomíra a její synové*). A major figure in Tyl, Václav has only a small part in Škroup's opera; twenty years later in Šebor's *Drahomíra*, based on Šír's competition libretto, Václav does not even sing, though he appears silently in a mimed vision. Ludmilla does not appear in either opera – only in Tyl's play, where she is strangled on the instructions of her daughter-in-law Drahomíra. Boleslav, on the other hand, figures strongly in all three works.

That the two saints of the family have so little to do on the operatic stage was due not only to possible objections from the censor but also to the fact that the two murderers of the family, Drahomíra and Boleslav, presented more obvious operatic possibilities, Boleslav as a baritone villain and Drahomíra as a Medea-like sorceress. (In both operas she meets her death when the earth opens up and engulfs her in flames and thunder.) Erben, who was one of the panel in the Harrach competition, took particular exception in his report to the fact that Drahomíra appears as a witch, dressed in black with a witch's rod with which she invokes the spirits of darkness. He also made the point that, though successful in conventional operatic terms, the libretto was hardly the basis for a Czech national opera, since its only source of Czechness was the easily replaceable Slavonic names of the protagonists (Daněk 1983, 152).

After the strong rule of Boleslav and his son Boleslav II, the Czech throne was occupied by the latter's three sons: Boleslav III, Jaromír and Oldřich. Factional fighting among the three was encouraged by Bohemia's two powerful neighbours, the German emperor in the west, and the Polish king in the east, with the result that Jaromír and Oldřich held the throne two or three times each, according to changing deals and alliances struck with Bohemia's neighbours. Stability was achieved only after Oldřich's death in 1034 and when Jaromír, physically blinded by his ambitious brother and thus effectively incapacitated as a ruler, relinquished the throne in favour of Oldřich's son, Břetislav.

The Maýrs' *Jaromír* is set during the time of Jaromír's first brief occupancy of the Bohemian throne in 1003. It concerns an attempt made on his life, organized by a rival family, and how this is foiled by his trusty huntsman Hovora. The historian and archaeologist J.E. Vocel, one of the panel of judges in the Harrach competition, complained about the unhistorical aspects of this libretto, citing the presence of Boleslav II during the rule of his son and the fact the old king appeared as blinded (like his son Jaromír was to be) (Daněk 1983, 158–9). Vocel does not mention, however, that both details came from Hájek's chronicle (see below, pp. 136–8, 140).

### Oldřich and Božena, Břetislav and Jitka

None of the three sons of Boleslav II had any issue. While out hunting one day Oldřich, the youngest son, caught sight of a beautiful maiden and, since his own wife was barren, he resolved to wed her. Thus the humble Božena became the Bohemian consort, and gave to Oldřich the longed-for son – Břetislav. The tale of Oldřich and Božena was a great favourite in the Czech Revival. A 'patriotic Singspiel' on this subject was performed at the *Bouda* in 1786, but the earliest surviving dramatic version was Antonín Josef Zíma's five-act play, performed and published in 1789. Škroup's opera *Oldřich and Božena* (1828) is one of the earliest operas in Czech. Tomášek planned one even earlier, *Božena, Bohemian Princess*, to a libretto (described by Emingerová 1925, 36–7) by Václav Hanka. As is known from Hostinský's memoir, Fibich also considered writing an opera on this subject, but all he left was an independent overture. Smetana's delicious mock-serious overture *Oldřich and Božena* was written for one of the many puppet plays on the subject. A related puppet play, much adapted, lies behind Dvořák's first Czech opera, *King and Charcoal Burner (DČD* ii, 189).

The rather more complicated story of Oldřich's and Božena's son was the basis for Bendl's *Břetislav* (1870). Like Oldřich's courtship of Božena before it, the topic had already inspired several plays, beginning with Václav Thám's knightly drama *Břetislav and Jitka, or The Abduction from the Convent (Břetislav a Jitka aneb Únos z kláštera*, 1786). These mostly concentrate on Břetislav's dramatically rewarding abduction of his future bride, Judita (Jitka in Czech), the sister of the Duke of Schweinfurt. For Bendl's opera his librettist Krásnohorská supplied a large-scale Act 2 finale ensemble to encompass this scene. What follows in Act 3, the funeral oration by the blind Jaromír over the corpse of his dead brother Oldřich, and his acclamation of Břetislav as king, comes as something of an anticlimax. This act, however, like the retitling of the opera from *Břetislav and Jitka* (on the full score)[3] to *Břetislav* (so performed), was no doubt meant to stress that what was intended was not simply a dashing amorous adventure, but a historical pageant culminating in the coronation of one of Bohemia's most successful rulers.

The point was made rather more succinctly in Smetana's *Libuše*. When Wenzig came to write his text for Libuše's prophetic survey of Czech history, he relied not on Hájek, as had Krásnohorská and her predecessors, but on the first authoritative Czech history, František Palacký's monumental *History of the Czech Nation in Bohemia and Moravia* (*Dějiny národu českého v Čechách i v Moravě*), whose definitive version came out in instalments between 1848 and 1876. Palacký called Břetislav the 'restorer of Bohemia' and Wenzig gave Libuše, describing her first vision (a *tableau vivant*), these words to say about him:

> Here strides the hero who gave the sister state to the throne, and with one powerful blow won his bride, saved his holy body, and frightened away the terrible cloud in the west.

Though Wenzig included a passing reference to Jitka, the main reason for Břetislav's appearance here was his independent stance towards the Holy Roman Emperor (the 'terrible cloud in the west') and his ridding Moravia (the 'sister state') of Poles. Since Břetislav's time Moravia has been permanently linked to Bohemia.

### Brandenburgers, and other invaders

The winning entry in the Harrach competition, *The Brandenburgers in Bohemia*, was set in 1279, a time of great turmoil in the Czech state. Přemysl Otakar II, one of the greatest Bohemian kings, had died the year before, leaving his empire in disarray and his seven-year-old son, Václav II, on the throne. The Habsburg emperor Rudolf I quickly took over Moravia, much to the satisfaction of the large local German population, while Bohemia was overrun by the Brandenburgers who arrived with Otto of Brandenburg, nephew of the last Bohemian king and guardian to the young Václav. They devastated Bohemia, and Otto held the boy king hostage in Brandenburg. It was not until the Bohemian aristocracy had united against Otto that Václav was ransomed back to the country, Otto's 'guardianship' strictly controlled, and the Brandenburgers expelled.

Sabina's libretto was much criticized by the Harrach panel for its careless language and versification (Daněk 1983, 153–4). But in comparison with Šír's *Drahomíra* (the only libretto commended in the Harrach competition) or to the Maýrs' *Jaromír*, it was rather more soundly based historically, taking as one of its sources an up-to-date history of Prague (Sabina 1918, xii), rather than Hájek's chronicle, discredited as a reliable source since the end of the eighteenth century. Furthermore the subject was unequivocally nationalist.

This had not been the case, for instance, with Jan Nepomuk Škroup's similarly titled *The Swedes in Prague*. In 1812, at the height of the Napoleonic Wars, the Czech dramatist J.N. Štěpánek had written his popular play *The Siege of Prague by the Swedes, or Czech Faithfulness and Bravery* (*Obležení Prahy od Švejdů aneb Věrnost a udatnost česká*) as an expression of sincere nationalism within the framework of the Austrian Empire. The Swedes had invaded Prague many times during the Thirty Years' War, but their attempt in 1648, the last year of the war, was successfully repulsed by the citizens and thus allowed Habsburg rule to begin in earnest. That this essentially loyalist topic was equally acceptable to the Germans is demonstrated by German translations that were also performed and by the first operatic version, Georg Valentin Roeder's *Die Schweden in Prag*, given in Munich in 1842, three years before the performance of Act 1 of Škroup's opera (it was performed in full only in 1867). In contrast, *The Brandenburgers in Bohemia* was seen as anti-German and thus anti-Austrian. It reached back to powerful folk memories of a much-hated invasion. Even the eighteenth-century Moravian operas, reacting to a more recent German invasion, preserved the fear of the 'Brandenburgers' in the title *Landebork* (see p. 61). Some of Smetana's most patriotic lines were set in this opera, and ever since it was written it has created problems for any force occupying the country.

It is significant that all three historical librettos for the Harrach competition took their history from the rule of the Přemyslids, the only native Czech dynasty, which presided over the Czech lands from the early tenth century to the beginning of the fourteenth. Even in later Czech opera few other rulers are mentioned. The greatest Czech king of all, Charles IV, and at least a Přemyslid on his mother's side (his mother Eliška was the daughter of the second-last Přemyslid king), appears in only one Czech opera, Novák's *Karlštejn*, apart from his brief appearance, with Eliška and Přemysl Otakar II, in the third *tableau* at the end of *Libuše*.

### Non-dynastic historical operas

Other Czech 'historical' operas were content to make use of a historical background (usually 'medieval') against which to set an incidental, or even trivial topic. Thus, in the best-known Czech historical opera – Smetana's *Dalibor* – King Vladislav II (ruled 1471–1516) appears in the outer acts. In Act 1 he conducts Dalibor's trial, in Act 3 he condemns him to death. But though a commanding figure by virtue of his position, Vladislav is overshadowed as a stage personality by Dalibor, Milada, Jitka and even perhaps by the jailer Beneš. Rozkošný's *Záviš z Falkenštejna* similarly introduces a king, Václav II (ruled 1278–1305), the young Václav mentioned in *The Brandenburgers in Bohemia* and almost the last Přemyslid ruler. (His son,

Václav III, was murdered at the age of seventeen after a rule of one year, leaving no issue and no male relatives.) But in *Záviš* Václav figures even less prominently than Vladislav in *Dalibor.* He appears in only one of the four acts, and there as a small boy (sung by a mezzo). The opera is not about him, but instead about Záviš and his machinations to acquire the throne for himself. In Sabina's libretto to *The Templars in Moravia* the action takes place merely 'in the thirteenth century', i.e. before the suppression of the order in the Czech crownlands in 1312. One of the characters in the opera is a queen (a king is mentioned, but does not appear), but she is unnamed. Unlike the Brandenburgers, the Templars are not portrayed as marauding foreigners (the opening chorus has them toasting '*our* Czech land'). Instead their appearance in the opera was more a matter of the Romantic possibilities they could offer in terms of colourful costumes and ceremonial: a Romantic 'medieval' background against which to depict a story of knightly challenges, insulted maidens and their champions.

Some Czech historical operas introduce historical figures other than rulers. For instance some of the characters in Jirásek's historical novel about the Chod rebellion in 1695 find their way into Kovařovic's *The Dogheads.* Smetana's *The Devil's Wall*, set 'in the middle of the thirteenth century', has as its chief character Vok Vítkovic, head of the main rival family to the Přemyslids, and an important part is played in this opera by his nephew Záviš z Falkenštejna. Since Smetana's opera is set some thirty years before Rozkošný's *Záviš*, it is Záviš this time who is the youth sung by a mezzo. However, Krásnohorská's facts were unreliable: Záviš was born after Vok's death (and in the cast list 'nephew' became unaccountably turned into 'uncle'). Another Krásnohorská libretto, *Karel Škreta*, wove an imaginative fantasy around the life of Bohemia's greatest Baroque painter.

While there was undoubtedly nationalist mileage to be had in the portrayal of a Czech ruler, speaking Czech, running his own affairs, and presiding over the country with due pomp and circumstance, the most effective way of rousing nationalist sentiment, and with a potent moral attached, was to show the state at a time when threatened – and saved by the heroic actions of its citizens. One such time was the Brandenburgers' invasion in 1279. Even more appealing were the foreign invasions during the Hussite era of the fifteenth century.

### Hussites

The burning of Jan Hus at the Council of Constance in 1415 had consequences more terrible than Pope Clement V or the Holy Roman Emperor Sigismund, on whose guarantee Hus had gone to Constance, could ever have imagined. The martyrdom of the leader of the reformist, Wycliffe-influenced sect united the country and its vacillating king as no other event could have done, and when in 1420 at the Pope's behest the Emperor sent an army to root out the Hussite heretics, it was roundly beaten off largely by Czech peasants shaped into an efficient fighting force by a commander of genius, Jan Žižka. For the next decade the Czechs were invincible in the face of some five assaults by imperial and crusader armies; it was only when the various factions of Hussites began to feud among themselves and the more moderate wing joined forces with the Catholics against the hardline Taborites that the latter were beaten at the Battle of Lipany in 1434 and their leader Prokop (who succeeded Jan Žižka) was killed. This defeat led not to the rooting out of Hussitism but to a compromise whereby articles of Hussite faith were tolerated by Rome, and Hussites and Catholics lived side by side, if a little uneasily.

The one element of faith on which all Hussite factions agreed (ironically not stemming from Hus himself) was the insistence of communion in both kinds for the laity, not just the bread as is normal Catholic practice. The chalice became a militant Hussite symbol, appearing on their banners and flags (see illustration 9). More radical sects believed in common ownership; the powerful Taborites, centred on what became the town of Tábor in southern Bohemia, rejected all forms of worship and dogma not based on the bible, and waged numerous local wars to persuade others of their view. Twenty years after the Battle of Lipany a Hussite king, Jiří z Poděbrad, was elected to the Bohemian throne (1458-71) – the only native king to rule the Czech lands after the Přemyslids. One and a half centuries later, after the defeat of the Bohemian nobles at the Battle of the White Mountain (1620), Catholicism was finally reimposed on a reluctant populace.

Hussitism, with its heady mixture of religious independence and national heroism, was viewed with the gravest suspicion by the Austrian state, especially once the Napoleonic wars (when Hussite battle hymns began to be sung again) had fanned into life the embers of Czech nationalism. Since Hus himself still counted as a heretic he and his movement were zealously proscribed by the state's Catholic censors, and thus the most fervently national of all Czech historical subjects did not appear on the Czech stage at all for the first two thirds of the nineteenth century, except for a brief period in 1848-50, when censorship was relaxed sufficiently to allow the staging of a few plays on the Hussite movement, in particular Tyl's *Jan Hus*, which received six well-attended performances. The subject, however, was taken up enthusiastically abroad, even in Vienna, where Salieri's 'Schauspiel' *Die Hussiten vor Naumburg*, based on Kotzebue's play, was given at the Court Theatre in 1803. In Protestant Germany Hussitism was espoused as a symbol of liberal nationalism, vividly illustrated, for instance in Carl Friedrich Lessing's 'Hussite Sermon' (1836), which depicted a Hussite preaching in the open air (with a church burning in the background) to a group which included all social classes (Honour 1979, 226-7). In France

9  The Hussite army, a drawing by the painter and illustrator Mikoláš Aleš in 1904, based on a picture in the Jenský Codex (1490–1510). The strange 'agricultural' weapons (e.g. the flails) represent the peasant element in the army. The important Hussite symbol of the chalice, seen on the banner and added by Aleš in the bottom righthand corner, emphasizes the basic Hussite tenet of the laity's right to take communion in both kinds, and not just the bread (carried in a flaming monstrance by the priest leading the procession). Like his exemplar, Aleš depicted the Hussite leader Jan Žižka (on the horse) incorrectly as blind in both eyes and included the most famous Hussite chorale, 'Ktož jsú boží bojovníci'. Despite the Gothic script and old spelling Aleš used a half-modernized version of the words and added the music in a modern notation, though constantly changing clef to avoid leger lines.

George Sand wrote three historical novels on the Hussite periods. But in Bohemia factual knowledge of Hus and the Hussite movement was minimal until the publication of Palacký's history and a more relaxed attitude towards the movement by the authorities (partly brought about by the Prussian invasion of 1866) allowed the subject to surface again, for instance in the composition of musical works based on Hussite themes (Lébl 1981, 112–13).

Smetana included 'Tábor' (1878) as one of the tone poems of *Má vlast*, and two of the five *tableaux* of Libuše's prophecy are given over to Hussite topics; the war leaders Žižka and Prokop appear in the fourth *tableau*, and the Hussite king, Jiří z Poděbrad in the fifth. Hussites might seem less likely to appeal to a composer as Catholic and conservative as Dvořák, but even he celebrated the movement in his *Hussite Overture* (1883).

Several phases of the Hussite movement are represented in Czech opera. The defeat of the Taborites at Lipany (1434), effectively the end of the Hussite wars, is the scene of Šebor's *The Hussite Bride* (1868). Bendl's *The Child of Tábor* (1892), to a libretto by Krásnohorská, based partly on Kotzebue's play *Die Hussiten vor Naumburg*, portrays a fictitious incident in 1430, when the Taborites were at the height of their power. Janáček's *The Excursion of Mr Brouček to the Fifteenth Century* (1920) deals with the first Hussite victory, on 14 July 1420.

Šebor's and Bendl's operas depict the conflict of love and duty against a wider historical canvas. In Šebor's opera, the Hussite hero loves a Catholic girl; in Bendl's opera, the 'child of Tábor' attempts to find her (non-Hussite) mother in the town the Taborites are besieging, and in so doing causes not only her own death but those of her Hussite betrothed and a non-Hussite suitor. Both operas are further complicated by somewhat unlikely paternity problems. Jaroslav's 'Hussite bride' turns out to be his sister (incest is prevented only by their deaths on the battlefield); while the orphan Hagar discovers she is not just the 'child of Tábor', but in fact also the child of the Taborite leader, Prokop, who has one of the main parts in the opera.

It may seem curious that of the three Hussite operas, Mr Brouček's drunken dream is the most soundly based in fact. This is largely because F.S. Procházka's libretto is carefully adapted from Svatopluk Čech's novel (1888), which achieves much of its effect by its mixture of sheer fantasy (the resolutely nineteenth-century, bourgeois Mr Brouček transposed into the fifteenth century) and minute historical detail. Contemporary references abound: Domšík's daughter Kunka enthuses over the sermon of Jan z Rokycana, later to become the Hussite Archbishop of Prague; Žižka, while not given the singing part that his successor Prokop has in *The Child of Tábor*, appears in a triumphant procession; another contemporary figure, the Emperor Sigismund (Zikmund), does not himself appear but leaves his trace as the chief offstage villain (Brouček is at first accused of being his

spy); the warring Hussite faction is portrayed in the doctrinal arguments between Miroslav, Vojta and the Student that give so many problems to contemporary producers of the opera. And while the other two operas were fuelled by the love–duty conflict that makes the Hussite background virtually indistinguishable from any other historical canvas, *Brouček* is an opera specifically about patriotism (see below).

Šebor's opera was the first musical work to make use of the famous Hussite battle hymn 'Ye who are God's warriors' ('Ktož jsú boží bojovníci'), made available in a modern transcription only in 1861 (Štědroň 1953, 74). The tune was to become even more famous after Smetana (in 'Tábor' and 'Blaník') and Dvořák (in his *Hussite Overture*) had exploited it instrumentally. Janáček could hardly avoid using it in his opera, in a powerful unison version as the men go off to battle. Unlike the other Hussite operas, however, Procházka's libretto also incorporated the words of three more Hussite chorales. For all of these Janáček wrote new tunes, such as the male voice chorale 'Attend, knights of God!' ('Slyšte rytieři boží'), heard at first from afar *pianissimo*. Its final, resplendent, organ-accompanied *fortissimo* repetition provides the rousing curtain to the first act of Mr Brouček's Hussite excursion.

### Founding legends

A final group of Czech historical operas is based on legends, or myths, about Libuše, the legendary founder of Prague, and about the war that raged after her death.

Czech legends tell of a mythical founder, Čech, who gave his name to his people and, Moses-like, brought them to a land flowing with milk and honey, establishing a successful settlement under the shadow of the sacred hill Říp, some forty miles north of Prague. Čech was followed by another ruler, Krok, and on his death Krok was succeeded by the youngest and wisest of his three daughters, the prophetess Libuše. At first Libuše was accepted as a ruler, but on one occasion her judgement in a boundary dispute was contested (see illustrations 10a and 11). Women have long hair but short understanding, the loser declared, and it is an outrage that the Czechs are ruled by one. Angered and humiliated, Libuše offers to marry in order to give her people a male ruler. The next day she gives instructions on how her future husband is to be found. Beyond the mountains is a stream, Bielina (Bílina), and on its bank stands a village named Stadice. There they will find a man ploughing with two piebald oxen (see illustration 10b). They are to take her robe and symbols of office and bring him back as ruler and as her husband. His name is Přemysl, and his descendants will reign in the land for ever.

All these signs are fulfilled and Přemysl himself adds more. 'Go whence

135

10 Libuše and the Maidens' War; woodblock illustrations by unidentified artists, dated 1539 and 1540, from the *Czech Chronicle* (1541) of Václav Hájek z Libočan.

10a Libuše, in a stylized attitude of melancholy (perhaps based on Dürer's well known engraving, *Melencolia*), sits in judgement on the brothers Chrudoš and Šťáhlav. Her palace of Vyšehrad (high fortress) is on the right. From the smoke in the chimneys it would appear to be winter.

10b The delegation sent by Libuše to search out her future husband, Přemysl, depicted here in the foreground ploughing with two piebald oxen near the village of Stadice.

10c  Omens confirming Libuše's choice of husband and Přemysl's suitability as future leader. At Přemysl's bidding his oxen 'vanish' (in an intriguing zodiacial conflation, upper left); the hazel rod sprouts branches with leaves (five rather than three) while Přemysl entertains members of the delegation at his 'iron table' (the upturned plough).

10d  The women construct their fortress at Děvín.

10e   The maidens' war: the women invincible.

10f   The maidens' war: the women defeated.

11 Libuše as depicted in Emil Zillich's drawing (published in *Světozor*, 1883) of scenes from Smetana's opera. Centre panel: Libuše's judgement (Act 1, cf Illustration 10a); top panel: the delegation to Přemysl (Act 2, cf Illustration 10b); bottom panel: the reconciliation of the brothers (Act 3).

you have come', he says to the oxen, and they immediately vanish (see illustration 10c). The hazel rod which he thrusts into the earth grows three branches, with leaves and nuts; two wither, but the third shoots up tall and broad. A sign, Přemysl explains, that the royal family will have many sons but only one will rule. Clad in the robe of office, Přemysl returns with the delegation. He marries Libuše and together they found the first Czech princely dynasty, the Přemyslids.

This version of the Libuše myth comes from Cosmas, a high-ranking church diplomat and dean of the Prague chapter, who wrote his *Chronica Boemorum* at the end of his long life (he died in 1125 at the age of about 80). During the Middle Ages it became the chief source for the early history of the Czech state and was copied freely into other histories and chronicles. Best-known of these was Václav Hájek z Libočan's *Czech Chronicle* (*Kronika česká*, 1541), which, published in a German translation in 1596, achieved wide currency.

Elements of the story percolated through into a variety of Baroque entertainments, in Prague, Vienna and, in 1666, Dresden and thence to the first operas on the subject, *La Libussa* (Wolfenbüttel, 1692), and Albinoni's *Primislao primo rè di Bohemia* (Venice, San Cassiano, 1697; see Trojan 1976). The Wolfenbüttel opera provided the model for the first opera on a Czech subject to be performed on Czech soil, Bartolomeo Bernardi's *La Libussa*, given in Prague during the 1703–4 season (Trojan 1979). But all these works use little more than the names of some of the Czech characters in their elaborately contrived and totally imaginary plots. The first Libuše opera clearly based on Cosmas-related sources (carefully detailed in Helfert 1936, 161–73) was *Praga nascente da Libussa e Primislao*, staged by Count Sporck's company in Prague in 1734. The libretto was by Antonio Denzi, Sporck's impresario, the composer possibly Bioni, the resident composer of the company. The Libuše legend became well established in German literature from the seventeenth century onwards (Kraus 1902, Chapter 2, gives a comprehensive list). It became the subject of plays by Brentano (1814) and Grillparzer (completed in 1847); a Czech translation of an earlier play by Steinsberg (see illustration 13a) introduced the subject to the Czech stage in 1787. Kreutzer's opera *Libussa*, to a German text by J.C. Bernard, was performed in Vienna in 1822 and brought to Prague a year later. Škroup's Czech opera, *Libuše's Marriage* (composed 1835), was heard complete in 1850. But it was only with Smetana's *Libuše* that the subject was invested with its full nationalist resonance (see pp. 3–4).

Apart from his recourse to Palacký for Libuše's visions, Wenzig's text for Smetana's opera was based largely on two sources: Cosmas's chronicle and the Green Mountain Manuscript (Zelenohorský rukopis). The latter was 'discovered' in 1818: four leaves of parchment containing two fragments, one of them concerning Libuše's judgement, purporting to be written in the ninth to tenth centuries. Together with the Queen's Court Manuscript (Rukopis Královédvorský, 'thirteenth century'), it is now considered to be a fake, made to provide Czech with a longer pedigree as a written language. Cosmas's account of Libuše was not the first; it was preceded by a brief mention in Christianus's life of St Václav and St Ludmilla. While Christianus mentions Přemysl by name (as Premizl) and his previous occupation as a ploughman, Libuše's name does not appear, nor any of Cosmas's details of her life – the judgement and her marriage. Přemysl is merely said to be called to the throne on the advice of a 'prophetess', whom he then marries. Such a deflation of the Czechs' most vibrant national legend led to disputes over the age and authenticity of the manuscript, though the most recent discussion, in Jaroslav Ludvíkovský's critical edition of 1978, accepts a dating of the late tenth century, about 130 years before Cosmas. The discrepancy between the two accounts, usually explained by the unconvincing proposal that Cosmas was recording tales still alive in ancient folk memory (cf Očadlík 1939, 17), has led to speculation that the vivid detail of the Libuše legend was the work of Cosmas himself. Libuše could have been based, it has been suggested (Karbusický 1966, 32-40), on the matriarchal Matilda of Tuscany (1046-1115; Cosmas supplies a contemporary anecdote about her elsewhere in his chronicle) and on elements from contemporary Minnesinger ballads.

Similar reservations have been expressed about the legend of the 'maidens' war' (dívčí válka). Women's power, in decline after Libuše's marriage, diminished further at her death and commentators have seen in these legends a metaphor for the transition from a matriarchal to a patriarchal society. In protest the girls took themselves off, built a fortress (see illustration 10d) called 'Děvín' (etymologically associated with the word for girl in Czech), and there trained an army of warrior women which, to the men's surprise and consternation, turned out to be invincible (see illustration 10e).

Cosmas provides the earliest source for this myth (there is nothing of this in Christianus) and once again it has been suggested that this colourful passage in his chronicle was his own invention, a reflection of his classical knowledge of Penthesilea, of the Amazon warriors of Scythia and so on, and that the maidens' fortress was merely another elaboration of a favourite medieval myth found elsewhere in Europe, such as Magdeburg ( = the maiden's castle) (Karbusický 1966, 69-77).

Cosmas's tale of the maidens' war was elaborated in the earliest Czech chronicle, the fourteenth-century chronicle of Dalimil. It is in Dalimil that the names of the maiden warriors first appear, notably that of their leader Vlastislava (or Vlasta). Hájek in turn confidently dated the maidens' war to 736-44 and in the substantial section he devoted to it in his chronicle it acquired much greater significance. His version, unlike Cosmas's, ends bloodily, with the defeat of the women on the battlefield (see illustration 10f).

The central figure of the war is Vlasta but she attracted rather less musical attention than one of the members of her army, Šárka. Though several Czech plays about Vlasta were presented in the earlier part of the century (they are listed in Lébl 1981, 110–11), there is only one completed Vlasta opera (by Ostrčil) as against two Šárka operas (Fibich's and Janáček's) and Smetana's tone poem 'Šárka' in *Má vlast*. In fact Dvořák, Smetana and Fibich all showed some interest in Vlasta. Early in their acquaintance Smetana inquired about Krásnohorská's Vlasta libretto (Očadlík 1940, 26). He was working at the time on *Libuše* – *Vlasta* would have been a sequel had the libretto not been committed to Krásnohorská's brother-in-law Hynek Palla. Two years before he died Smetana was offered another Vlasta libretto, *The Death of Vlasta* by Karel Pippich, who, on Smetana's refusal, then offered it to Fibich and in 1885 published it with a dedication to him (Nejedlý 1935a, 115–16). Fibich allegedly sketched a few scenes for Act 1, but ultimately turned it down, as Hostinský revealed (1909, 139), because of the inhibiting similarity of Vlasta to Brünnhilde. In 1900 Dvořák made some sketches for Pippich's libretto; they appear in his sketch book immediately before those for *Rusalka*, to which some are related in mood (Šourek 1916, iv, 100–4). But in the end it was Fibich's pupil Ostrčil who set Pippich's text, and the work finally reached the stage in 1904.

Pippich's libretto concerns the very end of the maidens' war. Vlasta alone has escaped the fury of the Přemysl's forces, and before being hunted down and killed she manages to cause the death of one male warrior and cause another to fall in love with her. The Šárka incident, on the other hand, is a separate, earlier episode in the maidens' war. In order to kill Ctirad, the bravest and most dangerous of the male warriors, Šárka has herself tied to a tree at a place in the forest where Ctirad will pass (see illustration 12). He discovers her and learns from her that she has been left by the women to die there. His pity is aroused, and then his love. Too late he realizes that this is an ambush: Šárka's horn brings on the rest of the women, hidden nearby. But Šárka has been caught in her own trap; she has fallen in love with Ctirad. In Zeyer's version (set by Janáček) Ctirad is killed there and then. In Schulzová's and Fibich's version, Ctirad is led off by the women and later Šárka helps the men rescue him, after which she remorsefully throws herself off a cliff. In Zeyer's *Šárka* she leaps instead on to Ctirad's funeral pyre.

In *Libuše* erotic love is confined to subsidiary characters (and Wenzig was blamed for allowing it even there). Any love between the central characters, Libuše and Přemysl, was magical or at any rate dynastic: unsullied, Libuše pursues an almost saint-like existence. While Škroup's *Libuše's Marriage* draws to a triumphant conclusion – reasonably enough – with Libuše's wedding celebrations, Smetana's *Libuše* closes with Libuše's prophecies of the nation's history and its glorious future. This *tableau vivant* is one of the most exciting parts of the opera and its chief *raison d'être*. In contrast, the most memorable part of both Fibich's and Janáček's *Šárka* is the central encounter between Ctirad and Šárka in which Šárka's conflicting feelings of love and revenge are depicted. It is this central erotic moment that seems to have appealed to both composers, a moment that quite overshadows the nationalist trappings of the original myth.

12  Šárka's trap for the brave Ctirad: cover illustration by Antonín König for the four-hand piano arrangement (published by Urbánek in 1880) of Smetana's tone poem 'Šárka'. Šárka is bound seductively to a tree, stripped of her armour, though a horn to summon her followers (preparing their ambush on the left) dangles from her waist. Ctirad and his band approach innocently on the right. A snake in the bottom right-hand corner provides a clue to Šárka's intentions.

# God and nature

## *Christianity*

Christianity came to the Moravians (and to the Czechs, who formed part of the Great Moravian Empire) from Byzantium through the mission of SS Cyril and Methodius. The eastern rite and Cyril's script did not, however, last long among the western Slavs. Rome, through its Bavarian episcopate, drew the Czech lands into its sphere of influence at the death of Methodius in 885, bringing with it Latin and the western rite. This early dislocation in denominational affiliation left no more trace than some interesting archaeological sites in southern Moravia and a romantic Pan-Slav hankering, demonstrated, for instance, by Janáček's Slavonic Mass, whose appealing title 'Glagolitic' refers to an early version of the cyrillic script.

Later changes went deeper. By the early seventeenth century Jan Hus's popular brand of Protestantism had been adopted by some nine-tenths of the Czechs. The enforced re-Catholicization under the Habsburgs reversed this so successfully that very few Czech-speakers – less than 2% – returned to Protestantism after Joseph II's Patent of Toleration in 1781.[4] Doctrinal differences, much more than their distinctive language, had set the Czech Hussites apart from their adversaries, and in the fifteenth century religious and national fervour had gone hand in hand. But in the next surge of national awareness, the Czech National Revival of the nineteenth century, the predominant if nominal religion of the Czechs – Catholicism – was also that of their adversaries. Denominational differences could not be the national rallying force that they assumed for the Czechs' neighbours, the fervently Catholic Poles. Religion consequently played little part in the Czech National Revival and religious reference was not as important a feature of Czech opera as it was in Italian and French nineteenth-century opera.[5]

Nevertheless Czech historical operas of the 1860s and 1870s in their employment of French grand opera clichés did not make an exception of those connected with the church. Sabina's libretto for Šebor, *The Templars in Moravia*, includes the Templars themselves and their resonant, quasi-religious rituals, and, in the very next scene, the heroine's flight to seek refuge in a nunnery. Set evocatively against a storm, this scene offered its composer the *embarras de richesses* of an offstage 'Ave Maria' (with organ accompaniment), the sudden arrival of the terrified heroine, the anxious response of the nuns, the ominous knocking and subsequent intrusion of her pursuers, the brave resistance of the nuns and the venerable mother, the desperate ringing of alarm bells, the agonized decision of the heroine to take the veil, and the final hymn of thanks of the nuns. Smetana's *The Brandenburgers in Bohemia*, again with a Sabina libretto, has nothing quite on this scale, but nevertheless included two 'prières' – in Act 1 set to an Andante religioso for three female soloists and chorus, and in Act 2, as a chorale, at first unaccompanied, for bass and chorus.

Two years later, in 1868, Krásnohorská's first libretto for Bendl compounded the debt to French grand opera. Set in Catholic Spain of the late fifteenth century, *Lejla* assembled a cast that included the Grand Inquisitor (just a year after Verdi's *Don Carlos*), monks and nuns. It ends with a scene outside a cloister, though here it is an offstage nuns' chorus (rather than the monks of its model, *Robert le diable*) that provides the background to the onstage action. Krásnohorská's next libretto for Bendl, *Břetislav*, included an abduction from a nunnery (with many of the same ingredients as the nunnery scene in *The Templars in Moravia*) and in the final act, set in Prague's St George's Cathedral, a 'Miserere mei Deus' intoned over Oldřich's coffin by a chorus of monks.

In fact most of Krásnohorská's librettos contain some form of religious reference.[6] Even Smetana, characterized by Plavec as 'certainly one of the least religious types in the whole world of music' (Plavec 1929, 135), and who after *The Brandenburgers in Bohemia* had not set any libretto with religious connotations,[7] was presented with them in his last two operas, to Krásnohorská librettos. *The Secret* has an offstage religious procession in Act 2 (Smetana seems to have grumbled about it (Očadlík 1940, 99) but nevertheless produced a convincing Marian hymn). In *The Devil's Wall* the hermit Beneš and his double, the devil Rarach, provide opportunities for quasi-ecclesiastical vocal stylizations as does the 'miracle' at the end – the destruction of the Devil's wall, celebrated by the ceremonial ringing of the monastery bells and an offstage hymn of thanksgiving.

Fibich, to whom Christianity was 'somewhat foreign' (Schulzová 1902, 19; Nejedlý 1911, 126, described him as a 'pagan of pantheistic character'), also found himself dealing with overtly Christian subject matter in a Krásnohorská libretto. In her *Blaník* the religious ingredients went deeper than the trappings of Romantic religious atmosphere beloved by French grand opera to the plot itself, which deals with the bitter religious division of the nation after the Battle of the White Mountain. The possibilities it offered are well exemplified by the poignant chorus 'The chalice is already taken down' ('Již kalich sňat'), sung soon after the opening of the opera by the Hussites as they see their symbol torn down from the Týn Church by the victorious Catholics. Fibich's next stage works, however, were all set to librettos far removed from opportunities for Christian reference, so that it comes as rather a shock that his last opera, *The Fall of Arkona*, deals with the confrontation of the German Christians and the Slavonic pagans, and that it is the conflict of religions rather than that of nations that is stressed. The opera ends with a maestoso Te Deum sung in unison by the full chorus celebrating the victory of the Christians.

Dvořák, as the only major Czech composer of this period to retain his faith and to write liturgical music into his maturity, might have been expected to view Christian reference in his operas with rather more favour, but his practice here is little different from Smetana's – i.e. rare, and dependent on his librettists. Thus the Angelus ending to Act 1 of his *King and Charcoal Burner* was added as late as the final version, when Novotný revised the text. *Armida*, dealing with the conflict of Christian crusaders and heathens, is naturally the richest in Christian reference among his operas, though not one that he seems to have written easily (Kvapil 1932, 232), and it is the heathens rather than the Christians who have the more memorable music. Otherwise the only Christian references in Dvořák's operas are in the two with librettos by Marie Červinková-Riegrová: the offstage hymn with onstage commentary which opens *The Jacobin* (set in a town square, with a church visible) and the Russian Orthodox figures of the Patriarch and his priests, which form an important faction of opinion in *Dimitrij*. The chant style of some of the choruses in *Dimitrij* provides the most distinctly Russian-sounding feature of the score.

An echo of Orthodox ceremony can be found in Janáček's last opera *From the House of the Dead*, where he introduced into the festivities of Act 2 a Russian priest, who blesses the prisoners before their meal (this passage was left in Russian), and the church-like bells which announce his entrance. For all Janáček's professed atheism there are more Christian references in his operas than in those of his compatriots, even the pious Foerster, who came from a strongly Catholic background and whose faith was an important part of his musical personality (Plavec 1929, 144ff). Foerster's first opera, *Debora*, is awash with Christian reference from the Good Friday hymn of the opening to the organ-accompanied offstage Resurrection hymn in Act 2 to the Angelus bells in Act 3. All this, however, comes from Mosenthal's play, which concerns Christian prejudice against Jewish refugees, or from the librettist's adaptation. In his next opera, *Eva*, which he adapted himself from Preissová's text, Foerster systematically omitted all references to Lutheranism, an important feature of the play since Eva's hopes for marriage with the married (and Catholic) Mánek depend on his becoming Lutheran too and being able thus to obtain a divorce. In contrast, Janáček particularly stressed the deep religious feelings of his Kát'a Kabanová. One of the great moments of the opera is in the scene where Kát'a tells Varvara of her vision in church: of angels, with the sun streaming down through the incense-filled cupola, while Janáček's music begins to evoke the sexual dreams that are plaguing her – a subtle statement of the thin line that divides religious from sexual ecstasy.

Janáček's next opera, *The Cunning Little Vixen*, is one of the few Czech operas to depict a priest on stage (and much more sympathetically than, for instance, the unappealing clerics in Foerster's *Debora* or Bendl's *Lejla*) while even in the contemporary, cosmopolitan *The Makropulos Affair*, Janáček made Čapek's offhand reference to the Lord's Prayer in Greek (Pater hemon) into a striking, twice-repeated and touching symbol of Emilia Marty's approaching end. Janáček's Jenůfa similarly repeats the Lord's Prayer (in Czech) to calm herself at the disappearance of her child, much in the same way that Kunka and Kedruta do when their menfolk have gone off to fight (*The Excursion of Mr Brouček to the Fifteenth Century*). *Jenůfa* is full of religious references, not least in the central figure of the Kostelnička, Jenůfa's foster-mother, and the stern arbiter of village mores. Her name indicates her office of sacristan, a female version (in a native Czech form) of the 'Sakristán' in *Brouček*. In Act 3 Christian blessings are given to the young couple before they go to the church to be married, first by the Grandmother and then by the Kostelnička, during which the dramatic news breaks out of the discovery of a child's corpse, Jenůfa's baby son murdered by the 'godly' Kostelnička.

In fact in all his operas from *Jenůfa* onwards except *Fate*, Janáček included Christian reference. Since he was his own librettist for all these operas (he had some outside help with *Brouček*) and could easily have expunged many of the references, their presence is even more arresting than the few in Smetana, Dvořák and Fibich, which go back directly to particular librettists. It is tempting to speculate that Janáček's monastery upbringing left more of a trace on his outlook than is generally accepted. It is also striking that Janáček's first two 'traditional' operas are his only ones, together with the experimental *Fate*, that lack Christian reference altogether, another confirmation of the absence of any national religious links in Czech nationalist opera. Where a link might have been expected, in the Hussite operas of Šebor and Bendl, these operas confined themselves to the military and nationalist elements of Hussite movement. Janáček's own Hussite opera, *The Excursion of Mr Brouček to the Fifteenth Century*, in contrast, includes many references to the religious nature of the movement, for instance in Kunka's warmly lyrical description of Jan z Rokycana's sermon, or in the doctrinal arguments that break out soon after.

### Pagan gods

No pagan gods actually appear in Czech opera. With the early conversion of Bohemia and Moravia to Christianity (more than a century before Poland and Russia), less trace remained there than anywhere else in the Slavonic world of its pagan, pre-Christian religion. Pyerun, the Slavonic god of thunder and lightning, was venerated by most Slavs (Prince Vladimir of Kiev cast an idol of Pyerun into the Dnieper on his conversion to Christianity in 988), but evidence of his cult in Bohemia and Moravia is scanty, and the Czech form of the name, Perun, is a nineteenth-century borrowing (Machek

1957). Thus the few references to him in *Libuše*, usually of a 'by Perun!' nature, are trivial, and intelligible only to those Czechs who had come across the name in literature, rather than from a shadowy folk memory. Svantovít, the chief god of the Polabian and Baltic Slavs, was similarly foreign to the Czechs, despite the helpful overlap of his name with Svatý Vít (St Vitus). His cult in Arkona, on the Baltic island of Rügen, was the most developed, or at any rate the best recorded, of any Slav god, and its destruction formed the subject of Fibich's last opera, *The Fall of Arkona*. Slav paganism was characterized here by Schulzová and Fibich as alien and unsympathetic: its chief priest Dargun is the chief villain of the opera.

The only other Slav god with a claim to a wide distribution was the sky god Svarog. Anežka Schulzová, who wrote the libretto for *The Fall of Arkona*, provided an extensive invocation to 'Svaroh' in the first act of *Šárka*, but the vagueness of the attributes she ascribes to him only emphasizes that she, better educated and more widely read than many Czechs of her time, had no knowledge of him apart from what she had gleaned from Erben and from Máchal's *Outline of Slav Mythology* (*Nákres slovanského bájesloví*, 1891; see Pala 1953, 32). Other Czech writers ignored him altogether. Curiously, a version of the name does seem to have survived in popular vocabulary, if it is accepted that by a taboo-exchange (a substitute for a taboo word), it became *raroh* (a type of falcon), corrupted to *rarah* (a devil). The word *raroh* casts long shadows back to Indo-Iranian mythology (whose concepts and vocabulary influenced Slav mythology), in particular to the falcon form used by the ancient Iranian god Vrthragna. As *rarach* and its diminutive *rarášek* (e.g. in Stroupežnický's comedy *Zvíkovský rarášek – The Imp of Zvíkov*, made into an opera by Vítězslav Novák) and other regional forms the word has a venerable folk history, with virtually all of its mythological meaning shorn off, leaving only the concept of a devil or demon (Jakobson 1949, 1026; Machek 1957, 508–9). Krásnohorská's Rarach in *The Devil's Wall* is essentially a devil, and her original prose synopsis called him that – *čert* (Očadlík 1940, 133ff). Unlike Schulzová's 'Svaroh', his accomplishments are specific, for instance his ability to change shape, usually to that of the hermit Beneš (on which many of the comic complications of the plot depend), but also to that of an old shepherd, conjuring up visions to confuse the weary Jarek, or, at the end of the opera, to his full satanic majesty to summon up monsters to dam the Vltava. Smetana responded to Krásnohorská's Rarach not only with the celebrated pantomime-melodrama laugh (Chapter 6, Ex. 3) – this was, after all, intended to be a comic opera – but also with a full-blooded, augmented-chord Lisztian musical demonism, for instance in the Mephisto waltz of the dam building.[8]

While Smetana and his librettist could count on the audience's familiarity with the Czech *rarach*, the responsorial chorus addressed to his elevated ancestor 'Svaroh' in Fibich's *Šárka* Act 1 would have been as exotic to Czech audiences as the Egyptian priests and their rituals in *Aida* were to the Italians. All in all, references in Czech opera to pre-Christian Slav mythology are few. Significantly the most varied collection occurs in an opera whose libretto is not Czech but Polish in origin, Dvořák's *Vanda*. Not only Perun and Svantovít are invoked, but also Černoboh, depicted here as the primitive god of evil his name suggests (*černý* = black; *bůh* = god). However, as Máchal pointed out (1891, 36–7), the etymology of the word suggests a more recent, possibly folk, origin.

### Folk mythology

It has been suggested (Larousse 1959, 303) that there were in fact two Slav mythologies, a heroic mythology of war gods (Pyerun, Svarog, Svantovít) that served the leaders and possibly the townsfolk, and an informal regional mythology preserved in the fairy tales and superstitions of the rural population, by far the greater proportion of the people. While the 'official' war gods disappeared with the conversion of the establishment to Christianity, the folk gods who inhabited the lakes and the woods, the homes and the farms, proved far more durable. Many folk beliefs managed to co-exist with Christianity or were reinterpreted by the Catholic clergy (often of peasant origin themselves) and survived in local superstitions into this century (see Germer 1984). If Czech opera librettists and composers sought a supernatural sphere with rich and suggestive associations for Czech audiences, they found it less in Christianity or in the pre-Christian war gods than in this humbler folk mythology of the Czech countryside. And while the Czech townsman may have forgotten these myths and folktales, they were revived for him, in the decades preceding the flowering of Czech opera, by the localized supernatural elements of the fairy-tale (*báchorka*) plays of Klicpera and Tyl and in the writings of K.J. Erben and Božena Němcová.

It should be stressed, however, that Erben, Němcová and others in the folktale movement that began in Bohemia of the 1830s under the influence of Herder and the Grimm brothers created a new literature rather than providing authentic documentation of raw folk material (Tille 1909, 159–61). Němcová's popular *Folk Tales and Legends* (*Národní báchorky and pověsti*, 1845–6, 1854–5) were based to some extent on local tales which she recorded herself, but Erben's collection of *One Hundred Slavonic Folk Tales and Legends in Original Dialects* (*Sto prostonárodních pohádek a pověstí slovanských v nářečích původních*, 1865) were simply his own prose stylizations of foreign material. Erben's best-known work, *A Garland of National Tales* (*Kytice z pověstí národních*), has rather different origins. Written over a couple of decades and published as a collection of twelve ballads only in 1853, it was not so much an attempt to imitate folk poetry as to create a new Czech poetry, but in a national style: art poetry rather than the folk poetry of which Erben had an unrivalled knowledge (see pp. 209–10). In many cases his ballads owe just as much to other Slavonic literature, such as the ballads of the Polish poet Juliusz Słowacki (Dolanský 1970, 109–11 and *passim*). Erben's ballads – some of the most perfect and evocative examples of their type – became familiar to every Czech through innumerable editions and through the paintings and the musical settings they inspired. Dvořák alone set one (*The Wedding Shift – Svatební košile*) as an oratorio and based tone poems on four others.

The world depicted in Erben's *Garland*, in particular its wrathful supernatural beings ready to take a terrible revenge on mortals who tangle with them, became so much part of Czech national consciousness that when writing his libretto to *Rusalka* Jaroslav Kvapil sought to transform his principal source, Friedrich de la Motte Fouqué's *Undine* (1811), largely through reference to Erben's world.

There is much of the Czech folk element in my fairy tale and in the spirit and form I have tried to follow the unsurpassable example set by our ballads. My fairy tale is much closer to Erben, to his *Lily* [*Lilie*], his *Water Gnome* [*Vodník*] and *The Golden Spinning Wheel* [*Zlatý kolovrat*; all from Erben's *Garland* – Dvořák based tone poems on the last two] than to many foreign models. It is perhaps this very characteristic of my work that led that great master of the arts, Dvořák, to choose it.                    (Kvapil 1901, 8)

Kvapil's libretto begins by the edge of a lake. This allows him the following cast list: the three Wood Sprites (the first voices heard in the opera), the Water Gnome (Vodník) who, Alberich-like, tries to catch them, and the Water Nymph (Rusalka), who with the aid of the Witch Ježibaba acquires her human soul. Human characters in the form of the Prince, with whom Rusalka has fallen in love, and his retinue appear only towards the end of the act. In the second act Rusalka is unhappy and unsuccessful as a human; in the third act she is back in the water.

Kvapil's departures from *Undine* are at once evident when his libretto is compared with those of the German operas that were also made from Fouqué's tale, the settings of *Undine* by Hoffmann (1816) and Lortzing (1845). Despite its supernatural core, the story in these works is seen entirely through human eyes and human reactions to its central non-human character. Undine is first encountered with her human foster-parents, not, like Rusalka, in her original watery environment. Undine's uncle Kühleborn, a river sprite capable of creating floods and storms, appears in the German operas in the human disguise in which he watches over her, unlike Kvapil's Water Gnome, who is confined to the water and needs a handy pond to find his way into the otherwise 'human' Act 2 of Kvapil's libretto. Even the Undine–Rusalka figure is different. Fouqué's Undine, and in turn Hoffmann's and Lortzing's, is a skittish child, whose supernatural dimension is suggested by her mercurial changes of mood. In contrast, Rusalka is a suffering Slavonic heroine, in this sense nearer the Rusalka of Dargomyzhsky's opera (1856, given at Prague's National Theatre in 1889). Based on Pushkin's unfinished poetic drama, and before that on Russian folk legends, Dargomyzhsky's Rusalka is a human girl who becomes a water nymph when she drowns herself, betrayed by her aristocratic lover.

Kvapil's Czech equivalent of the fierce Kühleborn was a figure immortalized by Erben's ballad *The Water Gnome* (*Vodník*), which Dvořák had already set as a tone poem in 1896 and Fibich before him in 1883 as a melodrama. Erben's Water Gnome, based more on Lusatian Sorb and Slovenian sources than on Czech ones (Dolanský 1970, 248), is violent and sadistic, revenging himself upon his human wife by decapitating their child and flinging its body against her mother's house where she has taken refuge. Kvapil's gentle, pessimistic creature, full of concern for Rusalka, could hardly be more different. Kvapil's version is in fact nearer the folk perceptions of water gnomes recorded in Bohemia by the Grimm brothers (e.g. *Deutsche Sagen*, no. 52) or by Slavia, the Czech folktale collection circle (Dvořák 1984, 262–71). While water gnomes were best avoided (the origin of the figure is probably a type of cautionary tale to prevent children going near dangerous pools – see Ward 1981, i, 334), there are stories of them seen in a more friendly light, fraternizing with the local populace, securing and rewarding the services of human midwives and godparents, and wooing – rather than seizing, as in Erben – human girls. Unlike Kvapil's figure, Czech folk water gnomes could walk on land and were virtually indistinguishable from humans but were given away by a continual drip from the left coat-tail.

Kvapil's witch, however, with no counterpart in Fouqué, seems just as malevolent as Erben's *Noon Witch* (*Polednice*), although, as Kvapil explained in his preface to the libretto, she also owed something both to Andersen and to Gerhard Hauptmann (including her name – the Czech translation of the witch in *Die versunkene Glocke* calls her 'Ježibaba'). She is in fact a land version of Andersen's Sea Witch. Ježibaba gives Rusalka her 'land legs' just as the Sea Witch gives the Little Mermaid a potion to transform her tail into legs. And the price is the same: the Sea Witch asks for the Little Mermaid's beautiful voice and accordingly cuts out her tongue; Rusalka is similarly mute in her dealings with humans. Fouqué's Undine has not had to make any bargain of this kind, and explains her origins very lucidly to her baffled Prince. However, the end is much the same. Undine and Rusalka are rejected by their respective princes, who ultimately pay for their unfaithfulness with their lives. Only the Little Mermaid cannot bring herself to kill her Prince, but is nevertheless given a second chance, this time as an air spirit.

The effect of the folk periphery with which Kvapil transformed Fouqué's *Undine* is particularly noticeable when compared with Rozkošný's earlier *St John's Rapids*, which has some similar elements, notably the 'Vltavka' (the

Vltava sprite) who charms the hero when rejected by his human sweetheart and who, when later rejected by him, takes her revenge on the pair. But for all the localized connections with the Czech river Vltava (many of them reinterpreted in Smetana's famous tone poem – see Srba 1985, 73fn) the work is much nearer the German Undine operas in spirit. This is hardly surprising. The opera's librettist, Eduard Rüffer, was German; furthermore, earlier appearances of the Vltava sprite on the Czech stage in the guise of *The Water Sprite from the Vltava* (*Vodní žínka z Vltavy*) were in fact translations (in 1804 and 1847) of Kauer's Singspiel *Das Donauweibchen* (Laiske 1974, nos. 488, 497, 1617).

Many pagan beliefs were absorbed into Christianity in localized conceptions of the 'devil'. While Krásnohorská's Rarach in *The Devil's Wall*, despite his name, owes more to her than to folk sources, Czech folk traditions are responsible for much of the appearance (in hunting gear) and character of Marbuel in *The Devil and Kate* (Wenig's libretto is based on one of Němcová's folktales). Even the devil in Ostrčil's *Johnny's Kingdom*, despite the Russian origins of the plot, owes much to Czech folktales.

Folk legends and superstitions also lie behind the mummery figures of St Nicholas, an angel and a devil in Sabina's libretto for Rozkošný's *Mikuláš* and provide the basis for the plot of *In the Well*. Here Sabina made use of the popular folk belief (not of course confined to Bohemia) of a girl being able, through sorcery at specified times of year, to conjure up her future bridegroom. The Grimms' *Deutsche Sagen* (nos. 115–17) offer several examples, on the eves of St Andreas, St Thomas, Christmas and the New Year. A similar incident is recorded in Němcová's *The Grandmother* on St John's Eve, a time of particular folk celebration in Bohemia, for it coincided both with the ancient Slav Kupala festival and the summer solstice. When he set his libretto for *In the Well* at this time Sabina was thus drawing on a particularly rich source of folk custom. The season also allowed him the outside setting of the opera (the girl has to see her lover's face in the well) and for its comic complication: the heroine's unwanted suitor, overhearing talk of this myth, decides to advance his chances by climbing the tree overhanging the well so that his reflection can be seen in the water – but since he is too heavy for the branch his reflection is soon joined by his ungainly form.

The same legend, but with a tragic outcome, had been popularized by Erben in his *Garland*. Here it takes place on Christmas Eve, which as Erben himself pointed out (Dolanský 1970, 160), allowed it to draw on the Christmas Eve customs of the Slavs in general, and in particular those of Russians, Poles and Serbs. Erben's *Christmas Eve* (*Štědrý den*) was set several times by Czech composers, most magically by Fibich as a melodrama in 1875.

## Nature

The natural habitat of the folk gods – the woods, rivers and lakes – became by association the object of a mystic, pantheistic reverence which was to find expression in Czech music of the twentieth century, by Suk and Novák for instance, and especially in Janáček's *Glagolitic Mass* ('Everywhere the scent of the damp forests of Luhačovice – that was my incense. My cathedral grew in the giant size of the mountains and the misty distances of the vaulted sky. . .'; Janáček 1958, 60). Whether the number of Czech forest plays (many by Klicpera) and Czech forest operas stem from this source is more difficult to say. Awareness of nature was not a purely Czech phenomenon in the nineteenth century, and the forest setting of operas with attendant hunters' choruses and horn calls must have been influenced by neighbouring German culture. Nevertheless Czech treatment of the genre was enthusiastic and distinctive. It was the nocturnal forest scene at the beginning of Act 2 of *The Kiss* that first attracted Smetana's attention to the libretto (Bartoš 1939, 138) and he responded with the Smugglers' Chorus which, potentially comic, is instead magical and mysterious in the atmosphere it evokes. It is against this nocturnal world of the forest that the deepening drama of Lukáš's and Vendulka's relationship is enacted. Both escape to the forest from each other and from themselves; both find themselves, and each other, in the forest. As in *A Midsummer Night's Dream*, the forest acts both as metaphor and as physical surroundings.

Janáček's *Šárka*, uncomfortable in its first-act trappings of Czech mythology, finds an authentic voice only in Act 2, set in the deep forest in which Šárka seduces Ctirad. Fibich, himself the son of a forester, had much the same response in his own opera on the same topic. Towards the end of his life Janáček was to write an even more personal forest opera, *The Cunning Little Vixen*. The changing seasons of the forest, its different aspects at different times of day and the stirring of life within it drew from the composer one of his most magical scores and one that climaxes in the great pantheistic affirmation of the Gamekeeper's final monologue.

Dvořák's first Czech opera, *King and Charcoal Burner*, opens 'in a clearing in the deep forest' (the Křivoklátsko forest, the largest in the interior of Bohemia). According to its first stage direction, 'horns resound from the forest, summoning the hunters. Groups of the king's hunting retinue suddenly converge.' Dvořák responded with an evocative orchestral introduction based on open fifths, offstage horn calls and colourful pedal-harmony effects. Similar devices portray the two hunters in Dvořák's *The Cunning Peasant*. Twenty years later much the same harmonic effects, again with offstage horns, accompany the arrival of the Prince in *Rusalka* (he is hunting in the forest), but the unsophisticated hunting choruses of *The Cunning Peasant* give way to a single offstage and mostly unaccompanied hunter, whose contribution owes more to *Tristan*'s Sailor than to the robust hunting choruses of *Der Freischütz*. A final echo of this tradition can be found in the exuberant fanfares for four horns that Janáček inserted in *The Cunning Little Vixen* between the second inn scene and the Gamekeeper's return to the forest.

Whatever these hunting scenes owe to German models, the extensive use of the horn to evoke such scenes is an apt feature for Czech opera since the development of the functional hunting horn into the orchestral 'french' horn owes much to Count Sporck, who introduced the *cor-de-chasse* to Bohemia, and to the schools of Bohemian horn players who took up the instrument (Fitzpatrick 1970, esp. 9–25). Significantly, the first great German forest opera, *Der Freischütz*, is set on Bohemian rather than German soil. The heavily forested border region between Bohemia and Germany provided the settings for Smetana's *The Kiss* and *The Secret*. Smetana and his librettist were unconsciously avoiding German tradition by allowing into these two operas only one forester/hunter – Kalina's son Vít, though his occupation, apart from a reference in Blaženka's Act 2 aria, passes virtually unnoticed.

Czech nationalist opera had good reason to avoid hunters since their aristocratic associations were inappropriate to the more democratic world that most Czech opera was trying to evoke. The conservative Dvořák seemed the most attracted to them, but even his hunting Prince (in *Rusalka*) and King (in *King and Charcoal Burner*) are essentially fairy-tale characters, and the appearance of other characters in hunting outfits – Marbuel in *The Devil and Kate* or Ladislav in *The Two Widows* – seems to be intended satirically, deliberately avoiding the patriotic–sentimental resonances of hunters in much German opera. Even the humbler occupation of the forester or gamekeeper is treated as comic material in Czech opera. The tradition starts with the garrulous and self-important Mumlal in *The Two Widows* (which would give it a French origin: Labaraque, the corresponding figure in Mallefille's play, was also a 'garde-chasse'), and continues into the final decade of the century with Mudroch (*The Beginning of a Romance*) and the Gamekeeper in *Rusalka*. The only forester in Czech opera whose occupation emerges clearly and who is essentially a serious character is Janáček's Gamekeeper in *The Cunning Little Vixen*. While his presence is a localizing device, as in many German Romantic operas, he is also much more than a figure of local colour. Janáček aptly used his Gamekeeper as an example of a human who learns, during the course of the work, to be in tune with nature; and it is into the Gamekeeper's wise mouth that Janáček inserts some of the more general philosophical reflections from Těsnohlídek's novel.

Here, as in most Czech opera, the forest and its supernatural periphery is essentially friendly, unlike in German opera where a darker side is also evident, as in the Wolf's Glen scene of *Der Freischütz*, which initiated a whole genre of German operatic *Schauerromantik*. Several nature scenes in Czech opera are particularly exultant. The great C-major sunrise that introduces the final scene of *The Kiss*, and Barče's ecstatic song soon after, in which she greets the new dawn, prophesies in its mood the chasing away of the shadows that threaten Lukáš's and Vendulka's happiness. Shadows are chased away even more literally at the end of *The Devil's Wall*:

> With his staff Beneš makes the sign of the cross in the air. The wall crumbles with a roar, Rarach and his monsters flee, the sky becomes clear, the waters recede and return to their river bed, and a beautiful morning dawns. A rosy sky. Bells toll joyfully from the monastery.

And once again Smetana's music attempts to depict not just the natural phenomena described in the stage directions, but also, for instance in the rapt five-part ensemble (Andante amoroso and espressivo), the hushed inner joy that breaks out in the closing pages of this opera.

# Society

## *Range*

Unlike Poland or Hungary, which had native aristocracies but little in the way of a middle class, the Czech lands by the nineteenth century had few native aristocrats but an increasingly prosperous Czech middle class and Czech proletariat. Perhaps it is for this reason that most of the aristocrats depicted in Czech opera are either foreign or historical, appearing primarily in operas based on cosmopolitan subjects such as *Armida* or *The Bride of Messina*, or on the dynastic subjects described above. Those few Czech operas based chiefly on courtly amorous intrigue in 'medieval' times, from Fibich's early *Bukovín* to Kovařovic's *The Bridegrooms* and Novák's *Karlštejn*, have seldom sustained a permanent place in the repertory, perhaps because such events and such people were of little interest to their audiences or even to their composers. Smetana came nearest to this sort of formula in *The Devil's Wall*, but even here the aristocratic characters make up only half the cast and there are other important elements in the work.

While no durable Czech operas have casts exclusively made of aristocrats, several Czech operas exist with casts of villagers, something that reached the mainstream of European opera only with the *verismo* movement in the 1890s. The most famous example in Czech opera, *The Bartered Bride*, is slightly flawed in this respect in that in Act 3 there is the intrusion of the circus, but Sabina's village libretto for Blodek, his very popular *In the Well*, has a cast only of countryfolk, as does his village libretto for Rozkošný, *Mikuláš*. The cast of *The Stubborn Lovers* is similarly made up only of countryfolk. Smetana's *The Kiss* depicts the inhabitants of a village in the Krkonoš mountains.

The action of most of these operas hinges entirely on comic intrigue within the enclosed society, but some operas provide a fuller picture of the society itself, its occupations and hierarchies. *The Bartered Bride*, for instance, carefully distinguishes between two farmer fathers: Krušina, the father of Mařenka, is a *sedlák* (a common word for a farmer); Mícha, the father of Vašek and, as it turns out, of Jeník, is a *gruntovník* (the owner of a *grunt*, a plot of land, i.e. a smallholder) and in debt to Krušina. Several decades later another village opera, Janáček's *Jenůfa*, went much further in this respect. As in most Czech village operas, there are songs and dances, but here they are limited to 'realistic' contexts, namely ceremonies associated with recruiting and with weddings. The social hierarchies and tensions within the Burjovka mill form an important part of the action; subtle distinctions of property ownership are made particularly precise. Grandmother Burjovka is not only housekeeper at the mill but also a *výminkářka*, which means, in her case, that she has legally made over the mill she once owned to Števa, her favourite grandson, on condition that she receives food and accommodation there. Her status is roughly that of a pensioner. Village characters depicted in the opera include the 'sacristan' (*kostelnička*), the mayor and his snobbish family, a shepherd boy and a cow-woman.

This sort of social detail, but in a small-town context, can be found in Smetana's opera *The Secret*. There is a chorus of threshers, bricklayers and councillors as well as 'neighbours and boys and girls'; the soloists, apart from the rival councillors Malina and Kalina, include a forester, a ballad singer, a bell-ringer, a publican, and a master builder. All except the forester are seen engaging in their occupations, for instance in the genre scenes at the openings of the outer acts. There is also an old soldier, Bonifác, who (like the Grandmother Burjovka), has right of abode in his former house, now made over to Kalina. *The Jacobin* similarly has a number of small-town functionaries in its cast, and a chorus that includes musicians, schoolchildren, soldiers and countryfolk. But where this opera differs from those mentioned so far is that it also has representatives of the local aristocracy, Count Vilém z Harasova, his son Bohuš, and Adolf his nephew.

*Class tensions*

There is no attempt in *The Jacobin* at a critical examination of the relationship between the classes. The Count is greeted enthusiastically on his arrival in Act 1, and is serenaded with dances and a specially composed cantata at the end of the opera. There is no suggestion that the people do not approve of him or grudge him his place in society. If the Count's nephew Adolf is disliked it is because he behaves badly, not because of his class.

In his first Czech opera, *King and Charcoal Burner*, Dvořák set a text which, as its title suggests, is primarily concerned with the relationship between a king and one of his most humble subjects, a charcoal burner. But the relationship is shown as idyllic: a wise, magnanimous king and his kindly subject, brought together by chance, find that they have much in common. Their common name Matěj provides a symbol for the bond between them. Dvořák's *The Cunning Peasant* is no more critical, despite the fact that here the leading aristocrat is shown to be a worthless philanderer, wishing to take advantage of a pretty village girl. His defeat is engendered by the principal women in the cast, who, rich and poor, band together against him; the same sex is a greater bond than class-difference a barrier.

In these three operas, *King and Charcoal Burner*, *The Cunning Peasant* and *The Jacobin*, Dvořák chose texts by three different librettists and found the same ingredients in all: a full range of society, with friendly relations between the classes and all reconciled to their place in it. Even in *The Devil and Kate*, where the aristocracy is shown to be corrupt, wicked and exploitative, the iniquities are naively put right by the sudden decision of the Princess (urged on by the shepherd Jirka) to abolish the *robota* (forced labour). It is true that Dvořák's Princess does not come across particularly warmly, possibly because of the dull aria she is allotted on her belated first appearance in Act 3, and it is equally true that in *The Jacobin* Count Vilém and his nephew are two of the least memorable characters in the opera. But the philandering Prince in *The Cunning Peasant* receives one of Dvořák's most affecting numbers, his aria in Act 1. No one singing such a piece, with its ravishing middle section, could be anything other than sympathetic. With rather more justification King Matěj in *King and Charcoal Burner* similarly emerges as a highly attractive character, with one of the finest lyrical numbers in the work, the aria towards the end where he recalls his dead daughter.

It would not be unreasonable to distil a political philosophy from this: Dvořák seems not to have noticed social tensions, and treated his aristocrats as sympathetically as his peasants. It is not possible to trace such a consistent view through Smetana's operas. His political outlook, clear enough from his diaries (Nejedlý 1980, 175–8), is hardly reflected in the strange bunch of librettos that he took on. His passivity in the choice of subjects (see Chapter 4) resulted in his setting, all seemingly with equal relish, dynastic operas by an oldfashioned patriot, a bourgeois comedy, and Krásnohorská's small-scale observations of town or village life. His only librettist with a political stance similar to his own was Sabina, and it was through this connection that at the beginning of his career Smetana set one of the most revolutionary (in terms of class struggle) of all Czech nineteenth-century librettos, *The Brandenburgers in Bohemia*.

The Czech society Sabina depicted excludes aristocracy, has several representatives of the middle class (including a knight and a mayor) and quite exceptionally includes an urban proletariat, exemplified by Jíra and the 'rabble' (*luza*). During a lull in its looting of Prague the mob sings

> Nechtěli nám ve dne dáti,
> oč jsme snažně žádali,
> přišli jsme si proto v noci,
> sami jsme si nabrali.
> Nejsme více chudina!
> Přišla naše hodina!
> Žebráků už v Praze není,
> jsme si rovní, chlap i pán!

(Since you wouldn't give us what we begged for during the day, we have come for it at night and taken it ourselves. We're poor no longer, our hour has come! There are no more beggars in Prague; we're all equal, man and master!)

The compassionate side of the mob is also shown. When Ludiše and her sisters run in, seeking protection from Jan Tausendmark, a Prague burgher, the people agree to help them, only to be told by their realistic leader Jíra that they are powerless without weapons. However, by a ruse Jíra manages to take possession of Tausendmark's sword. It is at this moment that Ludiše's father enters with his retinue. Tausendmark accuses Jíra of abducting Ludiše and her sisters and despite his protests Jíra is led off for trial. Middle-class justice has believed one of its own, and not the 'vagabond' Jíra. When he attempts to defend himself at his trial Jíra claims bitterly:

> A Tausendmark, můj žalobník,
> z proklatého cizinců rodu,
> jest jeden z vás!
> Že však má peněz, protož právo
> a celé soudstvo při něm stůj!

(And Tausendmark, my accuser, from the accursed family of foreigners, is one of you! But he has money, and therefore rights, so let all the judges stand by him.)

When Tausendmark's crimes emerge in Act 3, Jíra's name is cleared and the whole company beg him to join them; he refuses, saying that he does not belong with them. Finally Ludiše's father, Volfram, enters and, also acknowledging Jíra's innocence, offers him his hand.

It is a fascinating question how much Jíra was intended by Sabina, the most politically radical of any Czech librettist, to serve as a representative of the Czech proletariat of the 1860s, and how much the clearing away of misunderstandings and the offering of a hand of friendship encoded a message from the Czech middle classes to the Czech proletariat. Whatever Sabina may have intended here, Smetana's response to Jíra and the rabble is a good deal milder than Sabina's words. The 'revolutionary' scene in the town square has nothing of the fervour of the virtually contemporary revolutionary scene in Musorgsky's *Boris*. Much of it in fact sounds rather jolly, so much so that Smetana was able to transfer the dance music from this scene to the circus scene in *The Bartered Bride* at some of its early performances until he wrote new music for it.

Erben's tart comments in his Harrach report on the mob scene of *The Brandenburgers in Bohemia* ('delightful company of communists of the basest sort') did not prevent his considering it the most successful passage in the piece ('clearly written *con amore*'; Daněk 1983, 153–4). Even so this sort of motif quite disappeared from Sabina's later librettos. His libretto for Bendl's *The Elderly Suitor*, for instance, contains a fleeting reference to the *robota* (forced labour) in a comic context (Mr Franc's entrance aria). For a darker view of the *robota* one has to wait for operas based on Jirásek's historical novels, for instance Kovařovic's *The Dogheads* or Novák's *The Lantern*.

Despite evidence of social concerns in the non-operatic works he wrote in the early years of this century, Janáček seems in his operas to have been more interested in character than in class. In adapting Ostrovsky's play *The Thunderstorm* into *Kát'a Kabanová* or Čapek's *The Makropulos Affair*, Janáček carefully suppressed much of these plays' social criticism in order to throw even more weight on his central heroines. Like Smetana's, most of his operas are limited to a single layer of society, whether rural (*Jenůfa*, *Vixen*) or bourgeois (*Brouček*'s earth scenes, *Fate*). The early and uncharacteristic *The Beginning of a Romance* is an exception and follows the Dvořák pattern. The emerging romance is between Baron Adolf and a village maiden, an affair cut short when the girl's father begins to hint at marriage. Instead of a work of social criticism that these ingredients might suggest, the girl is quickly paired up once more with her humble village swain and the opera ends, very cheerfully, with an ensemble in which everyone professes satisfaction with his station. Any touch of irony that the original short story by Preissová possessed has been squeezed out by the librettist.

The only opera Janáček set with a large range of class among its characters is *From the House of the Dead*, where Petrovič, even before he arrives, is branded as gentry by the other prisoners. It is a form of class tension that brings Act 2 to its powerful close, with the Tall Prisoner's envy of Petrovič and his tea-drinking erupting into violence. But this opera, with its male cast, inhabits a region quite different from the Czech nineteenth-century tradition and, with its social concerns, belongs instead to the twentieth century. Only a few years earlier Janáček set a similar class 'incident' satirically: the eviction of the Badger by the Vixen with approving help from the animal riffraff. Similarly the Vixen's 'political' speech to the hens has little hope, through its deliberately absurd context and Janáček's delicious exaggeration of the vocal rhetoric, of being taken at face value.

While large-scale social tension is absent from most nineteenth-century Czech operas, there is plenty of evidence of social climbing, usually by ambitious parents promoting their daughters' interests (e.g. in *The Bartered Bride*, Michálek in *The Devil's Wall*, Jurásek in *The Beginning of a Romance*, Benda in *The Jacobin*, or the fathers in *King and Charcoal Burner*, *The Stubborn Lovers*, and *Debora*). Some of these are gently humorous, such as Michálek's aria in which he imagines Vok, 'the king's chief marshal', as his son-in-law. In other cases poverty is shown as much more ominous, sowing the seeds of tragedy, as it nearly does in *The Secret*, or as it does in fact in *Eva*, where by ensuring that her son will not marry the poor seamstress Eva, Mešjanovka sets up the course of events that leads to Eva's suicide. Similarly in *Fate*, the impoverished composer Živný has been rejected as a suitor for her daughter by Míla's mother before the opera opens. When he begins living with Míla, her mother lapses into madness and dies violently.

*Foreigners*

If aristocrats were lacking from many Czech operas because there were few native Czech aristocrats by the nineteenth century, this is not true of another lacuna in the casts of Czech nineteenth-century opera librettos: foreigners. Unlike French grand opera, with its double choruses of warring peoples, or Russian opera, which disparagingly and with evident relish depicted its Polish enemies, Czech opera shied away from showing conflict with other nations. A comparison with Russian opera is of course misleading, since the Russians were an independent nation, while the Czechs were still subjects of an Austrian Empire, with censorship regulations that specifically forbade the depiction of conflict between nations. In *The Brandenburgers in Bohemia*, for instance, the sorrowing Czech masses are characterized as a strong vocal force, but not, however, their German oppressors. The only singing Brandenburger is their captain, Varneman, whose music – 'quasi marcia' with a ubiquitous dotted figure supplemented by the occasional jaunty trill (Ex. 1), makes him out to be not so much a German, or a villain, but a military man: he is simply carrying out orders. The real villain – and again Smetana's music tells us what to think of him (see Chapter 6, Ex. 1) – is the Prague townsman Jan Tausendmark, who sides with the Germans for his own ends.

That Sabina's and Smetana's thrust is not against foreigners so much as against traitors is a theme taken up in another patriotic opera written almost sixty years later – *The Excursion of Mr Brouček to the Fifteenth Century*. Brouček is taken entirely on trust by the upright Domšík and his family, but when it is discovered that he has not taken part in the fighting against the invaders he is thrown into a barrel to be burned. Janáček's response to this incident, on which hinges the question whether this second excursion should be taken as a satire like the first, or at its face value, was stern and violent. The music that he supplied as the Hussites demand vengeance on

Ex. 1

Varneman: Stand! Not a step further! [*The Brandenburgers in Bohemia*, 2.2.213–9]

Brouček is some of his most powerful. Confirmation of the music's message can be found in Janáček's savage words in his *Lidové noviny* article on the opera (see below), where he demands that the Czechs should eradicate the Broučeks in their midst.

For all the anti-Austrian gestures in his earlier life (not patronizing the German opera in Brno, not travelling on 'German' trams), Janáček's response to Germans in his later operas was surprisingly sympathetic and approving. There is the brief but poignant phrase, full of *Tristan*esque yearning, when Emilia Marty remembers her German reincarnation as 'Else Müller' (Ex. 2); while Skuratov's beloved Lujza, as becomes evident in

Ex. 2

Marty: . . . and Else Müller. [L. Janáček, *The Makropulos Affair*, 3 VS 163; C 1966 by Universal Edition AG, Wien]

his Act 2 monologue in *From the House of the Dead*, was a German (i.e. Luise); and no one in the opera, except for the much-wronged Akulina in Šiškov's story, has warmer or more poignant music than that with which Skuratov describes their affair.

If any foreign antipathy is lurking in Czech opera, it is not against their oppressors, the German-speaking Austrians, or invaders like the Brandenburgers, but against a neighbouring Slav nation, the Poles. The most blatant example is of course *Dimitrij*, where the Poles have exactly the same role as in several Russian operas, and Dvořák responded similarly with trivializing mazurka rhythms, and with edgy coloratura for their chief representative, the Polish princess Marina. Though her nationality is not specified, one suspects that Dvořák's 'Foreign Princess' in *Rusalka* was Polish, judging by her vocal resemblance to the Polish Marina; while the polonaise rhythms and the harsh glitter of the Prince's court also suggest that it may have been Polish. The aristocrats in another late Dvořák opera *The Devil and Kate* could well be Polish too, judging from the similarity of their court music. If Dvořák succeeds musically in making them unsympathetic, it seems it was because he made them Polish.

## The musician and the teacher

'What Czech does not love music?' says Beneš the jailer, when he grants Dalibor's request and sends him a violin. One of the features which distinguishes Smetana's opera from its well-known model, *Fidelio*, is the prisoner's love of music.[9] Moreover Milada, the Leonore figure who dresses up as a boy to gain access to Dalibor, gains her entrée into the castle as a singer (*lyrník* – the libretto specified a harp-player). The latter detail was Wenzig's contribution; but the sounds of Dalibor whiling away his time in prison on the violin (a couple of centuries before its invention) is one of the more durable elements of the Dalibor legend.[10]

Dalibor the violinist embodies one of the most potent of all Czech nationalist myths: the notion of the musicality of the Czechs and the achievements of their musicians. Unlike many other national myths this one had solid grounding in reality, from the international standing of the many Czech professional musicians forced to earn their living abroad to the traditions of the humble village schoolmasters who kept Czech culture and music alive in the darkest years of Austrian oppression. Foreign accounts of the widespread musical education among the Czechs and their love of music range from Burney's business-like reporting (in his *Present State of Music in Germany. . .*, 1775) of the role of music in Czech schools to Wagner's Hoffmannesque novella, *Eine Pilgerfahrt zu Beethoven* (1840). One of its most charming passages describes how on his pilgrimage to Vienna, Wagner's hero encounters a group of wandering Bohemian musicians who, for their own pleasure, give an open-air performance of Beethoven's Septet. In the nineteenth century the Czechs themselves zealously cultivated this image. Musicians became favourite figures on the Czech stage in the first part of the century, their presence an important localizing device (*DČD*, ii, 225–6; 79, 95). Tyl's play *Fidlovačka* (1834, with music by Škroup) included not only a couple of ballad singers in his portrayal of the 'typical' inhabitants of a Czech village, but also the blind fiddler Mareš, whose patriotic song 'Where is my homeland' ('Kde domov můj', see p. 66) is the central focus of the fair scene. Another play by Tyl, *The Bagpiper of Strakonice* (*Strakonický dudák*, 1847), had a musician as its hero. It was a huge success with the public and during the nineteenth century it ranked in popularity and influence with other Czech classics such as Erben's *Garland* and Němcová's *The Grandmother* (*DČD*, ii, 323). The fairy-tale elements in the play and the opportunities they provided for exotic spectacle and transformation scenes contributed to its success. So did widespread familiarity with the southern Bohemian folktale tradition which served as Tyl's source. But above all it was the central figure of the bagpiper (see Frontispiece) that seems to have struck a special chord in Czech audiences. Švanda the bagpiper, a Czech village Orpheus whose instrument has magic powers, personified the musicality of the Czech people; and the fact that Švanda was a folk musician, playing an instrument with purely folk connotations emphasized that his musicality was inherent, rather than learnt.

The figure of Švanda became the basis for several Czech operas, all called *Švanda the Bagpiper* (*Švanda dudák*), from Bendl's oratorio (1880, recast as an opera in 1895–6) and Hřímalý's opera (1885, performed 1896) to Weinberger (1927). Even Fibich considered a Švanda opera with Hostinský as his librettist, in which 'the magic power of music' should be the spring of the whole action (Hostinský 1909, 136–7). What is rather more revealing is the way the bagpiper figure crept into a number of other Czech operas. Bagpipers are specified in *King and Charcoal Burner*, *The Secret*, *The Devil and Kate*, *The Dogheads*, *The Black Lake*, *Fate* and *The Excursion of Mr Brouček to the Fifteenth Century*. In some cases the figure can be traced back to the literary source on which the opera is based; in others it has been clearly introduced by the librettist or, in the two Janáček operas, by the composer. Apart from Řehůřek in *The Dogheads*, the bagpiper plays no essential part in the plots of these operas. He appears merely as an incidental character brought in for local colour, for the rewarding opportunities he offered to the composer to imitate the sound of his instrument, and as a well-established guarantor of the work's 'Czechness' (Tyrrell 1984).

Other stage musicians are specified in *The Kiss*, *The Devil and Kate* (playing violin, clarinet and trumpet) and *Jenůfa* (village boys playing toy trumpets, and four violinists); in the last two operas the soloists ask the musicians to play dances for them. There are also several musician soloists in Czech opera. Krásnohorská provided in *Karel Škreta* a part for a young organist and in *The Secret* for the ballad singer Skřivánek, who appears with a guitar and has to compose ballads in praise of the rival councillors Malina and Kalina. There are musicians in two later Novák operas: three village musicians in *The Lantern* (these derive from Jirásek's play) and the composer hero of his final opera, *The Grandfather's Legacy*, whose inheritance is a violin. Živný, the central character of Janáček's *Fate*, is also a composer, but, like the poet, painter and musician in *The Excursion of Mr Brouček to the Moon*, he belongs to a quite different tradition: 'Bohemian' rather than Czech.

One of the earliest drafts for the libretto of *The Jacobin* began with musicians crossing the stage in preparation for the day's dancing (Kuna 1982, 255). The musicians here were ultimately omitted, but one element that was constant in the long gestation of Červinková-Riegrová's text was the idea that Julie was a singer, or at least an 'artist'. In one version of the libretto she establishes her credentials by displaying her 'bravurní koloratura' (Kuna 1982, 250). The same effect is achieved in a later version when Julie and her husband impress Benda by their intimate acquaintance with musicians such as Gluck ('well known to us') or Haydn (Julie's 'teacher') (Kuna 1984, 44). The final version of this episode, and the one that Dvořák set, was rather more homely and celebrated the Czechs' love of music in a more touching manner. Julie and Bohuš relate how when longing for their homeland during their exile abroad it was only in song that they found relief, a sentiment which Dvořák invested with poignantly emotive harmony (Ex. 3). The power of song is demonstrated even more crucially in the final act of the opera when, by singing a song beloved by the deceased Countess, Julie gains access to the Count and softens his heart, and thus effects a reconciliation with his estranged son.

But the most famous musician in this opera, and in all Czech opera, was Benda, the choirmaster of the late eighteenth-century Bohemian country town where the opera is set. At the beginning of Act 2 there is an entire choir-rehearsal scene of a cantata that Benda has composed. It is curious (even suspicious) that Dvořák's librettist Marie Červinková-Riegrová seems never to have mentioned Lortzing's *Zar und Zimmermann* in her extensive notes and correspondence on the opera (examined in Kuna 1982 and 1984). Lortzing's opera was performed both at the Provisional and the National Theatres and its choir-rehearsal scene was the obvious model for Benda's rehearsal. There are, however, significant differences. Lortzing's Van Bett is a comic figure and the scene showing him – the Mayor of Saardam – rehearsing the chorus in a home-made cantata is clearly farcical. Benda, on the other hand, is a professional and his choir rehearsal is to be taken seriously. If he comes across at all as a comic character it is not because he is self-important (and accident-prone) like Van Bett, but because of his fussy

Ex. 3

Bohuš:...only in song did we find sweet relief! [*The Jacobin*, 2.5. 1063–72]

attention to detail and because he is completely single-minded about his
'klasická muzika'. Unlike Lortzing, who provided an intentionally banal
parody, Dvořák composed an example of a typical rural cantata, old-
fashioned but quite elaborate in the florid demands it makes on its soloists.
It recalls with respect and affection a tradition of Czech village classicism

exemplified in the works of Brixi and other minor eighteenth-century Czech composers and which would have provided Dvořák with some of his earliest musical experience.

According to the list of characters Benda is a 'teacher, *regenschori* (choirmaster) and composer'. All this is summed up in a single word – kantor. This word is still used by Czech students to describe a schoolteacher, though its Latin origin suggests a singer. The linking of the choirmaster and schoolmaster, especially outside the large towns, was well established in Bohemia and Moravia in the eighteenth century. Up to Joseph II's school reforms teachers were often chosen chiefly for their musical abilities in the knowledge that they would be able to augment their tiny incomes by doubling as organist or choirmaster (*ČSV*, 110–11, 116). Dvořák, tempted by the idea of writing an opera which would establish him as an international composer not just of instrumental works but also of opera, was at first inclined to turn down Červinková-Riegrová's *The Jacobin* on the grounds that 'such a teacher–musician exists only here and just wouldn't be understood elsewhere' (Bráfová 1913, 107–8). Indeed many nineteenth-century composers in Bohemia and Moravia came from just such a background. Foerster and Suk were both from teaching families and were both the first of their families to be trained exclusively as musicians. Janáček, from a Moravian teaching family, was not so lucky. Both his father and grandfather were village teachers and musicians, and his initial training was as a teacher.

Just as images of musicians recur in Janáček's works, so do images of teachers. One of Janáček's finest choral pieces is his setting of Bezruč's powerful poem about 'Kantor Halfar', the schoolteacher in a disputed part of Silesia, whose only crime (barring him from promotion and even marriage) was to speak Czech. And if the little incident in *Jenůfa* in which Jano the herdboy dashes on to say that he can read stems from Preissová, Janáček's music gave it special prominence as one of the few really happy moments in Act 1, momentarily uniting the bickering cast. One of the most charming passages – entirely Janáček's invention – in *The Cunning Little Vixen* is where the Vixen instructs her cubs about the Gamekeeper's trap. And it can be no coincidence that in his final opera the relationship between Petrovič and the young Tartar boy Aljeja is cemented at the beginning of Act 2 by Petrovič's offer to teach the lad to read – an offer taken up with great joyous excitement. More professional teachers are depicted in *Vixen* (the lonely Schoolmaster) and in *Fate* (seriously in Act 3 with Živný seen addressing his students at the Conservatory and satirically in Act 1 when Miss Stuhlá rehearses her group of vacationing lady teachers).

Not all of Janáček's operas have teachers of course but most, from *Jenůfa* onwards, involve their central characters with some form of learning and coming to terms with their problems. *Jenůfa* is a wonderful example with no fewer than three of its central characters achieving wisdom and equanimity by the end. Preissová, rather than Janáček, is responsible for this but the importance that Janáček attached to it can be seen in the way his music bulks out the final scene and draws attention to the healing process that is completed there. Similarly the Gamekeeper (in *Vixen*) and Emilia Marty (in *Makropulos*) proclaim their new-found wisdom to some of Janáček's grandest music. Even Mr Brouček was originally to have sobered up at home after his moon excursion and accepted the realities of life (Tyrrell 1980a). *Fate* falls less easily into this pattern. The apotheosis-like music at the end of Act 3 foretells a kinship with the wise, reconciled beings at the end of Janáček's other operas. The words, insofar as they are intelligible, imply otherwise: Živný's tribulations seem to have taught him no more than self-righteous, artistic posturing. In Janáček's final opera, *From the House of the Dead*, we are not shown any particular reconciliation or wisdom achieved – the work does not operate through time – but instead it is Janáček's compassion which illuminates each grisly story, no better illustrated than by the tender *idée fixe* which drifts through Šiškov's narration.

It is in this sense, in his choosing and setting operas which deal essentially with the education and enlightenment of its characters, that Janáček shows a kinship with Smetana. The three operas written during Smetana's deafness became increasingly dark. They were all intended as comedies, but all deal with relationships in a profound manner that overshadows the humorous element – music stifling the farce in the same unsettling way that Mozart's music casts strange shadows on Da Ponte's *Cosi*. There is an important difference in type between *The Bartered Bride* and Smetana's later operas. All depend for their conclusion on the overcoming of obstacles, but whereas the obstacle that stands in the way of Jeník's and Mařenka's marriage in *The Bartered Bride* is external (the two pairs of parents aided by Kecal and a reluctant Vašek) and can be removed by trickery, the obstacles that prevent the union of Vendulka and Lukáš in *The Kiss*, or Kalina and Roza in *The Secret*, or even Hedvika and Vok in *The Devil's Wall*, are internal, namely defects of character in the hero or heroine, which need to be remedied by re-education. In all cases the re-education is shown symbolically rather than literally. In *The Kiss* the quarrelling lovers come to their senses in the dark forest; in *The Secret* Kalina has to tunnel through the earth to find himself – and his beloved. In a post-Freudian age these healing journeys of moral re-education might be regarded as symbols of the womb – the characters are in a sense born again – though it is more likely that Krásnohorská's symbols came from Shakespeare's late comedies and romances. Hedvika's hazardous journey over the dammed-up Vltava, literally defying the forces of Hell, is another powerful psychological symbol: Vok's self-containment and isolation is such that only a truly dramatic gesture can reach him.

These last operas may seem to have quite a different purpose from Smetana's early, more overtly nationalist works. But the re-education of the central characters that they propose (rather than the comic humiliation of some of the others) could be considered a stern nationalist lesson: only with radical changes of attitude would the Czechs be able to assume success-fully the responsibilities that independent statehood would thrust upon them. It was an attitude which Janáček was also to espouse when he came to writing *Mr Brouček's Excursion to the Fifteenth Century*. In a newspaper article he wrote for the work's première, he explained some of his motives for writing the opera:

> We can see among the Czechs as many Broučeks as there are Oblomovs among the Russians. I wanted us to be disgusted by such people, to destroy them when we come across them, to strangle them – but, above all, to destroy the Brouček *in ourselves*, in order that we might be reborn with the heavenly purity of mind of our national martyrs. We must not suffer on account of the Brouček mentality in the same way that the Russians suffered for their Oblomovs. (Janáček 1958, 52)

Of all major Czech composers, Janáček (together with Ostrčil in *The Bud* and *Kunála's Eyes*) came nearest to continuing the spiritual message of Smetana's late operas. With the exception of the Shakespeare-based *The Tempest*, Fibich's operas are mostly fate-wracked tragedies with their central characters at the end neither enlightened nor reconciled – simply dead. In some of Dvořák's early operas the re-education of their stubborn or errant central characters is achieved comically and clumsily, with none of the illumination of character that is such a feature of this type of work in Smetana or Janáček. Four operas, including his last two, are tragedies. This leaves only *The Jacobin* and *The Devil and Kate*. *The Jacobin*, with the reconciliation achieved between the Count and his son Bohuš at the end, is the nearest Dvořák came to setting this sort of opera. *The Devil and Kate* may at first sight seem to be similar. The Princess's abolition of the *robota* at the end could perhaps suggest that she has learnt something. So perhaps has Kate, judging from her music when she receives the Princess's bounty. It has all the gentleness of a wise, reconciled individual, with the voice arching to its highest note in one of Dvořák's most beautiful phrases (Ex. 4). The words, however, do not tally. There is no question of Kate's under-standing herself better or coming to terms with the fact that she is a gar-rulous, unattractive spinster. Now that she is rich, she says, she will have no problem finding herself a bridegroom.

In Tyl's play *The Bagpiper from Strakonice*, the hero Švanda, despairing of ever being able to marry his sweetheart Dorotka (her father has already rejected him as too poor for a suitor), sets out with his magical instrument into foreign lands, where he becomes rich and famous. But he also forgets his roots, his sweetheart, and his native goodness of heart. He loses every-

Kate: [if however I now have a house and money, bridegrooms will compete for me] as though I were the most beautiful girl in the whole village [*The Devil and Kate*, 3. 953–67]

thing and returns home, no richer but much wiser. Tyl's play portrays his progress as a human being and his achievement of wisdom through learning hard lessons. Another play by Tyl, *Through the Middle of the Earth to Africa* (*Středem země do Afriky*), takes his characters on similar journeys of education. Here it is in fact the whole family that, one by one, sets off into exotic climes. At the end the father is reconciled with his son (who is then able to marry his faithful sweetheart) and with his wife. The wife has a particularly bad time of it: she is reduced to penury during her husband's absence and then shares with him the dangers of the North Pole. They share hardships together and only then begin to value one another.

These fairy-tale plays about educational journeys were not in themselves particularly Czech. The earliest source of the Švanda legend appears to have derived from the German Faust legends; Tyl's *Through the Middle of the Earth to Africa*, was simply an adaptation of Gustav Räder's *Die artesische Brunnen*. In the latter, there is also a magic instrument – this time a violin – and this, like Švanda's bagpipe, helps to emphasize the close relationship of Bohemian theatre in the early nineteenth century to that of Vienna. The fairy-tale play, with its heroes engaged in an educational quest, and with music featuring strongly in the form of inserted numbers and even in stage props, was a well-established Viennese genre. Modern audiences are acquainted with its most elevated examplar, *Die Zauberflöte*.

The line that stretches from Tamino's and Pamina's trials of fire and water to the ordeals of Laca and Jenůfa a century later may seem a tenuous one given Janáček's lack of interest in Mozart. It is, nevertheless, a line that is consolidated by a whole genre of popular Czech fairy-tale plays in the earlier part of the nineteenth century. It is a line that Krásnohorská, perhaps quite unconsciously, picked up when she wrote the librettos for Smetana's last three operas. It is a line that Smetana clearly responded to and to which he held firm, despite all efforts to prise him away from his librettist. And it is a line that Janáček pursued right into the twentieth century, selecting plays or other material that allowed him to continue it, and where necessary adapting such material to allow this. To argue that a strong tradition of Czech nineteenth-century opera derives not so much from any of the mainstream contemporary operatic traditions as from a popular Viennese genre of magical plays with music may seem perverse. It was however the one genre that allowed to flourish a central Czech preoccupation not with high tragedy or low comedy, but with learning, with wisdom, and with coming to terms with problems.

# 6. Characters

## Smetana

At the heart of Smetana's comic operas is a relationship between two characters, the exposition and ultimate resolution of which provides the central core of each opera. Thus, *The Bartered Bride* tells the love story of Jeník and Mařenka and how, despite the opposition of their parents, it ends happily. The plots of Smetana's last four operas differ only in one sense: that while resistance to Jeník's and Mařenka's union is external (their parents' plans), in the later operas the resistance to marriage is internal – Anežka's devotion to her late husband (*The Two Widows*), Lukáš's and Vendulka's stubbornness (*The Kiss*), Kalina's pride (*The Secret*), or Vok's inaction and lack of confidence that anyone could love him at his age (*The Devil's Wall*). Whereas the duping of Kecal, and thus of Mařenka's parents, is a comic mechanism, the overcoming of these personal problems in Smetana's later operas is a sign of the characters' spiritual growth, an occasion not for laughter but for joy.

Smetana's historical operas are not so clear cut in their central preoccupation, particularly not in *The Brandenburgers in Bohemia*, where it is difficult to say who the central character is.[1] Apart from a Captain and a few extras, the Brandenburgers of the title do not appear on stage, and most of the information about them in the opera comes second-hand. Certainly the most interesting character is Jíra, the leader of the Prague mob, and he dominates those scenes in which he appears. In Smetana's only opera with a tragic ending, *Dalibor*, Milada and Dalibor form a central couple though Milada's rescue attempt results in their deaths, not their marriage. But the nature of the opera, which provides little time or opportunity to chart the development of any relationship between the two, ensures that it is less about Milada's and Dalibor's relationship than about their heroic bearing in adversity. Similarly *Libuše* is about more than Libuše's marriage to Přemysl. Even the final act, where Libuše and Přemysl are brought together, has as its climax Libuše's prophecies, invoking Czech pride in the past and hope for the future, and this, rather than Libuše's wedding, is the message that the audience takes home. Libuše marries for reasons of state; if her heart moves in that direction too, we hear very little about it.

*Dalibor* has a secondary pair of lovers, as do all of Smetana's operas thereafter except for *The Kiss*. The presence of these young pairs suggests that the central couples are older and more experienced. This is certainly true of all Smetana's operas from *Libuše* onwards, if not also of *Dalibor*. Only in two early operas, *The Brandenburgers* and *The Bartered Bride*, are the central couples obviously young. In *Libuše* the central couple comprises a female ruler and a well-established gentleman farmer; in Smetana's next operas one partner is either a widow (Anežka) or a widower (Lukáš in *The Kiss*, Kalina in *The Secret*), or long unmarried (Roza in *The Secret*, Vok in *The Devil's Wall*). While the young couples in Smetana's first two operas, and the secondary couples in all later operas, are sung by a lyric soprano and a lyric tenor, the only tenor–soprano central couple in the later operas is Lukáš and Vendulka in *The Kiss*. In the later operas the increased age of the central couple begin to be reflected in lower voices. Thus Ladislav, though a tenor (and young and ardent), loves a mezzo[2] widow (Anežka); Roza is a contralto; and her eventual partner Kalina, like Přemysl (in *Libuše*) and Vok, is a baritone.

Unlike Verdi's or Wagner's operas, Smetana's have few baritone villains. The only unambiguous candidate is in Smetana's first opera, *The Brandenburgers in Bohemia*. Here Jan Tausendmark, the Prague townsman who sides with the German forces, exploits the confused situation to force his unwelcome attentions on Ludiše. He has her and her sisters taken prisoner, and it is on his false evidence that Jíra is imprisoned for this crime. In Smetana's next serious opera King Vladislav is also a baritone and a 'villain' in the sense that he has the hero Dalibor imprisoned. But Vladislav comes across as a reasonable, if cautious ruler, forced to react to the charge that Dalibor has killed Milada's brother. Wenzig's libretto lacks a vengeful Pizarro figure. Budivoj (baritone), the commander of the royal castle guard who gives instructions to the jailer, has only a tiny, episodic part, and any notion that Vladislav could serve as villain is dispelled by Smetana's music. While Tausendmark's part contains stereotyped 'villainous' vocal gestures (Ex. 1; note the many accented notes, especially on climactic top Fs, and the

Ex. 1

Tausendmark (with drawn sword): Ha! In vain your flight! You will not escape me again, Ludiše, even if I have to burst the bolts of heaven, even if the gates of hell were to stand in my way! [*The Brandenburgers in Bohemia*, 1.10.1352–60]

emphatic syncopations on 'Ty' and 'brány'), Smetana's music makes Vladislav the embodiment of dignified authority, a mouthpiece of the legitimate establishment (Ex. 2; note the low brass accompaniment, the 'tranquillo'

Ex. 2

Vladislav: Law and order must prevail, the land suffers most through misrule, our duty is the law. [*Dalibor*, 1.5.939–48]

marking and the opening in slow, even notes). The 'villain' of *The Devil's Wall*, the devil Rarach, is of course a comic villain, complete with melodramatic laugh (Ex. 3).

In Smetana's hands, in fact, the baritone soon ceased to be a potential villain and reverted instead to a noble, if somewhat inactive, figure – the *padre nobile* of Italian opera. At the end of the line of baritones in Smetana operas is the noblest and most inactive of them all, Vok in *The Devil's Wall*. He is well born, the lord of the Rožmberk estate and the highest marshall in the land, and has music of dignified poignancy, but is so inactive that others have to conspire to find him a wife and lure him out of monastic seclusion to marry her. Between Vladislav and Vok there is Přemysl, chosen

Ex. 3

(Un poco animato, ♩ = 72)
RARACH (objeví se v poustevnickém hávu mezi balvany a zase zmizí)

Ha ha   ha  ha  ha   ha  ha  ha!

*p* str (vn, va tremolo)
  ob, cl, bsn

Rarach (appears in a pilgrim's habit among the rocks and then disappears): Ha ha ha ha ha ha ha ha! [*The Devil's Wall*, 1.1.68]

by Libuše for a husband rather than the other way round, Tomeš in *The Kiss*, and Kalina in *The Secret*. The most active of these is Kalina. The key to his character is his feeling of inferiority that has caused the rift with his old love Roza and, in an expression of defiance, has led him to build an opulent house for himself that he cannot afford. Kalina – for instance at the opening of Act 2 – comes the nearest of any Smetana baritone to the complex 'divided' baritones of German Romantic opera, with a multi-tempo, multi-mood *scena* to express his conflicting emotions. This character, however, is something of a sport among Smetana's serious baritone roles.

For buffo singers Smetana used both basses (including bass-baritones – Smetana himself never used the term) and tenors. *The Bartered Bride* contains well-known examples of both: the shy stuttering suitor Vašek (tenor) and the marriage broker Kecal (bass). The buffo element in Vašek's part comes musically chiefly from his expertly handled stutter. This is a unique comic device in Smetana and the comic elements of later buffo tenors such as the castellan Michálek in *The Devil's Wall* are confined to what the librettist could offer in the way of situational or verbal comedy. Krásnohorská clearly felt it was necessary to eke this out with repeated tags such as Michálek's much-repeated 'tuze' (an outmoded word for 'very'), which, as Foerster wrote of the première (1929, 213–14) soon becomes tiresome. Kecal, however, is quite another matter. His entrance music tells us within seconds what we are to think of him. A bustling *moto perpetuo* in the orchestra introduces and at the same time debunks his first vocal utterance, some thirty notes sung solemnly (in mostly equal notes) to just three pitches. In the next six bars the voice takes up the buffo patter of the orchestra with a single phrase 'všecko je hotovo' ('everything is ready'), repeated so frequently that it degenerates into circular, meaningless patter: '-vo je ho-to-vo je ho-to-vo'. Ex. 4, a little later, creates a similarly portentous impression with its climactically repeated 'můj hled' (my gaze) and, after more quaver patter to repeated phrases, ridiculously wide jumps and a cadential trill.

Ex. 4

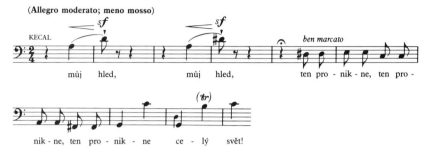

Kecal: . . . my gaze penetrates the whole world! [*The Bartered Bride*, 1.4.1274–83]

Exactly the same comic devices characterize the part of the gamekeeper Mumlal in *The Two Widows*. In the refrain of Mumlal's strophic song in Act 2, Smetana particularly exploits coloratura devices such as melisma, turns and trills, all comically inappropriate to a low, heavy voice. And both parts are ruled by the same comic mechanism: an assertive, officious, somewhat bullying personality is set up dramatically and musically, specifically in order to be taken down a peg by the other, more sympathetic characters. However, while it is true to say that while Kecal comes across as a genuinely comic creation, Mumlal, despite their similar names (Kecal = one who prattles; Mumlal = one who mutters), is something of a failure in this respect. In Kecal's case his portentous vocal gestures have behind them the menacing fact that he, acting for their parents, can upset Jeník's and Mařenka's marriage plans. Mumlal, however, provides no such threat to Anežka's and Ladislav's union (the obstacle is Anežka's own attitude) and his brand of musical humour appears not only second-hand and tiresomely exaggerated, but, more importantly, lacks the underlying aggression which is an element of most humour.[3] Even weaker is the character of the Foreman in *The Secret*. Like Michálek he is provided with a 'comic' verbal and musical tag, 'Nu jářku!' ('well I say!'), which is heard each time he appears. Its inflexibility dominates the Act 2 ensemble and even breaks up the Act 3 trio, but since he is completely irrelevant to the plot and poses no threat to anyone his 'humour' is impotent, and, like Mumlal's, tedious.

Seen in this context the handling of Father Paloucký in *The Kiss* is particularly interesting. He seems to have been intended as a comic character (see, for instance, Krásnohorská's commentary in Očadlík 1940, 55) and indeed his part contains many of the same musical hints used to instruct the audience on how to regard Kecal. Though he is introduced in the genial bustle of the opening of the opera, his part soon assumes solemnity as he contemplates his future 'journey into eternity', and the orchestra with its 'Baroque' double dots and extravagant flourishes appears to set up his solemn warning (Ex. 5) as a target for comic puncturing. And when he interrupts the quarrelling lovers with his aria 'Jak jsem to řek'!' ('Just as I said!') we could be back with Kecal, with its mixture of portentous gesture (the descending sevenths of the Baroque sequences), its 'unsuitable' melismas and trills, its fussy semiquaver figures, and its repetitions such as the opening tag 'Jak jsem to řek'!', as ubiquitous as Kecal's 'Všecko je hotovo'. Yet Father Paloucký does not come across as a comic character, and we are inclined to take his solemnities seriously. While Kecal's pomposity expressed self-importance, Paloucký's concern is for his daughter. His repeated 'Jak jsem to řek'!' is no comic tag but instead expresses exasperation and impotence in the face of potential tragedy.

In contrast to Smetana's serious, inactive baritones, many of his female parts are strikingly energetic. In *The Bartered Bride*, for instance, both Jeník and Mařenka explore ways of averting her marriage to Vašek. Though it is Jeník's plan that succeeds, his union with Mařenka almost comes to grief when she refuses to listen to his explanation of his behaviour. Her anger arises from her not being consulted or being treated like an equal partner. High-handed male behaviour is the underlying cause of the argument in *The Kiss*. The plot stands on a simple disagreement between the couple, Vendulka regarding her opinion as equally valid and refusing to change it. And Vendulka becomes the dominant partner when Lukáš is forced to seek her out and apologize. In two of Smetana's operas the prospective husband is actually rescued, or nearly rescued, by the prospective wife. Hedvika (in *The Devil's Wall*) saves Vok from the mounting waters of the Vltava, and in so doing proves her love and gains a husband. The case of Milada and Dalibor is even more striking. The story parallels that of Fidelio, with Milada dressing up as a boy and seeking service with the jailer in an attempt to reach Dalibor. While Leonore, after pointing her pistol at Pizarro, collapses into Florestan's arms, relying on the famous trumpet call to forestall any further action from his would-be murderer, the Czech Milada is made of sterner stuff. She gallops sword in hand at the head of her followers, and dies in the attempt to rescue Dalibor.

Women are the energetic prime movers in *The Two Widows* (Karolina's arrangements ensure that her cousin Anežka marries her man) and in *The Kiss*, where the resourceful Martinka (more than a match for the border guard) takes Vendulka off with her on her smuggling expedition and thereby sets in train the events that will lead to Vendulka's reconciliation

Ex. 5

Father Paloucký: You are hotblooded, and Vendulka is no different; what will come about is not my fault! [*The Kiss*, 1.3.441–50]

with Lukáš. The most dominant of all Smetana's female characters is of course Libuše. No male ruler was ever depicted on the Czech operatic stage with such force; no Czech male ruler was ever the focus for such blatant national pride.[4]

As Krásnohorská determined so many other aspects of Smetana's operas, it seems possible that the vocal stereotypes of the later operas were also suggested by her. This is definitely so in *The Devil's Wall*. Smetana's first encounter with the subject, Krásnohorská's prose sketch, was preceded by a list of characters including specified voices (Očadlík 1940, 133). All of these were observed in Smetana's setting begun a year later. Similarly in their earliest collaboration, on *Viola*, Krásnohorská stipulated the voices (and even some of the singers) in advance in order, so she said, to plan ensembles (see p. 107). Only in *The Secret* (where the original libretto has disappeared) can there be doubts about this procedure, since in her letter to the composer of 1 February 1878 Krásnohorská asked whether Smetana had composed Blaženka for a dramatic or a 'naive' singer, and whether Roza was written for a low or high voice (Očadlík 1940, 105). Vocal stereotypes, however, run through all Smetana's operas, not just those with Krásnohorská librettos.

To some extent these stereotypes were derived from the system of stock characters that had long existed in drama and opera and even today finds expression in film and television typecasting or in the *Fächer* into which German singers are sometimes divided. Mr Crummles's theatrical company in *Nicholas Nickleby* included actors to play 'low-spirited lovers', 'comic countrymen', 'calm and virtuous old men' and 'irascible old men'; similarly Weber's handover notes for his successor in Prague in 1816 included an account of the company which assigned his singers to parts such as 'naive, cheerful and similar roles', 'character parts', 'trouser roles', 'comic old women' (Němec 1944, 187). The Czech parentage for Vašek, the simpleton son of rich countryfolk, can be traced through a succession of Czech plays stretching back into the eighteenth century (*DČD*, ii, 78-9). Similarly Kecal clearly owes something to Van Bett in *Zar und Zimmermann*, an opera Smetana much admired, and to which, when requesting a comedy element in *The Devil's Wall*, he directed Krásnohorská's attention together with Dr Bartolo in *Il barbiere di Siviglia* (Očadlík 1940, 102). In Smetana's last completed opera, *The Devil's Wall*, the mezzo casting of the youth Záviš ('about seventeen' according to Krásnohorská's prose sketch – Očadlík 1940, 133) had a number of *travesti* models to choose from in the Provisional Theatre repertory, such as Cherubino, Jemmy in *Guillaume Tell*, Urbain in *Les Huguenots*, Siebel in Gounod's *Faust*, Vanya in *A Life for the Tsar*, or Oscar in *Un ballo in maschera*. There was also a Czech precedent from an earlier opera with a Krásnohorská libretto, Bendl's *Břetislav*, where the boy king Vaclav II is allocated to a mezzo (Bendl went on to use the same voice type in three later operas); while a year or two later, to another Krásnohorská libretto, Smetana had composed scenes from his unfinished *Viola* in which, following nineteenth-century theatrical practice, Sebastian was played by the same performer as Viola – in this case a mezzo.

While it is possible to argue that many of Smetana's voice types were either modifications of European models, in some cases suggested to him by Krásnohorská, the single most important factor in determining the type that Smetana chose in the end was what voices were available at the Provisional Theatre. This aspect is more important in the later operas than in the earlier ones, especially *The Brandenburgers in Bohemia*, which is generally uncharacteristic of Smetana's use of voices, perhaps because of his inexperience at the time and because of its special circumstances as a competition entry. Even *Dalibor*, produced two years after Smetana joined the Provisional Theatre as its chief conductor, was hardly realistic in its demands for large dramatic voices for the parts of Milada and Dalibor, and at the première Milada had to be taken by a mezzo, who coped poorly with some of the higher reaches of the part. But by the time that Smetana wrote his three last operas with Krásnohorská he had worked closely as conductor with the Provisional Theatre singers for eight years. His deafness meant that he heard none of the newer ones, and it was the earlier voices which he thought of when he wrote the operas. As he wrote to Adolf Čech, suggesting the casting of *The Devil's Wall*: 'During composition I always had in mind those esteemed members [of the company] which I was still lucky enough to hear' (Teige 1896, 136).

## The Provisional Theatre singers

In a tradition that went back to the earliest days of Czech theatre, use was sometimes made of actors rather than singers in musical works. The prime field for this was of course operetta, but this tradition is also evident in the original casting of *The Bartered Bride*. The fact that this opera originally employed spoken dialogue rather than sung recitatives made this use of actors more logical. It is interesting that when sending Smetana her outline for a libretto of *Viola* Krásnohorská suggested that

the comic figures of Tobiáš [Sir Toby Belch], Ondřej [Sir Andrew Aguecheek] and Marie [Maria] (three characters that are in any case roles for half-actors and half-singers) could make very good use in places of spoken dialogue.                    (Očadlík 1940, 29)

In the first production of *The Bartered Bride* Vašek was sung by Josef Kysela, a member of the acting company making his only appearance in any Smetana opera, and Esmeralda was played by the soubrette Terezie Ledererová. Ledererová was originally a member of the drama company, used especially in farces, but was also outstanding in operetta (Bartoš 1938,

13a Changing images of Libuše:
Libuše as Amazon warrior (with helmet, breastplate, shield and spear), an engraving by G. Balzer for the title page of the 1779 edition of Guolfinger von Steinsberg's play *Libussa, Herzoginn in Böhmen*, one of a long line of German plays and operas based on the Libuše legend. The illustrator appears to have confused Libuše with her warlike successors in the maidens' war.

38). For her Smetana wrote his only 'soubrette' role, clearly characterized, for instance, in the duet that he added later for her and the Circusmaster. (Late in life Smetana had to protest that Mařenka, the heroine of the same opera, was not a soubrette – although sometimes played as such, but a 'dramatic' role; Očadlík, 1941a, 17.) Esmeralda's close cousin, Barče in *The Kiss*, was similarly created by a singer used more in operetta than in opera, Marie Laušmannová. Here Smetana not only overruled the Provisional Theatre intendant's objections to using her, but added a rare coloratura aria for her, Barče's 'Lark' song in Act 2.

The part of the Circusmaster in *The Bartered Bride* was created by Jindřich Mošna, one of the foremost Czech comic actors in the second half of the nineteenth century. Mošna had virtually no singing voice. For anything high or low, he slipped into parlando. The original part contained much more speech than song, and when Smetana, in his later revisions, replaced the spoken dialogue with recitative, he was careful to take Mošna's vocal limitations into account (Srba 1985, 98–9). Mošna proved by far the most durable member of the original cast, playing in the first 446 performances over the next thirty years (Pražák 1948, iv, 301).

The theatre's problem with tenors also dates back to an earlier period. Kittl, in his report on *The Brandenburgers in Bohemia*, suggested that Smetana's requirement for three tenors might cause problems in casting the

13b  Libuše as portrayed by Marie Sittová in the 1883 production of Smetana's opera. A century after Steinsberg's play the Libuše legend had been fully slavonicized in Wenzig's libretto (see pp. 3–4) though not, however, by Sittová's party dress (at that time soloists supplied their own costumes).

piece (Daněk 1983, 163). No doubt he remembered earlier times when Czech tenors were created by pushing baritones up into falsetto, or persuading foreigners to learn the parts in Czech. Smetana's predecessor Škroup had taken the easy option in his *Libuše's Marriage* by simply omitting tenors from the cast. The problem persisted into the 1870s, particularly as regards Heldentenors. After the defection of the talented Čeněk Vecko to the German theatre in 1865 and Arnošt Grund to Berlin in 1870, there were simply no Czech Heldentenors permanently employed by the Provisional Theatre; and for parts such as Robert (in *Robert le diable*) or John of Leyden

13c Libuše as prophetess; a famous Libuše at the turn of the century, Růžena Maturová (see pp. 191–2). Costumes and sets by Mikoláš Aleš for *Libuše* at the National Theatre in Prague in 1897 established a more historically acceptable conception of the work on stage.

(in *Le prophète*), the theatre was obliged to make use of amateurs such as Vincenc Cicvárek, the owner of a windmill (Heller 1918, 113–14; Bartoš 1938, 340–1, 360, 362). The chief tenor parts in Smetana's operas after *Dalibor* were taken by Antonín Vávra, who joined the company in 1871 as a young man of twenty-four and who remained there until 1888. The essentially lyric character of his voice is attested by the parts that Smetana wrote for him: from Ladislav in *The Two Widows* to Vít in *The Secret* and Jarek in *The Devil's Wall*, which Smetana himself, when allocating parts, described as 'almost overflowing with the lyricism which Mr Vávra has so often and so triumphantly given us' (Teige 1896, 137). In the latter part of his career, Vávra, *faute de mieux*, took on Helden parts such as Lohengrin in 1885 and Dalibor, when this opera was eventually revived in 1886. The first Dalibor, in 1868, was Vávra's teacher, Jan Lukes, another essentially lyric tenor though then nearing the end of his stage career.

There were similar problems with dramatic sopranos. After the departure of the Polish Helena Zawiszanka in 1865, the Provisional Theatre company lacked a true dramatic soprano. The result was that Smetana wrote his later soprano parts for smaller, lyrical voices. Libuše, usually reckoned to be a role for dramatic soprano, was entrusted, on the composer's advice, to Marie Sittová (see illustration 13b), originally engaged as a coloratura soprano. Sittová was one of the most versatile of the Provisional Theatre artists, including in her repertory most soprano roles from coloratura and soubrette to dramatic. In addition to Libuše, she created the parts of both widows in *The Two Widows* (the soprano Karolina in the 1874 première, and the mezzo Anežka in the definitive version of 1878), Vendulka (in *The Kiss*), and two essentially lyrical, ingénue roles, Blaženka (*The Secret*) and Katuška (*The Devil's Wall*).

Smetana's distaste for Italianate display led him to make little use of one of the Provisional Theatre's star singers, the coloratura soprano Eleonora z Ehrenbergů. It was not clear who was the more dismayed, z Ehrenbergů or Smetana, when they both discovered that she was to be the first Mařenka, a role that she considered beneath her with few opportunities to show off her talents, and one which she soon relinquished. Nevertheless, Smetana seems to have had her specifically in mind when he wrote the part of Jitka in *Dalibor*, with its surprising flourishes (for instance over the soldiers' chorus in Act 2). The part of the First Reaper in Act 2 of *Libuše*, with its elaborate melisma and trills was also entrusted to z Ehrenbergů at its première. Such melismatic and coloratura writing, however, is rare in Smetana, who included it occasionally only for specific singers such as z Ehrenbergů and Laušmannová, for particular characterization (for instance in the part of Karolina, the merrier of the two widows) or for comic effect in buffo bass parts. Almost the only instances of melisma in serious male parts came in those that Smetana wrote for his friend, the baritone Josef Lev.

Josef Lev was one of the pillars of the Provisional Theatre. After singing for some ten years in the chorus at the Vienna opera, he joined the company in 1864, and at once drew attention to himself as a singer of outstanding talents. In his *Národní listy* review of Lev's first appearance (as Conte di Luna in *Trovatore*) Smetana commended his technique, especially his well-placed tone and his use of portamento. He added:

his true account, full of feeling and yet without any striving for oversweet sentimentality and sheer effect, confirms our opinion. We can count ourselves lucky that he has been gained for our theatre. His voice is very soft and sweet, weaker in the bass than at the top, which however is no bad thing in a baritone. (Smetana 1948, 116)

Eighteen years later, having worked with Lev in the theatre and written many roles for him, Smetana's regard for him was even greater. Making suggestions for singers for his final opera to the conductor Adolf Čech Smetana wrote:

Vok Vítkovic definitely Mr Lev, not only because he is one of the leading singers any-where in the whole musical world, but because *the role of Vok* is extensive and demands both dramatic expression, and a mastery of purely musical style – for instance church style (old church music), that more lively motet style, modern lyricism and the greatest attention to declamation. (Teige 1896, 136)

Lev was particularly suited to high baritone roles, e.g. Luna in *Trovatore*, or Nevers in Meyerbeer's *Huguenots*. He was no actor, and his small stature and undistinguished appearance detracted from parts such as Don Giovanni, which he nevertheless frequently played. Patti, at a guest appearance in *Traviata*, took one look at the Germont that the Provisional Theatre had provided for her (she did not attend rehearsals) and decided to ignore him completely. His singing, however, won her over and at the end of the act she added her own tribute (a kiss on the unmade-up back of his neck) to that of the audience (Novák 1944, 356–7). His voice communicated a passion quite lacking in his acting; his other strengths included crystal-clear intonation, a magnificent *mezza voce* and a bravura technique that enabled him to sing, as a concert turn, a soprano coloratura aria from Isouard's *Le billet de loterie* (Dolanský 1918, 134).

His first part in a Smetana opera was Tausendmark in *The Brandenburgers in Bohemia*. Smetana subsequently added for him the third-act aria 'Tvůj obraz, dívko' ('Your likeness, my girl!'). Its elegiac character (it is marked 'largo amoroso, dolce con sentimento') and high tessitura were well suited to Lev's talents, though the piece goes against the nature of the part and presents Tausendmark in an unwarrantably sympathetic light. There was no obvious part for Lev in the two comedies, *The Bartered Bride* and *The Two Widows*, but he created all the main baritone parts in Smetana's other operas, from King Vladislav to Vok. There is ample evidence, for instance in the extra arias that Smetana added for him in these works, that Smetana took Lev's particular qualities – and his shortcomings – into account. Most of the writing is lyrical, undramatic and often slow-moving, allowing Lev to show off his sustained tone and his ability to convey heartfelt though passive emotion.

In the same letter discussing the casting of *The Devil's Wall*, Smetana assigned the part of Záviš to another key singer of the company: 'the pure alto, refined figure and importance of the role all point to Mrs Fibichová' (Teige 1896, 137). Betty Fibichová, Fibich's second wife, joined the com-pany in 1868 and sang under Smetana's direction for six years, excelling in such parts as Fides and Azucena. Smetana specified her for the part of Radmila in *Libuše*, and wrote parts specifically for her in the three Krásnohorská operas. He was put out when in fact she was not entrusted with Martinka in *The Kiss* at its première and insisted on her taking the part at its revival (Teige 1896, 51–2). Though she sang forty-seven performances from 1878, this energetic role was temperamentally unsuited to her personality (Nejedlý described her as 'essentially a completely passive singer'; 1935, i, 214). Similarly the trouser role of Záviš in *The Devil's Wall* was something of a miscalculation in its vocal tessitura, lying too high for her deep contralto, while dramatically the part was rather too lively and, furthermore, this most statuesque of Czech singers towered over the tiny Lev (Foerster 1942, 213–14). The most suitable part that Smetana wrote for her was the embittered spinster Miss Roza in *The Secret*.

Another singer that Smetana remembered in the casting of *The Devil's Wall* was the buffo tenor Adolf Krössing. Krössing joined the Provisional Theatre in 1870, excelling particularly in operetta, with his light, flexible voice and his talent for comedy, and in operatic parts such as Triquet in *Eugene Onegin* or Pedrillo in *Die Entführung*. From 1871 he began singing the buffo part of Vašek in *The Bartered Bride*, and went on to sing it for a total of 547 times until his retirement in 1914 at the remarkable age of sixty-six. Smetana wrote character parts for him in his last two operas, and in accordance with his talents both Skřivánek (the ballad singer in *The Secret*) and Michálek (the castellan in *The Devil's Wall*) demand not just a flair for comedy but the ability to project a sweet and sustained tone (for instance in Skřivánek's Act 1 ballad).

The lack of low bass parts in Smetana's operas also reflected conditions at the Provisional Theatre. Josef Paleček, a young and promising singer who created the part of the Elder in *The Brandenburgers in Bohemia* and Beneš in *Dalibor*, two of the lowest-lying bass parts in Smetana's operas, was lured away to St Petersburg in 1870, while František Hynek, the first Volfram in *The Brandenburgers in Bohemia* and the first Kecal in *The Bartered Bride*, left the company in 1866, returning only in 1881 (and then partly as a producer). Smetana's most favoured substitute was Karel Čech, brother of the Provisional Theatre conductor. He joined the company in 1868 and went on to create parts such as Mumlal (*The Two Widows*) and Father Paloucký in *The Kiss*. Smetana was keen to fill out the small part of Bonifác for him in *The Secret* (see p. 110), and wrote the important part of Rarach in *The Devil's Wall* for him. But these are all essentially bass-baritone parts. Čech's comparatively small and light voice could not cope with the demands of the bigger auditorium of the National Theatre, and it is thought that this and the competition with the fuller bass of František Hynek led to the illness which cut short his career.

In an interesting article comparing vocal tessitura of Smetana voice parts to those of Verdi and Wagner, Leo Jehne (1974) concluded that Smetana did not invent any new voice types, and that those he used corresponded to Verdian rather than Wagnerian practice. Smetana generally observed the optimum register for the voice, straining neither top nor bottom, with the main tessitura lying in the third quarter of the voice range (counting from bottom to top). Wagner's voice parts, with the main tessitura lying in the second quarter, tended to blur the traditional distinctions between, for instance, soprano and mezzo, or tenor and baritone. Jehne's findings are supported by an 'index' of the average register of a given vocal part (or section of such a part), a figure arrived at by counting the recurrence of individual notes: the greater the frequency of high notes, the higher the index. Jehne's index of the average tessitura of Dalibor's voice part varies between 14.16 (Act 1), 14.13 (Act 2) and 14.70 (Act 3). A particularly passionate aria, Dalibor's song of freedom 'Ha, kým to kouzlem' ('By what spell!'), reaches an index as high as 15.15. This is comparable with the index of Manrico's cabaletta 'Di quella pira' in *Trovatore* (15.64); in *Rigoletto* the Duke's 'Parmi veder' and its preceding recitative has the lower index of 14.48, 'Celeste Aida' and its preceding recitative only 13.32. In comparison the part of Lohengrin has an index of 13.03, and those of post-Tristan tenors in Wagner operas correspond more with baritones. Even 'Winterstürme' in *Die Walküre* has an index of only 11.73.

Figures like these appear more exact than they actually are and Jehne's indices, as he freely admits, do not take into account duration of notes. Nevertheless the figures do provide some guidance, and reinforce what is clear from a less statistical examination of Smetana's voice parts: that his vocal writing tended more to the lyric than the heroic, and that for all his reservations about Italian opera, Smetana was forced to take into account the Italianate training of many of his singers. This is particularly clear in the case of Josef Lev, for whom Smetana wrote some noticeably high-lying parts: the index of Přemysl's aria 'Ó vy lípy' (14.54) is comparable to the Conte de Luna's 'Il balen' (14.65) in *Il trovatore* rather than to Wolfram's 'Wie Todesahnung – O du mein holder Abendstern' (11.56) in *Tannhäuser* or the Dutchman's 'Die Frist ist um' (11.65). At the same time Smetana chose for Lev characters that suited him, Germonts rather than Ernanis, and thereby established his tradition of noble rather than villainous baritones.

'Placid, purely vocal, more lyrical than dramatic' was how Nejedlý (1935, i, 303) epitomized the singing style of the Provisional Theatre. And this was the style, whatever reservations he may have had, in which Smetana found himself writing: a little coloratura to placate Lev, and gentle parts, especially for tenors, so as never to tax the small-scale voices available and threaten the health of his singers, and thus the very existence of the tiny Provisional Theatre company (Srba 1985, 97–8).

# Fibich and Dvořák

## Plot types

After experimenting in his first three extant operas with a variety of subjects – light-hearted amorous intrigue in *Bukovín*, a love story against nationalist trappings in *Blaník*, a tragic incestuous triangle in *The Bride of Messina* – Fibich appeared, in his later operas, to settle for a type of plot with a central passionate relationship whose outcome, mainly tragic, forms the narrative core of the work. In all cases the lovers are sung by tenor and soprano; there is no suggestion either in the story, or in their voice types, that they are akin to the older, wiser people who inhabit Smetana's later operas (only Don Juan in *Hedy* is, of course, 'experienced'). Furthermore the lovers are always thwarted by external rather than internal circumstances: angry fathers or, more often, just fate. It is significant that while *The Tempest* could well have dwelt on Prospero and the wisdom he gains through experience, Fibich chose instead an adaptation of Shakespeare's play that concentrated on the love story of Miranda and Ferdinand. In their reduction, from a variety of sources, to an erotic core and the muting of other issues, Fibich's operas have more in common with the tendency in nineteenth-century Italian opera to draw on world literature for its stories of simple passion, than with the Czech tradition that Smetana had formulated. It is also possible to see in this trend a reflection of Fibich's own circumstances, especially since Anežka Schulzová wrote the librettos of his last three operas.

Dvořák's case is different. For all the variety of subject matter and the constant turnover of librettists (nine for ten operas), the fact that a number of trends run through most of his operas suggests that his choice of librettos was not so haphazard as it might appear. He seems to have been unattracted by the Fibich-type opera with a passionate relationship at its core (he turned down Zeyer's *Šárka*), and his operas such as *Vanda* or *Armida*, based on a love–duty conflict, are, despite incidental beauties, his least characteristic and least inspired. Even the Smetana–Krásnohorská type of plot, where love is a quest and its successful conclusion a sign of personal development, is not reflected in his œuvre. His comic opera *The Stubborn Lovers* may seem to resemble Smetana's *The Kiss* in that the union of the couple is temporarily frustrated by the couple's stubbornness. However, there is a crucial difference. In *The Kiss* the obstacle is removed by the characters' growth; in *The Stubborn Lovers* it is removed by Řeřicha's shrewd psychological trickery – a comic mechanism. This is the only one of Dvořák's comic operas to be essentially the story of a young couple's union. While in *The Bartered Bride* the young couple work in their various ways to steer their marriage plans to a successful conclusion, in Dvořák's *The Cunning Peasant* this activity is taken over by a consortium of women, whose leader, the Princess, has as her chief motive revenge on her philandering husband. That the young couple Bětuška and Jeník are united at the end is incidental, and Jeník, unlike his namesake in *The Bartered Bride*, is totally inactive in the affair. In Dvořák's first Czech opera, *King and Charcoal Burner*, the young couple are more enterprising, but even so this love interest is something grafted on to the original puppet play. Instead, the opera's title aptly sums up its main concern: the relationship between the two Matějs – the Charcoal Burner and his King. In *The Devil and Kate* there is no love interest at all.

Although both *Rusalka* and *The Jacobin* have ostensibly a loving couple at their centre, neither relationship provides the main focus of these operas. In *The Jacobin* the relationship between Bohuš (the 'Jacobin' of the title) and his wife Julie is not at stake, but instead it is his relationship with his estranged father, and the reconciliation that is finally achieved. *Rusalka* is never able to converse with the Prince until the very end of the opera. The Prince has rather more to do with the Foreign Princess and the seemingly central relationship is thus scarcely explored. Even if *Dimitrij* could be said to hinge on the tragic love affair between Dimitrij and Xenie, the triangle with Marina in fact conceals political implications. *Dimitrij* is not the simple story of a pretender's love affairs but is more about his position within the state: his repudiation of his Polish wife Marina and his taking up with the Russian Xenie reflect the changes in his political affections. He has important and powerful scenes with each woman, but most gripping of all is the final scene where Dimitrij's assumed mother Marfa is urged to swear to their relationship. Were the Act 1 'recognition' handled more adeptly, one might argue that Dimitrij's most important relationship was not with Marina or Xenie but instead with Marfa. As it is, this complex of issues tends to dissipate the power of what in many other respects is one of Dvořák's most notable operatic achievements.

### The impact of the National Theatre

Of Smetana's eight operas, only *Libuše* was written for and premièred in the National Theatre. The others, and even *Libuše* itself, increasingly took account of the Provisional Theatre and its limitations, and of the small band of devoted singers who sang there. With the definitive opening of the National Theatre in 1883 and Smetana's death a year later, a new era opened for Czech opera. At last the Czechs had a 'European-size' theatre. With it, however, they lost several of the distinctive features that had shaped their new operatic tradition. The size of the National Theatre allowed a greater concentration on visual aspects, with opulent new productions of European novelties. The artistic policies of Šubert and, in the twentieth century,

Kovařovic and Ostrčil meant a widening of the repertory which in turn created the need for new types of singers. Czech heroic/dramatic voices – a permanent lack at the Provisional Theatre – began to emerge for the Wagnerian repertory, just as a generation of acting singers (another weak point at the Provisional Theatre) had to be found for the *verismo* repertory and the new, more naturalistic methods of staging.

While a few of the prominent singers from the old guard – Sittová, Kröss-ing and Fibichová – remained, others found that their voices, nicely matched to the small stage of the Provisional Theatre, were not able to cope with the strain of filling a much bigger area, and singers such as z Ehren-bergů, Lev, Vávra and Čech were soon to disappear from the Czech operatic stage. New generations of singers replaced them. A larger body of singers, drawing increasingly on new talent that had gained experience in the Czech provinces, allowed double casting. While Smetana had at his disposal only one or two good singers for a particular *Fach* or voice type (or in some cases, none), later generations of composers were not so confined. But they could not rely on some of the best voices being always available. While some, like the great soprano Růžena Maturová, remained loyally with the company so that Dvořák and Fibich wrote roles especially for them, other prominent singers acquired European reputations that lured them away for long periods. Janáček hardly thought about specific singers at all. He wrote for Prague and beyond, yet for all but one of his operas had to settle for a Brno première. His new concept of the voice part, modified by his theories of speech melody, meant in fact that he was writing for a brand of singer that did not yet exist; with a few honourable exceptions, none of the great Czech singers of his day was prepared to sing his music at all.

Inevitably, the determination of voice types, and to some extent charac-ters, by particular singers was no longer the strong factor in post-Smetana Czech opera that it had been during his lifetime. And though some of his typical characters/voice types left a discernible trace in subsequent operas, developments such as the emergence of Czech dramatic voices meant fur-ther changes away from Smetana's models.

## Voice types

Mindful of the constraints of the Provisional Theatre company, Smetana was careful never to write another heroic tenor part after Dalibor. His successors did not need to be so scrupulous. The important Helden roles that Fibich and Dvořák included in their operas reflect not only a striking departure from Smetana's model in this respect, but also that there were now singers available who could take on such parts. Dvořák's *Dimitrij*, premièred two years before Smetana's death, has as its title role one of the most taxing heroic tenor parts in the Czech repertory. This, however, was written for Smetana's 'lyrical' tenor Antonín Vávra,[5] who achieved one of the great triumphs of his career with it, and was thereby encouraged to tackle the heavier repertory that he had hitherto avoided. From 1896 Czech composers could make use of Bohumil Pták, a tenor whose full, almost baritonish quality was immediately utilized at the National Theatre in *Dalibor* and *Lohengrin*. Pták was the first Ctirad in Fibich's *Šárka* and Rutan in *The Fall of Arkona*, the first Kozina in *The Dogheads* and Mánek in *Eva*. He created the similarly heroic tenor parts in *Rusalka* and *Armida*. (Although Dvořák wrote the part of the Prince in *Rusalka* with Pták in mind it was only indisposition that prevented an even more heroic tenor, Carl Burrian – one of the foremost Tristans of his day – from singing at the première.)

In *The Jacobin* tenor parts are confined to a lyrical tenor for the young suitor and a character tenor for the kantor Benda (it was taken by Krössing at the première). In Dvořák's other opera between *Dimitrij* and *Rusalka*, *The Devil and Kate*, the tenor part of the shepherd Jirka was, like the Prince in *Rusalka*, created by Bohumil Pták. At first sight this was a surprising casting. In fact the part has something in common with the slightly heavier voice that Smetana had employed in one of his most interesting tenor roles, Jíra in *The Brandenburgers in Bohemia*.

Smetana was lucky that the première of his first opera coincided with Arnošt Grund's brief period as leading tenor at the Provisional Theatre. His large voice was well suited to the middle Helden roles such as Radamès and Lohengrin that he took on after he left the company in 1870 and this, together with his acting abilities, made him an ideal choice for Jíra. Grund's distinctive energy is clearly apparent from Jíra's angry defence of himself at his trial (Ex. 6). Jíra differs from Smetana's lyrical tenors not simply by virtue of his forceful, more declamatory part, but also because he is not a romantic hero. He has no female partner and is motivated by poverty and social concerns. Smetana wrote only one more 'angry' tenor part of his sort, Šťáhlav in *Libuše*, though here the reason for the anger is sibling rivalry and jealousy. (Later angry tenors in Czech opera tend to be jealous ones, such as Lukáš in *The Kiss* whose outburst in Act 1 lies outside the generally lyrical character of much of his music.)

This type of 'angry' tenor occurs in some of Dvořák's operas. Jirka in *The Devil and Kate* is rather more genial than most, but he lacks a partner, and has moments of social anger both against his own poverty (he is thrown out of his humble job as a shepherd in Act 1) and against aristocratic oppression. Two of Dvořák's early comic operas contain examples of would-be lyrical tenors (young suitors), turned into heavier parts by the injection of a little anger. Toník in *The Stubborn Lovers* rebelliously does not want to obey his father's wishes for his marriage, although they coincide with his own. The part of Jeník in Dvořák's first Czech opera, *King and Charcoal Burner*, is even more interesting. He is not just an impatient young suitor, but one

Ex. 6

Jíra: Who is in control here? You or the law? The law! it is a dead letter here. [*The Brandenburgers in Bohemia*, 2.4.566–70]

with considerable independence of thought and action. This is nicely set off by Dvořák's music, for instance in his departure for the army, which provides the curtain climax to Act 2. Jeník's resolve to go away, sung 'with determination', was clearly intended by Dvořák to be a key moment in the opera since it brings back the opening music of the overture. When it is sung by Jeník, this music has, with its frequent *fermate* (sometimes on high notes, or on leaps to high notes), a distinctive swagger to it. In the final concertato, Jeník's voice is deliberately pitted against the rest of the cast, who plead with him to stay. But Jeník continues to sing 'broadly and with pain' that his beloved is faithless. His anger is fuelled by poverty, jealousy and pride.

While tenor parts in Czech opera grew heavier and more dramatic after Smetana, female parts, lyrical or, at the most, energetic in Smetana, turned into the full-blown tragic heroines of Fibich's and Dvořák's later operas – Hedy, Šárka and Radana (*The Fall of Arkona*), Rusalka and Armida, also Ostrčil's Vlasta or Foerster's Eva and Portia (in *Jessica*). These were mostly roles created by or directly written for the distinguished soprano Růžena

Maturová. A celebrated Libuše (see illustration 13c), Maturová may seem too dramatic a singer for the frail watersprite Rusalka, the quintessence of whose part seems to be the meltingly lyrical 'Hymn to the Moon'. However the part calls for a fair measure of vocal steel and appears more frail because of the contrast set up between her and the Foreign Princess.

This scheme, and indeed some of the music,[6] recalls an even more striking vocal opposition in *Dimitrij*, between the gentle Russian Xenie and the fierce Polish princess Marina. Xenie is always seen in a vulnerable position, escaping from the rabble that vows death to her family, threatened with rape by drunken Poles, a frightened suppliant for the life of her protector Šujský, and finally seeking refuge in a nunnery. Marina, on the other hand, initiates action with her inflammatory drinking song in Act 2, her

Ex. 7a

Rusalka: Oh moon, stay a moment! [*Rusalka*, 1.499–501]

Ex. 7b

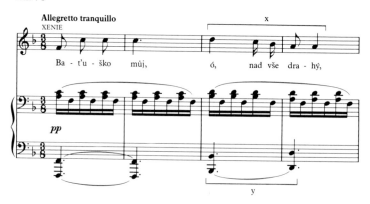

Xenie: My father, dear above all things! [*Dimitrij*, 2: scene change, 2]

Dimitrij: [I saw her, and] forgot the world! [*Dimitrij*, 3.1]

Ex. 7d

[*Rusalka*, 1.566–9] See p. 302 n.6 for commentary.

argument with Dimitrij over Xenie during which she reveals to him his real parentage, and her public denunciation of him in the final act. The contrast between the two characters is neatly encapsulated in the songs each sings in Act 2. Marina leads the Polish courtiers in an ebullient, provocative drinking song. Soon after, Xenie seeks refuge in the vault of the Uspensky Cathedral and sings a quiet, touchingly simple prayer, unaware that she is overheard by Dimitrij. For Marina's song, Dvořák provided some of his most elaborate and brilliant operatic vocal writing, with trills, melismata and other coloratura effects quite absent from Xenie's part (Ex. 8). There is little difference in the range of the two parts, though the tessitura of Marina's is generally higher. But while Xenie's most characteristic utterances are her simple strophic prayer and her soft despairing cries for help, Marina in contrast is distinguished by a number of powerful dramatic gestures and by the leading part she plays in ensembles. (Xenie, significantly, takes no part in any of the choral ensembles.)

Models for these actively malevolent female villains in Dvořák's operas – and there are similarly unpleasant female characters in his other operas,

Ex. 8

Marina: . . . only there [in Poland] they know how to laugh, to enjoy themselves and to rejoice! [*Dimitrij*, 2.2]

including two named witches – cannot be found in any of Smetana's operas, which are entirely without female villains, as are Fibich's, with the exception of the demonic Radana in *The Fall of Arkona*. And while the German tradition of evil, jealous ladies represented by Weber's Eglantine and Wagner's Ortrud may seem to offer similar character types, these are all dramatic mezzo roles (Göpfert 1977, 80–2 traces their origins) whereas the tessituras of Marina and the Foreign Princess are soprano. Dvořák's evil women tend to emphasize their natures not with the weight of an Ortrud, but with bright, steely voices able to use snatches of coloratura.

Similarly, the dignified figures of female authority in Fibich's early operas, all given to a contralto (the White Lady in *Blaník*, Donna Isabella in *The Bride of Messina*), have no real counterpart in Smetana (whose Libuše is a soprano) but were parts written for the voice, stature and character of his wife Betty (Hostinský 1909, 68, 99–100). It is noteworthy that with the breakup of his marriage and the arrival of Schulzová as librettist, Fibich's dominant female roles were henceforth written for dramatic soprano. Betty Fibichová also created the contralto parts in all three of Dvořák's early comic operas. Here Dvořák used the voice conventionally for older women, and wives, widows and so on. Interestingly he did not write the part of Marfa for mezzo, as one might have expected in view of her age and in view of the two major soprano parts given to Marina and Xenie; at the première Marfa was sung by z Ehrenbergů (now nearing the end of her long career). Dvořák's mezzo and contralto parts, unlike Fibich's, were not for

194

aristocratic older women. Thus, while the old housekeeper in *The Jacobin* is a mezzo, the Princess in *The Devil and Kate* is a soprano (Maturová again). With this last opera, the mezzo voice seems to have become for Dvořák an essentially comic or even grotesque vehicle: the unmarriageable Kate is a mezzo and so is the comically malevolent Witch in *Rusalka* (in contrast to Dvořák's earlier witch, the Ulrica-like Homena in *Vanda*, who is merely malevolent).

In his *Dimitrij*, Dvořák cast the villain Šujský as a baritone. It is Šujský who insists on Marfa's swearing that Dimitrij is her son (thus precipitating the final crisis) and who at the end shoots Dimitrij. Though the part is small, it is strongly characterized with a number of melodramatic, conventionally 'villainous' vocal gestures. Likewise, in his last opera, *Armida*, Dvořák cast the villain, the magician Ismen, as a baritone. Clear-cut male villains, absent from Smetana's operas after Tausendmark in *The Brandenburgers*, thus reappear in post-Smetana operas and, as in the European tradition, are generally assigned to energetic baritones. Before *Dimitrij*, Dvořák cast the Chief Priest in *Vanda* – like Šujský a custodian of the old order who spoils the happiness of the protagonist – as a bass. There are, nevertheless, proportionally few such baritone villains, and those that occur are often in operas on non-Czech plots. Dvořák's Šujský and Ismen are balanced by the 'noble' baritones in his operas with Czech plots, for instance the King in *King and Charcoal Burner* or Bohuš in *The Jacobin*. The latter fits easily into this tradition: he is well born (the son of a count) and is full of noble sentiments about his homeland and about liberty. He is also inactive in that when his plan to see his estranged father is thwarted and he is cast into prison, it is his resourceful wife Julie who finds a way of releasing him and bringing about the reconciliation with his father. Technically, the villain of the opera is Bohuš's cousin, Adolf, who is plotting to usurp Bohuš's position as heir to the count. His part – also written for a baritone – is, however, small and feebly characterized in comparison with the noble Bohuš, or with the comic characters like Benda and the Steward.

Fibich, in his most nationalist opera, *Šárka*, similarly followed Smetana's model in *Libuše* and cast the princely but inactive Přemysl (now a widower) as a 'noble' baritone, as he did Absolon, the Christian bishop in his other late-Slavonic opera, *The Fall of Arkona*, and Prospero in *The Tempest*. But in *Hedy* the heroine's pirate father Lambro (who sells her lover into slavery, precipitating her suicide) is also a baritone, the most actively malevolent baritone in Czech opera. Lambro's predecessors in Fibich's operas include Bořek in *Blaník* and Don Manuel in *The Bride of Messina*. The only non-baritone male villain in a Fibich opera is the high priest Dargun (bass) in *The Fall of Arkona*.

It cannot really be said, then, that either Fibich or Dvořák continued with

Smetana's distinctive voice types as far as their serious operas were concerned. Both made much more use of heavier, dramatic voices, and found a different role for the mezzo (or contralto). And while Smetana's noble baritones continue in several notable parts by both composers (possibly because the Lev tradition was carried on by such 'placid' baritones as Bohumil Benoni and František Šír), this casting vied with the baritone villain of European opera that had all but disappeared from Smetana's works. It should be stressed that Smetana's serious–heroic operas were written in the earlier part of his career, and that his most distinctive voice types emerged in the later operas – a strain of bitter-sweet questing comedies that neither of his major successors espoused. Fibich came nearest in his works with *The Tempest*, Dvořák in his early comic operas and in the later *Jacobin*. Dvořák's bass Steward Filip, for instance, is a more effective successor to Kecal than Smetana's own Mumlal, with elements of real menace to threaten the happiness of both couples and even a fully-fledged revenge aria. There are, however, enough clues to direct the audience to view his threat in a comic context. The first time we meet him his bass voice is fitted to unsuitably dainty minuet music; soon he is given the same comic trills that punctured Kecal's pomposity. In the same way, Dvořák's comic bass devil Marbuel (in *The Devil and Kate*) owes something to Smetana's comic melodrama 'villain' Rarach in *The Devil's Wall*, while the anxious, pessimistic father-figure of the Water Gnome in *Rusalka* has a family resemblance to Father Paloucký in *The Kiss*, his much-repeated phrase 'Ubohá rusalko, bledá, běda!' ('Alas, poor pale Rusalka!') operating not as a comic tag but, like Paloucký's 'Jak jsem to řek'!', as an expression of frustration and concern. While Dvořák's Benda in *The Jacobin* is too distinctive to be compared directly with anything in Smetana it is clear that his tremulous fussiness owes something, as does another tenor buffo part, the Gamekeeper in *Rusalka*, to Michálek in *The Devil's Wall* and to the creator of all three, Adolf Krössing.

# Janáček

## *Plot types*

Both Janáček's early operas have at their centre would-be loving couples whose union is either tragically frustrated (*Šárka*) or brought to a happy conclusion (*The Beginning of a Romance*). This, as much as any other factor, sets them apart from his mature works. Their successor, *Jenůfa*, appears to follow the Krásnohorská–Smetana pattern based on love developing between a central couple and ultimately fulfilled through their spiritual growth. From the passionate and impulsive girl in Act 1 to the wise, reconciled woman in Act 3, Jenůfa's growth is charted in her relationship with

Laca: from dislike to an awareness of his qualities and, finally, love. But Jenůfa's growth is also revealed in her relationship with her foster-mother, the Kostelnička. By the end of Act 3 she is able to comprehend what it cost her foster-mother to make her terrible confession, and can forgive and accept her. It is this relationship, rather than that with Laca, which is celebrated in the opera's Czech title – *Její pastorkyňa* (Her foster-daughter).

Some of Janáček's later operas have no central love interest: *From the House of the Dead* has none outside the narrations; *Brouček* has only a secondary pair of lovers. In others there is a central couple but, rather as in *Libuše*, one partner is more interesting and dominant than the other. This happens to some extent in *Káťa Kabanová*, more so in *Fate* and *Vixen*, and particularly in *The Makropulos Affair*. Marty has any number of would-be suitors; but she is a larger character than any of them, and three hundred years more experienced. Although erotic love is an issue in *Makropulos* and *Vixen*, both operas are even more concerned with old age, death and rebirth, and above all reconciliation. Janáček's final operas may lack the central loving couple of Smetana's late operas, but they share, unlike Fibich's, the concern of Smetana's late operas for reconciliation and the achievement of wisdom through experience. The change in perception in a central character and his or her acceptance of life and especially death is usually demonstrated in an extended solo towards the end of the opera, for instance those given to the Gamekeeper in *Vixen*, or to Marty in *Makropulos*.

## Voice types

The voice types in Janáček's first opera, *Šárka*, conform to the heavier, more dramatic type of voices that were being used in Prague in the 1880s. Janáček actually designated Šárka as a 'dramatic soprano', his only use of the term except for the special case of Emilia Marty.[7] But the Heldentenor conception of Ctirad persisted into many later parts, such as Laca in *Jenůfa*, or Živný in *Fate*, or Petřík in *Brouček*. In *The Beginning of a Romance*, however, Janáček went back to Smetana and to Dvořák's early comic operas for his voice types. This is evident, for instance in the bass role of Mudroch, which looks back to Dvořák's Řeřicha (and ultimately to Kecal), or in the part of Tonek, the helpless tenor lover whose characterless passivity relates him to Smetana's secondary tenor lovers such as Vítek in *Dalibor* or Vít in *The Secret* or especially the apathetic Jeník of *The Cunning Peasant*. Thereafter Janáček's passive tenors no longer sing in thirds and sixths with the soprano but become realistically tongue-tied like Janek in *The Makropulos Affair*, or nervously inhabit the higher reaches of the tenor range like Blankytný in *Brouček*, or Gregor in *Makropulos* (Ex. 9). Janáček, in an annotation to his copy of the printed vocal score, specified falsetto for comic effect in Blankytný's part (which he had originally conceived for an alto; Tyrrell

Ex. 9

Blankytný: To Beauty and Love! [L. Janáček, *The Excursions of Mr Brouček*, 1 VS 51; C by Universal Edition AG, Wien]
Gregor: I am crazy. I have never been so crazy. [L. Janáček, *The Makropulos Affair*, 1 VS 60; C 1966 by Universal Edition AG, Wien]

1968, 106), but may well have expected Gregor to use falsetto too, and indeed the effete sound here complements the character. It is surely significant that Janáček cast the two most helpless men in *The Makropulos Affair* as tenors. Both are infatuated with Marty, and both show their impotence by threatening to shoot themselves or, in Janek's case, by actually doing so. It is the two lawyers who succeed with Marty, either sexually (Prus) or by uncovering her secrets (Prus and Kolenatý); and Janáček made them both baritones.

The two men in Kát'a Kabanová's life, her husband Tichon and her lover Boris, are also tenors. It might seem odd that Janáček did not contrast husband and lover vocally, but in fact his choice of voice type helps to stress their unassertive characters. There is little to choose between their voice types, just as there is little to choose between their characters. In *Jenůfa* Janáček similarly made both suitors tenors: here, however, there is a clear differentiation between them. Števa is weak, passive (easily led astray, as his grandmother indulgently comments) and lyrical. Laca is active, jealous and angry, which is clear from the first time he sings (Ex. 10), a robust part with sharp rhythms.

Ex. 10

Laca (jealously): These days, grandmother, you see all sorts of things poorly!
[L. Janáček, *Jenůfa*, 1.1; C 1969 by Universal Edition AG, Wien]

The two types are also present in Janáček's last opera, *From the House of the Dead*, in the gentle Skuratov and in the surly Luka, imprisoned because he stabbed his commanding officer, a crime motivated by social injustice. Janáček emphasized the difference between the two by making Skuratov's often lyrical narrative into the prelude of the light-relief plays in Act 2, while it is Luka's grim narrative, with his description of the flogging he received, that brings Act 1 to its frightening climax. Janáček's invented continuation of their life stories in Act 3 divided the characters still further. Both are in hospital. Skuratov is impotently mad and is capable only of high-lying cries of 'O Lujzo!'. Luka is dying in great agony and, as he does so, he is revealed as the arch-villain of Šiškov's narration, Filka Morozov.

The line of noble baritones continued in Janáček's first opera, *Šárka*, with a baritone Přemysl comparable to that of Fibich's later opera, and of course to their common ancestor, in *Libuše*. In a sense, too, one could say that the baritone Gamekeeper in *The Cunning Little Vixen* belongs to the same breed. If he was an active, disruptive force at the beginning of the opera, seizing the Vixen, by the end he has turned into a 'noble' baritone, wise and at peace with himself, full of poignant resignation, and inactive: at the end we see him dropping his gun. Petrovič in *From the House of the Dead* also belongs to this line. He is aristocratic, resigned to his fate, and apart from his kindliness to the young Aljeja almost completely passive, a neutral figure whose arrival and departure provides the slender narrative frame of the opera.

Like Smetana, Janáček wrote few operas with male villains. There are only two candidates: the prison Commandant in *From the House of the Dead* and Dikoj in *Kát'a Kabanová*. Harašta, the poacher who shoots the Vixen, is hardly a villain. The Vixen herself provokes the shooting, and Janáček took great pains, in the laconic musical gesture after her death, to play down any tragic feelings that might have been aroused. Similarly the two lawyers who doggedly pursue Marty's fraud in *The Makropulos Affair* do so 'professionally' and at the end sympathize with her plight; Marty is up against bigger things than Kolenatý and Prus. These differences are made even clearer by Janáček's music. The more sinister of the two baritone laywers in *Makropulos* has music in his Act 2 confrontation with Marty possessing an oily menace that turns threatening at the end of the act (the trombone snarls); but by Act 3, under the double impact of his unsatisfactory night with Marty and his son's death, he is a broken man and contributes little to Marty's unmasking. Similarly, Harašta in *Vixen* is introduced on both his entrances with 'folksongs', the second a particularly genial one, and much of his scene with the Vixen is given over to a semi-comic sobbing lament over what his bride-to-be will say at the dispersal of his hens.

The music of the two 'true' villains, Dikoj and the prison Commandant, is rather different. Both are basses, not baritones, and the parts share outbursts of aggressive and sadistic malevolence (at least in Act 1 of *From the House of the Dead*; by Act 3 the Commandant has crumpled, like Prus, into maudlin self-pity and sentimentality). Dikoj's is the more extensive and active part, with a number of distinctly villainous gestures, but Dikoj himself is dominated by an even more formidable representative of the old order, Kát'a's mother-in-law, Kabanicha. This comes of course from Ostrovsky's play, which Janáček adapted for his libretto, but the music helps accentuate the unequal relationship by showing Dikoj, in the one scene where they are alone together, as servile and slightly comic.

Kabanicha is the most clear-cut villain in any Janáček opera and by far the nastiest character in his operatic gallery. It is the music of her triumph (after approvingly viewing Kát'a's corpse) which, together with the hammerblows of fate and the music of the Volga, brings the opera to its close. Her music is strongly contrasted with that of the heroine. While Kát'a has some of Janáček's most lyrical, fragile utterances (his model was in fact Madama Butterfly – Tyrrell 1982, 34), Kabanicha has a more fragmented, craggier line, with sharp leaps, accompanied by unsettled dissonant or whole-tone dominated harmony. Another guardian of the old morality, the Kostelnička, is the overt 'villain' of *Jenůfa*, in the sense that she murders her foster-daughter's child, and is accordingly given a rantingly melodramatic solo as she goes off to do the deed (Ex. 11). But she differs from other villains in that while acting out of pride, she also has in mind the ultimate happiness of her foster-daughter. Furthermore, evil or relentless fate is not triumphant at the end of the opera, as it is in *Dimitrij* or *Rusalka* or *Kát'a Kabanová*. The chief point of the opera is Jenůfa's spiritual growth which makes it possible for her to forgive her foster-mother's act.

In Janáček's next opera, *Fate*, Míla's mother plays a similar role to the Kostelnička in 'protecting' her daughter from a man she considers an unsuitable husband for her. But unlike the Kostelnička's murder of Jenůfa's child, which provides a dramatic axis for the work, the deaths caused by Míla's mother when she falls from the balcony taking Míla with her provides nothing more than a melodramatic curtain to the second act.

The most fascinating figure in this line is Emilia Marty in *The Makropulos Affair*. Though she causes much unhappiness and, during the opera, a death, she is not a straightforward villain like Kabanicha or Míla's mother. Like the Kostelnička, she becomes reconciled to her fate, and in the end there is understanding and compassion for her, expressed by the rest of the cast, just as the Kostelnička was forgiven by Jenůfa. Her part is as dominating as Libuše's. The 'strange light' which Janáček specified at her first appearance (presumably to add a supernatural dimension) is entirely unnecessary in view of the oddness of her story as it unfolds, and the fact that, more than any other dominant female part, Janáček set hers off with more 'old-fashioned' vocal gestures (sustained notes, melismata, trills) than

Ex. 11

The Kostelnička: I will take the boy to the Lord God. . . It will be shorter and easier! By spring, when the ice melts, there will be no trace. He will go to God before he knows anything (losing her senses in the peak of her excitement). They would attack me and Jenůfa! (cowering, she points to herself as one persecuted) Look at her, the Kostelnička! (she stealthily hurries into the bedroom and returns with the child and wraps it in a shawl). [L. Janáček, *Jenůfa*, 2.5; C 1969 by Universal Edition AG, Wien]

was generally acceptable within the conventions of his late operas. Her soprano voice also sets her apart from Kabanicha and Míla's mother, both contraltos. Janáček did not, however, limit the lower female voices exclusively to his female villains. The Housekeeper Kedruta in *Brouček* and the Gamekeeper's wife in *Vixen* are both 'older-woman' contraltos, while in *Káťa Kabanová* Janáček employs a mezzo for Varvara. The fact that he seems to have regarded this as a way of emphasizing the seductive and erotic side of her character seems clear from the way that at virtually the same time he revised his song cycle *The Diary of One who Disappeared*, making a mezzo out of the seductive gypsy instead of the original soprano (Wingfield 1984, 52).

In his later operas Janáček kept on finding himself attracted to woman-dominated subject matter. While he was writing *Káťa* he confessed to Kamila Stösslová that he was worried about writing too many 'women's operas', but nonetheless went on to write two more in which men are depicted as moths, helplessly fluttering around one central female. In *Vixen*, for instance, it is the Vixen, rather than the Fox, who initiates most of the animal action; the human males hover hopefully round the mysterious figure of Terynka (who never even appears). In *The Makropulos Affair* this image is even stronger: the immense figure of Emilia Marty is set apart by her extraordinary past from the males who flock round her. Only in his final opera, *From the House of the Dead*, did Janáček write a mature opera which was not women-dominated, largely because they were excluded from the cast.

Since Janáček's operas are mostly serious, there are only a few comic characters in them. Mudroch in *The Beginning of a Romance* is the usual meddling, bumbling bass-baritone in the Kecal tradition, complete with nudging trills in case we do not get the point. Context is vital as always, as is demonstrated in the various metamorphoses of the character of the Sacristan in *The Excursions of Mr Brouček*. In his earthly guise as a Sacristan he functions as irate father, a 'threat' (though complete with comic trills, Ex. 12) to his daughter's marriage with the impoverished painter Mazal. Similarly, it is clear from the absurd context when he becomes Lunobor on the moon, how seriously he should be taken, and any doubts are settled

Ex. 12

Sacristan: Oh, I will be revenged! (goes off into the Víkarka [inn]) [L. Janáček, *The Excursions of Mr Brouček*, 1 VS 14; C by Universal Edition AG, Wien]

by his nonsense 'chapters' which help bring Act 1 to a close, or the comically exaggerated phrase with which he introduces them (Ex. 13). In the fifteenth-century excursion the same character sings Domšík, the serious and sympathetic Hussite who takes in Brouček as a guest. His kindly

Ex. 13

Lunobor: I will read him three chapters. Traverse the moon's beauties in discipline, fight in love, love in fear; in discipline, in fear, do not get stuck! [L. Janáček, *The Excursions of Mr Brouček*, 1 VS 77; C by Universal Edition AG, Wien]

actions, his serious nature, his death while fighting for his ideals (movingly mourned by his daughter) lack any comic context and instead we take them at their face value. Even Janáček hardly believed he was dealing with the same voice and set the part in the first scene not for a comic bass, but as a lyric tenor, and had to rewrite it when he realized his mistake (Tyrrell 1973).

Most of Janáček's comic men, however, tend to be tenors. His Schoolmaster in *Vixen* is probably intended to be comic (note, for instance, his vocal coupling with the drunken Mosquito) but the comic mechanism hinges less on the fact that like Vašek he is an inappropriate suitor than on the juxtaposition of his 'learning' with his drunkenness on his journey after the first inn scene. His vocabulary of foreign musical terms ('staccato', 'flageoletto') in fact proclaim him to be a cousin of Benda, whose choir-rehearsal scene is peppered with similar foreign musical terms. The joke goes back to the original novel but if Janáček had Benda in mind this may have been a factor for the respective castings of the Schoolmaster and the Priest as tenor and bass. The Schoolmaster, as an inappropriate bass suitor, would have been in the comic company of the Steward (in *The Jacobin*) and the elderly bachelor suitors of *In the Well*, Mikuláš and *The Elderly Suitor* rather than in the touching company of Vašek and Benda.

The central tenor of Janáček's 'comic' opera *Brouček* does not conform to any of the comic tenor models in Czech opera. He is not an anxious father like Michálek in *The Devil's Wall* (or Janáček's own Vítek in *Makropulos*), nor an unworldly, preoccupied intellectual like Benda, nor even like the madman Hauk in *The Makropulos Affair* (cast, uniquely in Janáček, as an 'operetta tenor'); and, although he occasionally flirts with Málinka, he is not even an inappropriate suitor. By the moon excursion, he has become distinctly reluctant. On earth, especially in the tirade against life on earth, Brouček is something of an 'angry' tenor; on the moon, when placed in comic situations, the characters around him are so exaggerated that he begins to appear as the sympathetic voice of reason. In the fifteenth century he emerges almost as a tragic figure. The voice of reason against all the fanaticism around him rings a little hollow since Domšík (the main spokesman of the Hussite view) is so obviously a decent man, and Brouček so obviously a coward. In fact his shrieks of 'Smilování!' (Mercy!) as he is bundled into the barrel at the climax of the Hussite excursion have anything but a comic effect. Brouček lacks adaptability, and is unable to learn, unlike Jenůfa, Laca, the Kostelnička, the Gamekeeper and Emilia Marty.

If the title role in *Brouček* is too complex to fit neatly into earlier Czech vocal stereotypes, the trouser role of the Little Waiter (in turn the Child Prodigy on the moon and the precocious Student in the fifteenth century) looks back not just to Dvořák's Kitchen Boy in *Rusalka*, a few years earlier, but to a whole tradition of mezzo or soubrette youths (see pp. 178–9). It is not entirely clear what voice Janáček had in mind for the five-year-old Doubek in *Fate*, but *travesti* parts for mezzo or soprano occur in many of his operas from the herdboy Jano in *Jenůfa* to Aljeja, the Tartar lad in *From the House of the Dead*. Actual children's voices were used in Czech opera before Janáček's *The Cunning Little Vixen*, but only as part of the chorus. The most famous example is in the choir-rehearsal scene of *The Jacobin*, but the French provenance of the resource (in *Le prophète*) is however more evident from Bendl's use in *The Child of Tábor*. After the death of Prokop's daughter, the opera's 'big tune' is sung by a choir of children and young women and this, its heavenly choir suggestion emphasized by the orchestral accompaniment of harp, tremolando muted strings, soft flutes and so on, is enough to soften the heart of the rugged warrior and persuade him to receive the child embassy from the besieged town of Naumburg.[8] In *Vixen*, however, Janáček boldly specified children's voices for several of the animal and insect solo parts (most marvellously for the young Frog in the final bars); and when contemporary productions failed to provide them, he protested vigorously.

# Conclusion

Writing in German in 1843, the Czech critic and composer Ludvík Ritter z Rittersberku opposed the prejudice, common at the time, that Slav languages were unsuitable for singing because of the difficult pronunciation of consonants, and consonantal clusters (Zielecká 1926, 12). They gave, he argued, strong support to the 'characteristic expression' of the language.

In Czech clear vowel sounds predominate – *i*, *e* and *a* – so that Czech sounds the clearest and brightest among the Slav languages. Polish and especially Russian, on the other hand, have more dark vowels, chiefly *u* and *o*, which colour the voices. This, he stated, was apparently the cause of the greater disposition of lower notes, celebrated among the Russians. A full physiological study of this subject has yet to be made, but it is true that Czechoslovakia has tended to export sopranos and tenors to the world whereas Russia and Bulgaria have tended to export basses and mezzos.

To physical predisposition must be added training. Although Bohemia in the nineteenth century was part of the 'German' world, and certainly by the end of the century was training its singers for the German market – with some success (Destinn in Berlin, Burrian in Hamburg, Jeritza in Vienna), a clear Italian bias is evident in much of the singing teaching of the Provisional Theatre singers (see p. 32). The first conductor at the theatre, J.N. Maýr, drew the critic Smetana's anger for his penchant for Italian guests and the bel canto repertory, but Smetana the composer nevertheless wrote for Italianate voices rather than German ones, stinting only on coloratura. As Leo Jehne points out on the basis of tessitura analysis, Smetana's tenors and baritones have predominant tessituras respectively almost as high as those of Verdi's tenors and baritones, unlike Wagner's 'baritonal' Heldentenors and bass-baritones. Similarly Czech sopranos, even those usually categorized as dramatic sopranos (Libuše, Milada, Hedy, Šárka, Eva), are nearer the high Italian soprano than the mezzo-ish German dramatic soprano. This trait is even more pronounced in the work of Smetana's young contemporary, Karel Šebor. In his second opera, *Drahomíra*, the baritone villain Boleslav has a part which dwells constantly on high Fs and F sharps with occasional Gs, while the dramatic title role, described as mezzo by Hornové (1903, 290), goes up frequently to B flat and even C.[9]

But the presence of certain character traits, observed earlier in this chapter, ensured that Czech voice types were not simply Italian or German voice types transferred to the Czech opera stage, but a distinctive breed. Credit for observing and depicting such character traits must go initially to the librettists, but even more depends on the composer's response: his choice of this rather than that libretto, and the highlighting by his music of particular features. Furthermore, some of the character traits reach back even beyond the librettists. Dvořák's first strong woman (Alvina in *Alfred*), with warrior tendencies like Šárka and a saving mission like Milada (*Dalibor*) or Julie (*Jacobin*), came not from a Czech librettist's imagination but from a German play by Karl Theodor Körner (1791–1813). Rescuing women themselves came into prominence in French revolutionary opera (whence Beethoven's Leonore in *Fidelio*) and warring women, such as Amazons, go back even further. The difference is that while Verdi turned down Scribe's *Wlaska* ('The female soldiers made a strange impression on me', he wrote to

205

Scribe on 18 August 1852),[10] and set *Les vêpres siciliennes* instead, Czech composers seem to have sought out and responded positively to opera librettos with women rulers, warrior women, resourceful, rescuing wives and fiercely protective mothers or foster-mothers. Mothers in Czech nineteenth-century opera are more dominant and influential than fathers, wives more dominant than husbands, queens more charismatic than kings. Smetana's Libuše (in comparison to, say, his King Vladislav in *Dalibor*) illustrates the last point, but an even neater example can be found in a single opera, Šebor's *Drahomíra*, in which the saintly Václav I ('Good King Wenceslas') appears but does not sing, unlike his formidable mother, Drahomíra, who obviously caught the imagination of both librettist and composer.

Such preferences clearly determine the types of character most likely to be portrayed on the Czech operatic stage and the types of story in which they are best employed. Czech opera has few male villains and many male comics; conversely there are few female comics and several female villains. A good example can be found in attitudes taken in Czech opera towards the supernatural or to demonic characters. Czech opera frequently portrays devils, but invariably makes them out to be friendly, feeble, incompetent or comic: the one in Weinberger's *Švanda the Bagpiper* is simply the latest in a long line. Serious and malevolent demonic males are unusual in Czech opera – there is nothing in between Bendl's Almamen in *Lejla* (1868) and Dvořák's Ismen in *Armida* (1904), both based on foreign sources. On the other hand there is a plethora of female witches in Czech opera, both actual witches or *femmes fatales* (like Janáček's Emilia Marty) luring men to their death, shading into masterful women like the Kostelnička, who achieve their ends by sheer force of character. Whether the frequent occurrence of such women is simply an example of atavistic Slavonic matriarchy, as Stuckenschmidt (1954, 9) has suggested, or the contribution of Czech women librettists is difficult to say. Strong women are found equally in operas with male librettists, or in many of Tyl's plays in the first half of the nineteenth century, and even in Míča's opera of 1730, where the character of the energetic Hedvika, on which the plot revolves, seems to allude to the young Maria Theresa, the only Habsburg female ruler (Trojan 1974, 85). Another theory (Vacková 1940, 148–9) suggests that the lines of sharp-witted women like Mařenka (*The Bartered Bride*) or Karolina (*The Two Widows*), or headstrong women who need keeping in order such as Vendulka (*The Kiss*) or Kate (*The Devil and Kate*), reflect the popularity with Czech audiences of the time of two Shakespearean heroines, Beatrice (*Much Ado about Nothing*) and Katherina (*The Taming of the Shrew*). But this is another way of saying that such characters, and their Czech derivatives, found a deep and significant response in Czech audiences.

It is striking that Smetana's first opera, *The Brandenburgers in Bohemia*, and those written in the first few years of the Provisional Theatre – Bendl's *Lejla* and *Břetislav*, Šebor's serious operas, and Dvořák's somewhat later *Vanda* (1876) – comply with some of the patterns of contemporary European opera. All these operas have male villains, or at least 'divided' male anti-heroes: Tausendmark in *The Brandenburgers*; Bendl's Almamen and Torquemada in *Lejla*, and Ota in *Břetislav*; Šebor's Vraník in *The Templars*, Boleslav in *Drahomíra*, Radimský in *The Hussite Bride* and Vuk in *Blanka*; Dvořák's Chief Priest and Roderich in *Vanda*. Tausendmark, Roderich and all the Šebor characters except Radimský are baritones; but, interestingly, in his two operas mentioned above Bendl assigned these roles to basses (Paleček, a true bass, as Almamen, and the bass-baritone Karel Čech for the other two roles), while, even before Smetana, he had taken advantage of Lev's particular qualities to create 'noble' baritone parts. Both King Ferdinand and the last king of Granada, the indecisive Boabdil el Chico, were sung by baritones (the latter by Lev), as was the unfortunate King Oldřich in *Břetislav* (Lev again).[11] Bendl persisted with this pattern in his later operas such as *The Montenegrins*, where Lev once again was assigned to the noble ruler King Petr II, while the villainous Ljubota, the secret adherent of the Turks among the Serbs, was sung by a bass.

An active but divided character in Smetana, or for that matter in Janáček, was much more likely to be female – Milada changing her hatred into anger, Krasava feigning hatred for love, or Anežka torn between mourning her husband and acknowledging her love for Ladislav. And equally, during the 1870s and 1880s, the demonic or guilt-racked, 'divided' baritones of Weber, Marschner and Wagner are absent from Czech opera, which preferred instead to cultivate the placid, noble, inactive baritone. Lambro in Fibich's *Hedy* (1896) was the first major Czech work to breach this convention, followed by the baritone villains in Kovařovic's *The Dogheads* (1898), Dvořák's *Armida* (1904), and in some of Foerster's operas. In most nineteenth-century opera a male, angry with his lot or at odds with society, is likely to be a baritone (Ernani, Rigoletto in Verdi; in German opera, from Weber's Kaspar and Lysiart up to Wagner's Telramund and even Alberich). This, however, is not true of Czech opera after 1870, where such a character is more likely to be cast as a tenor. There are thus no anti-hero baritones who give their names to Czech operas in the manner of Don Giovanni, Hans Heiling, the Flying Dutchman, Macbeth or Simon Boccanegra. With the paucity of real basses there are no bass heroes such as Moses or Ivan Susanin. When a Czech opera is named after a single male character he is invariably a tenor, for instance in *The Tinker*, *Vladimír* (Skuherský), *Dalibor*, *Břetislav*, *Bukovín*, *Záviš*, *Dimitrij*, *Karel Škreta*, the Švanda operas of Hřímalý and Bendl, *Mr Brouček's Excursions*, and *Johnny's Kingdom*. The only baritones or basses to appear in the titles of Czech opera apart from Dvořák's early and German *Alfred* and the ambiguous case of the 'Jacobin' Bohuš, are comic, such as the title roles of *King and Charcoal Burner*, *The Cunning Peasant*, *The Elderly Suitor*, *Mikuláš*, *Zítek*, *The Devil and Kate*, and Weinberger's *Švanda the Bagpiper*. And though the tendency is surprisingly undeveloped in Smetana and Dvořák, later Czech operas from Fibich to Janáček are much more likely to be named after their women characters, no more tellingly demonstrated than in Vrchlický's and Foerster's renaming of *The Merchant of Venice* to *Jessica*.

# 7. Folk elements and the 'Czech style'

## Czech folksong up to the 1860s

As far as music and singing is concerned, I lay down as the first and the chief requirement, dependent *on the assiduous study of Czecho-Slavonic folksongs and the music ap-
pertaining to them*, that it should have a truly *national* character [original emphases].
Choruses, especially in a comic opera, should not be a mere diversion for the audience,
but by providing a living echo of folksongs, should encourage the audience's lively
participation. In a comic opera folkdances could perhaps be used to good effect.

(Harrach 1861, 45)

Even before Smetana and his contemporaries had begun writing operas,
theoreticians had pronounced on how Czech composers should go about
this task. The chief requirement of the music, and one clearly spelt out in
Count Harrach's competition rules above, was that it should be based on the
study of Czech folksongs. Admittedly, this was only a means to an end –
that, as Harrach put it, Czech opera should have 'a truly *national* character'.
Smetana and his adherents could maintain that there were other, more
appropriate, more artistically rewarding, ways of suggesting national
character. But folksong proved to be an easy slogan, and one that was
enthusiastically taken up by the conservative camp. The politics of Czech
opera polarized more openly here than on any other issue and had the effect
of charging with crucial importance something that might otherwise have
remained purely a matter of artistic choice for the composer. Is Vaughan
Williams's *Hugh the Drover*, with its string of English folksongs, a more
'English' opera than Britten's *Peter Grimes*? The question seems hardly
worth raising in view of the different aims and natures of the two works, and
yet it was this sort of question that almost cost Smetana his Harrach prize
and which continued to bedevil his operatic career until his death. What,
however, did Harrach mean by 'national character' and what was the general
perception at the time of Czech 'folksong'?

By the 1860s there was a wealth of easily accessible folksong material for
Czech composers to study. This decade saw the definitive publication of two
enormous collections (about 2500 songs each), one Moravian, one Bohemian. František Sušil's *Moravian Folksongs with Tunes Included with the Text*
(*Moravské národní písně s nápěvy do textu vřaděnými*)[1] completed its seven-
year serial publication in 1860; Karel Jaromír Erben's *Czech Folksongs and
Nursery Rhymes* (*Prostonárodní české písně a říkadla*) – dedicated, inciden-

tally, to Count Harrach – was published in 1862 (tunes) and 1864 (texts). Both projects were initiated considerably earlier, in an atmosphere stimulated by the publication in the 1830s of Polish, Ukrainian and Slovenian folksongs (the publication of Russian folksongs had begun fifty years earlier). Such publications formed part of the wider European movement whose origins are usually traced to the eighteenth-century collections of folksongs and folk poetry in the British Isles and to the writings of Herder. In the Czech lands Sušil's preparatory volumes in 1835 and 1840 of Moravian folksongs, and Erben's first volumes of Czech folksongs (1842, 1843, 1845) were themselves preceded by the three volumes of *Slavonic Folksongs* (*Slovanské národní písně*) published by the Czech poet F.L. Čelakovský between 1822 and 1827. Although Čelakovský, a leading poet of the Czech National Revival, published a few tunes in his second volume, his chief object was the regeneration of the language by means of its folk poetry. Similarly, though Erben took down tunes, he published only song texts: booklets of tunes, harmonized by Jan Pavel Martinovský, were issued separately. While all these projects were essentially patriotic – assembled by poets and clerics in their spare time – the initiative for the first substantial published collection of Czech folksongs (see illustration 14) had come from official sources. In 1819, at the behest of the Gesellschaft der Musikfreunde in Vienna, instructions were issued to regional governments to assemble collections of local folksongs. Of all the collections made, however, nothing was published at the time except for *České národní písně/ Böhmische Volkslieder*, 300 Czech and 50 German songs, and 50 instrumental dances, brought out anonymously in 1825 by Jan Ritter z Rittersberku and Friedrich Dionys Weber, using mostly material from the official collection in Bohemia (Markl 1968, 25; Vetterl 1973, 96–7).

What Harrach may not have realized when he recommended to potential Czech opera composers the assiduous study of Czech folksong, was that the music, as recorded by the 1860s, was not particularly Czech. Early secular song traditions had been heavily suppressed by the Church and went largely unrecorded, though popular elements made their way into the impressive hymnology of the Hussite era in the fifteenth century. At the end of the nineteenth century Hostinský unearthed the tunes of thirty-six Czech secular folksongs from the sixteenth century (*Třicet šest nápěvů světských písní českého lidu z XVI. století*, Prague, 1892). He derived these from instructions in contemporary hymnbooks to sing the hymns to well-known tunes whose opening words were quoted as a reminder. But the folksongs that were known from the Erben collection and that Harrach had in mind were mostly of more recent origin. References in them to contemporary events, to social conditions, to clothes, to lengths of service and conscription in the Austrian army (introduced in 1778 to replace voluntary enlistment), indicate that most of the texts of the songs collected by Erben go back no further than the eighteenth century (Horák 1937, 448–50; Karbusický 1958). Similarly, despite attempts by musicologists to discover ancient melodic strata beneath an eighteenth-century surface, few of the tunes exhibit archaic features. Those that can be traced back reliably to the sixteenth century amount, in the light of recent research, to a 'relatively modest group' (Vetterl 1978, 127).

One significant statistic of the Erben collection is that it contains 2583 texts (including variants), but only 811 tunes. Another, by Hostinský's reckoning (1906, 352), is that only a third of their words follow normal Czech stress patterns. The inference that folksong scholars draw from this is that Czech folk texts – in some cases several – were generally fitted to pre-

14 Music making in the village, a coloured lithograph by Antonín Machek after a drawing by Josef Bergler, the title page to the first published collection of Czech folksongs in 1825. The simultaneous combination of (left to right), hurdy-gurdy, singing, dancing, bagpipes, clarinet?, horn and cimbalom suggests a range of folk activities rather than a plausible ensemble. Rittersberk's folksong collection was published anonymously and was based on the collection made at the behest of the Austrian government in 1819.

existing tunes. These are overwhelmingly major (92% of materials published before 1935), frequently (60% of the Erben collection) in triple time, and 'stylistically their melodic invention is a reflection of the invention of Baroque and Classical art music with which the Czech people came into close contact in the seventeenth, eighteenth and nineteenth centuries' (Václavek 1950, 137–8). Coincidences of melody between Bohemian folksong and music of the Classical and pre-Classical eras have inevitably nurtured claims of borrowings either from art to folk music or the other way round (summarized by Karbusický 1968, 39ff). This is a popular, if emotionally charged, area of speculation, and conclusions tend to vary according to the ideologies of the writers. The fact is, as Karbusický makes clear, that large-scale systematic work on concordances has not been attempted, and that actual borrowings in either direction are difficult to prove conclusively.

Either way, by recommending to Czech opera composers the assiduous study of Bohemian folksong, Harrach was unknowingly advocating the study of music whose melodic and harmonic idiom had much in common with that of the main stream of art music of a couple of generations earlier, and had little, apart from its texts, to distinguish it from the folksong traditions of adjacent German-speaking areas. Both were based on the same type of Classical instrumental melody. The only difference that has been discerned is that German folksong sounds 'harsher' (to Czech ears) because of the greater incidence of triadic melody; Czech 'gentler' because of the greater incidence of adjacent notes (Karbusický 1968, 38).

Ironically, this type of origin for Czech folksong does not preclude its being able to evoke a national spirit. The signals which might lead contemporary audiences into perceiving a work as 'Czech' need not be specifically Czech themselves, or limited to Czech culture. To take a simple example: an accompaniment of drone fifths to a continuous tune played on oboe or clarinet can provide a recognizable imitation of a bagpipe.[2] Heard in an art music context, it may stand out as sounding 'different' and, in some cases, 'folk-like'. A musical signal like this may activate a Czech listener's associations with a favourite figure from Czech folk tradition, the bagpiper (see frontispiece), and lead to a perception of the music as 'Czech'. But drone fifths and bagpipe tunes are frequently used to evoke nationalist feeling by other musical cultures in which bagpipes are a common folk instrument, for example Polish, Scottish, Hungarian or Italian. As Carl Dahlhaus has observed (1974, 95), it is aesthetically 'perfectly legitimate to call bagpipe drones and sharpened fourths typically Polish when they occur in Chopin and typically Norwegian when they occur in Grieg'. This is another way of saying that 'national character' is often in the ear (and mind) of the listener. Indeed, nationalist messages are sometimes read into works whose authors and composers had no such intention.[3] The question of 'national' elements in music is often not so much a matter of what composers put into it as what audiences get out of it.

As Pospíšil and Ottlová point out in their analysis of references to 'Czechness' (*českost*) in music criticism of the 1860s (Ottlová 1979, 102), the concept was unstable and ill-defined. Signs of 'Czechness' were usually detected in passages which, purely because they were simple, were thought to resemble folksongs, whereas those passages which advanced the dramatic action were taken to conform to foreign models. Much depended on the musical background of the listener. For instance 'Wagnerian influence' was sometimes suspected in an opera simply because it was more thickly orchestrated or had longer orchestral interludes. This is probably the explanation for this damning accusation being levelled by the critic of *Politik* (18 November 1867) at Blodek's unassuming one-acter *In the Well*, usually taken as quintessentially in *The Bartered Bride* mould. Many of the chance associations that would have swayed a contemporary audience's perceptions are now lost and are impossible to reconstruct. Furthermore, what evidence survives of these perceptions of 'Czechness' comes only from a small part of that audience – from critics, or those well enough educated to describe their reactions in letters or memoirs, etc. But what, however, of the audience at large? This is an even more tricky and speculative area, and all that one can do here is to offer suggestions about the sort of inputs in the music which contemporary audiences might have taken as 'Czech'.

### Czech folksong and church music

In the first half of the nineteenth century (i.e. during the youth of the adult audiences of the 1860s) the chief opportunities for Czech speakers to hear music other than folk music would have been in church, or in taverns and dance halls.[4] It is possible that references to such music, or music in a similar idiom, might be taken as more 'Czech' than music in a more up-to-date operatic idiom. This notion is reinforced by the close connection that can be traced between Czech folk music on the one hand and Czech church music and popular entertainment music on the other.

It may be thought that vocal music in Czech churches was in Latin, hence 'international' and in no way exclusive to the Czech population. Music, however, was one of the weapons with which the Catholic Church in Bohemia and Moravia attempted to supplant the strong and popular traditions of Hussitism. Since these traditions included the singing of vernacular hymns by the congregation, the Church here was obliged to condone this practice, at least at an unofficial and local level, to a greater degree than elsewhere in Catholic Europe. In a response to an edict by Maria Theresa in 1756 by the Olomouc Consistory, it is clear that several Czech songs were sanctioned for use during Mass, and this practice, Jiří Sehnal believes, had already been current for at least eighty years (Sehnal 1985, 248–9).

The Catholic Church in Bohemia and Moravia permitted a surprisingly large folk element in its church music and many eighteenth-century hymns were sung to popular tunes (Sehnal 1985). The role of the kantor in giving a Czech character to local church music was crucial. These country musicians were responsible for the music that was performed in the church, but they also provided music for dancing in the taverns, while on the other hand their services were called for by the lesser nobility of the area. Their church music – a large number of kantors composed – reflected their wide range of musical activities, and not least their contact with folk culture. A revealing anecdote is provided by the Czech lexicographer Dlabač in his article about one of the most famous and accomplished kantors, F.X. Brixi. Brixi is said to have remarked to his friend the composer J.A. Koželuh that whenever he passed a church where one of Koželuh's masses was being performed, it seemed to him that he was hearing an Italian opera. To which Koželuh replied that when he heard one of Brixi's masses, he seemed as though he was going past the tavern (quoted in Trojan 1983, 51).

This story also serves to demonstrate that local church music was of a more elaborate nature than the typical fare in an Anglican parish church of the time. While in England some parish choirs outside the capital continued to sing unaccompanied into the nineteenth century, at the most adding a bassoon or cello to support the bass voice (Temperley 1979, i, 112, 151), parish choirs in Bohemia and Moravia had the support of what could sometimes amount to a small classical orchestra. As inventories of the time show, some country churches possessed up to twenty instruments, a number that would be augmented by those instruments – violins, flutes, oboes and, later, clarinets – in the personal possession of the players themselves (*HČD*, 229). Further evidence of musical activity in parish churches is provided by the large number of manuscript copies that survive of vocal and instrumental compositions for performance on Sundays and church festivals. The music in Bohemian churches often swamped the liturgy it was meant to adorn, and from time to time measures were taken against it. As Zdeňka Pilková reports (*HČD*, 229), Maria Theresa's ban in 1754 on trumpets and drums was not respected, as the contribution of military musicians at the larger church celebrations shows. The interventions of her son Joseph II in 1783 were more serious, but the fact that these sought to restrict the amount of instrumental music heard in churches on ordinary days is only further proof of the extent and popularity of such music. Furthermore, it had little impact on music in the country. Janáček tells a charming story – 'Without drums' – where he makes it clear that even in the tiny Moravian village where his father worked as the local kantor, a high mass on Easter Sunday without timpani was unthinkable, and in his view (he was seven at

214

the time – in 1861) fully justified stealing those drums from a neighbouring parish.

If Czech folk music seemed to be a simplified version of Classical instrumental and church music, the church music of the Czech kantors, even their mass settings, often has the character of stylized folk music (Markl 1963, 26). Nowhere is this more evident than in the Czech Christmas pastorella. This genre, which ranged from solo strophic songs to choral cantatas, attained its greatest popularity in the years 1775–1825. Its texts, generally in the vernacular, drew on the more human events of the Christmas story, in particular the reaction of the shepherds to the angels' announcement, and the cradling of the Christ-child. It was essentially a part of rural culture, its rustic tableaux enabling rural churchgoers to see themselves as participants in the celebration of the Christmas mass (Germer 1984). The characterization of the shepherds led to employment of pastoral (i.e. folk) references in the music and its instrumentation, and to the use of dialect in the text. The result was a unique blend of folk and art music, sacred and secular. No matter that this blend and many of its components could be found in neighbouring, non-Czech-speaking territories (Chew 1980); the music of this genre was seen as so quintessentially Czech that even Smetana was persuaded to include in *The Kiss* one of the best-known and linguistically most widely distributed pastorella tunes, *Hajej, můj andílku* ( = *Resonet in laudibus, Joseph, lieber Joseph mein*, etc).

In the pastoral mass, a genre closely related to the pastorella, portions of the liturgy may be replaced by freely texted sections. For instance, the Gloria of the 'Missa pastoralis Boemica' in C by the Moravian Josef Schreier (1718–?) retains the Latin text for just the first line, before lapsing into a vernacular text (and in a particularly opaque country dialect at that) about quite different matters; the Gloria combines the first eight lines of the Latin Creed (up to 'filium Dei unigenitum') with a dialect text mainly about sheep and goats. Such dialect interpolations naturally served to introduce references to local folk tunes (Trojan 1983, 46ff). In the best known pastoral mass of all, the Czech Christmas mass 'Hej mistře! ('Hail, Master!', 1796) by the Bohemian kantor Jan Jakub Ryba, the Mass ordinary is replaced entirely by a series of vernacular pastorellas.

### Czech folkdances and town dances

The connections between folk music and dance music are even clearer. In his unfinished Smetana monograph, Zdeněk Nejedlý (1924, iv, Chapter 4) painstakingly traced the wave of bourgeois dance which from the 1830s had overwhelmed the old, slower aristocratic dances such as the minuet, and threatened to supplant the traditional Czech folkdances. Among the newer dances the most significant in Bohemia were the *rejdovák-rejdovačka* (a dance in two sections, based on the same musical material, but presented first in 3/8 and then in 2/4), the *skočná* and the *sousedská*. The *skočná* was a fast dance in 2/4 of a light or comic nature; the *sousedská* a slower dance in 3/4 resembling the Austrian Ländler. By far the most important of the new dances was the polka, a dance in a fastish 2/4 with melodic movement mainly in quavers. Nejedlý cast doubts on the traditional explanation of its origins (first printed in the periodical *Bohemia*, in 1844), which carefully ascribes its invention to a high-spirited maidservant, Anna Chadimová, who, one Sunday afternoon in the small Bohemian town of Kostelec nad Labem, performed a new dance she had made up. Her audience included the local kantor, Josef Neruda, who took down and arranged the song that she sang as she danced. The dance became popular locally and soon made its way to Prague, where it acquired its name (Nejedlý 1924, iv, 363ff).

One of the difficulties with this story is that it offers no explanation for the name 'polka', though later descriptions mention the etymologically suspect derivations from the Czech word for half, *půl* (diminutive, *půlka*), referring to the dance's 'central half step' (Waldau 1859, 17), or from *pole* ( = field, i.e. a 'field dance'). Nejedlý argued for a quite different origin, as an adaptation of Polish *krakowiak* dance-songs, which were popular in Prague by 1835 (the first reference to the polka dates from this year). This is an attractive theory in that it is based on an attested source (an article by Jaroslav Langer in *Časopis českého musea*, 1835), and that the name 'polka' could in this case be taken as a reference to the dance's origins – a Polish dance – which, in the wave of sympathy that Poland attracted after its aborted 1830 insurrection, is all the more plausible (Nejedlý 1924, iv, 383–4). The chief problem is that there is little in common between the *krakowiak*, based on six-syllable verse lines with prominent syncopations emphasizing the second and fourth beats, and the purely instrumental polka with its emphasis on the third beat. What is certain is that the dance was an instant success, not just in Prague in the 1840s, but throughout the world, from Paris, to London and New York. Despite its appropriation by the leading ballroom dance composers of the day, its Czech origins were universally acknowledged and, for this reason, it became a symbol of growing national pride. The fact that it was essentially a two-in-a-bar dance clearly differentiated it from that other popular contemporary social dance, the waltz, which, for the Czechs, had German associations. When in 1847 Tyl put his Czech bagpiper on the stage, what could his magic instrument play other than polkas?[5]

The Czech kantors, responsible for so much of the local church music of the eighteenth and early nineteenth centuries, did occasionally try their hand at stage music, as in the folk Singspiels described in Chapter 3, and at least one kantor family, the Tučeks, made the transition from village music to professional stage music. With the kantors' awareness of (and even participation in) folk music, and the reflection of this in their own music, it is tempting to see in their works the beginnings of the 'Czechness' of Czech music in the second half of the nineteenth century. Indeed most accounts of their stage works inevitably comment on the 'Czech' qualities, or connections with folksong (Volek in *DČD*, i, 342, Sehnal 1961, 178). Direct links, however, are tenuous and it is difficult to see what effect the kantor tradition could have had on the essentially town-centred composers of Czech opera of the 1860s, which was steeped in the new romantic art music of Weber, Mendelssohn and Schumann, and even Liszt and early Wagner. But there is no doubt about the direct influence on Smetana of popular dance music. In his early years he wrote almost nothing other than dance music, though his polkas, like Chopin's waltzes, soon acquired a sophisticated stylization which lifted them above their functional origins. More than thirty years later, when Smetana sought to depict the influence of dance music on himself in his autobiographical quartet 'From my Life', he wrote the scherzo movement as a 'Quasi polka'. For the mainly urban audiences that heard Smetana's operas, familiar 'Czechness' may well have come not from references to folk music but from the incorporation of town dances, especially polkas, in his music. But by then the concept of 'Czechness' had become inextricably combined with the sound of Smetana's music itself.

## Folksong and Czech nationalist opera

### Smetana and folksong

What were Smetana's connections with folk music? Josef Srb-Debrnov recalled an evening when, in company that included Smetana and the intendant of the Provisional Theatre, František Rieger, conversation turned to the question of composing operas. A comic opera based on the life of the Czech people would be harder to write than a serious opera, Rieger declared ·(Smetana had just begun work on *The Brandenburgers in Bohemia*), and would certainly have to be based on Czech folksongs. Smetana countered this with the view that such an opera would be a mere collection of songs, a potpourri, and not a unified artistic whole. The argument became fierce and ended with Smetana's claiming that Rieger did not understand the matter; Smetana, as a musician, would have to show him (Bartoš 1939, 57). The theoretical basis for Smetana's views can be found in a draft for one of his *Národní listy* articles: 'imitating the melodic curves and rhythms of our folksongs will not create a national style let alone any dramatic truth – at the most only a pale imitation of the songs themselves' (Hostinský 1901, 112). Nejedlý (1908, 56) quotes this anecdote as a reason for dismissing the whole question of folksong in Smetana, but other, rather more sentimental arguments for avoiding the subject have also been proposed:

When he began to write Czech folk operas, Smetana could not rely on any theory of Czech song, for he did not know its characteristics. He was, however, a great genius, a musician in whose soul slumbered conscious sources of melody delightfully and faithfully Czech. He had no need to develop his Czechness, and with his first operatic note, he at the same time created a Czech dramatic style. [. . .] Smetana grew out of his Czech inner self, thereby solving at a stroke all questions of style: he wrote just as his enormous instinct led him.　(Branberger in *Čas* 24 and 26 January 1904, quoted in Němcová 1974, 143)

In view of such attitudes, common at the turn of the century and still a force in some Czech writing today (see for instance Holzknecht 1979, 189), it is not surprising that the question of folksong in Smetana has received little attention. The most comprehensive was a four-page article written by Otakar Zich eighty years ago (Zich 1909). He summarized his findings as follows. Smetana used folksong in two early instrumental works, the *Fantaisie sur un air Bohémien* for piano and violin (composed 1843), and the *Charakterische Variationen* for piano (composed 1846), based in both cases on a well-known folksong, 'Sil jsem proso'. In 1862 he wrote a *Fantasie concertante sur des chansons nationales tchèques* for piano. This last work seems to have been inspired by the publication that year of the tune-book to Erben's *Czech Folksongs and Nursery Rhymes*. Several fascicles of Smetana's copy survive though most of his annotations refer to his preparatory work for his Czech Dances of 1879, intended as a Czech response to Dvořák's Slavonic Dances (Očadlík 1960).

As far as Smetana's operas are concerned, Zich found only three conscious folksong quotations: the well-known use of the pastorella tune 'Hajej, můj andílku' in *The Kiss* mentioned above; the *furiant* from *The Bartered Bride*, based, Zich suggests, on the named *furiant* 'Sedlák, sedlák' in the Erben collection (Ex. 1); and an interesting example from *The Secret*. This

Ex. 1a

Farmer, once again farmer, farmer is a big shot: he has a belt on his belly and a tulip on his fur coat. [K.J. Erben: *Nápěvy prostonárodních písní českých*, no. 588]

218

Ex. 1b

[*The Bartered Bride*, 2.1.128–47]

occurs in Act 1 when, as the rival councillors suggest songs that the ballad singer Skřivánek might sing, they quote the beginning of 'Včera neděle byla'. The song that Skřivánek eventually sings, however, is rather different (Ex. 2).

The initiative for the inclusion of 'Hajej, můj andílku' in *The Kiss* came from Krásnohorská. On a sheet inserted into her libretto at this point, she wrote out the tune, which, together with the words, she took from Erben. Against Vendulka's second lullaby Krásnohorská noted that the metre was based on the rhythm of folksongs (Očadlík 1940, 50).[6] In this context it is

Ex. 2a

Yesterday was Sunday, I wasn't at home; I mowed the grass in the green meadow, I did not observe the holy day. [K.J. Erben: *Nápěvy prostonárodních písní českých*, no. 715]

Ex. 2b

Malina (aside to Skřivánek, giving him a tip): You will sing: (with comic expression) 'Kalina [= the guelder rose] is blooming.'
Kalina (aside to Skřivánek, giving him a tip: You will sing: (with comic pathos) 'Malina [= the raspberry] is ripening.'

Ex. 2b *(cont.)*

. . .
Skřivánek: (first verse) O, you faraway world, hear how our guelder rose is blooming; [*The Secret*, 1.3.402–9; 424–9]

interesting that in Smetana's previous opera, *The Two Widows*, Züngel had adopted much the same approach in the outer choral scenes. The words here include lines which are either direct quotations or adaptations of folksongs, and Züngel duly noted the originals (giving references to Erben) to remind the composer of the type of song intended (Züngel 1962, 18, 83, 100).

Two conclusions can be drawn from this: there are few overt references to Czech folksong in Smetana's operas; and most of them were suggested by his librettists. This has not prevented commentators from searching for further folksong echoes in these works. Zich himself mentions one 'unconscious' folksong reminiscence, the march of the circus people in Act 3 of *The Bartered Bride*, which he suggests could have been inspired by 'Ach ouvej náramné', no.78 of Rittersberk's collection (Ex. 3; cf the piccolo countertune in 3b with 3a). This, rather than its equivalent in Erben's collection (no.402, where it has different words), is particularly convincing in view of the aptness to the stage action of the last line of the song 'Play me you musicians a new march' ('hrajte mně, muzyční páni, vzhůru marš nový'; Zich 1909, 355). Brian Large similarly drew attention to two tunes from Erben's collection with melodic affinities to Ladislav's song 'Kdy zavítá máj' in *The Two Widows* (Large 1970, 256–7), another apt connection in view of Smetana's comments to his librettist on the revised version of the opera: 'almost a pendant to the lullaby in *The Kiss*. The song is completely in national style and I can say myself that it is a new national song' (Züngel 1962, 24). More recent treatment of the topic, inspired by Asaf'yev's influential theory of *intonatsia*, tends to emphasize generic similarities rather than specific models. Thus Jaroslav Smolka, in his study of Smetana's choruses, puts the drinking chorus at the opening of Act 2 of *The Bartered Bride* into the context of nine Czech and Moravian drinking songs, drawing attention to common traits such as the contrast between the lively, even-metred openings and the later sections with pauses on held notes (connected with the gesture of raising glasses). Smolka proposes that this is all evidence

Ex. 3a

Oh, woe, what a terrible headache: my beloved is angry with me; she is angry with me, she is looking on other men, play me you musicians a new march! [*České národní písně*, no.78; spelling modernized]

Ex. 3b

[*The Bartered Bride*, March of the Players, 3.2.100–15]

of how Smetana followed the 'typical intonation' of Czech folksongs (Smolka 1980, 179).

But just as important in Smetana's operas as the presence or absence of quotations from authentic folksongs was contemporary reception of the matter. As has been suggested, contemporary audiences may have sensed 'Czechness' in any of the simpler parts of the opera, in strophic songs for instance. Their absence in *Dalibor* may in turn have been interpreted as a lack of 'Czechness' and accounted for some of its initial unpopularity. In Smetana's other operas, there was usually at least one strophic song which stood out from the operatic framework as a deliberate 'song' (as opposed to aria), sung as it might be in real life, or at least as it would be in a play: Desdemona's Willow Song is a good example. Thus in *The Brandenburgers in Bohemia* Ludiše sings 'Byl to krásný sen' ('It was a beautiful dream') while waiting for her lover Junoš to appear. The piece is in three verses; Ludiše sings two, and Junoš (from his hiding place) adds a third. In its shortness and simplicity the song contrasts sharply with the 'operatic' trio that it follows. That it may have been intended to sound like a folksong is also suggested by its strophic construction and the plan of a slow, ruminative first half giving way to a faster, more regular second half (Ex. 4). Smetana evidently took some care over it; it is the only motif to be entered with a text in his 'Notebook of Motifs'. For his 'new national song' for Ladislav in *The Two Widows* (given, less suitably, to a rakish townsman rather than to a folk character), Smetana employed some of the same devices, a strophic song with a more declamatory first half (*espressivo*, with irregular metre) followed by a regular, more animated second half (*crescendo e poco animato*, regular 2/4 metre).

Ex. 4

Ex. 4 (*cont.*)

Ludiše: It was a beautiful dream, the glorious day of my first love! A cloud came, hid the sun, and my heart languished in its desires, the glorious day was over, my dream of love vanished! Where has it gone? [*The Brandenburgers in Bohemia*, 2.6.1032–50]

In all her librettos for Smetana Krásnohorská included strophic songs, many with folklike implications such as the Vendulka lullabies in *The Kiss*. *The Secret* has a particularly large number, with a variety of genre implications. Skřivánek, as a ballad singer, is allotted a strophic song, but here his more professional art is suggested both by the guitar accompaniment that Smetana specified (the guitar was not used as a folk instrument in Bohemia and Moravia), and by the elaborate melismatic decoration of the voice part. Act 2 has a simple pilgrimage hymn for Skřivánek and the women, and its demonic equivalent (at least in the dreaming mind of Kalina), a strophic ditty sung by the ghost of Barnabáš. Act 2 also has a strophic song for Bonifác, in which he attempts to woo Miss Roza by recounting his military exploits. Here the melismatic elaboration, unsuitably allocated to a bass voice as in Mumlal's strophic song in *The Two Widows*, suggests a comic intention, a hangover from the characterization of Kecal in *The Bartered Bride*. Finally, there are the two strophic songs in Act 3 sung to entertain the company gathered together to prepare the hop harvest. Skřivánek's song (to which Smetana added a counter-tune for Bonifác and a chorus refrain) is again a town song by the ballad singer, but Blaženka's song 'Což ta voda', with its *espressivo* first half (sung 'struggling against her tears') and an *animato* second half, instead suggests a more folklike world, and Smetana may have had it in mind when, in a letter to Adolf Čech, he mentioned the 'independent' songs in the opera, particularly those 'in a national style' (Teige 1896, 67).

It may appear remarkable that *The Bartered Bride*, Smetana's most popular opera and seemingly the most 'national', has no strophic songs, except for the two genre duets for Esmeralda and the Circusmaster (one later omitted) and the sad little song that Vašek sings at the opening of Act 3. The

225

latter, rather like Michálek's 'Ach pane, můj pane' in *The Devil's Wall*, is more of a set piece to characterize the singer than something intended to suggest a folk dimension. The music's power to suggest a folk milieu in *The Bartered Bride* derives instead from some of the choruses, especially the men's drinking chorus at the opening of Act 2, and from the dances (see below). All of these were additions, and their absence in early performances of the opera helps explain contemporary audiences' initial indifference to Smetana's new work. As in all nineteenth-century opera, Smetana used the chorus to support and punctuate the work of the soloists and to provide the basis for large-scale choral ensembles, from the Italianate finale ensembles in *The Brandenburgers in Bohemia* to the less traditional, though no less extensive ensembles in the three Krásnohorská operas. But in addition, all of Smetana's operas have choruses with specific genre associations, many of them overtly folklike. This is true equally of the operas with a folk setting, such as *The Bartered Bride* (the openings of Acts 1 and 2 for instance), and of those operas centred on courtly or bourgeois societies; in fact it is in this latter group that the folk choruses stand out the most. Thus Act 2 of *Dalibor* opens with a strophic chorus for the soldiers in a much lighter style than the rest of the work with a *più moto* 'la-la-la' refrain. Hostinský (1901, 258–9) characterized it as one of the self-evidently folk-sounding passages in the work; according to Procházka's report of the première it was one of the few numbers which were 'tumultuously received' (Procházka 1958, 37). The outer acts of *The Devil's Wall*, an opera mostly peopled by Czech medieval courtiers, also has a strong folk element, an echo chorus for the country girls in Act 1, and a substantial mixed chorus in Act 3 (characterized in Zelený's introductory article as a 'purely Smetana-esque polka [for the women]. . . which will surely soon be adopted as a folksong', followed by a 'gentle *sousedská*' for the men; Zelený 1894, 241–2). Perhaps most striking of all was the subsequently added folk frame (the opening and closing choruses) for *The Two Widows*. It is significant that in the operas Smetana revised most substantially after their first performances the folk content was particularly emphasized: *The Bartered Bride* acquired the drinking chorus and the dances; Ladislav's 'folksong', the folk choruses and two new folk characters, Toník and Lidunka, were added to *The Two Widows*.

### Smetana and dance

One evening, just after Smetana and my father [Ferdinand Heller] had played Beethoven's Seventh [Violin] Sonata, Neruda called out: 'And now that's enough of Beethoven! – Ferdáčku, play something to dance to! [. . .] Neruda taught everyone to dance the *beseda*[7] – Smetana happily joined in. However, after his 'rehearsal' Smetana made fun of the *'pargamyšky'*[8] – the folksongs and folkdances used in the *beseda*. . . .My father demonstrated to Smetana how they provided a foundation, drawing attention to their individuality, to their spirit, to the rhythm of the *furiant* etc. In these views he had an ally in Neruda, who enthusiastically defended and described Czech folksongs and dances, on which he was a particular expert. In return for Smetana's mockery of Czech folksongs and dances he dubbed Smetana's compositions 'Swedish music',' alluding to the atmosphere of Smetana's recent Swedish compositions, *Hakon Jarl*, etc. [. . .]

One day Smetana greeted my father during a free moment at the institute: 'You were right'. 'Why?', asked my father. 'Well, about the folksongs and dances'. . . He then brought and played through to my father his own 'Czech *pargamyška*': a polka from *The Bartered Bride*. When he had finished playing, he enquired: 'Well, what do you say to it? Haven't I reformed!'. . . When my father said 'Just go on writing like that!', Smetana beamed. . . 'I must play it to Neruda – what do you think he'll say?' And when he played it to Neruda the latter praised it, adding 'This is something different from that "Swedish" music'. Smetana wanted to know 'if it was all right'. Neruda proclaimed decisively: I should say so!'.

After that Smetana brought and played to my father almost every day some part of *The Bartered Bride* as soon as it was written: at random, simply according to his mood. He seldom forgot to add with a smile: 'Just another *pargamyška*'. . .But it was not mockery, according to my father, but hidden delight. [. . .] If my father did not like a particular passage Smetana would be taken aback, even unpleasantly offended. . .but the next day or so, he would bring the same piece corrected, if not completely reworked. 'How do you like it now?' When my father exclaimed: 'That's much nicer', and so on, Smetana derived a truly childlike pleasure. . . . During this period Smetana became so 'Czech' himself that he revised in a Czech manner sections of *The Bartered Bride* that were already written. (Heller 1917, 19–21)

This vivid account of the origins of the musical style of *The Bartered Bride* might be thought to provide welcome information in a sparse field, but its reliability has been questioned, for instance by František Bartoš (1955, 9–10), who pointed out a discrepancy in dating rehearsals for the *beseda*, and emphasized Smetana's refusal in principle to make direct use of folksong material in works such as operas. It should also be remembered that this account, published in 1917, describes at second hand events that took place in 1862–4, over fifty years earlier (the narrator is the son of Smetana's associate Ferdinand Heller, with whom he set up a music institute on his return from Sweden). Another problem is the mention of the 'polka' at a stage when the opera lacked any of the dances found in the final version (the polka now at the end of Act 1 was first introduced in January 1869). But for Czechs sharing the Branberger view (p. 218) the most serious objection to this account must be the inference that Smetana with his first opera, *The Brandenburgers in Bohemia*, had not written a thoroughly Czech opera and that it was only when he came into contact with Heller, Neruda and their dancing parties, and in particular the new dance that Neruda had invented, the *beseda*, that Smetana found his true Czech style.

What is particularly interesting about the *beseda* as far as a possible connection with Smetana's music is concerned is that, like the polka, it united social dance with Czech folk elements. The *beseda* was inspired by the quadrille, but incorporated steps based on Czech folkdances. Unlike the

French quadrille, which with one exception (in 6/8) was confined to simple duple time, the Czech *beseda* has two common motions, fast duple time or moderate to slow triple time. Although several different folkdances are involved, such as the *dvojpolka*, the *kalamajka*, the *obkročák*, the *hulán* and the *řezanka*, all these 2/4 dances were adapted to conform to the style and tempo of the polka. Karel Link, the author of the first manual on the *beseda*, suggests a tempo of 'Allegretto, M.M. $\downarrow$ = 92' not only for the polka in the *beseda*, but for all the above dances (Bonuš 1971, 54). The chief 3/4 dance was the *sousedská*, the name given in the early nineteenth century to a group of slowish triple-time dances whose character suggested a 'neighbourly' prudence (*soused* = neighbour), humour and gentle lyricism (Bonuš 1971, 32). The only dance in the *beseda* to stand outside these two basic motions was the *furiant*, a fast 3/4 with prominent syncopations giving the impression of 2/4 and danced 'con fuoco'. The Czech word has long lost its connection with 'fury' and today means a proud, swaggering person, or a dance in this style.

In the first version of *The Bartered Bride*, most of the individual numbers were separated by spoken dialogue (recitatives were minimal) and would thus have come across more as isolated musical entities than they do today. These pieces are extremely simple in form; few have tempo and metre changes other than perhaps a contrasting middle section, or a dramatic slowing down in important moments, or an increase of tempo at the end. But most striking of all in *The Bartered Bride* is the predominance of the two most frequent types of motion of the *beseda*: slow to moderate triple time, and moderate to fast duple time. Longer, more elaborate numbers, such as the bargaining duet for Kecal and Jeník, consist, like the *beseda*, of an alternation of the two. Apart from the slow 2/4 duet for Jeník and Mařenka, the following number (Kecal's entrance in a fast 4/4) and Vašek's entrance aria (a moderate 2/4), this pattern breaks down only in the middle of the last act, when the mood darkens, and Smetana runs several numbers together with more recitative-like material and multi-tempo sections culminating in the finale. The 6/8 opening of the finale is the first incidence in the score of compound time (equally rare in Erben's collection). It is at the beginning of the finale that Smetana's pencil sketch of the opera breaks off; the rest was worked out in full score and was thus unlikely to be presented to Heller for his approval. Significantly, this veering away from '*beseda* style' towards the end of the opera coincides with the abrupt change in verse metres in the libretto (see p. 273).

Though in subsequent revisions Smetana gave the appearance of continuity (and thus of more complex musical forms), by supplying linking recitatives to replace the prose dialogues, these new links were not the musically organic transitions such as are to be found in *Dalibor*. Furthermore, the existing dance element was much enhanced by the addition of three folkdances: the *furiant* near the beginning of the new Act 2, and two polka-type dances (the named polka at the end of Act 1, and the Circus-people's 'ballet' – a fast 2/4 *skočná*).

The difference in approach in *The Bartered Bride* becomes clear when it is compared with the newly written Czech operas of the 1860s that preceded it, Smetana's *The Brandenburgers in Bohemia* and Šebor's *The Templars in Moravia*. As was considered befitting to serious, historical operas, both works are continuously composed, with recitative rather than spoken dialogue between numbers. The numbers themselves are longer and more elaborate than anything in *The Bartered Bride*, and where they are not (as in Ludiše's 'Byl to krásný sen', discussed above) they invite interpretation as music influenced by folk elements. The overtly operatic associations of common structures in these operas, such as the concertato–stretta finales or the cantabile–cabaletta arias and duets, allies them more to the world of Italian and French opera, as do their long multi-tempo numbers (the long duet at the end of Act 1 of *The Templars in Moravia* has half a dozen changes of tempo and metre and many recitative interruptions). Where dance music is found in the operas, such as in Act 3 of *The Templars in Moravia* (or in Šebor's subsequent operas *Drahomíra* and *The Hussite Bride*), it comes from the world of the French grand opera, ballet rather than folkdance, and is presented as a *divertissement*, a point of relaxation in the main structure of the work. When Smetana added dances to later versions of *The Bartered Bride*, he was not weakening an operatic structure but consolidating one based essentially on dance.

It was several years before the success of *The Bartered Bride* with Czech audiences was established, but by the early 1870s the opera was the most popular and most performed opera by any Czech composer. It is possible to argue that many aspects of it, its melodic and harmonic style, but above all its essentially dance-based structure, took on an aura of 'Czechness' in themselves. The work was universally accepted as 'Czech', by Smetana's political opponents just as much as his adherents, so that further developments in style, which came naturally to a creative figure such as Smetana, were seen as ominous departures from this ideal of Czechness. The far richer harmonic idiom of *Dalibor*, its often declamatory discourse and the absence of short strophic numbers, all contributed to the disappointment that the work aroused among all but a few discerning critics. Conversely, when in *The Kiss* Smetana provided an opera with a folk setting, and incorporated a familiar folksong, he once again found favour with the general public. And though much more artfully integrated into the course of the music, the dance element here is not too difficult to find. In the overture Smetana introduces an 'Allegro à la Polka', which is then used extensively (often with added text, Ex. 5a) in the scene when the drunken Lukáš returns to torment Vendulka. The polka runs through the score, from its sym-

phonic development in the Act 2 prelude to its leitmotivic uses (Ex. 5b–c).
While there are other polka-based passages in the score (for instance the
scene with the border guard), and even some *sousedská*-like sections, where
*The Kiss* differs radically from *The Bartered Bride* is in its sheer rhythmic

Ex. 5a

Lukáš (twirling round the dancing girls in turn and lifting them): Play me your
liveliest [dance], play it specially merrily! For a kiss. . . [*The Kiss*, 1.1660–4]

Ex. 5b

230

Ex. 5b (*cont.*)

Lukáš: But I did this all in public, the whole village knows how I insulted her.
Tomeš: Hm, the whole village!? Now, then listen! (goes up to Lukáš). [*The Kiss*,
2.3.349–61)

Ex. 5c

Father Palouckỳ: I now have to disturb my soul, prepare for a courting and a
wedding, there is uproar beneath my window, jingling and dancing. [*The Kiss*,
2.7.1033–6]

variety: the quick duple and slow triple sections are only two of a large number of tempo-metrical types that Smetana employs.

Czech audiences, too, would have found similar constructions, had they looked a little harder at *The Two Widows*, the immediate predecessor of *The Kiss*, where once again a polka number (the sparkling Act 2 duet for the two widows), provides a generative element throughout the score.

### Folk elements in other Czech operas up to the 1890s

It is not quite true to say that there are no folk elements in Fibich. In the 1870s, before his strongly European orientation was consolidated, he went through a phase, apparently accentuated by his unhappy exile in Vilnius, of incorporating folk elements into his chamber works (Hudec 1971, 38–9), Even before his departure he wrote his *Wedding Scene* (*Svatební scéna*, 1872–4), a choral cantata which linked settings of ten wedding songs from Erben's *Czech Folksongs*. These works, however, are unrepresentative of the composer, and, with the exception of the cantata, he did not allow them to be published. His String Quartet in G, written in 1878, contains several folk references including a stylized polka which antedates the better-known examples in the string quartets of Smetana and Dvořák, but it is with this work that Fibich bade a definitive farewell to such experiments. The subject matter of most of his operas did not encourage the use of folksong elements; and where, in Schulzová's words, 'powerful folk scenes' are to be found, as for instance in *Hedy* (Richter 1900, 174), they adopt a cosmopolitan stance rather than a recognizably Czech one. Even in *Šárka*, when the hero Ctirad sings a song as he walks through the lonely forest in Act 2, the 'folksong' that Fibich assigns him is not one with familiar, sentimental associations, but instead one of the few ancient songs discovered by his friend Hostinský (Nejedlý 1911, 114; see also Richter 1900, 231–2): a sophisticated reference to contemporary research rather than a populist gesture.

It is likewise significant that the 'pantomime' in Act 3 of Fibich's *Hedy* is an elaborate ballet *divertissement* (here involving pirates, women vintners, hunters, harvesters and fisherwomen) rather than folkdances in *The Bartered Bride* mould. Similarly, in Rozkošný's *Cinderella*, one of the most frequently performed operas of the 1880s, the central ballet was labelled as such and was a characteristic depiction of the four seasons. It was only in much later works, after the impact of the folk movement of the 1890s, that Rozkošný was prepared to insert typical Czech dances into his works, such as the *sousedská* in *The Black Lake* (1906). Rozkošný's *Cinderella*, however, does betray an interesting departure in a couple of numbers sung by the heroine. Much of the music of the opera is continuously composed, so that the two 'songs' given to Cinderella, like the Act 3 ballet, stand out all the more. Her song in Act 1 'Měla jsem matičku milovanou' ('I had a beloved mother') has so many affinities with Smetana's second lullaby in *The Kiss* (Ex. 6) that one can only conclude that a conscious reference was intended to a work that in the eight years before Rozkošný wrote his opera had become familiar to Czech audiences. And if this is so, it might even be possible to suggest a reason for the insertion: this overtly 'Czech' music is sung by a despised individual, a simple girl who is then selected by a prince to be his bride. Might something comparable be in store for that Cinderella nation, the Czechs? While the popularity of the opera is generally ascribed to the lavish sets and effective ballet, it may also be that contemporary audiences picked up the 'message' embedded in Cinderella's lament, and liked it.

It seems odd that Bendl, who in *The Montenegrins* had incorporated features of south Slav folk music (a Serbian *kolo*, a *gusle*-player's song and so on), made so little attempt in his most consciously 'Czech' opera before

Ex. 6a

Vendulka (rocks the baby and sings): A little white dove was flying, and met God's little angel. [*The Kiss*, 1.7.1580–3]

Ex. 6b

Cinderella: I had a beloved mother, she was my greatest joy. [*Cinderella*, 1.4]

1890, *The Elderly Suitor*, to suggest its Moravian setting. Janáček pronounced that the style corresponded to neither Czech nor Moravian folksong, and when in one number Bendl did seem to quote a Moravian song, it
veered off in the second phrase to quite another one (Firkušný 1935, 51).
Bendl's use of polka rhythms in this opera is no more satisfactory in this
respect. The student Hovora, for instance, is allotted a couple of lively
numbers in duple time (for instance Ex. 7). But this is a trouser role, and
the effect of Hovora's 'polka', winsomely sung by a 'principal boy', is to
suggest French operetta rather than a Czech village.

The most conscious, not to say slavish, reference to Czech folk style came
in Šebor's last opera, *The Frustrated Wedding*. This was not his natural
habitat. His training and the 'European' style of his first four operas, all to
historical-romantic librettos, suggest a quite different orientation. But

Ex. 7

\* The top line is to be used if Hovora is sung by a soprano, the bottom if by a contralto.

Hovora: I wanted to test Mr Franc, how great his ardour, for if a bridegroom is three score years, then it's goodbye to love. I wanted to see how he would react when he learnt that there would be no mill. . . [*The Elderly Suitor*, 3.3]

Šebor, in uncongenial exile for almost a decade, could not afford to turn down the opportunity of writing again for the theatre, even if it meant setting a libretto quite different from any he had set before. The libretto was by Marie Červinková-Riegrová, daughter of František Rieger, who, although no longer intendant, still retained some influence at the Provisional Theatre. And, as is clear from Rieger's brush with Smetana on the matter, Rieger was one of the staunchest advocates of folksong-based opera. His daughter Marie studied peasant wedding ceremonies and songs (Bráfová 1913, 55) which enabled her to turn her adaptation of an indifferent French comedy into a 'Czech folk opera', and Šebor was persuaded to set it and to include folk material in it. When he did not seem to be making much progress, Rieger offered encouragement ('it will be a second *Bartered Bride*') and urged more folksong ('after all, "The Last Rose of Summer" in *Martha* is a Scottish folksong'). He also had some more general reflections:

It was also good for you that the folk text forced you to immerse yourself in the spirit of our folk music, of our songs. This is the soil from which our new art music must grow, and not just the lighter sort, not just comic opera, but also serious heroic opera! For we also have serious songs for serious music and some of them, those from the Tábor region, reach back to Hussite times. . .Europe will not thank us for producing copies and imitations of German music, let alone of Wagner himself. They will always be just copies, and the real thing will be preferred. It is for this reason that Dvořák's works, his Slavonic Dances and his duets and other works based mainly on the *ohlas* ['echo', see below] of Moravian and Slovak songs, are causing such a stir that German music publishers fight over his compositions, already much better known and sought after. . .than those of Smetana himself.

(Rieger to Šebor, April 1879, quoted in Bráfová 1913, 62–3)

In the end Šebor eschewed incorporating actual folk material in *The Frustrated Wedding*, declaring that he was quite capable of writing folksongs himself. The result was a poverty-stricken score, with none of the verve and distinction of his earlier operas. The folk-conscious numbers tend to be short slow waltzes, wretchedly simple structures that have none of the charm and none of the ingenuity of Smetana. The opera was not a 'second *Bartered Bride*' from either an artistic or a box-office point of view and when it became clear that Šebor was not making much progress with a second libretto from Červinková-Riegrová, *Dimitrij* (ironically much better suited to his talents), Rieger transferred the libretto and his hopes to Dvořák.

Of all the Czech composers of this period Dvořák would seem to have the best credentials for developing a folk-based operatic style. Unlike Smetana, he grew up in a Czech milieu and would have come quite naturally into contact with Czech folk music authentically performed, and at a formative period of his life, whereas Smetana's principal contacts were with printed collections. Unlike Fibich's operas, most of Dvořák's lend themselves through their village settings and characters to the incorporation of folk music. Only the consciously 'grand' operas, *Vanda, Dimitrij* and the late *Armida*, lack such opportunities.

At the beginning of his consideration of folk music in Dvořák's work (a study primarily connected with the composer's symphonic output, not the operas), Antonín Sychra made the point that Dvořák's personal style developed from the mid-1870s, in the middle of a decade in which the composer's vocal music was almost exclusively devoted to '*ohlasový*' works, i.e. works based on the *ohlas* (echo) of folk music through the use of folk texts or poems in folk style, or the quotation or imitation of folk melodies (Sychra 1959, 15–16). Research into Dvořák's deployment of folk music has concentrated particularly on the Slavonic Dances. Studies by Bonuš and Sychra point to direct borrowings, none of them ethnographically pure since, as the work's title implies, Dvořák drew on material from several Slav cultures, Bohemian, Polish, Ukrainian, South Slav, and especially Moravian and Slovak (Sychra 1959, 18–42). Sychra contended that Dvořák incorporated not just melodies, rhythms etc, but the 'content' that they invoked and this would not have been possible without Dvořák's complete assimilation of the world of the folksong – he grew from 'the same mushroom-spawn', as Sychra's colourful metaphor puts it (Sychra 1959, 21–2). More pragmatically, John Clapham (1962, 76–82) identified certain recurrent traits which can be found in both Dvořák's music and in Czech folksong. Among these he mentions the immediate repetition of opening phrases, three-bar phraseology, Lydian fourths (often associated with 'bagpipe' drones) and melodic patterns such as the leap up a fourth from the dominant to the tonic and back followed by a gradual descent to the lower tonic: the pastorella tune from Erben that Smetana included in *The Kiss* is a familiar example (Ex. 8).

Ex. 8

D = dominant note
T = tonic note

Vendulka: Go to sleep my angel, go to sleep! [*The Kiss*, 1.7.1549–56]

For all this, it is surprising how little overtly folklike material there is in Dvořák's early operas, even in *The Stubborn Lovers* or *The Cunning Peasant*, written at the height of his interest in *ohlasový* works. None of the strophic songs in them could be construed as folksongs. The King (of *King and Charcoal Burner*) has the only strophic song in this opera, a drinking song in

Act 3, which for all its clear phraseology and repetitive tunes clearly belongs to a different genre: its middle section, with its Baroque cycle of fifths, recalls Father Paloucký's 'Jak jsem to řek'!' in *The Kiss*, rather than the pastorella song of his daughter. Similarly in *The Stubborn Lovers*, Řeřicha's strophic song 'Nutit Tondu he, he, he!' ('Force Tonda, ha, ha, ha!') is a comic set-piece, its affinity with the world of Kecal and Mumlal clear from the wide jumps in the voice part, the comic melisma at the end, and the sequences and trills in the orchestra. The same opera abounds with solo songs in a light, Lortzing-like style, for instance Lenka's 'Na to bych se podívala' ('I'd have to see about that!'), or Jeník's 'Pantáta Lenku tak aby si vzal' ('My father to marry Lenka!'), none of them conveying the same sort of folk signals heard in Smetana's 'Byl to krásný sen'.

If folksong elements are to be found in these early operas it is not in complete numbers but rather perhaps in isolated features – a modal turn of phrase, an underlying dance rhythm, or details of orchestration. In many cases the idiom is not sustained enough to suggest a conscious folk signal to the audience; instead these brief flashes may well betoken unconscious influence at the 'mushroom-spawn' level. Of these features it is rhythm which is the most fundamental and pervasive. Martin's solo in Act 1 Scene 3 of *The Cunning Peasant*, for instance, seems to foreshadow the world of Dvořák's Slavonic Dances, written one year later. It is exuberant, highly rhythmic, with short repetitive phrases and plenty of dynamic contrasts. The voice gives the impression of being of secondary importance (note especially the swish of the orchestral triplets against the voice in the very first bar; Ex. 9). An even closer dance model can be found in *The Stubborn Lovers* where an aria for Toník provides 'a preliminary sketch for the languid opening of the twelfth *Slavonic Dance*' (Clapham 1966, 271). There are other similar dance-based passages in these scores, as well as a more conscious effort to introduce a Czech dance (complete with bagpipe drones in the introduction) such as the chorus and ballet ('quasi tempo di Polka') near the beginning of Act 2 of *The Cunning Peasant*, or the bagpiper episode in *King and Charcoal Burner*.

After the popularity of the Slavonic Dances, Dvořák made increasing use of dance in his operas both for formal dances, for instance in *The Jacobin* and *Rusalka*, and as an important element in the general construction of the score. The most striking example is *The Devil and Kate*, where Kate's delight in dancing provides a central feature of the plot. Act 1 is set among peasant dancing in a tavern and against this background the Devil tempts Kate on to the dance floor and whisks her off to Hell; Jirka dances her out of Hell in Act 2. Polka rhythms underpin the score in a similar way to Smetana's use in *The Kiss* (Veselý 1915, 101).

This late opera also provides one of Dvořák's few clear attempts to introduce folk signals through the use of a folklike strophic song. When

Ex. 9

Martin: That's right, go off to him you wretch, never return to your father you ugly thing! But grief will catch up with you. . . [*The Cunning Peasant*, 1.3]

Jirka the shepherd hero explains why he must leave the company, he does so in a strophic song with a simple, repetitive structure, poignantly swinging from minor to major and back again, against a folk-evocative accompaniment of initial drone pedal and clarinet counter-tune. Terinka's song in Act 2 of *The Jacobin* begins similarly with all the trappings of a folksong imitation (it was added to the score during the 1897 revisions, after Červinková-Riegrová's death, and the text was supplied by her father). Not surprisingly, in the light of his views on the value of folksong in Czech opera, Rieger's words have a folklike diction and Terinka announces her number as an 'old song'. The tune that Dvořák wrote for it is simple and repetitive with clear phraseology, and as in Jirka's song the accompaniment includes an orchestral pseudo-bagpipe with drone fifth in the bassoons and a continuous clarinet counter-melody. In the first interlude bagpipe-like mordents are heard in a middle part. However the illusion of a folksong is soon dispelled: the passionate refrain with chromatic harmony ('jen z jara') is in fact a quotation from Terinka's Act 1 duet with Jiří and although what

appears to be a second verse starts up, Dvořák soon disturbs the structure
and the folksong atmosphere, for instance in the surprise leap down on the
word 'mráz' (frost) with corroborative chromatic harmony (Ex. 10). Thereafter variations proliferate and the conventional folk signals of the opening
become skilfully absorbed into Dvořák's own style.

It is in fact surprising how few of Dvořák's strophic songs make any
attempt to sound as folklike as the two cited in *The Devil and Kate* and *The
Jacobin*. Dvořák seems consciously to have avoided most of the folksong
possibilities offered him by his librettists. A particularly significant ex-

Ex. 10

Terinka: In the autumn's hazel shrubs love gives no comfort, love belongs only to
the young world; only in the spring does true love blossom. To be sure, that old
man gives me the shivers. . . [*The Jacobin*, 2.1]

241

ample is Julie's song in Act 3 of *The Jacobin*. This crucial number, which has to bring about the old Count's change of heart towards his estranged son, could well have taken in folk elements. It is heard, after all, at third hand: Julie knows it from her husband, who in turn knew it from his mother, the late Countess. It must be simple enough to sound like a song, rather than an aria, and simple enough to be remembered and passed on. But this lullaby, like most of Dvořák's operatic songs, is simply too elaborate, too modulatory to suggest a folksong.

# The ethnographic movement of the 1890s

## *Bohemia*

It seems surprising that one of the most striking sources of perceived 'Czechness' – the visual aspect – reached the Czech stage only towards the end of the nineteenth century. The innovations in stage realism promoted by the Meininger Company (which visited Prague in 1878, 1879 and 1883, but whose influence was slow to affect the Czech stage; *DČD*, iii, 125) converged in the late 1880s and early 1890s with an increased and more scholarly interest in Czech folklore. Only then did Czech producers begin to take into account the exact location of a stage work, and to ensure that scenery and costumes were appropriate. The results were not immediately popular with the public, as is clear from the poor attendances during the first, brief run in 1887 of Stroupežnický's village play *Our Swaggerers*, the earliest consciously realistic production (by Josef Šmaha) on the Czech stage (*DČD*, iii, 220). Šmaha's productions of Preissová's *The Farm Mistress* (1889) and *Her Foster-daughter* (1890) included costumes based on authentic models from Slovak Moravia[10] (Hepner 1955, 82), though it was a few years before such methods were applied to opera. As late as 1883, when *The Bartered Bride* was first given at the National Theatre, the costumes and sets still betrayed an ignorance of the appropriate folk costumes and even of the appearance of a typical Czech village (Hepner 1955, 34).[11] But for the production which the National Theatre took on tour to Vienna in 1892 Edmund Chvalovský was despatched to the Plzeň area to bring back models of Czech village dwellings and of folk costumes of the area, and these formed the basis for the sets and costumes. In his production Šmaha attempted to depict on stage a faithful copy of a Czech village at fair time, adding for verisimilitude characters not actually specified in the libretto such as a priest, and a gypsy seen off by the village policeman (Nejedlý 1935, i, 353–4).

The success with the Viennese public of this approach did much for its consolidation as a model for future productions of the opera and of other Czech village operas. A few months later Prague saw an 'ethnographic'

15 Title page of the first vocal score (1872) of *The Bartered Bride*, the first venture by the newly-established publishing house Hudební matice. By this date the opera's librettist Karel Sabina was in disgrace (see pp. 117–18) and only his initials were allowed to appear. The decorative design shows young folk flocking into a tavern (left panel); Mařenka and Jeník (centre); and the marriage broker, Kecal, in top hat consulting with Mařenka's parents (right panel; later productions allotted the umbrella to Kecal as comic prop rather than to Mařenka's mother as a sign of seniority). A rather generalized approach is taken to folk costumes; it was only in the early 1890s that ethnographic authenticity began to be regarded as important.

production of *The Kiss*, based on local research by the designer and by the producer (Šmaha again) into the folk costumes of Podještědí and into smuggling habits of the area (Hepner 1955, 94–5). Even *The Secret* was given with village sets and costumes in spite of the town setting specified in the libretto (Nejedlý 1935, i, 412). By the time of the première of Kovařovic's *The Dogheads* (1898) such approaches were commonplace. For this production costumes were bought directly in Domažlice (the centre of the Chod region where the opera is set), or manufactured in theatre workshops according to original models in the Ethnographic Museum (Nejedlý 1935, i, 442).

Šmaha's attempts at greater stage realism went hand in hand with a more general awareness of Czech folk heritage. The ethnographic movement of the 1890s in Bohemia was different in kind from that which had culminated in the early 1860s. Now all aspects of folk culture (for instance costumes, decorative arts, folk architecture) attracted equal attention, and the consideration of folksong itself broadened into the investigation of less 'pure' genres such as military songs and commercial ballads adopted as folksongs. Folkloristic activities were no longer confined to the collection and publication of songs; their presentation at a more public forum was considered equally important. The Provincial Jubilee Exhibition (see p. 50), had included an unexpected attraction, a 'Czech cottage' containing an ethnographic display. Its success with the public led Šubert, the director of the National Theatre, to instigate the 1895 Czecho-Slavonic Ethnographic Exhibition and this second exhibition stimulated a number of associated scholarly ventures. A journal, *Český lid* ('The Czech people'), was founded in 1891, an Ethnographic Society in 1894 and an Ethnographic Museum in 1896. Otakar Hostinský, who had become a vital figure in the organization of the exhibition, was elected president both of the society and of the governing board of the museum. And folksong became an important new focus in his research and writings (Jůzl 1980, 221–6). Hostinský's essentially scholarly approach, for instance in his work on the genealogy of Bohemian folksong, marked a shift from mere collecting and laid down the framework for much of Czech folksong research in the twentieth century (Holý 1982).

### Moravia

In Moravia, culturally more backward than Bohemia and with more durable folk traditions, it might be said that folksong research right up to the 1890s was merely a continuation of Sušil's work. Thus František Bartoš (1837–1906), the foremost Moravian folklorist of his day, was a schoolteacher who in the 1880s widened his studies of Moravian dialect and folk customs to include the collection of folksongs. He did so expressly as an addition to Sušil's great collection and, like members of the Erben-Sušil generation, was more interested in the words than in the music. He needed helpers to notate the tunes for his 1882 collection, *New Moravian Folksongs with Tunes Included (Nové národní písně moravské s nápěvy do textu vřaděnými)*; for a second collection in 1889 he had the assistance of a new colleague (since 1886) at the Czech Gymnasium in Old Brno, Leoš Janáček, and in all later collections, for instance the three editions of the *Garland of Moravian Folksongs (Kytice z národních písní moravských*, 1890, 1892, 1901), Janáček was expressly named as co-editor. Janáček did not only notate tunes, he also contributed extensive introductions on the musical aspects and later provided piano accompaniments for fifty-three songs from the *Garland* – one of his many efforts to promote Moravian folksongs to a wider audience. His organizational talents were drawn into the service of Moravian folksong for the rest of his life. With Bartoš he was on the Moravian committee of the Ethnographic Exhibition and personally got together a troupe of Moravian folk musicians to perform at the exhibition. From 1905 he headed the Moravian branch of the state-sponsored folksong project, working closely with his Prague counterparts, Hostinský and, later, Nejedlý. After the First World War the material assembled was taken over by the Institute for Folksong in Czechoslovakia, and Janáček continued on the executive committee and as president of the Moravian and Silesian committee. His edition (with Pavel Váša, 1930–36) of *Moravian Love-songs (Moravské písně milostné)* was one of the few major publications that the new institute published before the Second World War.

Moravian folksong, particularly in the border areas adjoining Slovakia and Poland, was not just a different type of Czech-language folksong with the slight idiosyncrasies one can expect from a particular district, but essentially different from Bohemian folksong in kind and in its origins. In the words of Robert Smetana and Bedřich Václavek, the modern editors of Sušil's collection, Sušil placed side by side songs which come from two quite different musical worlds and which speak two quite different musical languages (Václavek 1950, 245). One language, that of western Moravian folksong, was virtually identical with that of Bohemian folksong; the other language, that of the border regions, was foreign and exotic. For convenience only the latter is referred to here as 'Moravian'. Bohemian folksong is predominantly major; Moravian folksong is much more varied in mode and in its choice of melodic intervals: two thirds of the tunes in Sušil's collection employ minor or modal scales, particularly Mixolydian. Bohemian folksong seldom modulates; Moravian folksong does so frequently, often to quite distant keys. Moravian folksong is much freer than Bohemian in its metrical and rhythmic structures through the frequent use of irregular, unbalanced musical periods, internal pauses and sharply dotted rhythmic figures. This, taken together with the near match in numbers of tunes and texts, has led to the conclusion that Moravian folksong is essentially word-based, in contrast to instrument-based Bohemian folksong, which has many more texts than tunes. And furthermore, while most Bohemian folksongs are comparatively recent in origin, essentially folk-versions of Baroque and early Classical music, Moravian folksongs display distinctly archaic features, for instance in their admixture of plainchant elements or in the very ancient reaping songs (Václavek 1950, 245–51; see also Trojan 1980, 17–18). Moravian folk music, with its echoes of older musical traditions predating Baroque tonality and Classical symmetries, was able to offer Janáček a much more diverse and interesting musical fare than that which Czech composers, acting on Harrach's advice, would have obtained from Bohemian folk music. The close association of words and music in Moravian folksong had much to interest Janáček as a dramatic composer. His studies of the material planted the seeds of his theories of speech melody (see p. 292).

### Folk music in Janáček's operas

Janáček's employment of this repertory in the regeneration of his own style represented a considerable break with the past. Furthermore, he came to the material as a distinguished folklorist himself, with a record of collecting, editing and arranging folksongs, and of writing scholarly articles on their classification and analysis. No Czech composer could match him in these respects. The nearest parallel to him was his younger contemporary Bartók, whose folk studies, initiated almost twenty years later, similarly pointed the way towards a liberation from a Germanic idiom and helped shape a new musical vocabulary and grammar. Curiously, the material they studied had many common roots. The Moravian folksong that most interested Janáček looked east to Slovakia, which for centuries had been incorporated in Hungary. Unlike Kodály, Bartók did not limit his studies purely to Magyar folk music, but drew on many folk traditions, of which Slovak was one of the most important. Another was Romanian, which similarly left its mark on Moravia, in the 'island' of Valašsko, adjoining Janáček's native Lašsko: the name still commemorates Wallachian settlers. It is disappointing that no record exists of what passed between Bartók and Janáček at their single meeting in Prague in January 1925 (Racek 1962, 14). Although so different in outlook and temperament they would have much to discuss. Many of Bartók's words about the impact of folk music on his work (quoted in Griffiths 1984, 46) apply equally to Janáček and find their echo in some of his own statements.

Although a composer with strong regional roots, Janáček was trained in the musical orthodoxies of the time in Prague, Leipzig and Vienna, and wrote his first works in an idiom that betrayed little of his origins. Any interest in folksong at this early stage of his career seemed to go no deeper than the occasional *ohlasový* work, for instance his settings of folk texts in some of his male-voice choruses. But in 1886 Janáček published a review of the first volume of Ludvík Kuba's collection, *The Slavonic World in its Songs* (*Slavonstvo ve svých zpěvech*). This was Janáček's first important statement on folksong, and from the tone of his remarks it is clear both that he was well informed on the subject and, as Jiří Vysloužil has pointed out (Janáček 1955, 34–5, 37), that he had already begun collecting Moravian folksongs himself, at least two years before his first expedition with Bartoš in 1888. Even so, as late as 1887–8 Janáček's first opera, *Šárka*, made no concessions to a more folk-based style. It was only when hopes for the opera's production were dashed that Janáček's energies, fuelled by his work with Bartoš, were directed towards Moravian folksong in a much more direct and consistent way.

The impact of Janáček's folk studies on his operas falls into three distinct phases, represented respectively by *The Beginning of a Romance*, *Jenůfa* and *Fate*. The clearest model for the first phase is Janáček's ballet *Rákos Rákocsy*, written and performed in 1891 during the Jubilee Exhibition. Essentially a celebration of folk music, it consists of a string of orchestrated folksongs and dances loosely attached to a scenario. *The Beginning of a Romance*, written the same year, similarly includes well-known folksongs, introduced into the opera at appropriate points in the story. Other numbers consist of Janáček's earlier orchestrations of folkdances (similar to or even identical with those in the Lachian Dances – *Lašské tance*) to which words from the libretto have been added (Tyrrell 1967, especially 266–8). Only about a third of the score was freshly written. This is hardly the best formula for an opera and in later years Janáček renounced it and even attempted to destroy the score. The little work, however, proved popular with its Brno audiences. And it made a more convincing stage presentation of ethnography than for instance Bendl's opportunistic 'folk ballet pantomime' given in 1895 at the Ethnographic Exhibition. The scenario for Bendl's *Czech Wedding* (*Česká svatba*) was based on the folk customs accompanying a peasant wedding. The score he wrote to this, however, was thoroughly conventional with only sporadic glances in the direction of folk music.

Janáček began *Jenůfa* in 1894, in the same year as the stage production of *The Beginning of a Romance*. He completed it almost a decade later, by which time his style had undergone a profound change: it was during the long gestation of *Jenůfa* that Janáček found his individual voice. Like *The Beginning of a Romance*, *Jenůfa* was based on a text by Gabriela Preissová set in the same folklore-rich area of southern Moravia. But in *Jenůfa* Janáček played down connections with folk music, even to the extent of claiming that there was 'not a note of foreign or folk music' in it (Štědroň 1946, 180–1). The misnamed Recruits scene in Act 1 (they are in fact conscripts) or the bridal chorus in Act 3 offered opportunities for the wholesale incorporation of folk material, especially since the words of the songs here can be traced back to Moravian folksong collections. Preissová took the bridal chorus directly from Sušil, and Janáček himself added the words for the two songs in the Recruits scene from Bartoš. In all three cases the tunes, however authentic-sounding, were different from those in the collections. Czech scholars have searched for years for sources for them and still disagree about the extent of Janáček's direct reliance on folk models (cf Štědron 1968, 155–62 and Vetterl 1968, 237–40). What is certain, however, is that instead of lifting folk materials virtually intact, as he did in *The Beginning of a Romance*, Janáček allowed the distinctive melodic intervals, the rhythms and metrical structures of Moravian folk music to permeate his style as a whole. Janáček was now working, like Dvořák, at the 'mushroom spawn' level, but the spawn was of a different, and most distinctive variety.

This close relationship allowed the folkloristic scenes to become easily and unobtrusively absorbed into the score. It has also provided generations of Moravian musicologists with the rewarding pastime of hunting for parallels between individual passages in *Jenůfa* and elements of Moravian folksong. Rhythm, phraseology and, particularly, modal inflection and harmonization are all favoured topics (cf Firkušný 1938, Vysloužil 1966) but the most interesting of all is undoubtedly the influence on aspects of Janáček's style such as accompaniment and tone colour (Trojan 1980, 12–13). Janáček took especial interest in folk harmonizations. He was one of the first scholars of Moravian folksong to notate the accompaniments of its distinctive *hudecká muzika*, the small peasant bands made up, at the simplest level, of two violins and a bass. The type of decoration played against the tune by the *kontráš* (second violin) is represented in the accompaniment to 'Všeci sa ženija' in the Recruits scene in *Jenůfa* (see figure 'x' in Ex. 11). And it is these short-breathed 'interruptions' and ostinatos that become such a feature of Janáček's own style. The tension between foreground tune (*primo*) and disruptive background (*kontráš*) is an essential element in the explosive energy of Janáček's music from *Jenůfa* right up to his late works, as is shown in Ex. 12, from the overture to *The Makropulos Affair*.

By Janáček's next opera after *Jenůfa*, *Fate*, the elements of Moravian folksong had penetrated Janáček's music to such a profound level that it becomes difficult to disentangle personal style from folk input. And most significant of all, Janáček no longer needed the crutch of visual associations with folk costumes, customs and architecture that provided the inspiration for *Jenůfa*. When he wanted the audience to hear something literally as a folksong, he simplified the structure, most obviously in the strophic or quasi-strophic songs that can be found right up to his final works. Here 'folksong' is not used for patriotic resonance but chiefly as a means of differentiating some of his characters. In his two Russian operas strophic folk-

Ex. 11

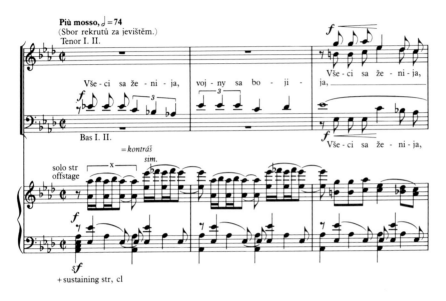

Chorus of recruits offstage: Everyone is getting married, they fear war. [L. Janáček, *Jenůfa*, 1.4; C 1969 by Universal Edition AG, Wien]

Ex. 12

Ex. 12 (*cont.*)

[L. Janáček, *The Makropulos Affair*, Prelude; C 1966 by Universal Edition AG, Wien]

songs help characterize the more carefree world of Varvara and Kudrjáš, the light-headed Skuratov, or the yearning aspirations of prisoners. In *The Makropulos Affair* the demented Hauk recalls his ancient affair with Marty with a 'Spanish' song. Some of *Káťa Kabanová* may sound 'Russian' but ethnographical purity was hardly Janáček's aim when for instance in Kudrjáš's waiting song in Act 2 Scene 2 he substituted a translation of a Ukrainian version of a well-known Russian folksong to fit the music he had originally written for Ostrovsky's song from the Volga region. And the music itself, as Polyakova (1974, 268–9) points out, is based on a scale that does not occur in Russian folksong. Despite his polite enthusiasm for 'A Lass that Loved a Sailor' on his London trip, Janáček – unlike Bartók – was not much interested in folksong outside his home territory (Vetterl 1968, 241 fn. 3). The most convincing 'folksongs' in his later operas come from the only one set in Moravia, *The Cunning Little Vixen*. In this opera Janáček again used folksong to characterize the 'lighter' figures, the comic poacher Harašta, or the Foxcubs with their delicious Lydian nursery rhyme.

It is equally revealing to follow the deployment in Janáček's later operas of another element favoured by Harrach for the establishment of Czech opera – the chorus. No Czech composer until the end of the nineteenth century risked omitting the chorus; in this respect Čelanský's chorus-less *Kamilla* of 1897 was a radical and innovatory work. Here Janáček was more traditional. Vestiges of choral finales haunt his late operas, even if the chorus has to be banished to an offstage, 'symbolic' realm (e.g. the conclusions of *Káťa Kabanová* and *The Makropulos Affair*). *The Cunning Little Vixen* has a full-blooded choral conclusion to the end of Act 2, and the two post-*Jenůfa* experimental operas, *Fate* and *Brouček*, are the most chorus-rich of all. *Brouček* has substantial choruses on earth and on the moon and, in the fifteenth century, makes thrilling use of Hussite chorales that would have pleased even Rieger.

It is in these two experimental operas that the dance element in Janáček takes on a new life. As in Janáček's later use of folksong, this has quite a different aim from his use of dance in his folkloristic operas. After *Jenůfa*, folkdances give way to the waltz, a social dance with no folkloristic implications for Bohemia or Moravia. Instead of exploiting dance for its potential as patriotic referent Janáček instead used it as a constructional and a characterizing device.

A strong, moderately fast triple metre provides the structural backbone of the opening scenes of *Fate* and *Brouček*. *Fate* begins with an infectiously vibrant choral waltz – a suggestion of the spa band, which provides an effective foil to the subdued entrance of Míla, when the metre subsides into duple time. Fast triple rhythms persist even longer in *Brouček*, from the teasing quarrel of Málinka and Mazal to the appearance of Brouček 'in a rosy mood' and the Artists' chorus soon after. On the moon Etherea makes her entrance with a radiant waltz song with full choral accompaniment. To judge from his annotations in his copy of Čech's novel, it seems that stressing the dance element on the moon was Janáček's way of suggesting the effects of lighter gravity mentioned in the novel (Tyrrell 1968, 106). In *The Cunning Little Vixen* the dance element is even more pronounced. The opening scene specifies 'ballets' for the Flies, the Blue Dragonfly, the Cricket, the Grasshopper, the Mosquito and, at the end, the Blue Dragonfly again. While many of the ballet scenes are for the non-singing cast, the entry of the Foxcubs in Act 3 is also designated a 'ballet'. The music for these scenes ranges from the strongly rhythmical polkas and waltzes (the Mosquito's waltz is in effect a *rejdovák-rejdovačka*, see pp. 215–16) to the metrically free arabesques for the Blue Dragonfly. The ballets help to provide musical continuity to an episodic libretto; but they also help suggest a different level of reality (i.e. the animal and insect world) and distinguish it from the world of humans.

The originality of Janáček's integration of dance and ballet into opera is no better illustrated than in this charming work, and his imaginative redeployment in it of folksong, dances, and other 'Czech' elements is in striking contrast to those operas of his younger contemporaries who continued to use folkloristic elements in their works. One has only to consider Novák's *The Grandfather's Legacy* (1926), Weinberger's *Švanda the Bagpiper* (1927), Ostrčil's *Johnny's Kingdom* (1934) or even works by the new avant-garde generation such as E.F. Burian's *Maryša* (1940) and Hába's quarter-tone *The Mother* (1931) to see how folkloristic elements persisted in fairly traditional ways in Czech opera right up to the Second World War (see especially Trojan 1972, 170 and Vysloužil 1974, 209–12). As a stage producer Burian was one of the most innovatory figures in Czech musical theatre of his time, but his opera *Maryša* is little more than a slightly updated *Jenůfa*. Ostrčil's final opera caused a riot when staged in Prague in 1935 but the cause was the text (which upset the radical right at a time of international tension; see Lébl 1959, 299–300) rather than the music, with its polkas and other dances, a soldiers' chorus and even a small village band. Such elements have their place in reinforcing the opera's humanitarian message, something which can hardly be said for their deployment in Weinberger's *Švanda*. His high-gloss exploitation of powerful national symbols includes the central figure of a bagpiper, a polka (several times) and sentimental 'folksongs' such as its hit tune 'Na tom našem dvoře' (presented, on its final hearing in the last bars of the opera, in a 'grandioso' version for soloists and full chorus). For all its success abroad, Weinberger's opera did not achieve popular success in Prague and it has not been heard at the National Theatre since 1933. Its fate serves to demonstrate that there is a limit to the currency of nostalgic patriotism and that its symbols, however skilfully presented, will not in themselves be enough to ensure acceptance.

# 8. Czech, metre and word-setting

What is Czechness in music, and how is it achieved? As Michael Beckerman has pointed out in a stimulating article, virtually all major Czech composers from Smetana onwards have at some stage stressed the Czechness of Czech music; they all seem to have known what it was. Why is it so difficult for us to define and explain it? A simple search for particular traits seems to lead nowhere:

> let us postulate that "Czechness" is composed of certain musical traits which can be objectively verified and analytically defined [. . .] These devices can be found in Czech music in abundance; yet they are also found elsewhere – in Liszt's Hungarian Dances, for example, in Copland's ballet scores, and Schubert's string quartets. There are also many "*bona fide*" Czech compositions that lack these characteristics. Are they then, temporarily, "not Czech?" And are composers who exhibit these details in greater concentration "more Czech" than other composers? Must we consider Liszt, Copland and Schubert "honorary Czechs"? (Beckerman 1986, 64)

Inevitably the subject of 'Czechness' in music exercised the chief Czech aesthetician of the nineteenth century, Otakar Hostinský. He did not believe that Czechness resided in specific subject matter and significantly both of his completed opera librettos, *The Bride of Messina* and *Cinderella*, were provocatively non-Czech at a time when this was unfashionable. Czech folksong, urged from the 1860s as a useful source of Czechness, he regarded as a positive hindrance to the development of opera. Hostinský did not, however, regard the pursuit of Czechness in music as a worthless goal nor as an impossible one:

> Let us first of all consider what we take to be the real basis of nationality, how we recognize it, and how we distinguish one nation from another. The *contents* of our thoughts are becoming increasingly common to all nations, more cosmopolitan; the more educated classes of virtually all European nations are drawing continually closer, and have more and more contact and thus more mutual exchange of thought. Psychological character (like the external features of the body) of course used to be much more defined and distinct among different nations, but even that has become generally eroded and has lost much of its meaning. Going on character and temperament alone it is impossible to distinguish a nationality with absolute certainty, especially in the places where there are most contacts. We have, however, one unmistakable, absolutely clear sign which is virtually a *symbol* and in many respects even the *basis of nationality* – namely the *mother tongue*. (Hostinský, writing in 1870, reprinted in Hostinský 1901, 169–70)

Whatever the subject matter, whatever the basis of the style, an opera would come across as Czech if written in Czech. Hostinský's view on this matter had become even firmer when in his later essay on Czech declamation he wrote 'National character in music depends largely on the rhythmic and melodic motifs which have a characteristic predominance in one's mother tongue' (Hostinský 1882, 277). Smetana said as much when he wrote to Krásnohorská that 'he who looks for *Czech style* only in [folk]songs and not in the characteristic declamation of *Czech words* will certainly be none the wiser' (Očadlík 1940, 162, Smetana's emphases). It is time, then, to examine the peculiarities of the Czech language.

What are the distinctive features of Czech as a language? To foreign eyes Czech looks heavily consonant-prone. Not only are there words which lack written vowels altogether (*vlk* – wolf, *srst* – fur, *pln* – full) but also unfamiliar consonantal groupings, sometimes further complicated by diacritical signs (*žhl, čtvr, hř*). The lack of vowels in words such as *vlk* and *srst* is an illusion – the *r* and *l* in each case imply an unwritten neutral vowel, e.g. *v(i)lk, s(i)rst*. Likewise the *háček* (hook) on *č, š, ž* etc conceals nothing more ominous than a differentiation of, say, 'sh' (*š*) from 's', or 'zh' (*ž*) from 'z'. While some of the consonantal clusters can be tricky, they are no more so than many English ones (e.g. 'sixths'). Despite appearances it is not its high proportion of consonants that makes Czech particularly distinctive so much as its stress system.

Unlike Polish, in which the stress falls normally on the penultimate syllable, and Russian, which has a movable stress, Czech stresses the first syllable of each word. In this respect it is not quite unique in Europe since Hungarian and a few western Slav languages such as Slovak and Lusatian share this characteristic. But in relation to all the major European languages, including all those with well-established musical cultures such as Italian, German or French, it is a powerful and immediately distinguishing feature. And it is something that proves constantly confusing to the foreigner. In order to get Germans to pronounce his name correctly, Smetana resorted to adding words to the opening of the overture to *Fidelio* (Ex. 1, quoted in

Ex. 1

Sme - ta - na,     Sme - ta - na,     Sme - ta - na sprich aus!

Bartoš 1939, 36). An apocryphal version based on Beethoven's Eighth Symphony makes the point even more clearly (Ex. 2).

Stress profoundly affects the rhythms of spoken language, and thus the music set to it. French has a weak, variable stress. Debussy's *Pelléas et*

Ex. 2

*Mélisande*, a musical setting which reflects its flexible 'half-tone' stresses, is a world apart from Strauss's *Elektra* written only a few years later, but to a text in German, a language with a strong, rigid stress pattern.[1] Likewise, the burst of energy at the beginning of a multi-syllable Czech word followed by a weakening patter of unstressed syllables is a distinctive feature of spoken Czech and of musical settings which take this into account. In Czech, however, there is another complication. Czech vowels can be long or short, the long indicated by an acute accent (*čárka*), as in *á, é, í, ó ú* (or *ů*) and *ý*. In Czech a long vowel is not necessarily a stressed vowel: the second syllable in 'Dvořák' has a long *á*, but it carries no stress; instead it is the first, short syllable that is stressed. In 'Janáček' stress and length again do not coincide: the first, short *a* is stressed, the second, long *á* is not. These names, correctly spoken, might suggest the following rhythms: (Ex. 3).

Ex. 3

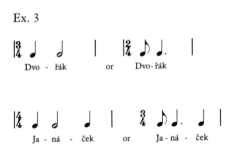

In both cases the foreign ear finds a short stressed first syllable followed by a longer unstressed syllable confusing and tends, wrongly, to regard the short first syllable as an upbeat. But it is these syncopations caused by the independence of stress and length that are so distinctive in Czech and any musical setting that reflects them will itself be distinctive – a perceptible source of Czechness, perhaps. What Hostinský and most subsequent commentators did not say, however, is that all operas in the nineteenth century were written to librettos in verse, rather than in prose (except of course for some recitative passages and spoken dialogue). Before opera composers could begin setting Czech words those words had already passed through a metrical mesh forcing the distinctive rhythms of Czech to conform to specific metrical patterns, some of them alien to the language.

## Verse metres in Czech

Czech prose comes naturally in a mixture of trochees and dactyls. Here, for instance, are some lines of Czech nineteenth-century prose, the first from a serious play, the second from a satirical novel.

Tu|poto|pil se | Finn | do modrých | vod, | do jejichž | tůně | měsíc | stříbro | lil, a | dole | v houští | z bledých | chaluh | obrovských | uviděl | reka | ležet.[2]

Zeyer: *The Legend of Erin*, Act 1 Scene 1

(Then Finn dived into the blue waters, into whose pool the moon poured its silver beams, and below in the undergrowth of huge pale seaweed he caught sight of the hero lying there.)

Ležel | z pola | odstrojen | na své | posteli | a byl by v té | chvíli | celý | výlet | do měs|íce | pokládal | za pouhý | divoký | sen, | kdyby se | nebyly |hlásily | následky | děsného | pádu: |

Čech: *The True Excursion of Mr Brouček to the Moon*, Chapter X

(He lay half undressed on his bed and at that moment would have considered the whole excursion to the moon simply as a wild dream, if the consequences of his terrifying descent had not manifested themselves.)

Because of first-syllable stress all Czech words come in 'falling' rhythms. Two-syllable words such as 'bledých' or 'ležel' are natural trochees (– ⌣) in Czech irrespective of their different vowel lengths; three-syllable words such as 'obrovských' and 'odstrojen' are natural dactyls (– ⌣ ⌣) Four-syllable words, with a subsidiary stress on the third syllable, break down into two trochees. Single-letter prepositions such as 'v' (in) or 'z' (from) are elided into the next word. Longer monosyllabic prepositions such as 'do' (to, into) and 'na' (on) are also grouped with the next word but in this case take its initial stress, just as the reflexive 'se' usually acts as the last, unstressed, syllable of the word before. Thus 'na své' is a trochee (– ⌣), 'do modrých' a dactyl (– ⌣ ⌣) and 'potopil se' a double trochee (– ⌣| ⌣̄ ⌣). The stress of non-prepositional monosyllables is more flexible and depends on context and individual interpretation.

Note that because of varying vowel lengths not all Czech trochees or dactyls are equal. Each trochee of 'celý výlet' has a different rhythm (short–long/long–short). The three dactyls 'hlásily', 'pokládal' and 'divoký' all differ from one another because of the differently positioned long vowel, respectively in first, second and third place.

Iambs (⌣ –) and anapaests (⌣ ⌣ –) do not occur naturally in individual words in Czech. But it is possible to create an iambic line by starting with a monosyllable (or, irregularly, with a trisyllable) and then continuing in trochees. For instance 'Tu' could be considered unstressed to give an iambic opening:

Tu po|topil| se Finn |

The conjunction 'a' (and) could be regarded as the unstressed second syllable in a foot beginning with 'lil', thus forming part of a line of trochees:

lil a|dole|v houšt í|z bledých|chaluh|

Conversely 'a' could be regarded as the unstressed first syllable of an iambic foot:

a do|le v hou|št í z ble|dých cha|luh

(This line provides an excellent example of the independence of stress and length: most of the stressed syllables are short ('do', 'z ble-', 'cha-') and some of the unstressed syllables are long ('-ští', '-dých').)

The accented syllables, originally on the odd-numbered positions (the condition for trochees), are now out of phase, on the even-numbered positions, and the foot, which in Czech generally corresponds to individual words, now runs across the word-breaks. Some writers have maintained that a genuine Czech iamb is impossible, and that the so-called iambic line in Czech is nothing more than a trochaic line preceded by an anacrusis or upbeat (an argument discussed fully by Král 1923, 674–87). However one regards such a line, the essential point is that the line now contains an opening monosyllable which musically can be set as an upbeat.

To write verse in which every line begins with a monosyllable is a tiresome restraint, even with the flexible word-order of Czech. In view of this difficulty one might think that Czech poets would automatically choose falling metres (trochees, dactyls or a mixture of the two) as their normal verse metres. This is not so, partly because some early traditions of Czech verse were based not on patterns of strong and weak syllables (accentual verse) but on patterns of long and short syllables (quantitative verse, known in Czech as *časomíra*), which made rising metres such as iambs easier to achieve. Czech quantitative verse had the distinction of a classical pedigree but also the disadvantage of often having to disregard the characteristic stress patterns of the language. It was not until the second half of the nineteenth century, however, that a clear consensus in favour of accentual verse prevailed; before then Czech prosody was confused. In opera this situation is well exemplified by the rival translations – accentual and quantitative – that were made early in the century of *Don Giovanni* and *Die Zauberflöte* (discussed, respectively, in Jirát 1938 and Ort 1939). Another reason for the prevalance of Czech iambic verse was the existence of foreign models such as Shakespeare and Schiller. Though some of Schiller's earlier plays such as *Die Räuber* are in prose, all his plays from *Don Carlos* onwards are in blank verse. Shakespeare was even more influential and much effort was expended in translating his plays into Czech. The first translations were usually in prose, but Tyl's version of *King Lear* (1835) was in blank verse (*DČD*, ii, 230). Iambic pentameters became the standard for any Czech dramatist aiming at the high style (*DČD*, ii, 139).

Even Sabina, working in haste on his first libretto seems to have felt the need to write iambs. The opening lines of *The Brandenburgers in Bohemia* are in almost regular iambs, formed by monosyllablic starts and mostly two-syllable continuations (only the second line contains some dactyls).

> Oldřich Já a|le pra|vím: Nel|že déle |
>
> tu | trpěti | cizácké | sbory. |
>
> Už po|třebí | se cho|pit zbraně |
>
> a vy|hnat z vla|sti Bra|nibory, |
>
> již hu|bí zem, | náš ja|zyk tupí, |
>
> pod je|jichž me|čem ná|rod úpí! |

(For a translation see p. 1)

The pattern continues for about twenty lines, mainly of eight or nine syllables each. But soon the verse deteriorates into trochees, or into nothing very much in particular. As Erben tartly commented in his Harrach adjudication, many of the lines were simply prose 'divided into short lines to deceive the eye' (Daněk 1983, 154).

## Trochaic/dactylic librettos

In view of these attitudes, it is perhaps not surprising that there are so few predominantly trochaic librettos in Czech opera in the nineteenth century. Significantly, the two that Smetana set were comic operas, *The Bartered Bride* and *The Two Widows*, and both, in their original versions, contained spoken dialogue. Here is one of Züngel's typical trochaic quatrains, from Karolina's aria in Act 1 Scene 2 of *The Two Widows* (as in all such examples in this chapter, the metrical markings refer to stressed and unstressed syllables):

> Kážu | orat, | sít i | žít,
>
> řídím | vino|brání, |
>
> všecko | musí | tak se | dít,
>
> jak chce | vzácná | paní. |

(I give orders for the ploughing, the sowing and the reaping; I direct the wine harvest. Everything must be done exactly as the distinguished lady wishes.)

Züngel's trochees are made up of two-syllable words (natural trochees in Czech), of monosyllables grouped in twos and of one four-syllable word ('vinobrání'), which provides two trochees. There are no three-syllable words, which are awkward to use in Czech trochaic verse because their third syllable receives an unwanted stress. Lines 2 and 4 contain six syllables – three complete trochees – but lines 1 and 3 contain seven syllables and

Ex. 4

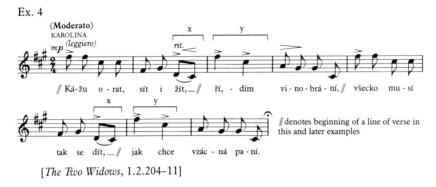

[*The Two Widows*, 1.2.204–11]

so end on stressed monosyllables – the first half of an incomplete fourth trochee.

Smetana's setting (Ex. 4) establishes a basic rate of one crotchet beat to every trochaic foot. The incomplete feet at the ends of lines 1 and 3 are also allotted a whole crotchet (or rather a two-quaver melisma – marked x); the six syllables (three trochees) of lines 2 and 4 are made up to the metrical equivalent of four trochees by allotting two crotchet beats (instead of two quavers) to the first foot of each line (marked y). This results in regular two-bar phrases for each line – a polka rhythm that derives very obviously from the regular trochees of the verse.

Trochees are Züngel's basic metre in *The Two Widows*. He used them so consistently that Očadlík speculated that a trochaic libretto may have been a specific requirement by Smetana (Züngel 1962, 19), citing the most famous 'polka' of the opera, the Act 2 duet 'Rozhodnuto, uzavřeno'. Smetana composed the music for this in his 'Notebook of Motifs' (*Zápisník motivů*, Smetana 1942, 34) in September 1864, almost a decade before the opera. The eight- or seven-syllable trochaic lines that Züngel wrote for it match so well (unlike other previously written material used in *The Two Widows*) that it seems likely that he heard the number before he began work. The trochaic quatrain he supplied for it may well have provided a basic model for his verse patterns in the libretto. Once again he avoided three-syllable words, but here made greater use of double trochees arising from four-syllable words. There are strong endings (on monosyllables) in the third and fourth lines.

Rozhod|nuto, | uza|vřeno, |

zamít|nuto, | postu|peno! |

Děj se | tedy | vůle | tvá,

když ho | nechceš | mým být | má.

(Decided, concluded, refused, proceeded on! Let your will be done, if you don't want him, he will be mine.)

Naturally not every trochaic quatrain was mirrored in the music so closely as in these examples. A composer of Smetana's resourcefulness was able to find many ways of varying the pattern. For instance the opening of Karolina's aria (immediately preceding Ex. 4) is metrically identical with the first quatrain quoted:

$$\overline{\text{Sa}}\text{mo}|\overline{\text{stat}}\breve{\text{ně}} \mid \overline{\text{vlá}}\overline{\text{dnu}} \mid \overline{\text{já}}$$

$$\overline{\text{vše}}\breve{\text{mi}} \mid \overline{\text{stat}}\breve{\text{ky}} \mid \overline{\text{svý}}\breve{\text{mi}}, \mid$$

$$\overline{\text{svrcho}}|\overline{\text{va}}\breve{\text{ná}} \mid \overline{\text{moc}}\ \breve{\text{je}} \mid \overline{\text{má}}$$

$$\overline{\text{na}}\breve{\text{de}} \mid \overline{\text{podda}}|\overline{\text{ný}}\breve{\text{mi}}. \mid$$

(Independently I administer all my estates; I have supreme power over the serfs.)

But Smetana's setting of it has a completely different rhythm (with much variation in note values) and even a different metre (Ex. 5). Nevertheless,

Ex. 5

[*The Two Widows*, 1.2.194–201]

whatever variation Smetana was able to conjure out of these trochaic quatrains, he seldom overrode one basic feature of Züngel's trochaic verse: the strong-beat beginnings. This is an important point. Trochees and dactyls when set 'as they come' lead naturally to music with downbeat beginnings and (except with incomplete feet) upbeat endings. They form an exact parallel to the Czech language with its first-syllable stress and weak word-endings. Music that reflects this pattern might be said to be more 'Czech' than music with upbeats and strong endings. Očadlík suggested (Züngel 1962, 19) that the metrical structure of the libretto (and the librettist's attempt to imitate the character of folk texts) was an important way of making the originally 'neutral' material more Czech.

An entirely trochaic libretto, however 'Czech' it might be, would be metrically monotonous and unstimulating to the composer, so Züngel also provided some metrical contrasts. He did this in specific areas amounting to about 15% of the libretto. He used iambs for set pieces that needed to be clearly differentiated: in the two numbers that he designated 'songs' in the libretto (for Mumlal and Ladislav), and in Ladislav's ballad in Act 1. Otherwise, for about 10% of the time, he used dactyls or a trochaic–dactylic mixture. This metre seldom occurs in solo sections, and is instead found in the ensembles and choruses. A frequent pattern, for instance, in Mumlal and Ladislav's duet in Act 1 and in the trios and quartet in Act 2, is for the ensemble to begin in trochees and culminate in a dactylic refrain, often set to a fast patter. About two thirds of all duets, ensembles and choruses have dactylic sections. The Act 2 quartet provides an example of this type of dactylic–trochaic refrain, with dactyls set as triplets in a regular 2/4 metre (Ex. 6).

Ex. 6

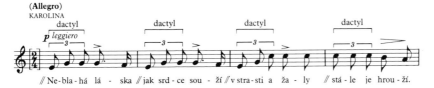

Karolina: As fatal love troubles the heart it constantly plunges it into grief and woe! [*The Two Widows*, 2.9.1427–30; three lower parts omitted]

It is not by chance that Züngel presented a clearly thought-out metrical strategy for his libretto. He was an immensely experienced man of the theatre with many translations of opera librettos to his credit before he wrote *The Two Widows* for Smetana (see p. 101). In view of the first-syllable stress in Czech by far the most natural plan for a Czech opera libretto was the one that he chose: trochees as a basic metre, with dactyls and occasionally iambs as contrasting metres. The only comparable figure to Züngel in this respect was Jindřich Böhm (1836–1916). Like Züngel, Böhm was an experienced translator of foreign librettos, and seems to have come to similar conclusions. Like Züngel, too, he used trochees for his main metre, but whereas Züngel used dactyls as a relief metre for ensembles and iambs only in a few songs, Böhm, perhaps because of the serious nature of his librettos *Drahomíra* and *Záviš z Falkenštejna*, avoided dactyls (which tend to have a more rollicking, even comic effect). Though he used a few dactyls in *Drahomíra*, for instance in Krůvoj's angry outburst in Act 3 'Zděšena výrokem hle dcera šílená' ('See my mad daughter, terrified by this statement'), he generally employed iambs as his relief metre. Böhm's comic libretto for Hřímalý, *The Enchanted Prince*, is written relentlessly in trochees, with little metrical relief.

Sabina's 'relief metre' in *The Bartered Bride* was prose. Unlike Züngel, whose spoken dialogue in *The Two Widows* was generally in rhyming trochaic couplets, Sabina simply wrote the dialogue in prose and the sung portions in trochees (or in a trochaic–dactylic mixture). But there is an interesting difference in Smetana's setting. While *The Two Widows* follows Czech patterns impeccably, *The Bartered Bride* frequently goes against them. Some of these accentual errors can be traced back to the librettist. At the beginning of Kecal's duet with Jeník, Sabina wrote the following quatrain:

Kecal: Nuže, | milý | chasníku |

dopřej pak | slovíčku! |

Jeník: Raději bych | poseděl |

tam při svém | pivíčku. |

Kecal: Now, my dear fellow, a word with you please!
Jeník: I would rather sit down there with my beer.

The most plausible scansion would be as shown. If 'tam' is more strongly stressed than 'při' then lines 2 and 4 can be completely dactylic, while lines 1 and 3 begin with two trochees and end in trisyllabic dactyls. The only way of setting these words with correct word-stress is to interpret the metrical scheme as a trochaic–dactylic mixture. Smetana, however, took it as straight trochees. By beginning on the half-bar, furthermore, he arranged to have a down-beat strong ending on the final (unstressed) syllable of each line (each underlined in Ex. 7). The pattern continues for the rest of this section, with the result that virtually every word at the end of a verse line is incorrectly stressed.

Ex. 7

underlining draws attention to mis-stressed syllables in this and later examples

[*The Bartered Bride*, 2.4.612–20]

It was this sort of example that Krásnohorská had in mind when she wrote, in 1871, that 'the composer need not, in fact must not follow the metre, for in the majority of our poems can be found in accentual verse some remains of *časomíra*, which simply is not suitable for music. The composer should follow only the natural accents, reading the poem as if it were prose' (Krásnohorská 1871, 17).

It is perhaps being over-generous to suggest that the irregularities in Sabina's verse arose from following *časomíra* rather than from lack of care. It is true, however, that behind many of the mis-stressings that can be found in Czech vocal music of this period lurk the theoretical disputes about the nature of Czech prosody, on whether metrical patterns in Czech verse should be based on vowel length or on stress. Confusion reigned among poets, librettists, composers and theoreticians at the time of Smetana's early operas and some examples of word-setting which from the point of accentual verse are incorrect have at least a theoretical justification according to the quantitative theory of Czech prosody. In the case of the quatrain quoted above, the fourth line might be said to consist of regular *časomíra* trochees (taking long vowels as stressed syllables):

$$\overline{\text{tam}} \; \breve{\text{při}} \mid \overline{\text{svém}} \; \overline{\text{pi}} | \overline{\text{víč}} \breve{\text{ku}}. \mid$$

But the first line would be irregular, if, according to *časomíra* rules,[3] one takes the long vowels as stressed syllables, since the iambic pattern that this suggests would need the short 'že' of Nuže' to be long.

$$\breve{\text{Nu}} \overset{?}{\breve{\text{že}}}, \mid \breve{\text{mi}}\overline{\text{lý}} \mid \breve{\text{chas}}\overline{\text{ní}} | \breve{\text{ku}}$$

Furthermore, although it is sometimes stated that Smetana followed *časomíra* in his settings, he clearly was not doing so here, since he set Sabina's line with a stress on the first syllable of each word, rather than on the long vowels stressed in *časomíra*.

While many of the mis-stressings in *The Bartered Bride* can be laid at Sabina's door, or at Smetana's uncritical rhythmic response, some have other causes. It could be argued, for instance, that there are deliberate mis-stressings for comic effect in Kecal's part or in Vašek's stammer. In a few cases there is clear evidence that Smetana first conceived a number instrumentally, and then fitted a text to it. Few of the motifs in his 'Notebook of Motifs' come with words attached. Smetana used the notebook for over twenty years, jotting down ideas, carefully dated, some of which subsequently found their way into his works. The three numbers that related to *The Bartered Bride*, for instance (the opening chorus, the 'věrné milování' theme from Jeník and Mařenka's duet and the duet in the last act for the Circusmaster and Esmeralda), were all originally entries in the 'Notebook', written well before he received Sabina's libretto. All have problems with word-setting, in the last instance because Smetana attempted to fit Sabina's irregular verse to a clearly trochaic tune (Ex. 8). Though Smetana continued to use the 'Notebook' in this way until his last operas, he soon learnt the trick of putting his instrumentally conceived themes into the orchestra and letting the voices recite against them.

Ex. 8

Esmeralda: We will make a dear little animal out of you. [*The Bartered Bride*, 3.2.510–13; Circusmaster's part omitted]

Another explanation for Smetana's poor word-setting offered by Czech writers (with understandable reluctance) is that the father of Czech opera, because of his German education and the years spent in Sweden, did not in fact speak his mother tongue correctly.[4] Like any foreigner struggling with Czech Smetana may in his speech have stressed syllables with long vowels rather than initial syllables. Some evidence of the way he spoke can be deduced from his spelling (Očadlík 1940, 14), which apart from confusion between letters such as 's' and 'z' is revealingly haphazard in the placing of the *čárka*, the length sign. If Smetana's speech was different from what today would be considered correct Czech, he was not alone. Many of the higher classes of Czech society of the time – gentry, administrators, officers, clerics – spoke a type of Czech which betrayed the influence of German stress patterns and of the unnatural declamation of ecclesiastical Czech (*DČD*, ii, 190). The great Czech historian František Palacký believed that the word 'opravdu' (really) in a question should be stressed 'o*pra*vdu', while the grammarian Josef Jungmann was convinced that '*ci*zinci' (foreigner) and '*spa*nilou' should be pronounced 'ci*zin*ci' and 'spani*lou*' (Král 1923, 680).

## German librettos

Rozkošný's *The St John's Rapids* (1871) was one of the most popular Czech operas of its time and one of the earliest to be published in vocal score. The score has a dual text, Czech and German, fitted beneath the voice parts. This may suggest that a German translation had been made and added in the hope of attracting a German market for the opera, as occasionally happened with other early vocal scores of Czech operas (for instance *The Bartered Bride* and Blodek's *In the Well*). But in fact the libretto was written in German, and the metrically equivalent Czech text was a translation.

The librettist of *The St John's Rapids* was Eduard Rüffer (1837–78). He was born in Prussia, descended from a Czech family which had emigrated after the Battle of the White Mountain. Although educated in German, he found a place in Czech cultural life; from 1864 he lived continuously in Prague, working as a writer fluent in German, Czech and French. He wrote his librettos for *The St John's Rapids*, and for Šebor's *The Hussite Bride*, in

German. Here is an example of his verse, with its equivalent in Šubert's translation.

| Du hast | ein Töch- | ter-chen | so wun- | der-schön, |
| Máš dce- | ruš- ku, | tu jed- | nou vi- | děl jsem, |

| ich lie- | be sie | seit dem | ich sie | gesehn; |
| a spa- | ní-lej- | ší pro | mne ne- | má zem; |

| drum bitt | ich dich | gib sie | zum Wei- | be mir, |
| i žá- | dám, | i sna- | žně žá- | dám tě, |

| drum bitt | ich dich | gib sie | zum Wei- | be mir. |
| a- bys | za chot' | mně ji | při- slí- | bil. |

(translation of the German text: You have a most beautiful little daughter. I have loved her from the moment I saw her and therefore ask you to give me her for my wife.)

Rüffer's lines are written in iambic pentameters, which Šubert's translation mirrors exactly except for the single syllable in place of 'bitt ich' in line 3 and 'Weibe' in line 4. Šubert also provided a new fourth line to correspond to Rozkošný's repetition of the third German line. In both German and Czech, the iambs are achieved by initial monosyllables, which Rozkošný's setting reflects with anacruses. The one exception, 'abys' in the last line, results in a mis-stress. The strong ending on 'mir' in the German is fine, but not its Czech equivalent – the unnatural stress on the final syllable of 'příslíbil' (Ex. 9).

Ex. 9

[*The St John's Rapids*, 1.6 VS 48–9]

Apart from a few of the more folklike items written in trochees (choruses at the openings of Acts 2 and 4, and a song for Horýmír in Act 2), the libretto, including other choruses and all the ensembles, is iambic. Iambs are easier to write in German than in Czech and it is not surprising that Rüffer's German libretto was written in what was the standard dramatic

German metre of the period. Rüffer's earlier libretto for Šebor's *The Hussite Bride* was more liberal in its use of trochees. Most of the choruses are trochaic (perhaps suggested by the use of the trochaic Hussite chorale 'Ktož jsú boží bojovníci'), so are a few, but not all, of the songs; the final ensemble of Act 3 begins in trochees, but soon goes into iambs.

The metrical patterns of a German libretto have an inevitable effect on the music written to it. A generally iambic metre, unless treated with much care, will result in upbeat starts and strong endings. Typical 'Czech' features – weak endings and downbeat starts – will be automatically precluded unless there are irregularities. A Czech-sounding opera written to such a libretto is not of course impossible but the composer setting it will start off at a disadvantage. It seems all the more surprising, then, not just that two librettos set by Smetana, *Dalibor* and *Libuše*, were written originally in German, but in particular that it was a high priority for Špindler when he translated them, to reproduce as far as possible the exact metrical scheme of each line.[5] The reason for the metrical matching is clear from a letter Smetana wrote on 20 April 1865 to his Swedish friend P.J. Valentin about *Dalibor*: 'Since the text exists in both German and Czech, it will also be possible to perform the opera outside Bohemia' (Kraus 1906, 408). Here are a few lines from Act 1, Scene 4 of *Libuše*:

```
Der   Äl- | ter bin ich, |
Jsem star - | ší bra- tra, |

Der Erst - | ge-burt Recht |
dle    to- | ho prá- vem, |

Wie's bei | den deu- | tschen Nach- | barn gilt, |
jakž  u | sou-sed- | ních Něm- | ců zní, |

Nehm' ich | in An- spruch. |
mám dě- | dit vše- chno! |

So      | steht's fest bei | mir, |
Pe-vně | bu-      |  du  | stát |

Fest, wie der | Vy- še-hrad | steht, |
ja-  ko že | sto-jí  ten | hrad, |

Ob die | Son- ne | auf ihn | nie-der- | lacht, |
nech i | slun-ce | naň se | u- smí- | vá, |

O- der | ihn um- | stür- met | Wet-ter- | macht! |
ne- bo | bou- ře | hrud' mu | ro- zrý- | vá! |
```

(translation of the German text: I am the older and claim my right as the first-born, as is recognized by the neighbouring Germans. I stand fast by it as Vyšehrad stands, whether the sun laughs down on it or stormy weather rages around it.)

This example gives a fair idea of Wenzig's verse. The lines vary in length but are generally short, unrhymed and metrically irregular. Although the earlier lines begin with monosyllables (as do well over half the lines in *Dalibor* and *Libuše*), normally an indication of iambic metre, the last two lines are trochaic and the line before, 'Fest wie der Vyšehrad steht', is dactylic. Špindler, in his translation, matched the number of syllables per line in identical metres and reproduced the rhyming couplet at the end. In other passages he was not always quite so successful. In Act 1 Scene 5 of *Dalibor* King Vladislav pronounces sternly on the need for law and order. Here Wenzig wrote regular iambs with a rhyme scheme of aabccb for the six lines:

Wladislaw: Ge-sétz | und Órd-|nung mü-|ssen wal-ten, |

Zum Heil | sie auf-|recht zu | er-hal-ten, |

Das ist | der Herr-|scher heil'-|ge Pflicht. |

Das Herz | be-zäh-|me sein | Be-geh-ren, |

Die Schuld | kann Gu-|tes nicht | ge-bä-ren, |

Und end-|lich trifft | sie das | Ge-richt. |

This is Špindler's equivalent stanza, marked off in metrical feet according to normal Czech stress patterns:

Vladislav: Po-řá-dek, | zá-kon | vlá-sti | mu-sí, |

zlo-zrá-dem | zem | nej-ví-ce | zku-sí, |

tož | po-vin-nost | nám | zá-ko-nem, |

by-chom | pře-slech-li | ňa-der | hla-sy, |

zlo-čin | ne-smí-ří, | ne-u-|ha-sí, |

jen kdo | jej schvá-|tí or-|te-lem! |

(translation of the German text: Law and order must prevail, to maintain it for the general welfare is the sacred duty of rulers. Let the heart tame its desire, wrong cannot bring forth good, and will eventually meet with justice.)

The first two of Špindler's Czech lines employ the useful device of starting an iambic line not with a monosyllable, but with a trisyllable, an irregularity that generally ensures that the remainder of the line will have its strong syllables on even-numbered syllables (the condition for iambs). The fourth and fifth lines are metrically irregular ('bychom přeslechli' and 'zločin nesmíří' are mis-stressed if the lines are considered iambic as in Wenzig's German rather than as a trochaic–dactylic mixture). The last line, apart from the final trisyllable (which will receive an unwanted stress on the final syllable) is iambic.

It is interesting to see how Smetana's music fits the two texts. The vocal score was published in 1884 with a single, Czech text. In Ex. 10 the equivalent Wenzig text has been added. In the Czech setting there is only one four-syllable word ('ne-u-ha-sí', which wrongly receives its strongest stress on its

[*Dalibor*, 1.5.939–67]

third syllable). Nearly all the three-syllable words are wrongly stressed: 'pořádek', 'zlořádem', 'přeslechli' and 'nesmíří' receive first-beat stresses on their second syllables; 'nejvíce' a half-bar stress on its second syllable; and 'povinnost' on the third. As can be seen, all these mis-stressings arise from metrical irregularities in Špindler's Czech translation. When Smetana failed to take them into account and instead set the six-line stanza as regular iambs, as in the German, mis-stressings automatically occurred. Some attempts were made in the printed librettos of the time to correct the mis-stressing (for instance by rewriting the fifth line; Wenzig 1944, 49, fn. 99) but the damage was already done. The six lines of the German fit Smetana's voice part extremely well, with no misaccentuations of any kind.

Where Czech and German verse metres were exactly the same, Smetana's music fits both equally well. But in those cases where Špindler deviated from the German metrical framework the setting fits the German suspiciously better than the Czech. In view of this it is hard to resist the thought that Smetana had the German text in mind much of the time (he did in fact write the German text of *Dalibor* into his full score for the first few scenes of the opera; Šilhan 1909, 110). The result can hardly be claimed to be distinctively Czech. If one considers just the rhythm in *Dalibor*, the work could just as well have been German.

The final word of this passage, 'ortelem', received a substantial stress on the final syllable to provide a strong end to the phrase. The climactic stressing of final syllables is a useful indicator of changing attitudes towards word-setting in Czech. Because initial stress is the rule in Czech words, only a monosyllable can legitimately carry stress on a final syllable of a line. Ends of phrases, unless ending with monosyllables, will produce weak endings if the correct stress pattern is maintained: two-syllable words yield feminine endings, three-syllable words triple endings. It is the feminine, and especially the triple, endings that are so characteristic of Czech and which set it apart from the strong endings more common in German or Italian. The ending of Milada's Act 2 aria ('Radostí nesmírnou', Ex. 11) with 'dostane' set correctly as a triple ending, provides an interesting pointer towards things to

Ex. 11

Milada: O Lord, if you can hear the cry of a human breast, o heavens grant that he receive his freedom through me! [*Dalibor*, 2.4.726–32]

come. It concludes an important, large-scale aria, and the climax is heightened by the written-out vocal cadenza. Here, almost for the first time in such an exposed position, Smetana risked a Czech triple ending ('*dostane*', set with a prominent appoggiatura on the first note) rather than the final-syllable ending ('dosta*ne*') that one might have expected.

'Orte*lem*' rather than '*dostane*' is however the rule in *Dalibor* and this, together with the many musical anacruses, are two tell-tale signs of a German libretto. These features are so prevalent in *Dalibor* that their virtual elimination in *Libuše*, Smetana's next opera, is astonishing, particularly as it originates from an identical source and in an identical way (the same German librettist and Czech translator). There had obviously been a clear change of attitude towards word-setting by Smetana, a shift which is corroborated by a study of the earliest drafts of the opera. Jiránek (1976, 65) has calculated that half of the word-stresses were incorrect in the first sketch of the opening of Scene 1 of *Libuše*. By the final version 83% of the words are correctly stressed. Smetana's awareness of the importance of correct word-stress can be traced to 1869 when, in composing a new aria for Mařenka in *The Bartered Bride* with mainly iambic lines, he wrote fewer vocal upbeats than in comparable passages in *Dalibor*. The impulse may have come from Hostinský, who in April 1869 (at the age of 22) gave a lecture on Czech prosody at the Umělecká Beseda (Jůzl 1980, 16) and the next year published his first thoughts on Czech prosody in music in *Hudební listy*. In 1871 Krásnohorská, already then in negotiation with Smetana, published in the same journal her even more practical comments, including some direct criticism of Smetana's declamation in *The Bartered Bride*. The writing of *Libuše* provides an eloquent testimony of Smetana's striving towards an almost flawless accentual declamation of the text. Ten years later he was still making tiny changes to it:

By chance, through weariness and boredom, I went through the vocal score of *Libuše* and discovered faults in the endings of many words, especially of three- and four-syllable words. – A work like *Libuše* must be *impeccable*. I will let you know my corrections, and ask you to stress in the Hudební Matice that the vocal score, in any *new* edition should incorporate my recent corrections. I will myself put the corrections into the full score when I next visit Prague. Just to show you now what I mean, in the *first* scene of the *first* act (p. 12), third system, Radmila begins at the half bar 'by srovnali zlou hádku', i.e. continuing her previous lines, viz: [Ex. 12]. This is bad, the syllable 'li' acquires undue importance, and it should be corrected thus [Ex. 13]. Thus the F of the second bar falls away, and it begins with a crotchet rest and a crotchet C flat on the word 'zlou'.

I will bring the revised work with me on my next visit to Prague; I think that such bars can be easily corrected in the printed score, i.e. in its engraving. Luckily there are few such stupid places in *Libuše*, and those that I have left *on purpose* must remain as they are, for not only the declamation *by itself* is the determining factor, but also the *melody*, the *polyphonic* part writing, gradation, etc – and sometimes the number of unmusical five- (and more) syllable monsters in the text.

(Smetana to Srb, 25 May 1882; Teige 1896, 132–3)[6]

Smetana may have had melody and gradation in mind when in *Libuše* he permitted a mid-bar strong beat to fall on the second syllable of 'nestála', thus preserving the ascending sequence, but distorting the first-syllable stress (Ex. 14). Part-writing must likewise have been a consideration when the chorus takes up Radovan's 'Ať' po zemi' (Ex. 15). Radovan's part itself is

Ex. 12                              Ex. 13

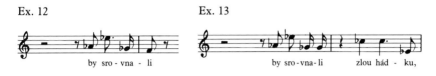

Ex. 14

Chrudoš: Alas when the evil viper creeps up on the birds, woe to him ruled by a woman so inconstant! [*Libuše*, 1.4.701–4]

Ex. 15

Radovan and chorus: Let the voice of bliss sound throughout the land! [*Libuše*, 1.4.901–4]

271

correctly stressed with the preposition 'po' receiving greater stress than the word it governs ('zemi'), whereas the imitative choral entries give a greater mid-bar stress to the first syllable of 'zemi'.

These passages, however, are scarcely serious blemishes. Against these and a small number of similar ones, there are many more examples of sensitive and imaginative word-setting. In the passage for Radmila (Ex. 16), just

Ex. 16

Radmila: Prophetess of the future! Gifted by the gods with wisdom which settles disorders! For the last time I commend both my brothers to your favour! [*Libuše*, 1.1.22–9]

after the example quoted to Srb, Smetana handles impeccably all words of three syllables ('věštkyně', 'od bohův' ( = preposition plus noun, regarded as a single word), 'moudrostí', 'poroučím') and of four syllables ('budoucnosti', 'obdařená', naposledy'). Virtually any page of *Libuše* will reveal similar felicities in the word-setting.

## Iambic librettos

There are no librettos in Czech operas that are wholly iambic any more than Züngel's libretto for *The Two Widows*, with its 15% of dactyls and iambs, was wholly trochaic. Even Sabina, while writing a trochaic libretto for *The Bartered Bride* had a remarkable change of heart in the middle of the final act: at Mařenka's sudden entrance, he moved unexpectedly into iambs. This change of metre coincides with the darkening of the plot, at the point where Mařenka learns that Jeník has apparently 'bartered' away his claims on her. Though the ensemble in which Kecal and the two sets of parents try to comfort her is written in Sabina's usual trochaic–dactylic mixture, Mařenka's bitter reflections and heated exchanges with Jeník follow in iambs; and the finale is also mainly iambic. Sabina's subsequent additions to his libretto were similarly non-trochaic: the aria for Mařenka in Act 3 is iambic, the drinking chorus which opens the second act (of the definitive, three-act version) is dactylic.

The additions to *The Bartered Bride* suggest that Sabina was beginning to take more trouble over his verse and his later comic librettos. For instance in his librettos for Blodek's *In the Well* or Bendl's *The Elderly Suitor*, there is much more variety in the verse metres. The opening of Act 2 of the latter opera is fairly typical in its sequence of metres: opening chorus – trochaic-dactylic; Hanička's recitative – iambic; Hanička's aria – dactylic; Hovora's song and dialogue with Hanička – mainly iambic.

### The Krásnohorská librettos

The librettos for Smetana's last three operas were all written by Eliška Krásnohorská, in whom Smetana found his most conscientious collaborator. A revealing glimpse of her attitude towards the combination of words and music was offered in a story she related in her autobiography (quoted in Očadlík 1940, 19). When she was sixteen Smetana asked her to translate some Schumann duets into Czech. She did this without the music, but as soon as she saw how poorly the words fitted, she immediately offered to do the job again. Smetana was apparently surprised; he had been perfectly happy with the first translation. A few years later, and with several librettos to her credit, she wrote up her very practical comments on word-setting in Czech in the *Hudební listy* article mentioned above. Such reflections were mostly directed at the composer. But from her criticisms of librettos such as Pippich's *The Death of Vlasta* (in a letter to Smetana, see Očadlík 1940, 177), it is clear that she also had firm views on the duties of the librettist, one of which was to provide metrical variety. In her own work she graduated from the predominantly iambic *Lejla* and predominantly trochaic *Viola* to the elaborate schemes of her later librettos for Smetana, where she carefully matched metres to particular moods, characters or sections.

A major difference from Züngel's scheme lay in the number of iambic lines Krásnohorská employed. Whereas *The Two Widows* is written mostly in falling metres with iambs making up less than 5% of the total, Krásnohorská's librettos for *The Kiss*, *The Secret* and *The Devil's Wall* are predominantly iambic. Iambs account for over half the lines in *The Kiss*; this figure rises in *The Secret* and still more in *The Devil's Wall*. Her next comic libretto, *Karel Škreta* for Bendl, continues this trend: almost 80% of its lines in Act 1 are iambic. Her serious librettos, from the early *Blaník* for Fibich (by 1874) to *The Child of Tábor* for Bendl (by 1888), are unashamedly in the high style, with even fewer passages in trochaic or dactylic metres.

Züngel's predominant metre in *The Two Widows* was trochaic: if ensembles were to be differentiated metrically, they went into dactyls. Since Krásnohorská's predominant metre was iambic, she could make use of both trochees and dactyls for ensembles. (In the large Act 3 chorus of *The Devil's Wall*, for instance, where the women go to offer themselves as potential brides for Vok and their menfolk restrain them, the women sing in trochees, the men in dactyls.) Thus not only does the percentage of iambic lines increase from *The Kiss* to *The Devil's Wall*, but also the percentage of dactylic lines, from 7.5% in *The Kiss* to almost double in *The Devil's Wall*. The percentage of trochees correspondingly declines, from over 40% of *The Kiss* to under 20% of *The Devil's Wall*. What had been the predominant metre of *The Bartered Bride* and *The Two Widows* accounts for less than a fifth of the lines in Smetana's last opera.

In *The Kiss* Krásnohorská made use of different metres for characterization. Trochees provide the chorus metre and the 'masculine' metre. The minor characters, Tomeš, Matouš the smuggler, and the Guard, sing almost exclusively in trochees, as do Father Paloucký and Lukáš in their more rumbustious scenes. Martinka bustles away in dactyls much of the time; Vendulka's lines are predominantly iambic. Her long scene with Lukáš begins in trochees (36 lines), but as the differences between the two become more apparent, the trochees turn to iambs. Characterization by metre, which partly explains the higher proportion of trochees in *The Kiss*, disappears from Krásnohorská's later librettos, though in *The Devil's Wall* some of the supernatural is handled with non-iambic metres.

Since the falling metres, trochees and dactyls, are more natural to Czech than are iambs, Krásnohorská often used them for 'lighter' sections, for 'songs' for instance, especially with folkish associations. This approach dates back to her first libretto, *Lejla*, where Zorajda's Romance in Act 3 and the song with the girls that precedes it are trochaic. The tendency is best exemplified in *The Kiss*, where Vendulka's two 'folksongs' (see p. 219) are dactylic; the drinking song for Tomeš and the chorus, Lukáš's 'polka' and Barče's song that opens the second scene in Act 2 are trochaic. This is also true of Blaženka's trochaic 'folksong' in Act 3 of *The Secret*, though the two songs for the ballad singer Skřivánek in this opera are iambic, perhaps to suggest his professional status. There are fewer such opportunities in *The Devil's Wall*, but this trend continues into the later *Karel Škreta*, where Bobeš's mock-Italian aria and Gabriela's song, both in Act 3, are written in trochees.

A striking metrical feature of *The Secret* is the way Krásnohorská used metrical contrasts to break up a long number, well demonstrated by Kalina's aria at the beginning of Act 2.

| 11 lines | iambs | Kalina laments his poverty |
| 4 lines | trochees | – what is this promise of a treasure? |
| 8 lines | alternation of dactyls and trochees | – why go on suffering? |
| 12 lines | dactyls | – I want happiness and gold! |
| 6 lines | trochees | – why all this longing after mammon? |
| | | – It is all for Roza's sake! |

This clearly suggests a *scena* with contrasts of mood differentiated by contrasts of metre.

### Smetana's response

In his last operas Smetana was thus working with a librettist who, whatever the dramatic shortcomings of her texts, was able to offer him librettos of considerable metrical variety which, unlike the haphazard prosody of *The Brandenburgers in Bohemia*, *Dalibor* or *Libuše*, was carefully thought out and tailored to different moods, situations and characters. Smetana responded with enthusiasm. His scene for Kalina in *The Secret* matches Krásnohorská's plan as follows:

| 11 lines | iambs | 4/4 Moderato; Quasi andante |
| 4 lines | trochees | 4/4 Più animato |
| 8 lines | alternation of dactyls and trochees | 3/4 Lento non troppo |
| 12 lines | dactyls | 2/4 with many triplets (in effect 6/8) Più vivo; Meno Allegro; Più vivo (reprise); Più animato |
| 6 lines | trochees | 3/4 Quasi andantino |

This is self-evidently far more more interesting metrically than the fast polkas and medium–slow waltzes that make up *The Bartered Bride*. But it is also further away from the dance roots of Smetana's earlier style, and thus represents a further draining off of a source of perceivable 'Czechness'. But this was to some extent compensated for by Smetana's metrical response. Whereas in his earlier operas an iambic libretto would have resulted in upbeat starts and strong endings (that is, the perceived characteristics of an opera with a 'German' libretto such as *The St John's Rapids*), in his later operas he seems to have made a conscious attempt to avoid this.

During his work on *Libuše* Smetana apparently began to regard vocal upbeats (and particularly any multi-syllable word beginning before the beat) as 'un-Czech' and thus to be avoided. In *Libuše* voice parts are more likely to begin on the first beat of the bar, at the half-bar, or just after either, rather than on the final upbeat of the bar. When, a few years later, Smetana began his first opera to a Krásnohorská libretto, with many iambic lines to contend with, he was well able to deal with the metrical problems they presented.

In her *Hudební listy* article Krásnohorská had emphasized that iambic lines could be set correctly and attractively in Czech and gave an example from a song by the Czech composer Alois Jelen.

Ǎch k̄ to|bě lá|sky žár |

m̄ou du|ši za|nímá. |

Jelen's solution (Ex. 17) was to put the initial syllables 'Ach' and 'mou' not before the beat as anacruses but on the beat, following them with longer notes (syncopated, over the half-bar) for the stressed syllables. The solution is satisfactory enough for a short song, but how did Smetana deal with this problem on a much larger scale, in a whole scene for instance?

Ex. 17

*// Ach k to - bě lá - sky žár // mou du - ši za - ni - má.*

Oh the warmth of my love for you fills my soul!

In the middle of Act 1 of *The Kiss*, Vendulka and Lukáš are left alone to sort out their differences. Their long dialogue is initiated with thirty-six trochaic lines, and then continues in iambs. The iambic section begins with a solo for Vendulka in 6/8, which is a comfortable and unobtrusive metre for iambs, its upbeats not so sharp as upbeats in 2/4 or 4/4. Half of Vendulka's sixteen lines start on quaver upbeats, though two of these occur in run-on lines, where this is not so noticeable. But the remaining eight lines employ whole-beat starts of the opening monosyllable, or, in two cases, start on the third quaver of the bar. It is interesting that the majority of the upbeat starts occur in the latter eight lines, almost as if by then Smetana had become weary of trying to avoid them. Here are the first four lines (Ex. 18). Line 1 begins on the first beat of the bar, lines 2 and 3 on the second beat, and line 4 on the third quaver. This variety characterizes the subsequent exchanges between Lukáš and Vendulka, but when, later, the anger between the couple mounts and their differences become more apparent, Smetana let this manifest itself in extremes of handling the initial monosyllables: either all aggressive upbeats (Ex. 19) or all emphatic first beats (Ex. 20). In the

Ex. 18

Vendulka (timorously): It is the glow of sunset, – hark before the darkness starts how from her sleep in the grave the mother arises to see her child. [*The Kiss*, 1.5.909–17]

Ex. 19

Lukáš: Do I have to wait until my wedding? Ay, ay, you want to frighten me! How well it befits my little wife! [*The Kiss*, 1.5.999–1011]

Ex. 20

Lukáš: I want no more than to kiss your cheek, resistance is useless, no more arguments! I won't beg where I might take; [*The Kiss*, 1.5.1050–5]

latter case the short four-syllable lines are each compressed into single bars. Another pattern for dealing with iambs in this scene comes seventy-five bars later where the eight-syllable lines now in 4/4 are set beginning on a crotchet second beat (Ex. 21). This of course is also a type of anacrusis, but a long one, moving towards a downbeat three beats away.

By his final opera, *The Devil's Wall*, avoiding upbeats had become part of Smetana's vocal style. Lines that start on the second beat are a feature of Míchálek's aria in Act 2 (Ex. 22). Even more frequent are lines that start a quaver after the first beat (Ex. 23), while those that start on the first beat are

Ex. 21

Lukáš: Surely the woman is usually the gentler!
Vendulka: However the man ought to be the wiser!
Lukáš: Why must it be just as you want?
Vendulka: And must you always be right? [*The Kiss*, 1.5.1160–7]

Ex. 22

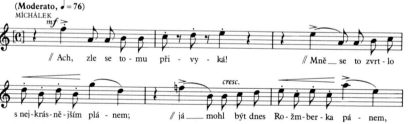

Míchálek: Oh, it is difficult to get used to it! My most wonderful plan has gone wrong; I could today have been the lord of Rožmberk. [*The Devil's Wall*, 2.2.274–9]

Ex. 23

Míchálek (threatens): That woman's face! When happiness rained directly on me and held me firmly in its fist, [*The Devil's Wall*, 2.2.326–36]

used only for particular verbal emphasis (Ex. 24: 'Já' (I), 'Pán' (Lord)). And Vok's great solo at the end of Act 1, a serious example from the same opera – despite its more flexible handling of note values – contains exactly the same devices.

Ex. 24

Míchálek: I am the old castellan Míchálek, I could have said to the lords: 'Vok, Lord of Rožmberk – my son-in-law; the highest marshall in the kingdom – my son-in-law!' [*The Devil's Wall*, 2.2.296–310]

An important aspect of Smetana's word-setting is how he dealt with internal irregularities. How, for instance, in a succession of trochees, would he treat a dactyl? In his earliest operas it usually went unnoticed: Smetana nonchalantly mis-stressed his way through metrically irregular lines. In the middle section of the opening chorus of *The Bartered Bride* Sabina introduced the following lines among what had hitherto been trochees:

$$\overline{\text{Ko}}\text{něc} \mid \overline{\text{ra}}\text{dos}\text{ti!} \mid$$

$$\overline{\text{Hr}}\text{nou se} \mid \overline{\text{sta}}\text{ros}\text{ti,} \mid$$

Smetana ignored the dactylic implications of these lines and set them mostly in continuous crotchets, consequently mis-stressing not only the final syllable of 'radosti' but also the first two syllables of 'starosti' and the unstressed reflexive 'se'.

$$\overline{\text{Ko}}\text{něc} \mid \overline{\text{ra}}\text{do}|\underline{\text{sti!}}$$

$$\overline{\text{Hr}}\text{nou} \mid \overline{\text{se}}\text{ sta}|\underline{\text{ros}}\text{ti,} \mid$$

The prose recitatives on the other hand (added to the opera in 1870) show some recognition of the varying trochee and dactyl patterns in Czech, as in Ex. 25, where the trisyllable 'odebral' is given a triplet semiquaver to be followed immediately by regular semiquavers. This mixture of twos and threes

Ex. 25

Jeník: I took myself off into the world, and. . .[*The Bartered Bride*, 1.2.619]

is a direct reflection of Czech stress patterns. There are of course other ways of setting interpolated dactyls (a quaver and two semiquavers, for instance) but the triplet semiquavers here provide a more idiomatic way of doing it. It is interesting to observe Smetana's increasing use of internal triplets for interpolated dactyls in *Dalibor*. They occur in recitatives and the more declamatory passages but also begin to be exploited as a characteristic rhythm, as in Milada's entrance (now dressed up as a young boy) in Act 2, where the librettist provided short 'breathless' lines, usually of five syllables (a dactyl and a trochee), which Smetana set with triplet quavers interspersed in the 4/4 metre (Ex. 26).

Ex. 26

Milada: Everything's ready, sit down here! Lots of sausages, there's good meat here, butter, bread, cheese, beer for everyone. [*Dalibor*, 2.3.569–73]

This free alternation of twos and threes, so characteristic of the Smetana of *Dalibor* and *Libuše*, did not disappear in the Krásnohorská operas, but its occurrences were rarer. This is because its chief *raison d'être* – the mixed metres of the earlier operas – gave way to Krásnohorská's more technically accomplished verse, where only occasionally (for instance when she was working in dactyls), did she find it difficult to stick to a consistent metre.

Smetana's lack of awareness of correct Czech declamation in his early operas makes the assumption of a consistent 'Czech' style derived from the Czech text difficult to defend. There is more evidence of a Czech style in *The Bartered Bride*, whose trochaic–dactylic lines coincide with the natural rhythms of Czech speech, than in *Dalibor*, whose libretto is metrically no different from a German one. But while he was composing *Libuše*, Smetana began to achieve a more idiomatic setting of the text. He largely eliminated the upbeats suggested by the monosyllabic beginnings of lines. This led to emphatic beginnings (prolonging the initial monosyllable – often for comic or emotional purposes) or beginnings just after the main beat of the half-bar. Often triple or compound metres helped overcome the long start or, if necessary, smoothed down the upbeat. Occasional dactyls were subsumed with interpolated triplets. He exchanged final-syllable endings for feminine and triple endings. All these characteristics, together with the syncopations produced by the interplay of first-syllable stress and long vowels on unstressed syllables, can be said to derive from the Czech language, or at one remove, from the constraints that a regular metre imposes on it. By the time Smetana began working with Krásnohorská his technique was quite ready to handle her predominantly iambic lines without recourse to the upbeats and strong endings they suggested.

Such characteristics are the hallmarks of the type of stylized Czech word-setting which Smetana bequeathed to his successors. Fibich, with his literary talents, did perhaps best of all. He never needed his librettists to make special efforts to accommodate his music and he set texts ranging from Krásnohorská's iambs to Schulzová's irregularly trochaic verse with equal aplomb. Hostinský (1909, 7) reports that having spent four years abroad, Fibich was at first unable to get the word-setting in *Bukovín* right and needed help with it when the work was accepted for performance. This was true to a lesser extent of *Blaník*, though by the time Fibich had made many small corrections Hostinský could declare that it was, after Smetana's works, the Czech opera with the best word-setting (Hostinský 1909, 66–7). In their own collaboration on *The Bride of Messina* Fibich asked Hostinský to underline the stresses as a check for his own instincts but by this stage such a procedure was quite unnecessary (Hostinský 1909, 84–5): impeccable declamation in Czech had become a hallmark of Fibich's vocal style and his overriding concern. In his reminiscences of the composer, Foerster (1929, 351) related that Fibich's main interest, when he took his songs to him, was to correct slips in the word-setting. In fact Fibich looked further than Foerster suggests. In an account of what may have been the same incident, Boleška (1903, 302) wrote that Fibich believed that the composer's task did not end with getting the stress of individual words right but needed equally to take into account the declamation of the verbal sentence as a whole.

Dvořák too achieved an idiomatic and expressive Czech word-setting in his later operas. But there is no doubt that impeccable declamation was not such a high priority with him. For all the many examples in his works of triplet groups, verbal syncopations, appoggiatura endings and other characteristic rhythms deriving from the Czech language, Dvořák always seemed happy to sacrifice natural word-setting in the interests of a good tune. All his later librettists report receiving strict and specific instructions on metre, for more or fewer words, and for monosyllabic ends to lines (Kvapil 1911, 431–2, Kundera 1933). Bráfová's description of the composer at work is the most graphic. In describing his dealings with her sister Marie Červinková-Riegrová she wrote, 'Dvořák would say to her every so often: "See here, I need this sort of rhythm" and instead of saying iamb, trochee, dactyl and so on he would begin to whistle a melody or would take some paper and write a melody on it' (Bráfová 1913, 82).

Despite such variations in approach among his successors, Smetana's style of setting Czech verse librettos survived through to the twentieth century. The metrical bases of Czech librettos did not change much either. Even the naturalistic school that grew up towards the end of the century followed the pattern of iambic librettos. This is true of Čelanský's conversational *Kamilla*, no less than in Bendl's veristic *Mother Míla*. Perhaps most remarkable of all is the fact that in his second opera, *Eva*, Foerster rewrote Preissová's 'realistic' prose into metrically regular iambs. Only Janáček, in his handling of similar material, took a different path.

## Prose librettos

The librettos to Janáček's first two operas were both written in verse. Zeyer's *Šárka* (1887) is iambic; apart from some inserted trochaic folksongs, Tichý's libretto (1891) for *The Beginning of a Romance* is also iambic, though with shorter lines, usually of seven or eight syllables in rhyming couplets, in contrast with Zeyer's blank verse.

Janáček could hardly have paid much attention, though, to the original metre of *The Beginning of a Romance*, since, as was shown in Chapter 7 (p. 247), much of the text was fitted to pre-existing music. Even in those numbers written to original music, for example Poluška's opening solo, there are instances of vocal upbeats and final-syllable stresses reminiscent of Smetana's pre-*Libuše* word-setting; whatever the gains in Czech declamation in Prague in the 1870s and 1880s they seem not to have penetrated to Brno by the early 1890s. The only indication of any feeling for natural accentuation is to be found in the recitatives (which, as in *The Bartered Bride*, had been originally conceived as spoken dialogue). The first words between Poluška and Adolf come in short notes and, despite the iambs, have on-beat beginnings, no final-syllable stresses and some sensitivity to long vowels (e.g. the longer notes on the 'á's of 'děvčátko', 'drobátko' and 'čekáš').

Soon after the première of *The Beginning of a Romance* in 1894 Janáček embarked on *Jenůfa*, this time making the adaptation himself. Setting Preissová's play as it stood meant that he was working with a prose text, the first Czech composer to do so. His example was followed a few years after the 1904 première of *Jenůfa* by Ostrčil in *The Bud* (1911) and later in *The Legend of Erin* (1921) but significantly in his final opera, *Johnny's Kingdom*

(1934), Ostrčil and his librettist replaced their first prose version with a verse libretto (Mařánek 1934, 6). Novák, too, returned to verse librettos for his final operas after setting prose librettos in *The Imp of Zvíkov* (1915) and *Karlštejn* (1916), while Foerster set nothing but verse librettos all his long life. The prose librettos of Janáček's last four operas are surprisingly rare for Czech operas of the period.

As in any full-length play converted into an opera libretto, there had to be extensive cuts in *Jenůfa* – whole scenes and incidents disappeared to bring the work to manageable proportions. But Janáček's adaptation is also characterized by detailed small-scale work, involving reshuffling of word-order (very flexible in Czech), the substitution of shorter or longer synonyms (with more convenient numbers of syllables), some tiny cuts, and considerable repetition of words, phrases and even whole sentences. What emerged when he had finished was a sort of quasi-verse, trochaic–dactylic in metre, based on a regular number of stresses (rather than syllables) per 'line'. Jenůfa's reproaches to Števa in Act 1 provide a good example. Here is Preissová's original text:

. . .beztoho bude pak ještě výčitek od mamičky dost. Víš, kterak si na mně zakládá – včils ju měl slyšet. Nevím, co by pak udělala, kdybys ty si mne v čas nesebral – a nevím, co by udělala taky já!

(Apart from that there will still be plenty of reproaches from mother. You know how proud she is of me – you ought to hear her now! I don't know what she would do if you didn't marry me in time – and I don't know what I would do!)

Janáček's adaptation has the same sequence of thoughts; the only change is to substitute a repetition of 'I don't know what I would do' for 'I don't know what she [i.e. Jenůfa's foster-mother] would do'. Musically Janáček organized the passage into a short 'aria' of what is now twenty-six bars (he omitted four purely orchestral bars when he revised the work for publication in 1908). Every bar of the accompaniment is based on a short four-note motif (marked 'x' in Ex. 27), rhythmically constant, melodically varied.

Ex. 27

283

Ex. 27 (*cont.*)

Ex. 27 (cont.)

[L. Janáček, *Jenůfa*, 1.6; C 1969 by Universal Edition AG, Wien]

The verbal text is set out below, one bar a line. Those bars/lines where the voice part is also based on the motif are marked 'x'. Numbers of syllables per bar are given. Where these are more or fewer than four (the length of the motif) Janáček needed to make adjustments to accommodate them. His solutions are described in the final column.

| Bar/line | Text as set | Motif | Syllables★ | Comments |
|---|---|---|---|---|
| 1 | Bez-to-ho bu-de | x | 5 | triplet on 'beztoho' |
| 2 | od ma-<u>mi</u>-čky | x | 4 | |
| 3 | těch vý-či-tek | | 6 (4) | 'pak ještě' (then still [more]) omitted; 'těch' (those) added |
| 4 | dost, dost! | x | 1 (2) | 'dost' repeated with melisma each time |
| 5 | – | | | |
| 6 | Víš, jak si | x | 3 (4) | melisma on 'Víš'; 'jak' replaces 'kterak' |
| 7 | na mně za-<u>klá</u>-dá, | x | 5 | extra note on (usually silent) first beat |
| 8 | včil, včils | | 1 (2) | 'včil(s)' repeated |
| 9 | ju měl sly-šet, | x | 4 | |

| Bar/line | Text as set | Motif | Syllables* | Comments |
|---|---|---|---|---|
| 10 | včils měl sly-šet! | x | 5 (4) | line repeated, now with 'ju' omitted to make 4 syllables |
| 11 | – | | | |
| 12 | Ne-vím, ne-vím, | x | 2 (4) | 'nevím' repeated to provide 2 more syllables |
| 13 | ne-vím, ne-vím, | x | 2 (4) | line 12 repeated |
| 14 | co bych u-dě-la-la | x | 7 (6) | 'pak' (then) omitted; last 4 syllables set twice as fast |
| 15 | kdy-bys ty mne | x | 5 (4) | 'si' (=reflexive) omitted; first part of 'x' now 2 quavers |
| 16 | včas ne-<u>se</u>-bral! | x | 4 | first part of 'x' now 2 quavers |
| 17 | ne-vím, ne-vím, | x | 2 (4) | see lines 12–13; lines 17–18 are |
| 18 | ne-vím, ne-vím, | x | 2 (4) | half a bar out of phase, but are phased in with the next line. |
| 19 | co bych u-dě-la-la | x | 7 (6) | as line 14, but begins later so last 4 syllables are 4 times as fast |
| 20 | ta-ké já, | x | 3 | melisma on 'já' |
| 21 | ta-ké já, | x | 3 | repetition; as line 20 |
| 22 | ne-vím, | | 2 | |
| 23 | co bych u-dě-la-la | x | 7 (6) | similar to line 19 |
| 24 | ta-ké já! | | 3 | |
| 25 | – | | | |
| 26 | – | | | |

* Janáček's modifications in brackets

It is clear that Janáček had little trouble in organizing Preissová's prose text into short units, each with two stresses and usually four syllables per unit. Sometimes Janáček achieved this by repeating words (line 12–13), or leaving out others (lines 10, 14, 15). Underlength lines could be accommodated with melismas (line 4); in overlength lines Janáček sometimes used a triplet to absorb three syllables in place of two (line 1) or four semiquavers in the place of two quavers (line 14), or made use of the usually silent first beat (line 7). In some cases he could not avoid a slight mis-stress in the middle of the bar (see underlined syllables in lines 2, 7 and 16).

The text itself is occasionally reshuffled (compare lines 1–4 to the first sentence of the original); some words disappear; 'kterak' (how) is replaced by a monosyllabic synonym 'jak' (line 5), and there are several repetitions of phrases. Given this amount of flexibility, it is not surprising that there are many similar sections of the opera – arias, duets or even trios in all but name – which depend on the balanced metrical units which Janáček constructed through this sort of small-scale tinkering with the prose text. Act 1 even has a full-scale ensemble built up on a single, slightly reshuffled and much repeated sentence. Acts 2 and 3, which have fewer such numbers, were written somewhat later and show the beginnings of a shift in the relationship between voice part and accompaniment. Here is a short passage from Act 2 of the play in which the Kostelnička tells Laca about Jenůfa's disappearance:

Jenůfa, bědná děvčica, nebyla jakživa ve Vídni, já ji po ten celý čas tu v komoře schovávala. Ona před týdnem dostala chlapca. . .

Jenůfa, poor girl, was never ever in Vienna; I have been hiding her all this while in an inner room. A week ago she gave birth to a boy.

Janáček's setting is shown in Ex. 28. As in the last example the music is based on a single-bar motif (x), repeated here in the accompaniment six times note for note, then twice modified. The voice part matches the motif in the first bar, and is thereafter linked to it only loosely with occasional reminiscences. This solution, depending on the orchestra's maintaining the simple underlying structure while the voice recites freely though melodically against it, allowed Janáček to stick more closely to Preissová's original text: the only differences are the emphatic repetition of 'celý čas' (all the while) and the omission of 'v komoře' (in an inner room).

Ex. 28

Ex. 28 (*cont.*)

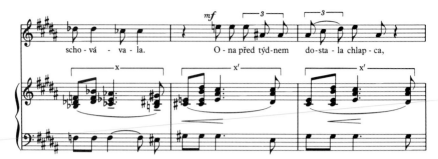

[L. Janáček, *Jenůfa*, 2.4; C 1969 by Universal Edition AG, Wien]

As Exx. 27–8 show, Janáček's word-setting in *Jenůfa* is a considerable improvement on that of *The Beginning of a Romance*. Final-syllable stresses are avoided, or were by the time Janáček had finished the score. Jenůfa's opening lines for instance (Ex. 29a) were originally set with a final-syllable stress for the end of the phrase 'a Števa se nevrací' (Ex. 29b). This was corrected to Ex. 29a only on the proofs of the vocal score.[7] Vocal anacruses, though infrequent, are however by no means excluded in the final score as the upbeat setting of 'a' (and) in Ex. 29a–b demonstrates. One curiosity is the setting of the heroine's name. Most versions in the final score follow the pattern of Ex. 30a, with the main stress on the first syllable as in standard Czech. But this was another change of mind at proof stage. Originally Janáček wrote Ex. 30b, and many other examples (among them Exx. 31 and 32) follow the same trend. Janáček spent much of his time on the *Jenůfa* proofs adjusting the declamation. Some of the mis-stressing arose from the tendency observed in Ex. 27 of fitting words to instrumental motifs. But another factor was the possible intrusion of Janáček's native dialect which, under the influence of neighbouring Polish, tended to stress the penultimate syllable ('Jenůfa') rather than the first, as in standard Czech.

Ex. 29

Jenůfa: and Števa is not back yet! [L. Janáček, *Jenůfa*, 1.1; C 1969 by Universal Edition AG, Wien]

Ex. 30

Grandmother Buryjovka: And you, Jenůfa, aren't you going inside with your mother? [L. Janáček, *Jenůfa*, 1.3; a: C 1969 by Universal Edition AG, Wien]

Ex. 31

Števa: Are you talking to me, Jenůfa? [L. Janáček, *Jenůfa*, 1.5; a: C 1969 by Universal Edition AG, Wien]

Ex. 32

Grandmother Buryjovka: And you, Jenůfa, don't cry! [L. Janáček, *Jenůfa*, 1.6; a: C 1969 by Universal Edition AG, Wien]

As *Libuše* did for Smetana, *Jenůfa* marks the turning point in the composer's approach to word-setting. The revisions for the publication of the vocal score in 1908 are evidence of his continual striving to improve the declamation, just as Smetana's similar efforts are documented from his earliest sketches for *Libuše* right up to the letter to Srb quoted on p. 270. Janáček, however, went further than Smetana in his emphasizing and exploiting the rhythmic quirks of Czech. He often exaggerated the speed and energy of the delivery of words of three or more syllables. When the

289

Kostelnička is waiting for Števa in Act 2 she recalls how she has prayed to God for Jenůfa's child not to be born (Ex. 33a). Janáček set the text exactly as Preissová wrote it except for the repetitions of the words 'namodlila' (prayed) and 'napostila' (fasted). It is significant that although the structure of the orchestral accompaniment would have allowed the complete phrases to be repeated Janáček chose to repeat merely the four-syllable words in them. And it is the energy of these repeated four-note groups (sung at twice the speed of the other notes in the voice part) that dominates this passage. At proof stage Janáček corrected the mis-stressing of the final word 'nepoznalo' (would not know) from Ex. 33b and in doing so unified the passage with yet another rapid four-note group. Initial stress at the beginning of a word-group is similarly sometimes emphasized by a leap down (usually by a perfect or diminished fifth) to the remaining notes of the group (Exx. 34a–f).

Ex. 33

The Kostelnička (desperately): How I have prayed, how I have fasted so that [the child] should never know the world! [L. Janáček, *Jenůfa*, 2.2; a: C 1969 by Universal Edition AG, Wien]

Ex. 34a

Števa: Is he already born? [L. Janáček, *Jenůfa*, 2.3; C 1969 by Universal Edition AG, Wien]

Ex. 34b

Laca: But I saw a young man go in [L. Janáček, *Jenůfa*, 2.4; C 1969 by Universal Edition AG, Wien]

Ex. 34c

The Kostelnička: She returned. [L. Janáček, *Jenůfa*, 2.4; C 1969 by Universal Edition AG, Wien]

Ex. 34d

Laca: Sharpen it for me!
The Foreman: I'll sharpen it! [L. Janáček, *Jenůfa*, 1.2; C 1969 by Universal Edition AG, Wien]

Ex. 34e

The Kostelnička: I will leave the door ajar, [L. Janáček, *Jenůfa*, 2.1; C 1969 by Universal Edition AG, Wien]

Ex. 34f

The Kostelnička: No, she did not speak to him. [L. Janáček, *Jenůfa*, 2.4; C 1969 by Universal Edition AG, Wien]

Though Janáček achieved more flexibility in the later acts, and in his revision of the opera jettisoned many of the 'rhyming repetitions' (more disappeared, too, in Kovařovic's revision for the Prague première), he was still structuring his music in regular units dominated by the voice part and consequently needed fairly regular units of text, i.e. a line of verse, or 'quasi-verse', for the voice to sing. In view of this it is not so surprising that for all his brave words about prose opera in *Jenůfa*, he gave instructions to the librettist of his next opera, *Fate*, to turn his prose draft into 'Pushkinesque

291

verse'. From the librettist he received iambic lines usually of eight or nine syllables, often with quite elaborate rhyme schemes. By the time Janáček had finished with it little of this verse structure can be detected. He over-rode the rhymes, abandoned the iambs, and subjected the text to a more radical restructuring than even his rewriting of Preissová's prose in *Jenůfa*. There were of course good reasons for Janáček's revising Bartošová's text, but it is odd, in view of his original instructions to her, that he made so little use of what it had to offer metrically. And in the light of this, it is even odder that the early history of his next opera, *The Excursion of Mr Brouček to the Moon*, was dominated by a long and fruitless search for a suitable librettist to adapt Svatopluk Čech's novel for him. The librettist was expected to write verse and it was only when one of the reluctant candidates fobbed Janáček off with the remark that his prose suggestions for Čaroskvoucí's song could perhaps remain in prose (Tyrrell 1968, 114) that Janáček settled for what became the final solution: compiling the text himself in prose directly from the novel and making use only occasionally of songs and other material that he coaxed out of his assortment of librettists. For his last operas Janáček relied on prose librettos which he arranged himself.

Janáček's radical change in attitude towards word-setting in *Jenůfa* prob-ably coincides with his discovery of 'speech melodies'. From about this time Janáček jotted down in his notebooks in a rough musical notation the frag-ments of speech and other sounds he heard about him, and wrote many arti-cles about them in which he asserted that the melodic curves of a person's speech revealed moods and emotions often unexpressed by the speaker's words alone – a 'window into a person's soul' – and that such a study was essential for a composer of operas. How much of the vocal style of *Jenůfa* derives from this study is impossible to say. The dating of his discovery of speech melodies is in dispute (on five occasions Janáček suggested five different dates),[8] and while the advance in style on *The Beginning of a Romance* is undeniable, many other factors were also at work.

A surer way of assessing the impact of Janáček's study of speech melodies on his word-setting and vocal style is to compare the second, 1888, version of his first opera, *Šárka* (which superseded a completely different version written the previous year), with his revision of the opera in 1918. Since Zeyer had refused to allow Janáček to use his text the opera lay forgotten for thirty years and it was only after the triumphant production of *Jenůfa* in Prague in 1916 that the composer remembered it and decided to revise it with a view to production. He left the overall structure of the opera in-tact, making only a few cuts, chiefly in the choral passages. Significantly, Janáček's revisions mostly affected the solo voice parts. He made his changes simply by erasing the old 1888 parts and writing in new ones over them, leaving the accompaniment untouched.[9] (In most cases, however, the old parts are easy enough to reconstruct.) The 1888 version was written before his interest in speech melodies had any impact on his composition. The 1918 revision was made long after Janáček had described his study of speech melodies and brought it to bear on at least two operas. Šárka thus provides a pre-speech-melody and a post-speech-melody version of what is otherwise identical music. How do the versions differ?

At the simplest level, as in the haunting chorus of maidens at the beginning of Act 2, Janáček simply adjusted the declamation to avoid a final-syllable stress, and to do so used a triplet, ending just before the new bar (Ex. 35). Ex. 36, with two triplets, is similar except that the voice now enters after the strong beat. One of the most noticeable characteristics of the 1888 voice parts is their emphatic on-beat starts. In contrast, the 1918 voice parts tend to start just after the strong beat. Ex. 37 shows a revision with an

Ex. 35

Warrior maidens: O how mysterious [Šárka, 2]

Ex. 36

Přemysl: What does it mean? [Šárka, 3]

Ex. 37

Warriors: What news does he bring? [Šárka, 1]

off-beat beginning and another triplet, allowing Janáček to correct the setting of the final trisyllable. Instead of the six dull crotchets of the original Janáček varied the note values from triplet crotchets (in 5/8) to a held note of five quavers on the central word – another feature of the 1918 revision is the much greater variation in note length. This is well exemplified by Ctirad's greeting in Act 1 (Ex. 38), which incorporates both shorter and longer note

Ex. 38

Ctirad: Glory to you great Přemysl! [*Šárka*, 1]

values than the original, with a triplet to avoid the final-syllable stress on 'Přemys*le*' and longer notes for the long vowels. The only difference in pitch between the two (apart from the final note) is the effective leap down a sixth for the second syllable of 'Sláva' (glory). Unusually for 1918, the revision now begins on the beat, giving a particularly heroic emphasis.

The second bar of Ex. 39 illustrates a similar leap down, untypically emphasizing 'padne v prach' (fall to the ground). Note the energy given by the triplets, here with no corrective function for the declamation. This is a good example of an obvious feature of the 1918 revision: the voice parts are generally quicker. The old parts tended to move with the orchestra, mirroring its regular phraseology and the even minim–crotchet movement; the new ones, written in shorter note values, seldom stretch over the entire

Ex. 39

Šárka: [I want the hero] to fall to the ground without a fight! And Trut's hammer and shield [will be my booty.] [*Šárka*, 2]

original length and thus create gaps where the orchestra shows through. Since the phrase climax remains in the same place, the lines bunch towards it, both beginning later and ending earlier. This is demonstrated in Ex. 40, the three bars of the original (identical with the orchestral tune) compressed into two triplets, or in Šárka's prayer, where the multi-syllable groups, the four-syllable 'slitování' (mercy) and three-syllable 'plameny' (flames), are speeded up (Ex. 41).

Ex. 40

Šárka: That woman is Vlasta [*Šárka*, 2]

Ex. 41

Ex. 41 (*cont.*)

Šárka: Have pity, moon, on your priestess, tame the spirit of my wild flames!
[*Šárka*, 2]

The rather dull rhythmic pattern of the 1888 voice parts of *Šárka* was often matched by an equally dull melody, sometimes limited to just one or two notes. Ex. 39 shows how the voice part became transformed melodically as well, moving over a wider and often higher range, showing a greater feeling for contour and climax. Ex. 42 provides another instance, here with the voice part much more dislocated from the original. Note the exciting leap up to 'žízním' (I thirst) and the leap down on the three-syllable group 'hrdého' (proud). For the most part, the gain in Janáček's revision is immense. An obvious result is a far more dramatic and energetic expression, more suited to the voice than the quasi-instrumental tunes which made up much of the 1888 version.

In general the 1918 revisions show how Janáček unhitched the voice from the orchestral accompaniment. Its part became speeded up, irregular, more interesting. It moved over a wider range, and made use of a greater variety of rhythms (often reflecting multi-syllable stress patterns in Czech). Heavy on-beat starts gave way to lighter off-beat starts, and final-syllable stresses were corrected, usually with triplets, as the vocal phrase shrank at both ends towards the phrase climax in the middle. The emphasis of Janáček's 1918 voice parts tends to be at the middle of the phrase; the emphasis in the 1888 ones at the outer ends. The 1918 parts of *Šárka* are not quite a compendium of Janáček's vocal style on the eve of his final great decade since allowance must be made for the iambic text and for the fact that Janáček was revising a pre-existing voice part and that its successor still needed to be in

Ex. 42

Šárka: I thirst for the blood of a hero! [*Šárka*, 2]

loose harness with an accompaniment that moved according to the 1888
phraseology. This last factor is the least important of the three. Much of
Janáček's later operatic music depends on a similar core of a regular
phraseology enunciated by the orchestra which allows the voice part to roam
freely above it in a more or less realistic stylization of spoken Czech.

This stylization is undoubtedly more natural and hence perhaps more
'Czech' than the settings of the Czech language in nineteenth-century verse
librettos. For when Hostinský advocated the Czech language itself as a
source of Czechness in opera, he was advocating, as far as the nineteenth
century was concerned, settings of Czech frequently metrified into rhythms

little different from German verse patterns and, since they went against the grain of the language, often resulting in mis-stressings of words. Even the impeccable settings in Smetana's later operas are in effect highly stylized solutions for accommodating iambic verse in Czech. There is no doubt that many of the solutions themselves, from late Smetana to Fibich and Dvořák, are rhythmically distinctive; with Janáček's prose settings of Czech they make up one of the more convincing bids for 'Czechness' though not one that would be free of Beckerman's strictures given at the beginning of this chapter. It would be perfectly possible for any non-Czech composer to imitate such rhythms himself.

Czechness in music, Beckerman argues, is more a context than an objective collection of musical materials. It arises from the association of music with national 'treasures' such as 'the shape of the Moravian hills, the sound of the Czech language in its many dialects, the burning of Jan Hus, the view of Prague from Hradčany, and all the folk songs and ancient chorales'. Thus,

the opening chords of *Má vlast* are not specifically Czech: $I–vi–V_6–I$ in the key of E♭. . . Yet when Smetana juxtaposes the opening chords with the image of the great rock Vyšehrad, and that image is further abstracted into a symbol of the enduring quality of the Czech people, the chords become imbued with a sensibility, and the sensibility becomes tied to something concrete. (Beckerman 1986, 66, 72–3)

The list of 'treasures' that Beckerman gives could of course be greatly extended. Many of them have been explored in earlier chapters of this book, notably the types of subject matter and characters favoured by Czech opera. But equally distinctive is the close relationship (arising from the widespread musical education among the Czechs during the eighteenth and early nineteenth century) between the high culture of the educated classes and popular culture resulting in a subtle interplay between Czech 'folk music' and 'art music'. Similarly there is the body of rhythmic strategies for setting the Czech language, whether more or less 'naturally' as in Janáček's prose settings or constrained by verse metres as in the nineteenth-century operas. But none of these 'treasures' are alone in themselves uniquely 'Czech'. Even such an eloquent symbol as the Czech bagpiper, doubly potent through his distinctive appearance and the distinctive sound of his music, has no national resonance outside the interpretation of this symbol in a context of national self-assertion. Without the rich accretion of associations bequeathed him by successive representations in folktales, pictures, stage plays and operas, Švanda would be no more Czech than Libuše without her glorification in Smetana's opera and a century of ceremonial performances.

# Notes

## 1 Czech Nationalism

1 Some of the most fruitful recent trends in Czech research in this area have been Vladimír Lébl and Jitka Ludvová's study of the cultural background to Smetana's *Má vlast* (Lébl 1981), Marta Ottlová and Milan Pospíšil's criticism of research methods in Czech nineteenth-century studies (Ottlová 1978) and their consideration of the question of 'Czechness' in Czech nineteenth-century music (Ottlová 1979), Bořivoj Srba's reassessment of Smetana's operas in the light of theatrical conventions of the time (Srba 1985) and Jitka Ludvová's and Petr Vít's various studies drawing attention the place of German culture in nineteenth-century Bohemia (Ludvová 1983 and 1984; Vít's treatment of the period 1810–60 in *HČD*).

## 2 Theatres

1 This section draws chiefly on two histories of the Czech theatre: *DČD* i–ii and Vondráček 1956 and 1957. Other references are given in parentheses.
2 Sehnal 1974 provides an excellent summary of the sources for early opera in Moravia.
3 Weber's Prague repertory is listed in Němec 1944, 168–206.
4 The libretto is printed in Kneidl 1964, 176–9; the poster is reproduced in *DČD*, ii, 247; the music is described and analysed in Sehnal 1961.
5 I am grateful to Mr Freeman for this information from his forthcoming dissertation *The Opera Theatre of Count Franz Anton von Sporck in Prague* (University of Illinois at Urbana-Champaign).
6 Czech operatic repertory 1824–34 is discussed in Vondráček 1957, 9–94 and in Plavec 1941, 92–101.
7 Škroup's roles are listed in Plavec 1941, 106.
8 The fullest account of opera at the Provisional Theatre is in Bartoš 1938. Details of the theatre's construction and capacity are drawn from Jareš 1979. The day-by-day operatic repertory is listed in Smaczny 1987.
9 Many of the stories of Smetana's incompetence as a conductor stem from prejudiced sources. One of the most sympathetic (Heller 1917) nevertheless makes clear that Smetana was temperamentally unsuited to the systematic and repetitive work involved in training an inexperienced orchestra.
10 Performance statistics are from Smaczny 1987; numbers of performances whether in the text or the tables refer only to complete performances and take no account of the performances of individual acts of operas. Smetana's opinions are from his reviews in *Národní listy* (reprinted in Smetana 1948).
11 Information in this section is based on *ČSHS* (articles 'Národní divadlo v Praze', 'Šubert, František Adolf'), *DČD*, iii, Heller 1918, Hepner 1955, Hof 1868, Javorin 1949, Kimball 1966, Nejedlý 1935 and Němeček 1968. The entire repertory of the National Theatre 1881–1983 is listed in Konečná 1983.

12 Here the ironies proliferate. The work regarded as an almost sacred operatic embodiment of Czech nationalism was composed to a text originally written in German and had been intended by Smetana to celebrate the belated coronation of Franz Josef as King of Bohemia (briefly promised in 1871). When this hope disappeared Smetana held the opera in readiness for the opening of the National Theatre. The added 'apotheosis' of Prince Rudolf's marriage was planned to take place at the end of the opera but 'only the sheer lack of tact of the Crown Prince, who had decided that he could not sit through the whole opera, meant that this apotheosis was repositioned to the beginning of the performance. Thus the Czech Theatre was spared the disgrace of making an act of homage to the Habsburg dynasty the culmination of Libuše's prophecy' (Srba 1983, 184).

13 Němeček 1966; see also Černý 1985.

14 Information in this section is based on *ČSHS* (articles 'Divadlo J. K. Tyla v Plzni'; Státní divadlo v Brně'), *DČD*, ii and iii, Procházka 1965, Vondráček 1956, 561–90, Vondráček 1957, 381–97, Bezdíčková-Ingerlová 1975, Nováková 1956, Němcová 1963, Němcová 1971, Přibáňová 1971, Telcová-Jurenková 1960, Hudec 1983 and Vratislavský 1971.

### 3 Composers

1 There is an excellent survey by Tomislav Volek in *DČD*, i, 331–45, with detailed bibliography of sources, p. 379. Most information on the Czech eighteenth-century operas has been drawn from here, from Trojan 1981, and from the introductory essays in Petrů 1985, where the librettos of four of the best-known 'Moravian Singspiels' are printed.

2 The *Grove* 6 article on the Tuček family clarifies the relationship between Jan and Vincenc, hitherto amalgamated into a single individual.

3 Autograph full score in Brno, Moravian Museum, Music History Division, A 8 545.

4 Both Foerster and Janáček recall Skuherský in their memoirs, but the fullest and most vivid account of Skuherský's teaching methods at the Prague Organ School comes from another student there, Ladislav Dolanský (1918, 41–57).

5 See Harrach 1861 for the initial announcement. Information on the subject has until recently been confined to speculation on the basis of press reports and Hostinský's own guesses. But the discovery of the judges' reports (reported in *HV*, vii (1970), 209–11) has allowed much more accurate comments. See Vejdělek 1982 for identifications of contestants' mottoes and Daněk 1983 for transcripts of judges' comments. The entries are listed on p. 126; Harrach's advice to composers is quoted on p. 209.

6 Autograph vocal score in Brno, Moravian Museum, Music History Division, A 21 502a–c.

7 Milan Pospíšil: 'Czechoslovakia: a contemporary of Smetana', *Opera*, xxxiii (1982), 184–5; see also Tomislav Volek: 'Plzeň s novým festivalem a sympoziem' [Plzeň with a new festival and symposium], *HRo*, xxxiv (1981), 264–5.

8 by Rozkošný, however, many years later; at the time of the première of *St John's Rapids* Rozkošný wrote to Šebor about Smetana's opinion of his work in quite a different vein (information from Milan Pospíšil).

9 Copyist's vocal score in Prague, National Theatre, Opera Archive, no. 28.

10 Copyist's vocal score in Prague, National Theatre, Opera Archive, no. 9–27.

11 Pospíšil (1987) shows that towards the end of his life Dvořák acknowledged the qualities of the first version and regarded both versions as equally valid.

## 4 Librettists

1 Šilhan 1909, 213; Očadlík 1939, 67-8; Josef Bartoš in Wenzig 1944, 28-30 and in Wenzig 1951, 42; Jiránek 1984, 243-5, 338-9.

2 The Smetana-Krásnohorská correspondence is printed in Očadlík 1940.

3 See for instance Krásnohorská's MS libretto for *The Kiss*, Smetana Museum (now National Museum in Prague, Museum of Czech Music, Music Archive), shelf-mark Tr xxiii/17.

4 This did not prevent some librettists of historical operas of the period making use of older materials. In the words of Lébl and Ludvová, librettos of this type 'stem totally from the older layer of domestic plays and often have the character of a montage of favourite elements which had proved themselves in performances at the Provisional Theatre and, especially, at the arenas' (Lébl 1981, 120-1).

## 5 Subjects

1 See the libretto of *Kamilla* (Prague, 1897) and MS full score (Prague National Theatre, Opera Archive, no. 217), pp. 17-28 and especially 303-25; Straková 1956 and Vogel 1958, 168.

2 Czech Pan-Slavism, and Dvořák's in particular, is discussed in detail by Burghauser in Červinková-Riegrová 1961, 5-18.

3 See contemporary label on cover of bound full score (dated 29 September 1870), vol. 1 (Prague National Theatre, Opera Archive, unnumbered).

4 'Československo, XII: statistika obyvatelstva', *Masarykův slovník naučný* (Prague, 1925-33), i, 1063.

5 See for instance Peter Gradenwitz: 'Biblische Schauplätze und "Colorito sacro"', and Klaus Wolfgang Niemöller: 'Die kirchliche Szene' in *Die 'Couleur locale' in der Oper des 19. Jahrhunderts*, ed. Heinz Becker (Munich, 1976), 323-39, 341-69.

6 Although Krásnohorská was brought up in a pious Catholic family, there are no direct references to her own religious practices in her writings apart from a few child-hood memories. This was not unusual for a member of her intellectual generation, in which Catholicism was taken for granted, albeit with an admixture of scepticism. As an adult she may not have been an active church-goer but there is no evidence that she left the church or that she lost her religious faith. Her Christmas poem 'The Czech Statue of the Baby Jesus' ('České Jezulátko', 1889) may be patriotic and moralistic but it is wholly without irony. I am grateful to Dr Anna Šerých for this summary.

7 The only exception is a twelve-bar offstage chorus of monks near the end of *Dalibor*.

8 From his letter to Josef Srb-Debrnov of 11 November 1882 (Balthasar 1924, 215) it is clear that Smetana's models were Gounod's Méphistophélès and Meyerbeer's Bertram.

9 It would be interesting to know what other Czech composers and librettists made of the Dalibor legend, but neither of the Dalibor operas reported in Czech literature (by Kott, in German, and by Pozděna; see Guth 1879) are extant.

10 By the time of Wenzig's libretto the name of Dalibor was even more strongly linked to music as the name of one of the first Czech periodicals devoted to music. The first *Dalibor* was founded in 1858; the third periodical with this title survived until 1927; its first volume included an article on the Dalibor legend (Guth 1879) which describes Dalibor 'a Czech Orpheus', thus linking him with the figure of Švanda the Bagpiper (see p. 163).

## 6 Characters

1 The judges in the Harrach competition were confused on this issue (Daněk 1983, 172), but so, 120 years later, is the most recent commentator, Jaroslav Jiránek, whose exhaustive statistical analysis proves that in number of lines Tausendmark beats Jíra narrowly, but in terms of bars sung Ludiše is slightly ahead of the Prague mob (Tausendmark and Jíra take third and fourth place respectively), while in terms of individual appearances the chief characters are, in order, Ludiše, Tausendmark, Jíra and the Prague mob (Jiránek 1984, 96–102). Smetana himself described Jíra as the 'main role' (letter to Fröjde Benecke, 7 January 1866, printed in Kraus 1906, 358).

2 Smetana's 1882 revisions of *The Two Widows* for the Hamburg production, printed in the appendix of the critical edition of the full score (*Studijní vydání děl Bedřicha Smetany*, vii, Prague, 1950), take Anežka's part up to b″ and c‴ but generally provide lower alternatives.

3 See Arthur Koestler: 'Laughter and Emotion', *The Act of Creation* (London, 1964), 51ff. It is interesting that in Smetana's 1877 revision of the work, where a subsidiary couple was added, Mumlal was employed comically to interrupt their love-making. This may indicate that the authors realized that Mumlal's character lacked something, but the fact that the added 'threat' was brief and incidental hardly remedied this.

4 Libuše's part in the opera is proportionally so much greater than those of the other main characters that Jaroslav Jiránek, after his detailed statistical analysis, describes her as 'a sort of super-main character' (Jiránek 1984, 390).

5 Shortly before the première Vávra's young wife died and in his absence on compassionate leave his place was taken by an inadequate substitute. Vávra took over the part in the many subsequent performances of the work (Bartoš 1938, 382).

6 One of the most memorable phrases (figure 'x' in Ex. 7a; see pp. 192–3) in the 'Hymn to the Moon', together with its bass rising a third to the sixth degree of the scale (figure 'y'), is a direct quotation from Xenie's prayer (Ex. 7b). And when Dimitrij recalls Xenie in his Act 3 aria, the orchestra gives out a phrase (figure 'z' in Ex. 7c) which, in a slight rhythmic modification, haunts the coda of Rusalka's hymn (Ex. 7d).

7 Generally only Czech composers with experience of opera abroad, such as Foerster, used detailed vocal designations of this sort. For instance in his *Jessica* Portia is a 'dramatic soprano', Jessica a 'young-dramatic soprano', Lorenzo a 'lyric tenor', Gobbo a 'buffo tenor'.

8 See autograph full score, Prague, National Theatre, Opera Archive no. 238, vol. iii, pp. 132ff.

9 See autograph vocal score, Brno, Moravian Museum, Music History Division, shelf-mark A 21 487b–c.

10 Andrew Porter: '*Les vêpres siciliennes*: new letters from Verdi to Scribe', *19th-Century Music*, ii (1978–9), 99.

11 The male vocal spectrum of Bendl's early operas is particularly interesting in view of Krásnohorská's account (1897, 974) of how she had to persuade him to include basses and baritones at all – at first he wanted only tenors. However, he seems to have got his way in his last opera with a Krásnohorská libretto, *The Child of Tábor*, where the rival lovers, like those in *Jenůfa*, are both tenors.

## 7 Folk elements and the 'Czech style'

1 For the purposes of this chapter I have not thought it necessary to distinguish in English translations between three Czech adjectives, all commonly translated as

'folk', especially in connection with *písně* (songs): *národní* (literally 'national'), *prostonárodní* (literally 'simple-national') and *lidový* (literally 'folk'). Folksong collections up to 1860, including Erben's of 1842–5, were automatically described as *národní*, thus equating the (country) people (*lid*) with the nation (*národ*). But, especially after the 1848 Revolution, it became necessary to distinguish the country-folk from the urban proletariat, and the folksong of the countryside from the commercial ballads and market songs of the town dwellers. Erben excluded town songs from his definitive collection of the 1860s and stressed the fact by his use of the new term *prostonárodní* (Bejlovcová 1979, 22ff). A decade later Smetana applied the term *prostonárodní* to his opera *The Kiss* and until the end of the century *národní* and *prostonárodní* were both used to describe folksong collections. It is only in this century that *lidový* replaced them.

2 Erben, in his 1842 collection (*Písně národní v Čechách*, i, 184–5) even records a practice of vocal imitations of bagpipes with singers humming to provide drones and another singing the tune 'with a nasal tone'.

3 See Rosselli 1984, 165–7 for an instructive example of how two performances of *Norma* in Cremona in 1838 and 1848 respectively inspired demonstrations both in favour and against the Austrian Emperor. The line 'Sgombre saran le Gallie' (Gaul will be freed from the foreigner) 'had had its inflammatory significance read into it during the ten-year interval'.

4 Krásnohorská, in a characteristically trenchant aside, pronounced in 1872 (Krásnohorská 1956, 352) that 'the people understand no music other than dance music, church music and songs'.

5 Polka rhythms were heard throughout *The Bagpiper of Strakonice*: in the overture, several songs, and in the dance music which Švanda plays (Pensdorfová 1959, 67–8, 81–4).

6 The coincidence of the tune with six bars of a pastorella (noted by Holzknecht 1979, 309) seems to be fortuitous.

7 A *beseda* was originally somewhere to sit (*seděti*) outside the house, though the talking that presumably took place there must have been important since the word's primary meaning has become 'a friendly conversation, meeting, neighbourly gathering for a chat'. From this the word acquired in the nineteenth century a host of allied subsidiary meanings: a social organization (e.g. the Umělecká beseda – Artists' Society), a social gathering for cultural and entertainment purposes etc. Its meaning as a type of social dance is explained on pp. 227–8.

8 *Pargamyška* (plural *pargamyšky*) is a jocular coinage from *pergamen* (parchment) signifying old papers, old writings, old pieces of music.

9 A play on words: instead of the adjective *švédský* (Swedish), Neruda used an invented word *švecský*, derived from *švec* (a cobbler).

10 Slovácko, the Moravian border region adjoining Slovakia (Slovensko).

11 Things were evidently better in Plzeň. In her memoirs (quoted in Suchá 1974, 108–9), Krásnohorská reports how at the performance on 3 November 1869 attended by Smetana the amateur cast was attired in folk costumes borrowed from the surrounding villages; even the manner of walking was based on local observation.

## 8 Czech, metre and word-setting

1 As Romain Rolland put it in his correspondence with Strauss over the French version of Strauss's *Salome*, 'Our language has no connection with yours. You have very marked stresses, very strong and continual contrasts between the – and the ⌣ , between the strong and weak syllable. With you, it's either all one thing, or all the other. And it's precisely in the interval which separates the – from the ⌣, the *f* from

the *p*, that our poetry lies. It has an infinite number of shades in the half-tone – accents much less stressed than yours are, but more more varied, more supple, more flexible' (letter of 16 July 1905 quoted in *Richard Strauss and Romain Rolland: Correspondence*, ed. Rollo Myers (London, 1968), p. 37).

2 Scansion marks used in this chapter always denote stress, not length. – = stressed syllable; ⌣ = unstressed syllable; ◡̄ = syllable with a subsidiary stress (e.g. the third syllable in a multi-syllable word) serving as a stressed syllable in a trochee. Ambiguous monosyllables are unmarked. ⌢ = elision. ⌣⌣ʹ = preposition + noun group. Vertical lines mark off poetic feet.

3 The earliest complete system of *časomíra* prosody in Czech was formulated by Vavřinec Benedict Nudožerský in 1606. Král, in summarizing his rules (1923, 33–4), describes them as 'very precise and simple'.

4 Smetana himself provides the most moving evidence of this in his (German) diary entry for December 1861: 'With the recent growth of our national consciousness I am attempting to perfect myself in my home language so that I can express myself in Czech both in speech and in writing, since from childhood I was forced to learn everything in German according to the schooling regulations of the day. It would be thus high time to make these entries in Czech: but since I have begun to write them in German I will continue doing so until I am able to write everything correctly in Czech, in which venture I am strenuously practising' (quoted in Dolanský 1918, 244). Krásnohorská's correspondence with Smetana includes a discussion of her *Hudební listy* article in which she criticized some of the word-setting in *The Bartered Bride*: she mentioned that in comic scenes she sometimes detected a somewhat 'foreign accent', which brought to mind Smetana's long absence from his homeland (Očadlík 1940, 35).

5 See Wenzig 1944, 23–8. Most commentators from Šilhan onwards have emphasized how frequently Špindler used demonstratives such as 'ten', 'ta', 'to' ('this', in its masculine, feminine and neuter forms) at the beginnings of lines. Czech lacks both definite and indefinite articles; the demonstrative adjective was Špindler's solution for a metrical equivalent to 'der', 'ein' etc.

6 Bartoš, in his introduction to the critical edition of the full score *Studijní vydání děl Bedřicha Smetany*, vi, Prague, 1949, pp. xi–xii), mentions that a copy of the vocal score now in the Smetana Museum contains, in addition to corrections of printing errors, sixteen changes by Smetana mostly affecting the declamation. Only the first of these, quoted above, was incorporated in later editions (from the third edition of 1903 onwards, i.e. after Smetana's letter to Srb was printed in Teige's collection). Smetana did not write his corrections into the full score, despite the fact that the work was given a new production for the reopening of the National Theatre in 1883, when he could have insisted on changes. Bartoš speculates that Smetana may have changed his mind, or that his resolve was weakened by his illness.

7 First proofs of the first edition of *Jenůfa* (title page date-stamped 10.1.[1908]) with Janáček's copious corrections and revisions, Brno, Moravian Museum, Music History Division, shelf mark A 7425.

8 Janáček's dates for the beginning of his speech-melody studies are 1879, 1881, 1888, 1897 and 1901. But the earliest surviving notations are from 1885 and these simply record the highest and lowest notes used by actors in a performance of *Othello*. The primitiveness of this approach suggests that Janáček then could have been only at the beginning of his speech-melody studies. His enthusiasm for folk music intervened and the first evidence of any systematic notation of speech melodies dates from 1897, i.e. a few years into the long gestation of *Jenůfa* (Štědroň 1968, 117–18).

9 See the 1888 copy of the vocal score by Josef Stross with Janáček's 1918 corrections, Brno, Moravian Museum, Music History Division, shelf mark A 23 522.

# Bibliography

## Abbreviations

ČMM    *Časopis Moravského musea/muzea v Brně: vědy společenské* (Brno, 1916–)

ČSHS    *Československý hudební slovník: osob a institucí* [The Czechoslovak music dictionary: people and institutions], ed. Gracian Černušák, Bohumír Štědroň and Zdenko Nováček (Prague, 1963–5)

ČSV    *Československá vlastivěda*, x/3: *Hudba* [Music] (Prague, 1971)

DČD    *Dějiny českého divadla* [The history of Czech theatre], ed. František Černý (Prague, 1968–)

DČHK    *Dějiny české hudební kultury 1890/1945* [The history of Czech musical culture 1890–1945] (Prague, 1972–81)

DČK    *Divadlo v české kultuře 19. století: sborník sympozia v Plzni 10.–12. března 1983* [The theatre in nineteenth-century Czech culture: proceedings of the symposium in Plzeň 10–12 March 1983] (Prague, 1985)

DP    *Documenta pragensia: sborník materiálií z Archivu hlavního města Prahy* [Anthology of materials from the archive of the capital city Prague], iii (Prague, 1983)

Grove 6    *The New Grove Dictionary of Music and Musicians*, ed. Stanley Sadie (London and Washington, DC, 1980)

HČD    Jaromír Černý and others: *Hudba v českých dějinách* [Music in Czech history] (Prague, 1983)

HR    *Hudební revue* (Prague, 1908–20)

HRo    *Hudební rozhledy* (Prague, 1948–)

HV    *Hudební věda* (Prague, 1962–)

MČK    *Město v české kultuře 19. století: sborník sympozia v Plzni 4.–6. března 1982* [The town in nineteenth-century Czech culture: proceedings of the symposium in Plzeň 4–6 March 1982] (Prague, 1983)

OL    *Operní libreta Bedřicha Smetany* (Prague, 1918–)

OM    *Opus musicum* (Brno, 1969–)

PHSN    *Pazdírkův hudební slovník naučný*, i: *Část věcná* [Pazdírek's musical encyclopaedia, i: subject part], ed. Gracian Černušák (Brno, 1929)

SC    *The Smetana Centennial: International Conference San Diego March 29–31 1984*, ed. Jaroslav Mráček (in preparation)

SV    *Studijní vydání děl Bedřicha Smetany* (Prague, 1940–)

★    indicates the edition to which page-number references are made

Abraham, Gerald, 1985. 'The operas of Zdeněk Fibich', *19th-Century Music*, IX (1985–6), 136–44

Anderson, Benedict, 1983. *Imagined communities: reflections on the origin and spread of nationalism* (London, 1983)

anon. 1888. 'Jan Nep. Maýr zemřel dne 25. října 1888' [obituary], *Dalibor*, X (1888), 319

Balthasar, Vladimír, 1924. *Bedřich Smetana* (Prague, 1924)

# Bibliography

Bartoš, František (ed.), 1939. *Smetana ve vzpomínkách a dopisech* [Smetana in reminiscences and letters] (Prague, 1939, \*enlarged 9/1954; English trans., 1955)

1950. Introduction to full score of Bedřich Smetana: *Dvě vdovy* [The Two Widows] (Prague, 1950 = SV, VII), VII–XVII

1955. 'Ke genesi Smetanovy Prodané nevěsty' [The genesis of Smetana's *The Bartered Bride*], *Musikologie*, IV (1955), 7–31

Bartoš, Josef, 1938. *Prozatímní divadlo a jeho opera* [The Provisional Theatre and its opera] (Prague, 1938)

Beckerman, Michael, 1986. 'In search of Czechness in music', *19th-Century Music*, x (1986–7), 61–73

Bejlovcová, Eva, 1979. *Hudebně dramatická tvorba skladatelů českého původu ve fondech pražských hudebních archivů a knihoven 1769–1871* [The musico-dramatic works 1769–1871 of composers of Czech origin in the collections of Prague archives and libraries] (diploma dissertation, Charles University of Prague, 1979)

Bezdíčková-Ingerlová, Anna, 1975. *František Bedřich Kott a jeho zpěvohra Žižkův dub* [Kott and his opera *Žižka's Oak*] (diploma dissertation, University of Brno, 1975)

Boleška, Josef, 1903. 'O Zdeňku Fibichovi: několik vzpomínek na poslední desetiletí jeho života' [Some reminiscences of the last decade of Fibich's life], *Dalibor*, XXV (1903), 281–2, 289–90, 302–3, 314–15

Bonuš, František, 1971. *Český salonní tanec beseda: jeho historie a tvůrci* [The Czech salon dance, the *beseda*: its history and creators] (Prague, 1971)

Bráfová, Libuše, 1913. *Rieger, Smetana, Dvořák* (Prague, 1913)

Branberger 1934. Jan Branberger with Zdenka Münzerová: *Svět v opeře* [The world in opera] (Prague, 1934, \*4/1948)

Branscombe, Peter, 1980. 'Bondini, Pasquale', *Grove 6*

Brod, Max, 1962. *Die verkaufte Braut: der abenteuerliche Lebensroman des Textdichters Karel Sabina* (Munich, 1962)

Budiš 1963. Ratibor Budiš and Věra Kafková: *Bedřich Smetana: vyběrová bibliografie* [selected bibliography] (Prague, 1963)

1964. Ratibor Budiš: *Vilém Blodek* (Prague, 1964)

Burghauser, Jarmil (ed.), 1983. *Národnímu divadlu: vklad zakladatelské generace* [To the National Theatre: the investment by the founding generation] (Prague, 1983)

Burke, Peter, 1978. *Popular Culture in Early Modern Europe* (London, 1978)

Čechová 1984. Olga Čechová and Jana Fojtíková: *Bedřich Smetana (inventář fondu)* [Inventory of the Smetana collection] (Prague, 1984)

Čelanský, Ludvík, 1897. 'Několik úvah o moderní opeře' [Some reflections on modern opera], afterword to the libretto of *Kamilla* (Prague, 1897), 47–55

Černý, Miroslav K., 1985. 'Ohlas díla Richarda Wagnera v české hudební kritice let 1847–1883' [The response to the works of Wagner in Czech music criticism 1847–83], *HV*, XXII (1985), 216–35

Červinka, František, 1969. *Zdeněk Nejedlý* (Prague, 1969)

Červinková-Riegrová, Marie, 1961. *Dimitrij*, ed. Jarmil Burghauser (Prague, 1961 = Operní libreta Antonína Dvořáka, II)

Chew, Geoffrey, 1980. 'Pastorella', *Grove 6*

Chvála, Emanuel, 1886. *Ein Vierteljahrhundert böhm. Musik* (Prague, 1886; Czech version, *Dalibor*, IX (1887), \*published separately (Prague, 1888)

Chvalovský, Edmund, 1917. 'Premiera Smetanových "Dvou vdov"' [The première of Smetana's *The Two Widows*], Josef Schwarz and others: *Vzpomínky na Bedřicha Smetanu* (Prague, 1917), 47–61

Clapham, John, 1962. 'The National Origins of Dvořák's Art', *Proceedings of the Royal Musical Association*, LXXXIX (1962–3), 75–88

# Bibliography

1966. *Antonín Dvořák: Musician and Craftsman* (London, 1966)
1971. 'The Smetana-Pivoda Controversy', *Music and Letters*, III (1971), 353–64
1972. *Smetana* (London, 1972)
1979. *Dvořák* (Newton Abbot and London, 1979)

Dahlhaus, Carl, 1974. *Zwischen Romantik und Moderne* (Munich, 1974; *English trans. Berkeley and London, 1980 as *Between Romanticism and Modernism: four studies in the music of the later nineteenth century*)
Daněk 1983. Petr Daněk and Jana Vyšohlídová: 'Dokumenty k operní soutěži o cenu hraběte Harracha' [Documents concerning Count Harrach's operatic prize competition], *Miscellanea musicologica*, XXX (1983), 147–75
Dolanský, Julius, 1970. *Karel Jaromír Erben* (Prague, 1970)
Dolanský, Ladislav, 1918. *Hudební paměti* [Musical reminiscences], ed. Zdeněk Nejedlý (Prague, 1918, *2/1949)
Dvořák, Karel (ed.), 1984. *Pohádky a pověsti našeho lidu* [Our folktales and legends] (Prague, 1984)

Emingerová, Katynka, 1924. *Obrázky ze staré hudební Prahy* [Pictures from the musical Prague of old] (Prague, 1924)
1925. 'Dramatická díla' [The dramatic works], *Hudební dílo Václava Jana Tomáška* (Prague, [1925]), 36–40

Firkušný, Leoš, 1935. *Leoš Janáček kritikem brněnské opery* [Leoš Janáček as critic of the Brno Opera] (Brno, 1935)
1938. *Z lidové hudby moravské k Její pastorkyni* [From Moravian folk music to *Jenůfa*] (Prague, 1938)
Fischer, Otakar, 1915. 'K Smetanovým librettům: 1. K Daliboru'; 2. K Libuši', *HR*, VIII (1915), 153–62; 205–15
Fitzpatrick, Horace, 1970. *The Horn and Horn-Playing and the Austro-Bohemian Tradition from 1680 to 1830* (London, 1970)
Foerster, Josef Bohuslav, 1897. 'Zpěvohra německá a francouzská za posledních let' [German and French opera in recent years], *Dalibor*, XIX (1897), *passim*; XX (1898), *passim*
1929. *Poutník* [The Pilgrim] (1929) and *Poutníkovy cesty* [The Pilgrim's travels] (1932), *repr. as *Poutník* (Prague, 1942)
Fraser, G.S., 1970. *Metre, Rhyme and Free Verse* (London and New York, 1970)

Germer, Mark, 1984. 'The Pastorella in Historical Context', *SC*
Göpfert, Bernd, 1977. *Stimmtypen und Rollencharaktere in der deutschen Oper von 1815–1848* (Wiesbaden, 1977)
Gregor, Vladimír, 1983. *Obrozenská hudba na Moravě a ve Slezsku* [Music of the National Revival period in Moravia and Silesia] (Prague, 1983)
Griffiths, Paul, 1984. *Bartók* (London and Melbourne, 1984)
Guldener 1957. Bernard Guldener and Václav Juda Novotný: *Král a uhlíř* [King and Charcoal Burner], ed. Jarmil Burghauser (Prague, 1957 = Operní libreta Antonín Dvořák, I)
Guth, Jiří, 1879. 'Pan Dalibor z Kozojed' [Mr Dalibor of Kozojedy], *Dalibor*, I (1879), 180–1

Harrach, Jan hrabě, 1861. 'Vypsání cen za nejlepší dvě české opery a náležité k nim texty' [Competition for the two best Czech operas and their respective texts], *Dalibor*, IV (1861), 45

# Bibliography

Helfert, Vladimír, 1924. *Hudba na Jaroměřickém zámku: František Míča 1696-1745* [Music at the Jaroměřice castle] (Prague, 1924)

1936. 'Barokní zpracování pověstí o Libuši a Přemyslovi' [Baroque adaptations of the Libuše and Přemysl legends], *Mélanges P.M. Haškovec* (Brno, 1936), 15-80

Heller, Aleš, 1917. 'Vzpomínky Ferdinanda Hellera' [The reminiscences of Ferdinand Heller], Josef Schwarz and others: *Vzpomínky na Bedřicha Smetanu* (Prague, 1917), 9-35

Heller 1918. Servác Heller and others: *Založení Národního divadla 1868* [The founding of the National Theatre 1868] (Prague, 1918)

Hepner, Václav, 1955. *Scenická výprava na jevišti Národního divadla v letech 1883-1900* [Stage design at the National Theatre 1883-1900] (Prague, 1955)

Herrmannová 1959. Eva Herrmannová and Vladimír Lébl: *Soupis české hudebně dramatické tvorby* [A list of Czech musico-dramatic works] (Prague, 1959)

Hof, Karel Vít, 1868. *Dějiny velkého národního divadla v Praze od prvních počátkův až do kladení základního kamena* [The history of the large National Theatre in Prague from its earliest beginnings to the laying of the foundation stone] (Prague, 1868)

Holečková-Dolanská, Jelena, 1980. 'O deklamaci zpívaného slova' [The declamation of the sung word], *Živá hudba*, VII (1980), 315-54

Holý, Dušan, 1980. 'Odkaz Otakara Hostinského teorii lidové písně' [Hostinský's legacy to the theory of folksong], *Pocta Otakaru Hostinskému: Brno 1980*, ed. Rudolf Pečman (Brno, 1982), 187-95

Holzknecht, Václav, 1979. *Bedřich Smetana: život a dílo* [life and works] (Prague, 1979)

Homolová, Kvéta, and others (eds.), 1982. *Čeští spisovatelé 19. a počátku 20. století* [Czech writers of the nineteenth and early twentieth centuries] (Prague, 3/1982)

Honour, Hugh, 1979. *Romanticism* (Harmondsworth, 1979, *1981)

Horák, Jiří, 1937. Afterword to Karel Jaromír Erben: *Prostonárodní české písně a říkadla* [Czech folksongs and rhymes], ed. J. Horák (Prague, 1937), 443-54

Hornová, V. and J., 1903. *Česká zpěvohra* [Czech opera] (Prague, [1903])

Hostinský, Otakar, 1882. 'O české deklamaci hudební' [Czech musical declamation], *Dalibor*, IV (1882); published separately (Prague, 1886); reprinted in *Hostinský 1961, 257-97

1884. Introduction to the libretto of *Nevěsta messinská* [*The Bride of Messina*] (Prague, 1884), VII-XXIII

1885. 'František Škroup: k padesátilému jubileu písně "Kde domov můj?"' [František Škroup: on the fiftieth anniversary of the song 'Where is my homeland?'], *Osvěta*, XV (1885), 71-9, 149-64

1901. *Bedřich Smetana a jeho boj o moderní českou hudbu* [Smetana and his struggle for modern Czech music] (Prague, 1901, *rev. 2/1941, ed. Bohuslav Hostinský)

1906. *Česká světská píseň lidová* [Czech secular folksong] (Prague, 1906); *reprinted in Hostinský 1961, 299-410

1909. *Vzpomínky na Fibicha* [Reminiscences of Fibich] (Prague, 1909)

1956. *O umění* [About art], ed. J. Cisařovský (Prague, 1956)

1961. *Hostinský o hudbě* [Hostinský on music], ed. M. Nedbal (Prague, 1961)

1974. *Studie a kritiky* [Studies and reviews], ed. D. Holub, H. Hrzalová and L. Lantová (Prague, 1974)

1981. *Otakar Hostinský o divadle* [Otakar Hostinský on theatre], ed. M. Jůzl (Prague, 1981)

1986. *Z hudebních bojů let sedmdesátých a osmdesátých: výbor z operních a koncertních kritik* [From the musical battles of the 1870s and 1880s: selection of opera and concert reviews], ed. Eva Vítová (Prague, 1986)

Hostomská, Anna, 1955. *Opera: průvodce operní tvorbou* [Opera: a guide to operatic works] (Prague, 1955, *enlarged 7/1965)

Bibliography

Houtchens, Alan, 1984. 'Libuše and Vanda, legendary and operatic sisters', *SC*

Hrabák, Josef, 1955. *Úvod do teorie verše* [Introduction to the theory of verse] (Prague, 1955, *rev. 5/1978)

1973. *Poetika* (Prague, 1973, *2/1977)

Hrdina, Karel (ed. and trans.), 1947. *Kosmova Kronika česká* [Kosmas's *Czech Chronicle*] (Prague, 1947, *rev. 6/1975)

Hudec, Vladimír, 1966. *Fibichovo skladatelské mládí* [Fibich's compositional apprenticeship] (Prague, 1966)

1971. *Zdeněk Fibich* (Prague, 1971)

1983. 'K vývojové a axiologické problematice českého hudebního divadla na Moravě v 2. polovině 19. století [Evolutionary and axiological problems in Czech musical theatre in Moravia in the second half of the nineteenth century], *DČK*, 58–62

Hůlka, Karel, 1908. 'Z bojů o česká divadelní představení' [The battle for Czech performances in the theatre], *HR*, I (1908), 8–12, 70–5, 135–9, 185–8, 242–58, 289–300

Hutter 1951. Josef Hutter and Zdeněk Chalabala, eds.: *České umění dramatické: zpěvohra* [Czech dramatic art: opera] (Prague, 1951)

Jakobson, Roman, 1949. 'Slavic Mythology', *Funk & Wagnall's Standard Dictionary of Folklore, Mythology and Legend* (New York, 1949–50)

Janáček, Leoš, 1955. *O lidové písní a lidové hudbě* [On folksong and folk music], ed. Jiří Vysloužil (Prague, 1955)

1958. *Fejetony z Lidových novin* [Feuilletons from the *Lidové noviny*], ed. Jan Racek (Prague, 1958)

Jareš, Stanislav, 1979. 'Prozatímní divadlo v Praze' [The Provisional Theatre in Prague], *HV*, XVI (1979), 252–62

1984. 'Pražské městské divadlo v Kotcích 1738–1783: budova a provozní podmínky' [The Prague town theatre in the 'Kotce' 1738–83: the building and performance conditions], *HV*, XXI (1984), 155–64

Javorin, Alfred, 1949. *Divadla a divadelní sály v českých krajích*, I: *divadla* [Theatres and theatrical halls in Czech provinces, I: theatres] (Prague, 1949)

1958. *Pražské arény: lidová divadla pražská v minulém století* [Prague arenas: Prague folk theatres in the previous century] (Prague, 1958)

Jehne, Leo, 1974. 'K problematice smetanovských hlasových oborů a pěveckých typů' [The problem of Smetana's voice categories and types of singers], *HV*, XI (1974), 125–34

Jiránek, Jaroslav, 1963. *Zdeněk Fibich* (Prague, 1963)

1976. *Vztah hudby a slova v tvorbě Bedřicha Smetany* [The relation of music and words in Smetana's works] (Prague, 1976)

1981. *Muzikologické etudy* [Musicological studies] (Prague, 1981)

1984. *Smetanova operní tvorba*, I: *od Braniborů v Čechách k Libuši* [Smetana's operatic works, I: From *The Brandenburgers in Bohemia* to *Libuše*] (Prague, 1984 = Dílo a život Bedřicha Smetany, 3)

Jirát, Vojtěch, 1938. 'Obrozenské překlady Mozartova Dona Juana' [Translations of Mozart's *Don Giovanni* from the period of the Czech National Revival], *Slovo a slovesnost*, IV (1938), 73–90, 202–12; *reprinted in V. Jirát: *Portréty a studie* (Prague, 1978), 520–44

Jůzl, Miloš, 1980. *Otakar Hostinský* (Prague, 1980)

Kamper, Jaroslav, 1909. 'Švýcarská rodina' [*Die Schweizerfamilie*], *HR*, II (1909), 359–64

Karbusický, Vladimír, 1958. 'Datování lidových písní vojenských: příspěvek k dějinám naší lidové písně' [The dating of military folksongs: a contribution to the history of Czech folksong], *Český lid*, XLV (1958), 193–9

# Bibliography

1966. *Nejstarší pověsti české* [The oldest Czech legends] (Prague, 1966, *enlarged 2/1967)

1968. *Mezi lidovou písní a šlágrem* [Between folksong and hit song] (Prague, 1968)

Kimball, Stanley Buchholz, 1966. *Czech Nationalism: a Study of the National Theatre Movement, 1845-83* (Urbana, Illinois, 1966)

Kneidl, Pravoslav, 1964. 'K pražskému provedení první české zpěvohry před 200 lety' [The Prague performance of the first Czech opera 200 years ago], *Sborník Národního muzea v Praze*, C9 (1964), 173-86

Kočí, Josef, 1978. *České národní obrození* [The Czech National Revival] (Prague, 1978)

Kolár, Jaroslav (ed.), 1981. *Václav Hájek z Libočan: Kronika česká: výbor historického čtení* [Czech chronicle: a selection from the historic text] (Prague, 1981)

Konečná, Hana (ed.), 1983. *Soupis repertoáru Národního divadla v Praze 1881-1983* [List of repertory of the National Theatre 1881-1983] (Prague, 1983)

1984. Haná Konečná and others: *Čtení o Národním divadle: útržky dějin a osudů* [Readings on the National Theatre: fragments of history and fates] (Prague, 1984)

Kotek, Josef, 1986. 'Český hudební folklór 19. století' [Czech musical folklore of the nineteenth century], *HV*, XXIII (1986), 195-216

Král, Josef, 1923. *O prosodii české*, I: *Historický vývoj české prosodie* [The historical evolution of Czech prosody], ed. J. Jakubec (Prague, 1923)

Krásnohorská, Eliška, 1870. 'Český básník a hudební drama' [The Czech poet and music drama], *Hudební listy*, I (1870), 298-301; 306-10; reprinted in Krásnohorská 1956, II 339-50

1871. 'O české deklamaci hudební' [On Czech musical declamation], *Hudební listy*, II (1871), 1-4, 9-13, 17-19

1897. 'Z mladých let Karla Bendla: osobní vzpomínky' [From Karel Bendl's early years: a personal memoir], *Osvěta*, XXVII (1897), 959-76

1942. *Hubička* [The Kiss], ed. Mirko Očadlík (Prague, 1942 = OL, III)

1946. *Čertova stěna* [The Devil's Wall], ed. Mirko Očadlík (Prague, 1946 = OL, V)

1956. *Výbor z díla* [Selection of works] (Prague, 1956)

Kraus, Arnošt, 1902. *Stará historie česká v německé literatuře* [Early Czech history in German literature] (Prague, 1902)

1906. 'Bedřich Smetana v Göteborgu' [Smetana in Göteburg], *Věstník České akademie císaře Františka Josefa pro vědy, slovesnost a umění*, XV (1906), 1-8, 81-7, 283-9, 356-64, 401-13

Krupka, Jaroslav, 1923. 'František Antonín hrabě Sporck a jeho opera v Praze a Kuksu' [Count Sporck and his opera in Prague and in Kuks], *Dalibor*, XL (1923-4), 113-15, 125-8

Kuna, Milan, 1981. 'Ke vzniku Dvořákova Dimitrije' [The genesis of Dvořák's *Dimitrij*], *HV*, XVIII (1981), 326-41

1982. 'Ke zrodu Dvořákova Jakobína' [The birth of Dvořák's *The Jacobin*], *HV*, XIX (1982), 245-68

1984. 'Od Matčiny písně k Dvořákovu Jakobínu' [From *The Mother's Song* to Dvořák's *The Jacobin*], *HV*, XXI (1984), 32-68

Kundera, Ludvík, 1933. 'Jaroslav Vrchlický a hudba' [Vrchlický and music], *Tempo-Listy Hudební matice*, XX (1932-3), 286-95

Kvapil, Jaroslav, 1901. Introduction to the libretto of *Rusalka* (Prague, 1901), 5-8

1911. 'O vzniku "Rusalky"' [On the genesis of *Rusalka*], *HR*, IV (1911), 428-30

1932. *O čem vím* [What I know] (Prague, *1932, 2/1946-7)

Laiske, Miroslav, 1974. *Pražská dramaturgie, Česká divadelní představení do otevření Prozatímního divadla* [Prague dramaturgy: Czech theatrical performances up to the opening of the Provisional Theatre] (Prague, 1974)

310

# Bibliography

Large, Brian, 1970. *Smetana* (London, 1970)

Larousse 1959. *Larousse Encyclopedia of Mythology* (London, 1959)

Lébl, Vladimír, 1959. 'Dramatická tvorba Otakar Ostrčila a její jevištní osudy' [Ostrčil's dramatic works and their fate in the theatre], *Divadlo* (1959), 294–302, 333–9

1964. *Vítězslav Novák: život a dílo* [life and works] (Prague, 1964)

1981. Vladimír Lébl and Jitka Ludvová: 'Dobové kořeny a souvislosti Smetanovy Mé vlasti' [The contemporary roots and interconnections of Smetana's *My Fatherland*], *HV*, XVIII (1981), 99–141

Löwenbach, Jan, 1909. 'K rehabilitaci Fibichovy "Nevěsty messinské"' [The rehabilitation of Fibich's *The Bride of Messina*], *HR*, II (1909), 166–71

(ed.), 1914. *Bedřich Smetana a dr. Ludevít Procházka: vzájemná korespondence* [mutual correspondence] (Prague, 1914)

Ludvíkovský, Jaroslav (ed. and trans.), 1978. *Kristiánova legenda* [Christianus' Legend] (Prague, 1978)

Ludvová, Jitka, 1983. 'Německý hudební život v Praze 1880–1935' [German musical life in Prague 1880–1935], *Uměnovědné studie*, IV (Prague, 1983), 53–173

1984. 'Meyerbeer na pražském německém jevišti 1815–1935' [Meyerbeer on the German stage in Prague 1815–1935', *HV*, XXI (1984), 365–74


Máchal, Jan, 1891. *Nákres slovanského bájesloví* [An outline of Slav mythology] (Prague, 1891)

Machek, Václav, 1957. *Etymologický slovník jazyka českého* [An etymological dictionary of the Czech language] (Prague, 1957, *2/1968)

Macura, Vladimír, 1983. *Znamení zrodu: České obrození jako kulturní typ* [The sign of the birth: the Czech Revival as cultural type] (Prague, 1983)

Mařánek, Jiří, 1934. Introduction to the libretto of *Honzovo království* [*Johnny's Kingdom*] (Prague, 1934), 5–7

Markl 1963. Jaroslav Markl and Vladimír Karbusický: 'Bohemian folk music: traditional and contemporary aspects', *Journal of the International Folk Music Council*, XV (1963), 25–9

1967. Jaroslav Markl: 'Guberniální sběr písní z roku 1819' [The government collection of songs, 1819], *Český lid*, LIV (1967), 133–43

1968. 'Kolovratská sbírka lidových písní' [The Kolovrat collection of folksongs], *Český lid*, LV (1968), 25–35

Mazlová, Anna, 1968. 'Zeyerova a Janáčkova Šárka' [Zeyer's and Janáček's *Šárka*] *ČMM*, LIII–IV (1968-9), 71–88


Nejedlý, Zdeněk, 1901. *Zdenko Fibich: zakladatel scénického melodramatu* [Fibich: founder of the scenic melodrama] (Prague, 1901)

1908. *Zpěvohry Smetanovy* [Smetana's operas] (Prague, 1908, *2/1949, 3/1954)

1910. 'Operní pokusy a plány Z. Fibicha' [Fibich's operatic attempts and plans], *Památník Fibichův*, ed. Artuš Rektorys (Prague, 1910), 338–41

1911. *Česká moderní zpěvohra po Smetanovi* [Modern Czech opera after Smetana] (Prague, 1911)

1924. *Bedřich Smetana* (Prague, 1924-33, *2/1950-4)

1935. *Dějiny opery Národního divadla* [The history of opera at the National Theatre] (Prague, 1935, *2/1949)

1935a. *Otakar Ostrčil: vzrůst a uzrání* [Otakar Ostrčil: growth and maturity] (Prague, 1935, *2/1949)

1980. *O Bedřichu Smetanovi*, ed. Jaroslav Jiránek (Prague, 1980)

Němcová 1963. Alena Němcová and Svatava Přibáňová: 'Příspěvek k dějinám opery

# Bibliography

Národního divadla v Brně 1884-1919' [Contribution to the history of opera at the National Theatre in Brno 1884-1919], *ČMM*, XLVIII (1963), 261-82

1971. Alena Němcová: *Profil brněnské opery v kontextu s dějinami českého divadla v Brně v letech 1894-1904* [A profile of the Brno opera in the context of the history of the Czech theatre in Brno 1894-1904] (doctoral dissertation, University of Brno, 1971)

1974. 'Brněnská premiéra Janáčkovy Její pastorkyně' [The Brno première of *Jenůfa*], *ČMM*, LIX (1974), 133-46; German trans. in Jakob Knaus, ed.: *Leoš Janáček - Materialien* (Zürich, 1982), 7-22

Němec, Zdeněk (ed. and trans.), 1942. *Vlastní životopis Václava Jana Tomáška* [Tomášek's autobiography] (Prague, 1942)

1944. *Weberova pražská léta* [Weber's Prague years] (Prague, 1944)

Němeček, Jan, 1954. *Lidové zpěvohry a písně z doby roboty* [Folk operas and songs from the time of serfdom] (Prague, 1954)

1966. 'Komentář k premiérám Wagnerových oper na Národním divadle' [A commentary on the premières of Wagner's operas at the National Theatre], *HV*, III (1966), 676-96

1968. *Opera Národního divadla v období Karla Kovařovice 1900-1920* [The opera of the National Theatre during the Kovařovic era 1900-1920] (Prague, 1968-9)

Novák, Ladislav, 1944. *Stará garda Národního divadla* [The old guard at the National Theatre] (Prague, 1944)

Nováková, Eva, 1956. *Opera v Prozatímním divadle v Brně v letech 1884-1894* [Opera in the Provisional Theatre in Brno 1884-94] (diploma dissertation, University of Brno, 1956)

Očadlík, Mirko, 1939. *Libuše: vznik Smetanovy zpěvohry* [The origin of Smetana's opera *Libuše*] (Prague, 1939)

(ed.), 1940. *Eliška Krásnohorská - Bedřich Smetana: vzájemná korespondence* (Prague, 1940)

1940a. *Poslání české hudby* [The mission of Czech music] (Prague, [1940])

1941. 'Problémy operního libreta' [Problems of the opera libretto], *Rytmus*, VI (1940-1), 11-14, 33-4

(ed.), 1941a. *To, co my, komponisté, jako v mlhách tušíme* [What composers such as we vaguely suspect] (Prague, 1941) [collection of statements by Smetana]

1948. *Smetanovi libretisté* [Smetana's librettists] (Prague, 1948)

1950. *Rok Bedřicha Smetany v datech, obrazech, zápisech a poznámkách* [Smetana's year in dates, pictures, writings and remarks] (Prague, 1950)

1958. 'Soupis českých tištěných operních textů' [List of printed opera texts in Czech], *Miscellanea musicologica*, VII (1958)

1960. 'Malá Smetaniana: b. Smetanův exemplář Erbenových Nápěvů' [Minor Smetaniana: b. Smetana's copy of Erben's Tunes], *Miscellanea musicologica*, XII (1960), 82-6

1960a. 'Soupis dopisů Bedřicha Smetany' [List of Smetana's letters], *Miscellanea musicologica*, XV (1960)

Ort, Jan, 1939. 'Zrození české dikce operní' [The birth of Czech operatic diction], *Kritický měsíčník*, II (1939), 147-57

Ottlová 1978. Marta Ottlová and Milan Pospíšil: 'Uvažování nad situací v českém hudebně vědném bádání o 19. století' [Reflections on the situation in Czech musicological research into the nineteenth century], *HV*, XV (1978), 103-18

1979. 'K otázce češkosti v hudbě 19. století' [The question of Czechness in nineteenth-century music], *OM*, XI (1979), 101-3

1981. 'Český historismus a opera 19. století (Smetanova Libuše)' [Czech historicism and nineteenth-century opera: Smetana's *Libuše*], *Uměnovědné studie*, III (1981), 83-99

1981a. 'K problematice české historickě opery 19 století' [The problems of Czech historical operas of the nineteenth century], *HRo*, XXXIV (1981), 169-72; German trans. in *The Musical Theatre: Brno Colloquia XV 1980*, ed. Rudolf Pečman (Brno, 1984), 267-81

1983. 'Opera a podívaná v. 19. století' [Opera and spectacle in the nineteenth century], * *DČK*, 144-53; German trans. in *Die Musikforschung*, XXXVIII (1985), 1-8

1984. 'Smetanův Meyerbeer' [Smetana's Meyerbeer], *HV*, XXI (1984), 35-63

Pala, František, 1949. 'Foerstrovy opery' [Foerster's operas], *J.B. Foerster: jeho životní pout' a tvorba 1859-1959*, ed. Josef Bartoš and others (Prague, 1949), 170-97

1953. *Fibichova Šárka* (Prague, 1953)

1962. *Opera Národního divadla v období Otakara Ostrčila* [The opera of the National Theatre during the Ostrčil era], I-IV (Prague, 1962-70), V (Prague, 1983, by Vilém Pospíšil)

Pearson, Raymond, 1983. *National minorities in Eastern Europe 1848-1945* (London and Basingstoke, 1983)

Pensdorfová, Eva, 1959. *Klasický základ české hry se zpěvy a tanci: k problematice hudby k Tylovu 'Strakonickému dudákovi'* [The Classical basis for the Czech play with songs and dances: on the problems of the music for Tyl's *The Bagpiper of Strakonice*] (Prague, 1959)

Pešek, Josef B., 1903. *František Škroup: skladatel první původní české zpěvohry a národní naší hymny 'Kde domov můj?'* [František Škroup: composer of the first Czech opera and of our national anthem 'Where is my homeland?'] (Prague, 1903)

1906. *Prvá česká zpěvoherní představení* [The first Czech opera performances] (Vyškov, 1906)

Petrů, Eduard (ed.), 1985. *Copak to ale za mozeka hraje? Hanácké zpěvohry 18. století* [What sort of music is that playing? Eighteenth-century Singspiels from Haná] (Ostrava, 1985) [four librettos with introduction by Petrů and Alena Burešová]

Picka, František, 1908. 'O repertoiru opery Národního divadla' [The operatic repertory of the National Theatre], *HR*, I (1908), 26-9, 93-9

Plavec, Josef, 1929. 'K otázce náboženství díla Fibichova a J.B. Foerstrova' [Religion in the works of Fibich and Foerster], *Památník Foerstrův*, ed. Artuš Rektorys (Prague, 1929), 135-47

1941. *František Škroup* (Prague, 1941)

Pohanka, Jaroslav, 1958. *Dějiny české hudby v příkladech* [The history of Czech music in examples] (Prague, 1958)

Polyakova, Lyudmila, 1974. 'O "ruských" operách Leoše Janáčka' [Janáček's 'Russian' operas], *Cesty rozvoje a vzájemné vztahy ruského a československého umění* (Prague, 1974), 247-69

Pospíšil, Milan, 1979. 'Balada v české opeře 19. století' [The ballad in Czech nineteenth-century opera], *HV*, XVI (1979), 3-25

1984. 'Dramatická úloha Meyerbeerovy harmonie' [The dramatic role of Meyerbeer's harmony], *HV*, XXI (1984), 323-38

1987. 'Dimitrij als Editionsproblem', *Jahrbuch für Opernforschung* (in preparation)

Poštolka, Milan, 1980. 'Ryba, Jakub (Šimon) Jan', *Grove 6*

Pražák, Přemysl, 1948. *Smetanovy zpěvohry* [Smetana's operas] (Prague, 1948)

Přibáňová, Svatava, 1971. *Opera českého Národního divadla v Brně v letech před první světovou válkou* [The opera of the Czech National Theatre in Brno in the years before the First World War] (doctoral dissertation, University of Brno, 1971)

# Bibliography

Procházka 1965. Jan Procházka and Divadelní ústav v Praze, eds.: *Sto let 1865/1965 českého divadla v Plzni* [100 years of Czech theatre in Plzeň, 1865-1965] (Plzeň, 1965)

Procházka, Ludevít, 1958. *Slavná doba české hudby: výbor z kritik a článků* [A celebrated era of Czech music: a selection of reviews and articles], ed. Miloslav Nedbal (Prague, 1958)

Pulkert, Oldřich, 1979. 'Nad operou Švanda dudák Jaromíra Weinbergra' [Weinberger's opera *Švanda the Bagpiper*], *HRo*, xxxii (1979), 514-19

Purš, Jaroslav, 1959. *K případu Karla Sabiny* [The case of Karel Sabina] (Prague, 1959)

1980. Jaroslav Purš and Miroslav Kropilák, eds.: *Přehled dějin Československa* [A survey of the history of Czechoslovakia] (Prague, 1980- )

Racek, Jan, 1933. *Idea vlasti, národa a slávy v díle Bedřicha Smetany* [The idea of fatherland, nation and glory in the work of Smetana] (Brno, 1933; *enlarged 2/Prague, 1947)

1962. 'Leoš Janáčeks und Béla Bartóks Bedeutung in der Weltmusik', *Sborník prací Filosofické fakulty brněnské university*, F6 (1962), 5-16

Reisser, Jan, 1918. *Pěvecká kultura našeho divadla* [Singers and their training at our theatre] (Prague, 1918)

Rektorys, Artuš (ed.), 1949. *Korespondence Leoše Janáčka s F.S. Procházkou* (Prague, 1949)

(ed.), 1951. *Zdeněk Fibich: sborník dokumentů a studií o jeho životě a díle* [Zdeněk Fibich: anthology of documents and studies of his life and works] (Prague, 1951-2)

Richter, Carl Ludwig [=pseudonym of Anežka Schulzová], 1900. *Zdenko Fibich: eine musikalische Silhouette* (Prague, 1900)

Rosselli, John, 1984. *The opera industry in Italy from Cimarosa to Verdi: the role of the impresario* (Cambridge, 1984)

Sabina, Karel, 1918. *Braniboři v Čechách* [The Brandenburgers in Bohemia], ed. Zdeněk Nejedlý (Prague, 1918 = OL, i)

1930. *Prodaná nevěsta* [The Bartered Bride], ed. Zdeněk Nejedlý (Prague, 1930 = OL, ii)

Schulzová, Anežka, 1902. 'Zdenko Fibich: hrstka upomínek a intimních rysů' [A handful of memories and intimate characteristics], *Květy*, xxiv (1902), no.6, pp. 768-83, no.1, p. 67-84; *reprinted, ed. Ludvík Boháček (Prague, 1950); also in Rektorys 1951, ii, 141-99

Sehnal, Jiří, 1961. 'Hudba k české pantomimě Zamilovaný ponocný' [The music for the Czech pantomime *The Lovelorn Nightwatchman*], *Brno v minulosti a dnes*, iii (Brno, 1961), 170-91

1974. 'Počátky opery na Moravě' [The beginnings of opera in Moravia], *O divadle na Moravě*, ed. E. Petrů and J. Stýskal (Prague, 1974), 55-77

1985. 'Lidový duchovní zpěv v českých zemích v době klasicismu' [Folk sacred song in the Czech lands during the Classical period], *HV*, xxii (1985), 248-58

Séquardtová, Hana, 1978. *Konstanty a proměny ve Smetanově tvorbě: příspěvek ke studiu hudebně myšlenkových souvislostí* [Constants and transformations in Smetana's works: a contribution to the study of the coherence of musical thought] (Prague, 1978)

Šilhan, A[ntonín], 1909. 'Smetanův "Dalibor": příspěvek k historii jeho vzniku' [Smetana's *Dalibor*: a contribution to the history of its origins], *HR*, ii (1909), 209-17

1932. 'Opery Vítězslava Nováka' [The operas of Vítězslav Novák], *Vítězslav Novák: studie a vzpomínky*, ed. Antonín Srba (Prague, 1932), 281-305

# Bibliography

Šíp, Ladislav, 1983. *Česká opera a její tvůrci: průvodce* [Czech opera and its creators: a guide] (Prague, 1983)

Šípek, Karel, 1918. *Vzpomínky na Prozatímní* [Reminiscences of the Provisional Theatre] (Prague 1918)

Smaczny, Jan, 1982. 'The operas and melodramas of Zdeněk Fibich (1850-1900)', *Proceedings of the Royal Musical Association*, CIX (1982-3), 119-33

    1987. 'The repertoire of the Provisional Theatre', *Royal Musical Association Research Chronicle* (in preparation)

Smetana, Bedřich, 1942. *Zápisník motivů* [Notebook of motifs], ed. Mirko Očadlík (Prague, 1942)

    1948. *Kritické dílo Bedřicha Smetany* [Smetana's works of criticism], ed. V.H. Jarka (Prague, 1948)

Smolka, Jaroslav, 1980. *Smetanova vokální tvorba: písně, sbory, kantáta* [Smetana's vocal works: songs, choruses, cantata] (Prague, 1980 = Dílo a život Bedřicha Smetany, 2)

Šoučková, Milada, 1958. *The Czech Romantics* (The Hague, 1958)

Šourek, Otakar, 1911. 'Dopisy Antonína Dvořáka Jaroslavu Kvapilovi' [Dvořák's letters to Kvapil], *HR*, IV (1911), 430-2

    1916. *Život a dílo Antonína Dvořáka* [Dvořák's life and works], I-II (Prague, 1916-17, *rev. 2/1922-8, rev. 3/1954-5), III-IV (Prague, *1930-33, rev. 2/1956-7)

    1926. 'Dívčí boj v české opeře' [The maidens' war in Czech opera], *Listy Hudební matice*, V (1926), 94-6

    (ed.), 1938. *Dvořák ve vzpomínkách a dopisech* [Dvořák in reminiscences and letters] (Prague, 1938, *enlarged 9/1951; English trans., 1954)

    1939. *Episoda z osudů Jakobína* [An episode in the fate of *The Jacobin*] (Prague, 1939)

    (ed.), 1941. *Antonín Dvořák přátelům doma* [Dvořák to his friends at home] (Prague and Brno, 1941) [letters]

    1942. 'O zrození díla a jeho osudech' [On the genesis of the work (*The Devil's Wall*) and its fate], *Smetanův operní epilog*. . . (Prague, 1942)

    1943. 'Karel Kovařovic a Vrchlického "Armida"' [Karel Kovařovic and Vrchlický's *Armida*], *Hudební věstník Unie českých hudebníků z povolání/Smetana*, XXXVI (1943), 53-5

Špindler, Ervín, 1909. 'Několik vzpomínek na mistra B. Smetanu' [Recollections of Maestro Smetana], *HR*, II (1909), 248-53

Srb, Josef (Debrnov), 1891. *Dějiny hudby v Čechách a na Moravě* [The history of music in Bohemia and Moravia] (Prague, 1891)

Srba, Antonín, 1914. *Boj proti Dvořákovi* [The campaign against Dvořák] (Prague, 1914)

Srba, Bořivoj, 1983. 'Jevištní výprava představení Smetanovy Libuše v Národním divadle z let 1881 a 1883' [The stage sets for the production of Smetana's *Libuše* at the National Theatre in 1881 and 1883], *DČK*, 167-87

    1985. 'Bedřich Smetana a soudobá divadelní konvence' [Smetana and theatrical conventions of his time], *OM*, XVII (1985), 71-81, 97-107

Šťastný, Radko, 1974, *Čeští spisovatelé desetí stoletà* [Czech writers of ten centuries] (Prague, 1974)

Štědroň, Bohumír (ed.), 1946. *Janáček ve vzpomínkách a dopisech* (Prague, *1946; English. trans. 1955 as *Janáček in Letters and Reminiscences*)

    1947. *J.B. Foerster a Morava* [Foerster and Moravia] (Brno, 1947)

    1953. 'Husitské náměty v české a světové hudbě' [Hussite motifs in Czech and world music], *Časopis Národního musea: oddíl věd společenských*, CXXII (1953), 62-90

    1968. *Zur Genesis von Leoš Janáčeks Oper Jenůfa* (Brno, 1968, *enlarged 2/1972)

Stich, Alexander, 1984. 'O libretu Dvořákova Dimitrije' [The libretto of Dvořák's *Dimitrij*], *HV*, XXI (1984), 339-52

# Bibliography

Štolba, Josef, 1906. 'Libretto pro Bedřicha Smetanu' [A libretto for Smetana], *Z mých pamětí* [memoirs] (Prague, 1906-7), I, 243-59

Straková, Theodora, 1956. 'Janáčkova opera Osud' [Janáček's opera *Fate*], *ČMM*, XLI (1956), 209-60; XLIII (1957), 133-64

1973. 'Jaroměřice nad Rokytnou', *OM*, V (1973), 57-60

Stuckenschmidt, H.H., 1954. 'Leoš Janáček und seine Oper "Katja Kabanova"', *Musik der Zeit*, ed. H. Lindlar, no. 8 (1954), 5-10; abridged English trans. in *Opera*, II (1951), 227-34

Šubert, František A., 1908. *Dějiny Národního divadla v Praze* [History of the National Theatre in Prague] (Prague, 1908-12]

Suchá 1974. Milada Suchá and Marie Ulčová: 'Plzeňské počátky libretistické spolupráce Elišky Krásnohorské s Bedřichem Smetanou' [The Plzeň beginnings of Krásnohorská's collaboration with Smetana as librettist], *Bedřich Smetana: Plzeň 1840-1843* (Plzeň, 1974), 97-117

Sussex, Roland, 1985. 'Lingua nostra: the nineteenth-century Slavonic language revivals', *Culture and nationalism in nineteenth-century Eastern Europe*, ed. Roland Sussex and J.C. Eade (Columbus, Ohio, 1985), 111-27

Svobodová, Věra, 1953. 'Opery Karla Šebora v Prozatímním divadle' [The operas of Karel Šebor at the Provisional Theatre], *ČMM*, XXXVIII (1953), 150-62

Sychra, Antonín, 1959. *Estetika Dvořákovy symfonické tvorby* [The aesthetics of Dvořák's symphonic works] (Prague, 1959)

Teige, Karel, 1893. *Příspěvky k životopisu a umělecké činnosti mistra Bedřicha Smetany* [Contributions to the biography and artistic activities of maestro Bedřich Smetana], I: *Komentovaný katalog všech skladeb mistrových v chronologickém postupu* [Annotated catalogue of all the master's works in chronological order] (Prague, 1893)

1896. II: *Dopisy Smetanovy* [Smetana's letters] (Prague, 1896)

Telcová-Jurenková, Jiřina, 1960. 'Divadlo na Veveří ulici a jeho budova' [The theatre in Veveří street and its building], *ČMM*, XLV (1960), 199-214

Temperley, Nicholas, 1979. *The music of the English parish church* (Cambridge, 1979)

Teuber, Oscar, 1883. *Geschichte des Prager Theatres: von den Anfängen des Schauspielwesens bis auf die neueste Zeit* (Prague, 1883-8)

Thomson, S. Harrison, 1943. *Czechoslovakia in European history* (Princeton, 1943, enlarged 2/1953, *reprinted London, 1965)

Tille, Václav, 1909. *České pohádky do roku 1848* [Czech legends up to 1848] (Prague, 1909)

1929. *Soupis českých pohádek* [Catalogue of Czech tales] (Prague, 1929-37)

Trojan, Jan, 1972. 'Moravská lidová píseň v díle Vítězslava Nováka' [Moravian folksong in the works of Vítězslav Novák], *Národní umělec Vítězslav Novák: studie a vzpomínky k 100. výročí narození*, ed. Karel Padrta and Bohumír Štědroň (České Budějovice, 1972), 149-74

1974. 'Jak to dopadlo v Jaroměřicích' [How things turned out at Jaroměřice], *OM*, VI (1974), 82-5 [on Míča's opera *L'origine di Jaromeriz in Moravia*]

1976. 'Přemyslovská pověst na benátské operní scéně 1697' [The Přemysl legend on the Venetian operatic stage 1697], *HV*, XIII (1976), 350-61

1979. 'Libreto pana Sartoria [La Libussa]' [Mr Sartorio's libretto – La Libussa], *OM*, XI (1979), 76-8

1980. *Moravská lidová píseň: melodika, harmonika* [Moravian folksong: melodic and harmonic aspects] (Prague, 1980)

1981. *České zpěvohry 18. století* [Czech eighteenth-century Singspiels] (Brno, 1981)

1983. 'Missa pastoralis boemica Josefa Schreiera', *HV*, XX (1983), 41-58

# Bibliography

1984. 'Čeština na zámecké scéně v Jaroměřicích' [Czech on the castle stage at Jaroměřice], *OM*, XVI (1984), 101–5

1984a. 'Kantoři na Moravě a jejich hudební aktivita v 18. a 19. století' [Kantors in Moravia and their musical activities in the eighteenth and nineteenth centuries], *Sborník prací filozofické fakulty brněnské univerzity*, H19–20 (1984), 113–18

Tyrrell, John, 1967. 'The musical prehistory of Janáček's Počátek románu [*The Beginning of a Romance*] and its importance in shaping the composer's dramatic style', *ČMM*, LII (1967), 245–70

1968. 'Mr Brouček's Excursion to the Moon', *ČMM*, LIII–IV (1968–9), 89–124

1973. 'How Domšík became a bass', *The Musical Times*, CXIV (1973), 29–30

1980. Disc notes to Janáček: *Z mrtvého domu* [*From the House of the Dead*] (Decca, D224D 2, 1980)

1980a. 'Mr Brouček at home: an epilogue to Janáček's opera', *The Musical Times*, CXX (1980), 30–3

1982. *Leoš Janáček: Káťa Kabanová* (Cambridge, 1982)

1984. 'Švanda and his successors: the bagpiper and his music in Czech opera', *SC*

1987. 'The cathartic slow waltz and other finale conventions in Janáček's operas', *Music and theatre: essays in honour of Winton Dean*, ed. Nigel Fortune (Cambridge, 1987), 333–52

Urban, Otto, 1982. *Česká společnost 1848–1918* [Czech society 1848–1918] (Prague, 1982)

Vacková, Růžena, 1940. 'Současné české herečky' [Present-day Czech actresses], *Žena v českém umění dramatickém* [The woman in Czech drama], ed. Běla Veselá (Prague, 1940), 113–89

Václavek 1950. Bedřich Václavek and Robert Smetana: *O české písni lidové a zlidovělé* [Czech folksong and songs accepted as folksong] (Prague, 1950)

Vejdělek, Cyril J., 1982. 'Bejchorsko – kolébka naší zpěvohry i prvních pěvců' [Bejchorsko – the cradle of our operas and first singers], *OM*, XIV (1982), 265–7

Veselý, Richard, 1915. 'K boji proti Dvořákovi' [The campaign against Dvořák], *HR*, VIII (1915), 96–103

Vetterl, Karel, 1965. 'Lidová píseň v Janáčkových sborech do roku 1885' [Folksong in Janáček's choruses up to 1885], *Sborník prací filosofické fakulty brněnské university*, F9 (1965), 365–78

1968. 'Janáček's creative relationship to folk music', *Leoš Janáček et musica europaea: Brno III 1968*, 235–42

1973. 'Volkslied-Sammelergebnisse in Mähren und Schlesien aus dem Jahre 1819', *Sborník prací filosofické fakulty brněnské university*, H8 (1973), 95–121

1978. 'Stáří lidových nápěvů a formy jejich přežívání' [The age of folktunes and the forms of their survival], *HV*, XV (1978), 123–52

Vít, Petr, 1982. 'Libuše – proměny mýtu ve společnosti a v umění' [Libuše – the transformation of a myth in society and in art], *HV*, XIX (1982), 269–73

1987. 'Italská operní tvorba v českých zemích 19. století' [Italian opera in the Czech lands during the nineteenth century] *HV*, XXIV (1987), 26–32

Vogel, Jaroslav, 1958. *Leoš Janáček: Leben und Werk* (Prague, 1958; Czech original, 1963; English trans., 1962, *rev. 2/1981 by Karel Janovický as *Leoš Janáček: a Biography*)

Volek, Tomislav, 1973. *Mozart a Praha* [Mozart and Prague] (Prague, 1973)

1977. Tomislav Volek and Stanislav Jareš: *Dějiny české hudby v obrazech* [The history of Czech music in pictures] (Prague, 1977)

317

# Bibliography

1986. Tomislav Volek: 'Šporkovská opera' [The Sporck opera], *HRo*, XXXIX (1986), 135–7

Vondráček, Jan, 1956. *Dějiny českého divadla: doba obrozenská 1771–1824* [The history of the Czech theatre: the period of National Revival 1771–1824] (Prague, 1956)

1957. *Dějiny českého divadla: doba předbřeznová 1824–1846* [The history of the Czech Theatre: the period before the March revolution 1824–46] (Prague, 1957)

Vratislavský, Jan, 1971. *Neumannová éra v brněnské opeře* [The Neumann era in the Brno opera] (Brno, 1971)

Vycpálek, Jos., 1921. *České tance* [Czech dances] (Prague, 1921)

Vysloužil, Jiří, 1966. 'Modální struktury u Janáčka' [Modal structures in Janáček], *HRo*, XLX (1966), 552–5

1974. *Alois Hába: život a dílo* [Life and works] (Prague, 1974)

1980. 'Úvaha nad českou operou' [A reflection on Czech opera], *OM*, XII (1980), 193–9


Waldau, Alfred, 1859. *Böhmische Nationaltänze: Kulturstudie* [I] (Prague, 1859)

Wallace, William V., 1976. *Czechoslovakia* (London, 1976)

Ward, Donald (ed. and trans.), 1981. *The German legends of the Brothers Grimm* (London, 1981)

Wenzig 1944. Josef Wenzig and Ervín Špindler: *Dalibor*, ed. Josef Bartoš (Prague, 1944 = OL, v)

1951. : *Libuše*, ed. Josef Bartoš (Prague, 1951 = OL, VI)

Wingfield, Paul, 1984. 'On an Overgrown Path': A reappraisal of the sources and the editorial problems in the music of Leoš Janáček (MPhil. dissertation, University of Cambridge, 1984)

Wiskemann, Elizabeth, 1938. *Czechs & Germans: a study of the struggle in the historic provinces of Bohemia and Moravia* (London, 1938, *2/1967)


Zacek, Joseph F., 1969. 'Nationalism in Czechoslovakia', *Nationalism in Eastern Europe*, ed. Peter F. Sugar and Ivo J. Lederer (Seattle, 1969), 166–206

Závodský, Artur, 1962. *Gabriela Preissová* (Prague, 1962)

Zelený, Václav Vladimír, 1894. *O Bedřichu Smetanovi* (Prague, 1894)

Zíbrt, Čeněk, 1895. *Jak se kdyby v Čechách tancovalo: dějiny tance v Čechách, na Moravě a na Slovensku. . .* [How they used to dance in Bohemia: the history of dance in Bohemia, Moravia and Slovakia] (Prague, 1895, *2/1960, ed. H. Laudová)

Zich, Otakar, 1909. 'Bezprostřední styky skladeb Smetanových s lidovou písní' [The immediate contacts of Smetana's works with folksong] *Český lid*, XVIII (1909), 353–6

Zielecká, Olga, 1926. 'Památce zapomenutého vlastence, literáta a hudebníka Ludvíka Rittera z Rittersberku 1809–1858 [In memory of the forgotten patriot, literary figure and musician Ludvík Ritter z Rittersberku], *Dalibor*, XLII (1926); *published separately (Prague, 1926)

Žižka, L.K., 1939. *Mistři a mistříčkové: vzpomínky na české muzikanty let 1881–91* [Masters and lesser masters: reminiscences of Czech musicians 1881–91] (Prague, 1939, *enlarged 2/1947)

Züngel, Emanuel, 1962. *Dvě vdovy* [The Two Widows], ed. Mirko Očadlík (Prague, 1962 = OL, VII)

Zvonař, L[eopold], 1860. 'Slovo o českých národních písních' [A word on Czech folksongs], *Dalibor*, III (1860), 166–7, 182–3, 191, 199–200, 213–14, 229–30

# Note on list of Czech operas

This is not a complete list of Czech operas: simply those mentioned in the text. Operas by Czech composers in foreign languages are not generally given in the list except in a few cases where it helps avoid confusion or where, for instance in the case of Skuherský's German operas, Czech versions of these works were presented as new Czech operas. Some plays with songs and other musical numbers are included in cases where the musical element is particularly prominent. All titles are given in English, with cross references from their respective Czech titles. Alphabetization takes no account of accents and diacritical marks.

The following details of each work are given, as available:
*Title of opera*: in English [Czech title], genre*, number of acts, composer; librettist and source;
*Composition dates; place and date of first performance*;
*Publication*: first edition of vocal score, other important editions, most recent publication; full scores are listed where published; excerpts and pot-pourris for piano are listed if no vocal score was published. Publication dates are given in square brackets where the date is not stated on the print. Publication of the libretto simultaneously with the première can be assumed for all operas performed in Prague after 1862 (exceptions are noted).
*Discography* (33 rpm records only): recording company, date (conductor). Records of excerpts from full recordings are not listed; nor are individual arias. Works are sung in Czech unless otherwise stated. The date given is that of the actual recording (r), or its publication (p). Dates without r or p are review dates (in the United Kingdom) and may be several years after the recordings were originally released.

*genre* is provided for all operas, where specified. It is given as described on the vocal score, if published, failing that on the published libretto, theatre poster or autograph score. Genre descriptions in square brackets are editorial. The genre description is given in English translation except for the variant words for 'folk' which are kept in Czech (for an explanation of these see Chapter 7, fn. 1). The distinction between 'opera' and 'zpěvohra' is also retained here. The latter is a direct translation of the German word 'Singspiel', though it was often used to describe a continuously sung work, as a native Czech term for 'opera'.

## Abbreviations

(all theatres and publishers are in Prague unless otherwise stated)

| | |
|---|---|
| arr. | arranged |
| ed. | edited |
| ET | Estates Theatre [Stavovské divadlo] |
| FAU | Fr. A. Urbánek |

# Note on list of Czech operas

| | |
|---|---|
| HM | Hudební matice (to 1889); Umělecká beseda (to 1907); Hudební matice Umělecké besedy (1907–50) |
| HMV | His Master's Voice |
| MU | Mojmír Urbánek |
| NCT | New Czech Theatre [Nové české divadlo] |
| n.d. | no date |
| n.p. | no place |
| NT | National Theatre [Národní divadlo] |
| NTT | New Town Theatre [Novoměstské divadlo] |
| p | date of publication (of a recording) |
| perf. | performed, performance |
| pf | pianoforte |
| PT | Provisional Theatre [Prozatímní divadlo] |
| r | date of recording |
| rev. | revised |
| S | Supraphon |
| SNKLHU | Státní nakladatelství krásné literatury, hudby a umění [State publisher of literature, music and art] |
| SV | (for Dvořák's works): Souborné výdání [Complete Edition] (for Smetana's works): Studijní vydání děl Bedřicha Smetany [Study edition of Bedřich Smetana's works], ed. F. Bartoš and others |
| trans. | translated |
| UE | Universal Edition, Vienna |

# Czech operas mentioned in the text

*Alfred*, heroic opera, 3, Dvořák (in German); Körner: *Alfred der Grosse* (opera libretto, in 2 acts)
1870; Olomouc City Theatre, 10 Dec 1938 (in Czech)
overture (as Tragic Overture): Simrock 1912
*Apostat, Der*, see *Vladimír, God's Chosen One*
*Armida*, zpěvohra, 4, Dvořák; Vrchlický after Tasso's epic poem *Gerusalemme liberata*
1902-3; NT 25 March 1904
Dědici Dr. Antonína Dvořáka/HM 1941, 1951
Voce r1961 (Albrecht; in German)
*Armida*, zpěvohra, 4, Kovařovic; Vrchlický (same text as in Dvořák's *Armida*)
1888-95, incomplete (Act 1, fragment of Act 2)
*At the Old Bleachery* [*Na starém bělidle*], zpěvohra in 4 scenes, Kovařovic; Karel Šípek
after Němcová's novel *Babička* [The Grandmother]
1898-1901; NT 22 Nov 1901
HM 1902, 2/Orbis 1951 (ed. O. Šourek)
*Ave Maria*, [opera], 1, Rozkošný; V. Trapp?
Prague, privately performed 1855 or 1856

*Babička*, see *Grandmother, The*
*Bartered Bride, The* [*Prodaná nevěsta*], comic zpěvohra, 3, Smetana; Sabina
1863-6, rev. 1869-70; PT 30 May 1866 (in 2 acts with spoken dialogue); PT 25 Sept
1870 (definitive version)
HM [1872], Orbis rev. 2/1951 (ed. F. Bartoš), SNKLHU 1982; full score: Bote & Bock
[1893], Společnost Bedřicha Smetany 1932-6, ed. O. Ostrčil, SV I 1940, 2/1953
HMV r1933 (Ostrčil), reissued S p1980; Gramofonové závody r1952 (Vogel); Urania
1954 (Lenzer; in German); S r1959 (Chalabala); Philips 1961 (Gebré); Eterna 1962
(Suitner, in German); HMV 1963 (Kempe; in German); S r1974 (Hlaváček; 1866
version); S r1980-1 (Košler); Eurodisc 1982 (Krombholc; in German)
*Beginning of a Romance, The* [*Počátek románu*], romantic opera, 1, Janáček; Jaroslav
Tichý [pseudonym of František Rypáček], after Preissová's short story
1891; Brno PT 10 Feb 1894
Dilia/Alkor 1978 (reproduced MS)
Voce p1982 (Jílek, Brno Radio r1976)
*Black Lake, The* [*Černé jezero*], romantic opera, 3, Rozkošný; Karel Kádner after Adolf
Heyduk's poem *Dědův odkaz* [The Grandfather's legacy]
1904; NT 6 Jan 1906
*sousedská* arr. for pf: supplement to *Zlatá Praha*, VII (1903), 3
*Blacksmith of Lešetín, The* [*Lešetínský kovář*], opera, 3, Suda; Pavel Nebeský and Eduard
Šimek after Čech's verse novel

321

1900–2; Plzeň City Theatre 4 April 1903
excerpts: *Česká hudba*, XVII, XVIII, XX (Kutná Hora, 1911, 1912, 1914)

*Blacksmith of Lešetín, The* [*Lešetínský kovář*], lidová opera, 3, Weis; Ladislav Novák after
    Čech's verse novel
NT 6 June 1920
privately printed 1920

*Blaník*, zpěvohra, 3, Fibich; Kr snohorská
1874–7; PT 25 Nov 1881
FAU [1897]

*Blanka*, fantastic–romantic opera, 4, Šebor; Rüffer (in German), trans. ?
PT 8 March 1870

*Bloud*, see *Fool, The*

*Bouře*, see *Tempest, The*

*Božena, Bohemian Princess* [*Božena, česká kněžna*], libretto for Tomášek by Václav
    Hanka, unset

*Brandenburgers in Bohemia, The* [*Braniboři v Čechách*], zpěvohra, 3, Smetana; Sabina
1862–3; PT 5 Jan 1866
Družstvo ctitelů Smetanových/HM [1899], HM 1946; full score: SV IX 1952
S r1963 (Tichý)

*Braniboři v Čechách*, see *Brandenburgers in Bohemia, The*

*Břetislav and Jitka* [*Bretislav a Jitka*; performed as *Břetislav*], historical opera, 5, Bendl;
    Krásnohorská
NTT 18 Sept 1870
march arr. for pf: supplement to *Dalibor*, I (1873); Jitka's aria in Act 2 in Burghauser
    1983, 81–7

*Brewers, The* [*Sládci*], veselá zpěvní hra [sung comedy], 2, Vorel; Erben
Žebrák, Bohemia, 27 March 1837; NT 14 Feb 1903

*Bridegrooms, The* [*Ženichové*], comic opera, 3, Kovařovic; Antonín Koukl after Simeon
    Karel Macháček's comedy
1882; NT 13 May 1884
pf pot-pourri: FAU [1884]

*Bride of Messina, The* [*Nevěsta messinská*], tragic zpěvohra, 3, Fibich; Hostinský after
    Schiller's tragedy *Die Braut von Messina*
1882–3; NT 28 March 1884
HM/FAU 1884, HM 4/1950
excerpts: S r1950 (Krombholc); S r1984 (Košler)

*Bud, The* [*Poupě*], comic zpěvohra, 1, Ostrčil; Ostrčil after F.X. Svoboda's comedy
1909–10; NT 25 Jan 1911
HM 1911, 2/1950

*Bukovín*, romantic opera, 3, Fibich; Sabina
1870–1; PT 16 April 1874
Scene for pf: FAU 1872; duet from Act 1 for pf: supplement to *Dalibor*, I (1873); Žítek's
    song, Act 2 Scene 1: *Fibichova čítanka*, ed. H. Doležil (Prague, 1930), 40–43;
    no libretto published

*Butchers' Shops or Betting in the Lottery, The* [*Masné krámy aneb Sázení do loterie*], Sing-
    spiel, 2, V. Tuček; Prokop Šedivý
Prague u Hybernů Theatre 7 Feb 1796
libretto Prague 1796; no music survives

*Černé jezero*, see *Black Lake, The*
*Černohorci*, see *Montenegrins, The*
*Čert a Káča*, see *Devil and Kate, The*
*Čertova stěna*, see *Devil's Wall, The*
*Cesta oknem*, see *Way through the Window, The*
*Chapel in the Woods, The* [*Lesní kaple*], dramatic scene from country life, 1, Zvonař;
  V. Gábler
1862; NTT 1864 (concert perf.)
no libretto published
*Child of Tábor, The* [*Dítě Tábora*], tragic opera, 3, Bendl; Krásnohorská
1888; NT 12 March 1892
*Cinderella* [*Popelka*], zpěvohra, 3, Rozkošný; Hostinský, after the fairy-tale
1882 or ?1884; NT 31 May 1885
pf pot-pourri: FAU [1885]
*Comedy on the Bridge* [*Veselohra na mostě*], radio opera, 1, Martinů; Martinů after
  Klicpera's comedy
1935; Prague Radio, 18 March 1937; Ostrava State Theatre 9 Jan 1948
Boosey & Hawkes 1952 (English and German)
S p1984 (Jílek, Brno Radio r1973)
*Cunning Little Vixen, The* [*Příhody Lišky Bystroušky* = literally The Adventures of the
  Vixen Bystrouška], opera, 3, Janáček; Janáček after Těsnohlídek's novel *Liška
  Bystrouška*
1921–3; Brno NT 6 Nov 1924
UE 1924
S r1957 (Neumann); S r1970 (Gregor); S r1979–80 (Neumann); Decca r1981 (Mac-
  kerras); p1983 (Bakala, Brno Radio r1953)
*Cunning Peasant, The* [*Šelma sedlák*], comic opera, 2, Dvořák; J.O. Veselý
1877; PT 27 Jan 1878
Simrock 1882, Simrock/HM 1913; full score: Simrock 1882
S r1985–6 (Vajnar)


*Dalibor* [*Dalibor im Gefängnissthurm auf dem Hradschin in Prag*; *Dalibor, Die Gefängnisse
  auf dem Hradschin in Prag*], 3, Kott; Perger
one scene performed in Brno 1844?
lost
*Dalibor*, Pozděna; Sabina
? (before 1879), incomplete
lost
*Dalibor*, opera, 3, Smetana; Wenzig (in German), trans. Špindler
1865–7, rev. 1870; NTT 16 May 1868
Družstvo ctitelů Bedřicha Smetany 1884, HM 1950 (ed. F. Bartoš); full score: SV
  v 1945, 2/1960
S r1950 (Krombholc); S r1967 (Krombholc); S r1979 (Smetáček)
*Dearest Treasure, The*, see *Treasure, The*
*Death of Vlasta, The* [*Vlasty skon*], music drama, 3, Ostrčil; Pippich
1900–03; NT 14 Dec 1904
full score: Dilia 1966 (reproduced MS)

*Debora*, zpěvohra, 3, Foerster; Kvapil after Salomon von Mosenthal's play *Deborah*
1892; NT 27 Jan 1893
Foersterova společnost v Praze 1919

*Dědův odkaz*, see *Grandfather's Legacy, The*; see also *Black Lake, The*

*Destiny*, see *Fate*

*Devil and Kate, The* [*Čert a Káča*], opera, 3, Dvořák; Adolf Wenig after a folktale
1898–9; NT 23 Nov 1899
MU 1908, HM 3/1944 (ed. O. Šourek), Orbis 4/1951; full score: SV 1972
S r1955 (Chalabala); S r1979 (Pinkas)

*Devil's Wall, The* [*Čertova stěna*], comic-romantic opera, 3, Smetana; Krásnohorská
1879–82; NCT 29 Oct 1882
Družstvo ctitelů Smetanových/HM [1902] (with *Viola*), HM 6/1949; full score: SV XII
1959
S r1960 (Chalabala)

*Dimitrij*, grand opera 4, Dvořák; Červinková-Riegrová
1881–2, rev. 1883, 1885, 1894–5; NCT 8 Oct 1882; NT 7 Nov 1894
Starý 1886, HM 1912 (rev. Kovařovic), HM 3/1941 (ed. O. Šourek); full score in preparation (ed. M. Pospíšil)
excerpts: S r1980 (Štych)

*Dítě Tábora*, see *Child of Tábor, The*

*Dogheads, The* [*Psohlavci*], zpěvohra, 3, Kovařovic; Karel Šípek after Jirásek's novel
1895–7; NT 24 April 1898
HM 1898, HM 4/1950
excerpts: S r1950 (Folprecht)

*Drahomíra*, grand romantic opera, 4, Šebor; Šír, rev. Böhm
PT 20 Sept 1867

*Drahomíra* [originally *Bolemíra?*], romantic opera, 3, Škroup (in German); Václav Alois
Svoboda (Navárovský)
1840?; ET 20 Nov 1848

*Dráteník*, see *Tinker, The*

*Drunken Man, The* [*Opilý muž*], [Singspiel], Jan Tuček; Josef Galka
c 1780

*Dvě vdovy*, see *Two Widows, The*

*Elderly Suitor, The* [*Starý ženich*, originally called *Pan Franc* (Mr Franc)], operatic joke
(libretto), prostonárodní opera (vocal score), 3, Bendl; Sabina, rev. Gustav Eim and
V.J. Novotný
1871–4; Chrudim (Píštěk's Theatrical Company) 4 Feb 1882; NCT 20 Oct 1883
HM 1883

*Enchanted Prince, The* [*Zakletý princ*], comic opera, 3, Hřímalý; Böhm after *1001 Nights*
NTT 13 May 1872
pf pot-pourri: Starý (supplement to *Hudební listy*), III (1872)

*Eva*, zpěvohra, 3, Foerster; Foerster after Preissová's play *Gazdina roba* [*The Farm
Mistress*; literally: The Farmer's Wife – loose woman]
1895–7; NT 1 Jan 1899
HM 1909, Orbis 4/1951; as *Marja* UE n.d. (in German)
excerpts: S r1955 (Chalabala); complete: S r1982 (Vajnar)

*Excursion of Mr Brouček from the Moon to the Exhibition, The* [*Výlet pana Broučka z měsíce na výstavu*], [play with incidental music in 6 scenes], Kovařovic; František Ferdinand Šamberk after Čech's novel *Matěj Brouček na výstavě* [Matěj Brouček at the Exhibition]
NT 18 June 1894
Overture: FAU 1894; Havířská polka [Fireman's Polka] HM 1950, SNKLHU 1960; 'Slavnost chmelařská' [Hops celebration], arr. pf, Kočí a Finke, Plzeň, n.d.; many other arrangements for pf, wind etc, of these three items, especially the polka

*Excursion of Mr Brouček to the Moon, The* [*Výlet pana Broučka do měsíce*], operetta, 3 and epilogue, Moor; Vladimír Merhaut and Moor after Čech's novel
1909–10; Jaroměř, summer 1910
privately printed, n.p, n.d.

*Excursions of Mr Brouček, The* [*Výlety páně Broučkovy*], opera in 2 parts, Janáček: *The Excursion of Mr Brouček to the Moon* [*Výlet pana Broučka do měsíce*], 2, Janáček, with František Gellner, Viktor Dyk and F.S. Procházka after Čech's novel; *The Excursion of Mr Brouček to the Fifteenth Century* [*Výlet pana Broučka do XV. století*], 2, F.S. Procházka after Čech's novel
1908–17; NT 23 April 1920
UE 1919
excerpts: S r1954 (Jílek); complete: S r1962 (Neumann); S r1980 (Jílek)

*Fall of Arkona, The* [*Pád Arkuna*], opera: prologue (*Helga*) and zpěvohra (*Dargun*), 3, Fibich; Schulzová
1898; NT 9 Nov 1900
FAU [1899] (*Helga*) and [1901] (*Dargun*)

*Fate (Destiny)* [*Osud*], 3 novelesque scenes [tři obrazy románové], Janáček; Janáček and Fedora Bartošová
1903–5, rev. 1906–7; Brno Radio 18 Sept 1934 (broadcast perf.); Brno Stadion 30 Sept 1934 (concert perf.); Brno State Theatre 25 Oct 1958 (arr. V. Nosek)
Dilia/Alkor 1978 (reproduced MS)
excerpts: S r1954 (Bakala); complete: S r1975–6 (Jílek)

*Fidlovačka* (= name of a traditional spring fair), or *No Anger and No Brawl* [*Fidlovačka aneb Žádný hněv a žádná rvačka*], 4 scenes from Prague life [with overture and 21 musical numbers], Škroup; Tyl
ET 21 Dec 1834
Orbis 1951 (ed. K. Šolc)

*Fool, The* [*Bloud*], zpěvohra in 7 scenes, Foerster after Tolstoy's tale *Dva starika* [Two Old Men]
1935–6; NT 28 Feb 1936
Foerstrova společnost 1939

*Frasquitta*, see *Night of St Simon and St Jude, The*

*From the House of the Dead* [*Z mrtvého domu*], opera, 3, Janáček; Janáček after Dostoyevsky's novel *Zapisky iz myortvovo doma* [Memoirs from the House of the Dead]
1927–8; Brno NT 12 April 1930 (version by O. Chlubna and B. Bakala); Janáček's original gradually reinstated from 1964 onwards
UE 1930; full score UE 1930 (version by Chlubna)
Philips r1954 (Krannhals; in German, Chlubna/Bakala version); S r1957, 1959 (Bakala and Vogel; Chlubna/Bakala version; excerpts); S r1964 (Gregor; with original ending); S r1974 (Nosek; original ending and orchestration); S r1979 (Neumann;

original ending); r1980 (Mackerras; original ending and orchestration and Janáček's final corrections)

*Frustrated Wedding, The [Zmařená svatba]*, národní opera, 3, Šebor; Červinková-Riegrová after the French vaudeville *Le petit Pierre*
1876–9; PT 25 Oct 1879
overture arr. for pf: Wetzler, n.d.; 8 excerpts: Starý, n.d. [1885?]

*Grandfather's Legacy, The [Dědův odkaz]*, lyrical zpěvohra, 3, Novák, op. 57; Antonín Klášterský after Adolf Heyduk's poem
1923–5, rev. 1942; Brno NT 16 Jan 1926; NT 3 Jan 1943
HM 1926

*Grandmother, The [Babička]*, pictures from country life, 3 and epilogue, Horák; Wenig after Němcová's novel
1899; NT 3 March 1900

*Heart, The [Srdce]*, zpěvohra, 2, Foerster; Foerster
1921–2; NT 15 Nov 1923
Foerstrova společnost 1922

*Hedy*, zpěvohra, 4, Fibich; Schulzová after Byron's narrative poem *Don Juan*
1895; NT 12 Feb 1896
FAU [1895], 2/1912

*Honzovo království*, see *Johnny's Kingdom*

*Horymír*, see *Jaromír, Duke of Bohemia*

*Hubička*, see *Kiss, The*

*Hussite Bride, The [Nevěsta husitská]*, grand romantic zpěvohra, 5, Šebor; Rüffer (in German), trans. ?
NTT 27 Sept 1868
pf pot-pourri: FAU n.d.; love duet, Act 3: FAU n.d.; scene from Act 1 in Burghauser 1983

*Imp of Zvíkov, The [Zvíkovský rarášek]*, comic opera, 1, Novák; after Stroupežnický's comedy
1913–14; NT 10 Oct 1915
UE 1915

*Indian Princess, The [Indická princezna]*, operetta, 3, Bendl; Antonín Pulda
1876–7; NCT 26 Aug 1877; with new libretto (by Karel Mašek) NT 31 Aug 1906

*Indická princezna*, see *Indian Princess, The*

*In the Well [V studni]*, comic opera, 1, Blodek; Sabina
PT 17 Nov 1867
Starý 1878, 13/1946
S r1959 (Škvor); S r1981 (Štych)

*Invincible Ones, The [Nepřemožení]*, zpěvohra, 4, Foerster; Foerster
1906, 1917; NT 19 Dec 1918
UE 1918

*Jacobin, The [Jakobín]*, opera, 3, Dvořák; Červinková-Riegrová
1887–8, rev. 1897; NT 1 Feb 1889, NT 19 June 1898
HM 1911 (rev. Kovařovic), 4/1939 (1897 version, ed. O. Šourek), Orbis 1952; full score: SV 1966
excerpts: S r1952 (Vogel); complete: r1977 (Pinkas)

*Jan Zhořelecký*, zpěvohra, 3, Ostrčil; Antonín Šetelík
1896–8; excerpts: Smetana Museum 7 March 1939
no libretto published

*Jaromír, Duke of Bohemia* [*Jaromír, vojvoda český*], zpěvohra, 4, Maýr; Ujková by 1863
(submitted for Harrach competition); originally thought to be called *Horymír*

*Její pastorkyňa*, see *Jenůfa*

*Jenůfa* [*Její pastorkyňa* (Her foster-daughter) = Czech title], opera ('Moravian music
drama' on first poster), 3, Janáček; Janáček after Preissová's play
1894–1903, rev. before 1908, 1916 (rev. and reorchestrated Kovařovic); Brno NT 21 Jan
1904; NT 26 May 1916 (Kovařovic version)
Klub přátel umění 1908, UE 1917 (Kovařovic version), HM 1934 (original version ed.
V. Helfert); full score: UE 1917 (Kovařovic version), UE 1969 (Kovařovic version)
Kovařovic version: S r1953 (Vogel); HMV r1969 (Gregor); S r1977–8 (Jílek); original
version: Decca r1982 (Mackerras)

*Jessica* [*Jessika*], comic zpěvohra, 3, Foerster; Vrchlický after Shakespeare's play *The
Merchant of Venice*
1902–4, rev. 1906; NT 14 April 1905
UE 1909

*Johnny's Kingdom* [*Honzovo království*], musical play in 7 scenes, Ostrčil; Jiří Mařánek
after Tolstoy's tale *Skazka ob Ivane-durake i evo dvukh brat'yakh* [The Tale of Ivan the
Fool and his Two Brothers]
1928–33; Brno NT, 26 May 1934
Společnost Otakara Ostrčila 1936, HM 1950
excerpts: S r1956 (Krombholc); S r1979 (Jílek)

*Jora and Manda* [*Jora a Manda*], [Singspiel], 1, Josef Pekárek; Josef Mauritius Bulín
1783–4?
libretto in Petrů 1985, 96–109

*Kamilla*, opera, 1, Čelanský; Čelanský
1897; NT 23 Oct 1897

*Karel Škreta*, comic opera, 3, Bendl; Krásnohorská
NT 11 Dec 1883

*Karlštejn*, opera, 3, Novák; Otokar Fischer after Vrchlický's comedy *Noc na Karlštejně*
[A Night at Karlštejn]
1915–16, rev. 1925, 1930; NT 18 Nov 1916
UE 1916

*Káťa Kabanová*, opera, 3, Janáček; Janáček after Ostrovsky's play *Groza* [The Thunder-
storm] in the Czech translation of Václav Červinka
1919–21; Brno NT 23 Nov 1921
UE 1922; full score: UE 1921, 1971 (ed. C. Mackerras)
S r1959 (Krombholc); Decca r1976 (Mackerras)

*King and Charcoal Burner* [*Král a uhlíř*], opera (first and second version), comic opera
(final version), 3, Dvořák; B.J. Lobeský [pseudonym of Bernard Guldener] after a
puppet play; additions by V.J. Novotný
1871, second version 1874, rev. 1887; PT 24 Nov 1874 (second version); NT 15 June
1887 (final version); NT 28 May 1929 (first version)
HM 1915 (final version), 2/1929

*Kiss, The* [*Hubička*], prostonárodní opera, 2, Smetana; Krásnohorská after Karolina Světlá's short story
1875–6; PT 7 Nov 1876
FAU [1880], SNKLHU 1959 (ed. F. Bartoš); full score: Weinberger n.d.; SV III 1942
S r1952 (Chalabala); S r1980 (Vajnar)

*Král a uhlíř*, see *King and Charcoal Burner*

*Kunála's Eyes* [*Kunálovy oči*], zpěvohra, 3, Ostrčil; Karel Mašek after Zeyer's tale
1907–8; NT 25 Nov 1908

*Kunálovy oči*, see *Kunála's Eyes*

*Landebork* [ =corruption of 'Brandenburg'], [Singspiel], 1, Alanus [Ignác] Plumlovský
1757–8?
libretto in Petrů 1985, 63–83

*Lantern, The* [*Lucerna*], musical fairy-tale, 4, Novák; Hanuš Jelínek after Jirásek's play
1919–22, rev. 1930; NT 13 May 1923
HM 1923
excerpts: S r1957 (Škvor); complete: S r1984 (Vajnar)

*Legenda z Erinu*, see *Legend of Erin, The*

*Legend of Erin, The* [*Legenda z Erinu*], zpěvohra, 4, Ostrčil; Ostrčil after Zeyer's play
1913–19; Brno NT 16 June 1921
Foerstrova společnost 1920

*Lejla*, grand opera, 5, Bendl; Krásnohorská after Bulwer-Lytton's novel *Leila, or The Siege of Granada*
1867; PT 4 Jan 1868 (in 4 acts as *Leila*); PT 24 Sept 1874 (definitive five-act version)
HM Acts 1–2 1874, Acts 3–5 [1880]

*Lešetínský kovář*, see *Blacksmith of Lešetín, The*

*Lesní kaple*, see *Chapel in the Woods, The*

*Libuše*, ceremonial zpěvohra, 3, Smetana; Wenzig: *Libušas Urtheilsspruch und Vermählung*, trans. Špindler
1869–72; NT 11 June 1881
HM [1881], SNKLHU rev. 9/1955 (ed. F. Bartos); full score: SV VI 1949
S r1965 (Krombholc); S r1983 (Košler)

*Libuše's Marriage* [*Libušin sňatek*], zpěvohra, 3, Škroup; Chmelenský
1835, rev. 1849; ET 6 Dec 1835 (Act ?3), ET 11 April 1850 (complete)

*Libušin sňatek*, see *Libuše's Marriage*

*Liebesring, Der*, see *Lóra*

*Lóra*, romantic opera, 2, Skuherský; K. Krása after H.T. Schmid's *Der Liebesring*
1858; Innsbruck 26 Feb 1861 as *Der Liebesring* (in 3 acts); in Czech PT 13 April 1868 as *Lóra*

*Lovelorn Nightwatchman, The* [*Zamilovaný ponocný*], opera–pantomime (poster), Czech intermezzo (libretto), 1, Jan Tuček?
Prague, Kotzen Opera House 1763?
libretto in Kneidl 1964

*Lucerna*, see *Lantern, The*

*Lumír*, libretto for Smetana by Krásnohorská (1870?), unset

*Makropulos Affair, The* [*Věc Makropulos*], opera, 3, Janáček; Janáček after Čapek's comedy
1923–5; Brno NT 28 Dec 1926
UE 1926
excerpts: S r1955 (Vogel); complete: S r1965–6 (Gregor); Decca r1978 (Mackerras)

*Maréna and Kedrota* [*Maréna a Kedrota*], [Singspiel], 1, Josef Pekárek; Josef Mauritius Bulín
1783–4?
libretto in Petrů 1985, 85–95

*Maryša*, opera, 5 scenes, Burian; Burian after Alois and Vilém Mrštík's play
1938–9; Brno Provincial Theatre 16 April 1940
SNKLHU 1964
excerpts: S r1961 (Krombholc)

*Masné krámy*, see *Butchers' Shops, The*

*Máti Míla*, see *Mother Míla*

*Matka*, see *Mother, The*

*Matka Míla*, see *Mother Míla*

*Mikuláš*, comic opera, 1, Rozkošný; Sabina
1868–9; PT 5 Dec 1870
Overture arr. pf 4 hands: Em. Wetzler n.d.; pf pot-pourri: Jean Schindler n.d.

*Mintmaster's Wife, The* [*Paní mincmistrová*], Janáček; Janáček after Stroupežnický's play
1906–7, incomplete

*Montenegrins, The* [*Černohorci*], romantic opera, 3, Bendl; J.O. Veselý
1877; NCT 11 Oct 1881
pf pot-pourri: FAU n.d.

*Mother, The* [*Matka*], opera, 10 scenes, Hába; Hába
1927–9; Munich 17 May 1931 (in German); Prague Smetana Theatre 23 May 1947 (in Czech)
full score: Dilia 1963 (reproduced MS)
S p1965 (Jirouš)

*Mother Míla* [*Máti Míla; Matka Míla*], zpěvohra, 1, Bendl; Delmar (in German), trans. V.J. Novotný
1893–5; NT 25 June 1895

*Na starém bělidle*, see *At the Old Bleachery*

*Nejdražší poklad*, see *Treasure, The*

*Nepřemožení*, see *Invincible Ones, The*

*Nevěsta husitská*, see *Hussite Bride, The*

*Nevěsta messinská*, see *Bride of Messina, The*

*Night of St Simon and St Jude, The* [*Noc Šimona a Judy*; originally *Frasquitta*], comic opera, 3, Kovařovic; Karel Šípek after Alarcón's short story *El sombrero de tres picos*
1890–91; NT 5 Nov 1892
pf pot-pourri: A. Velebín Urbánek n.d.

*Noc Šimona a Judy*, see *Night of St Simon and St Jude, The*

*Oldřich and Božena* [*Oldřich a Božena*], zpěvohra, 3, Škroup; Chmelenský
1828; ET 14 Dec 1828
lost; two songs in *Věnec* (1835), (1837)

*Oldřich and Božena*, see *Udalrich und Božena*

*Opera about the Peasant Rebellion* [*Opera o sedlské rebelii*; many variant titles, e.g. *Opera de rebellion Boemica rusticorum*], [Singspiel], 1, Jan Antoš
1775–7
libretto and variants in Němeček 1954, 101–14, 145–57; excerpts in Pohanka 1958, 162–4

*Opera bohemica de camino a caementariis luride aedificato seu Pugna inter patrem familias et murarios* [title also in Czech; text in Czech; also known as *Operella iucunda*], [Singspiel], 1, Loos
before 1772
short score in Pohanka 1958, 152–61

*Opilý muž*, see *Drunken Man, The*

*Osud*, see *Fate*


*Pád Arkuna*, see *Fall of Arkona, The*

*Paní mincmistrová*, see *Mintmaster's Wife, The*

*Pargamotéka* [ = corruption of 'pragmatická', i.e. Pragmatic Sanction], opera, 2, Alanus [Ignác] Plumlovský
1747
libretto in Petrů 1985, 34–62; no music survives

*Počátek románu*, see *Beginning of a Romance, The*

*Poklad*, see *Treasure, The*

*Popelka*, see *Cinderella*

*Poupě*, see *Bud, The*

*Prague Brewers, The* [*Pražští sládci*], opera (1st perf.), Singspiel (2nd perf.), 2, V. Tuček; Prokop Šedivý
Prague u Hybernů Theatre 28 Sept 1795
libretto, Prague 1819; no music survives

*Pražští sládci*, see *Prague Brewers, The*

*Příhody Lišky Bystroušky*, see *Cunning Little Vixen, The*

*Prodaná nevěsta*, see *Bartered Bride, The*

*Psohlavci*, see *Dogheads, The*


*Recruiting at the Horse Fair* [*Verbování na koňskému trhu*], [Singspiel], Jan Tuček
performed at St Václav seminary, Prague, Carnival *c*1770
no music survives

*Rector and General* [*Rektor a generál*; *Der Rekrut*], comic opera, 3, Skuherský; Czech libretto by Züngel on E.B.S. Raupach's play *Vor hundert Jahren*
German version before 1866; Czech version, PT 28 March 1873
pf pot-pourri: Starý n.d.

*Rekrut, Der*, see *Rector and General*

*Rektor a generál*, see *Rector and General*

*Rusalka*, lyric fairy-tale, 3, Dvořák; Kvapil after Fouqué's tale *Undine*
1900; NT 31 March 1901
MU 1905, SNKLHU 1960 (ed. K. Šolc), 1981; full score: SV 1960
S r1952 (Krombholc); S r1961 (Chalabala); S r1982–3 (Neumann)

*Šárka*, zpěvohra, 3, Fibich; Schulzová
1897; NT 28 Dec 1897
FAU [1897], 4/1950
S r1953 (Chalabala); S r1978 (Štych)

*Šárka*, heroic opera [bohatýrská zpěvohra], 3, Janáček; Zeyer
1887, 1888, rev. 1918, Act 3 orchestrated by O. Chlubna 1918, rev. 1924–5; Brno NT
11 Nov 1925

*Satanella*, opera, 3, Rozkošný; Karel Kádner after Vrchlický's epic poem
1897–8; NT 5 Oct 1898

*Secret, The* [*Tajemství*], comic opera, 3, Smetana; Krásnohorská
1877–8; NCT 18 Sept 1878
HM [1892], SNKLHU 1958 (ed. F. Bartoš); full score: SV x 1953
S r1953 (Krombholc); S r1981–2 (Košler)

*Šelma sedlák*, see *Cunning Peasant, The*

*Sládci*, see *Brewers, The*

*Srdce*, see *Heart, The*

*Starý ženich*, see *Elderly Suitor, The*

*St John's Rapids, The* [*Svatojanské proudy*], romantic opera, 4, Rozkošný; Rüffer (in
German), trans. Šubert
1869; PT 3 Oct 1871
HM 1882

*Stoja*, opera, 1, Rozkošný; Otakar Kučera after J.D. Konrád's story
1893; NT 6 June 1894
pf pot-pourri: FAU n.d.

*Stubborn Lovers, The* [*Tvrdé palice*], comic opera, 1, Dvořák; Josef Štolba
1874; NCT 2 Oct 1881
Simrock 1882, Simrock/HM 1913

*Švanda dudák*, see *Švanda the Bagpiper*

*Švanda the Bagpiper* [*Švanda dudák*], opera, 3, Bendl; Vrchlický after the folk tale
as cantata NCT 16 May 1880; Prague Hlahol 18 Feb 1883 (rev. version); rewritten as an
'opera-ballet' 1895–6; NT 29 April 1907
cantata: FAU [1883]

*Švanda the Bagpiper* [*Švanda dudák*], lyric-romantic zpěvohra, 3 and prologue,
Hřímalý; Böhm (rev. Karel Želenský) after Tyl's play *Strakonický dudák* [The Bagpiper of Strakonice]
1885; Plzeň City Theatre 20 Jan 1896

*Švanda (Schwanda) the Bagpiper* [*Švanda dudák*], opera (described in German on dual-
language vocal score as 'Volksoper'), 2, Weinberger; Miloš Kareš with additions by
Max Brod
NT 27 April 1927
UE 1927
CBS p1981 (Wallberg; in German)

*Svatojanské proudy*, see *St John's Rapids, The*

*Švédové v Praze*, see *Swedes in Prague, The*

*Swedes in Prague, The* [*Švédové v Praze*], historical zpěvohra, 3, J.N. Škroup; Josef Pečírka
1845; ET 26 Jan 1845 (Act 1), PT 22 April 1867 (complete)

*Tajemství*, see *Secret, The*

*Tempest, The* [*Bouře*], zpěvohra, 3, Fibich; Vrchlický after Shakespeare's play
1894; NT 1 March 1895
FAU [1895]
excerpts: S r1957, 1960 (Bartl)

*Templáři na Moravě*, see *Templars in Moravia, The*

*Templars in Moravia, The* [*Templáři na Moravě*], romantic opera, 3, Šebor; Sabina
1865; PT 19 Oct 1865
pf pot-pourri: Wetzler n.d.

*Tinker, The* [*Dráteník*], zpěvohra, 2, Škroup; J.K. Chmelenský
1825; ET 2 Feb 1826
HM 1927

*Treasure, The* [*Paklad*], or *Dearest Treasure, The* [*Nejdražší poklad*], romantic comic zpěvohra, 3, Pozděna, an adaptation of Kott's *Žižka's Oak*
by 1863 (submitted for Harrach competition)

*Tvrdé palice*, see *Stubborn Lovers, The*

*Two Widows, The* [*Dvě vdovy*], comic opera, 2, Smetana; Züngel after Mallefille's play *Les deux veuves*
1873–4, rev.1877, rev.1882; PT 27 March 1874 (with spoken dialogue); PT 15 March
· 1878 (with recitatives and extra numbers)
Bote & Bock 1893 (in 3 acts, with extra numbers written for Hamburg), HM 1914 (1877 version), HM 7/1949; full score: SV vii 1950
S r1956 (Krombholc); S r1975 (Jílek)

*Udalrich und Božena*, romantic opera, 3, Škroup (in German); F.V. Ernst
ET 12 Feb 1833; trans. Tyl as *Oldřich a Božena*, ET 31 Oct 1847

*Vanda*, grand zpěvohra, 5 (revised to 4), Dvořák; Julian Surzycki, trans. V. Beneš Šumavský and František Zákrejs
1875, rev. 1879, 1883; PT 17 April 1876; PT 13 Feb 1880 (four-act version with new overture)
Mazurka arr. for pf: Cranz 1912; Overture: Cranz [1885]; Fantasie, pf MU n.d.
S p1985 (Dyk, Prague Radio 1951)

*Věc Makropulos*, see *Makropulos Affair, The*

*Verbování na koňskému trhu*, see *Recruiting at the Horse Fair*

*Veselohra na mostě*, see *Comedy on the Bridge*

*Viola*, comic opera, 3, Smetana; Krásnohorská after Shakespeare's play *Twelfth Night*
1874, 1883–4, incomplete; Academic Orchestra 15 March 1900 (concert perf.); NT 11 May 1924
HM [1902] (with *The Devil's Wall*), 3/1946 (alone)
S r1982 (Košler)

*Vladimír, God's Chosen One* [*Vladimír, bohův zvolenec; Der Apostat*], heroic zpěvohra, 4, Skuherský; H. Mostecký [pseudonym of Josef F. Frič]
1860 (in German); PT 27 Sept 1863
no libretto published

*Vlasta*, 3?, Hynek Palla; Krásnohorská
1870–81?, incomplete

*Vlasty skon*, see *Death of Vlasta, The*

*V studni*, see *In the Well*

*Výlet pana Broučka do měsíce*, see *Excursion of Mr Brouček to the Moon, The* (Moor), *Excursions of Mr Brouček, The* (Janáček)

*Výlet pana Broučka do XV. století*, see *Excursions of Mr Brouček, The*

*Výlet pana Broučka z měsíce na výstavu*, see *Excursion of Mr Brouček from the Moon to the Exhibition, The*

*Výlety páně Broučkovy*, see *Excursions of Mr Brouček, The*

*Way through the Window, The* [*Cesta oknem*], comic opera, 1, Kovařovic; Züngel, after Eugène Scribe and Gustave Lemoine's comedy *Une femme, qui se jette par la fenêtre*
1885; NT 11 Feb 1886
FAU [1885]

*Záboj*, historical opera, 3, Zvonař; A.V. Šmilovský
1859–62; excerpts only 1863, 1865
no libretto published

*Zakletý princ*, see *Enchanted Prince, The*

*Zamilovaný ponocný*, see *Lovelorn Nightwatchman, The*

*Záviš z Falkenštejna* [*Záviš of Falkenštejn*], grand historical–romantic opera, 4, Rozkošný; Böhm after Hálek's tragedy
1871–7; PT 14 Oct 1877

*Ženichové*, see *Bridegrooms, The*

*Zítek, čaroděj krále Václava*, see *Zítek, Magician to King Václav*

*Zítek, Magician to King Václav* [*Zítek, čaroděj krále Václava*], comic opera, 3, Blodek; Sabina
1869, incomplete; completed by F.X. Váňa, NT 2 Oct 1934
excerpts: S r1982 (Štych)

*Žižka's Oak* [*Žižkův dub*], romantic zpěvohra, 2, Kott (later adapted by Pozděna as *The Treasure/The Dearest Treasure*); Klicpera
Brno 28 Nov 1841

*Žižkův dub*, see *Žižka's Oak*

*Žmařená svatba*, see *Frustrated Wedding, The*

*Z mrtvého domu*, see *From the House of the Dead*

*Zvíkovský rarášek*, see *Imp of Zvíkov, The*

# Index

All operas are listed here under their composers, and librettos under their librettists. An alphabetical listing in English and in Czech of all Czech operas referred to in the book can be found on p. 321.

Index

# Index

# Index

Smetana, Bedřich (*cont.*)
chamber works
*Fantaisie sur un air Bohémien*, 217
String Quartet 'From my Life', 11, 71,
217, 232
'Notebook of Motifs', 224, 259, 263
orchestral works
*Hakon Jarl*, 69, 227
*My Fatherland (Má vlast)*, 10, 11, 69:
'Blaník', 135; 'From Bohemian Fields
and Groves', 107–8; 'Šárka', 142; 'Tábor',
134, 135; 'Vltava', 79–80, 152;
'Vyšehrad', 298
*Oldřich and Božena*, 128
*Richard III*, 69
*Wallenstein's Camp*, 69
piano works
*Charakteristische Variationen*, 218
Czech Dances, 128
*Fantasie concertante sur des chanson nation-
ales tchèques*, 218
*Six morceaux caractéristiques pour piano*, 68
Smetana, Bedřich: operas, 69–74
arias, 74: insertion arias, 110, 184
characters, singers, 33, 171–86, 195–6,
205: baritones, 172–4, 183, 186, 196,
205; basses, 185; buffo roles, 174–6,
185; female roles, 176–8, 183–4; tenors,
182, 186, 190–1, 205
choruses, 73–4, 226
duets, ensembles, 72–3, 104, 105,
109–10, 226, 229
folk elements, use of, 74, 217–32
foreign influences, 72, 73
patriotic affect in, 6–8
political philosophy, 73–4, 105, 157–9
Smetana's contribution to his librettos,
100–111
subject matter, 71, 109, 122, 145, 153–5,
156, 157, 167–8, 170, 171–2, 196
word-setting, 104–5, 258–64, 267–73,
275–81
*Ahasaver* (rejected libretto), 122
*The Bartered Bride*, 69, 71, 226–7, 321:
arias, strophic songs, set numbers, 73,
74, 225–6, 228, 270; characters, voice
types, singers, 155, 156, 172–80 *passim*,
183, 184, 185, 196, 197, 206, 226, 238;
choruses, ensembles, 73, 74, 226;
dances, 159, 226, 227–9; duets, 73,
228; and folk elements, 218–19, 222–3,
225–30; influence, 79, 82, 88, 213, 229,
236; libretto, *see under* Sabina, Karel;
music, 228–9, 276; productions, performances: in Prague, 38, 40, 46, 50,
52, 242, 243, elsewhere, 51, 55, 58,

102, 303 n.11; publication, xix, 78,
243; revisions, sketches, 71, 74, 102,
159, 225, 226, 228–9, 263, 270, 273, *see
also* spoken dialogue; reception, 226,
229; Smetana's comments, 103; spoken
dialogue, 71, 179, 180, 228, 258, 261,
279–80; subject matter, 103, 167, 171,
176, 187, 273; word-setting, 107,
174–5, 261–4, 270, 279–80
*The Brandenburgers in Bohemia*, 69, 71,
72, 76, 217, 322: arias, set numbers,
72, 74, 223–5, 228; characters, voice
types, 158, 160, 171, 172–3, 180, 184,
185, 190–1, 206–7; choruses, ensembles, 8, 72, 73, 144–5, 160, 226, 228;
folk elements, 74, 223–5, 229, 238;
foreign influences, 72, 104; libretto, *see
under* Sabina, Karel; music, 6–8, 72,
158–9, 228; patriotic words, 1, 6–8,
130; performances, productions, 30,
31; revisions, 74, 102; Smetana's comments, 302 n.1; subject matter, 71,
102–3, 129, 130, 145, 157–9, 171
*Dalibor*, 69, 71, 266, 323: arias, songs,
73, 74, 105, 186, 269–70; characters,
voice types, singers, 171–6 *passim*, 182,
183–6 *passim*, 196, 197, 205, 206, 207,
301 n.7; choruses, duets, ensembles,
72, 73, 105, 226; folk elements, 223,
226; German libretto, 2, 118, 266–70,
*see also under* Wenzig, Josef; music, 8,
105, 173, 228, 229; performances, publication, 30, 40, 50, 51, 113; reception,
223, 226, 229; revisions, 104–5; subject
matter, 71, 130–1, 162, 176, 177, 301
n.7; word-setting, 105, 267–70, 280
*The Devil's Wall*, 71, 108, 324: arias,
strophic songs, 108, 160, 226, 278–9;
characters, voice types, singers, 155,
160, 173–85 *passim*, 195, 203, 226;
choruses, ensembles, 72, 74, 110, 155,
226; folk element, 226; libretto, *see
under* Krásnohorská, Eliška; music,
145, 148, 155; performances, 31; revisions, 110–11; Smetana's comments,
109; subject matter, 109, 131, 145, 148,
167, 171, 176; word-setting, 278–9, *see
also under* Krásnohorská, Eliška
*The Kiss*, 71, 108, 328: arias, songs, 74,
110, 180, 225, 233; changes, 110;
characters, voice types, singers, 154,
156, 163, 171–7 *passim*, 180, 183, 184,
185, 190, 196, 206; choruses, ensembles, 72–3, 74, 109, 110, 153, 226;
dance element, 229–32; folk elements,
71, 74, 218, 219, 225, 229–32, 302–3
n.1; libretto, *see under* Krásnohorská,

348

# Index

351

# Index

# HEADLINES OF WORLD WAR I

Patience Coster

Evans

Evans Brothers Limited

# Contents

Pictures on page 4 show Captain Scott,
Book illustration, The *Titanic*,
George V and Queen Mary

Pictures on page 5 show Italian infantryman,
Tsar Nicholas II, Vladimir Ilyich Lenin,
Emmeline Pankhurst, signing the Armistice

**5**

# Introduction

World War I, the Great War, began in 1914 and ended in 1918. It marked the end of an old way of life in Europe. At the start of the twentieth century, wealthy landowners formed an upper class that kept up a high standard of living. They employed armies of servants to run their huge houses. These aristocrats sent their sons to private schools (called public schools in Britain). Here they were taught a strict code of behaviour. They were to become their countries' leaders. They believed it was right to die for the honour of one's family and one's country.

These young men became the officers on both sides in the war. They led their men 'over the top' of the trenches, and were often the first to die. The men they commanded had joined up with enormous enthusiasm. They, too, believed in their country, right or wrong. On both sides, they suffered appalling hardships. Millions died in the mud of France and Belgium and on the Russian (Eastern) front. Those who survived the horrors of World War I no longer believed in the notion of war as 'glorious'. They returned home believing that, from now on, things would be different.

As the dust of war began to settle, people started to question whether it had been worth fighting and why it had been fought at all. The immediate cause of World War I had been the assassination of an Austrian leader in the Balkans. But how had this regional event sparked a vast international conflict? Largely to blame were the old alliances and rivalries between European nations. These had become fragile and dangerous. Following the events in Sarajevo in June 1914, European states had tumbled one by one into a catastrophic and bloody war, like a house of cards falling.

In the USA, nobody wanted to go to war. But when the German U-boats continued to sink their ships, the USA joined the Allies. The USA survived World War I with her lands intact and her economy in good shape. In Europe and in the East, the survivors faced poverty and even starvation. Their towns and cities were in ruins. Men were clamouring for work, women were demanding voting rights, and a new struggle for personal equality was beginning. In Germany, Italy and Russia, leaders who promised a better world were certain of a following.

# 1910

# BUDGET ROW

February 14, London, England In the British Parliament a row is raging between the House of Commons and the House of Lords. Last year the Lords refused to agree the Liberal government's budget. The mainly Conservative Lords tend to vote against Prime Minister Asquith's government, which is not very strong.

# KING DIES SUDDENLY

May 6, London, England King Edward VII has died. Now there will be no quick solution to this government's problems. Mr Asquith had asked the King to allow 200 Liberals to be made peers (lords). Only the monarch may create peers. The King was considering this request when he fell ill.

# ELECTION NEWS

December 20, London The Liberals' success in the general election means that steps may be taken to reform Parliament.

# CRIPPEN SENTENCED

October 22, London, England Dr Hawley Crippen's trial for murder ended today. The jury heard how he poisoned his wife in January. He hid her body in his cellar and disappeared with his secretary, Ethel Le Neve. In July, Mrs Crippen's body was found. Dr Crippen and Miss Le Neve were discovered on board a ship bound for Canada. Crippen has been found guilty. He will be hanged next month.

Dr Crippen (with moustache) and Miss Le Neve leave the SS Montrose under arrest.

German and British royalty attend the funeral of King Edward VII.

# FUNERAL OF EDWARD VII

May 21, Windsor Castle, England Seven
European monarchs attended the
funeral of King Edward VII. The late
King's cousin, Kaiser Wilhelm II,
accompanied the Queen.

# US PRESIDENT IS HOME

June 19, New York, USA Former US president Theodore Roosevelt returned
home today after spending ten
months hunting in British East Africa.

esident Roosevelt (left, in hat) enjoys a picnic
h his family.

# ASSASSINATION ATTEMPT

June 15, Sarajevo, Bosnia-Herzegovina An attempt has been made on the life of the Governor of Bosnia, General Varesanin, during the state opening of parliament. A Serb student named Bogdan Zerajic fired five shots at the governor, but failed to kill him. Zerajic then shot himself. The dead student is said to be a member of the Black Hand, a group that wants Bosnia-Herzegovina to leave the Austrian Empire.

# FAMILY MEETING

November 4, Potsdam, Germany Tsar Nicholas of Russia is visiting Potsdam for a meeting with his cousin, Kaiser Wilhelm of Germany. The monarchs are discussing political issues concerning Russia and Germany. Following Austria's annexation of Bosnia-Herzegovina in 1908, the Tsar has been pleased to receive the Kaiser's assurance that Germany will not support Austrian ambitions in the Balkans.

# NEWS IN BRIEF...

## YOUNGSTERS PREPARE FOR ADVENTURE

February 6, New York Be prepared to meet America's first Boy Scouts! A group of boys met today to form a troop like those in Britain. American girls will be able to join a troop – the Camp Fire Girls.

## A FASHION SENSATION

September, London, England Fashionable women's skirts are now so tight at the ankle that walking is almost impossible. The Pope is shocked by the new fashion and has publicly condemned it.

Reduced to a 'Chinese toddle' in hobble skirts.

# PORTUGAL LOSES ITS KING

October 5, Lisbon, Portugal During the past hundred years, Portugal has been very unstable. Today there was a coup against King Manoel. After bloody fighting in the capital, the king fled to Gibraltar. The army and navy, who led the coup, have proclaimed Portugal a republic.

## HEAVENLY BODY

May 20, London, England Halley's comet, which visits our skies every 75 years, can be seen on clear nights. Comets are feared by some people as a bad omen.

# 1911

## THE SPIRIT OF UNREST
## STRIKING AND RIOTS IN BRITAIN

**August 17, London, England** About 200,000 British railway workers have come out on strike. Dockers at all the main ports have been on strike for two months. Shops are running short of food supplies. There is no coal or electricity in some towns and people have been rioting. The Home Secretary, Winston Churchill, has sent 50,000 troops to stop the riots. Armed soldiers are guarding railway stations and signal boxes. All over Europe, agricultural and industrial workers are striking and rioting for better pay and conditions. Governments may need to provide some social benefits for workers.

Troops and police arrive with armoured vehicles to confront strikers in Liverpool, England.

## HEATWAVE BRINGS TRAGEDY

August 30, London, England For once, the British weather has been too good. On August 8, the temperature soared to 36.7°C. More than 2,000 children have died in the heatwave.

## INSURANCE FOR ALL

December 16, London, England The government has announced that all low-paid workers in Britain are to receive health insurance. Now they can visit the doctor for free. Employers are complaining that they cannot afford to pay into this scheme, and many are cutting back on staff.

# ENGLISH ROYAL EVENTS

## THE KING IS CROWNED

June 22, London, England Today King George V and Queen Mary were crowned in Westminster Abbey. The Abbey was completely full. The congregation included lords, arch-bishops, members of parliament and representatives of the Empire. Motion picture cameras filmed the scene outside the Abbey, but they were not allowed inside.

The view from Buckingham Palace as the royal coach leaves for Westminster Abbey for King George V's coronation.

# CELEBRATIONS IN INDIA

**December 12, Delhi, India** Britain's King George V has been crowned Emperor of India before a huge crowd. The splendidly dressed princes of India were in attendance.

King George V and Queen Mary in Delhi.

# GERMAN TROOPS LAND IN MOROCCO

**July 2, Agadir, Morocco** Yesterday the Germans sent a gunboat, *Panther*, to the port of Agadir. Morocco has been under French protection since 1906, and Germany's action has alarmed France. Britain is concerned that Germany may establish a naval base at Agadir. With its large army, Germany is very powerful and the French and British are worried that it may be a threat to world peace. If Britain and France ally themselves against Germany, it is likely that war could follow. Talks between the three countries are planned soon. Meanwhile the Austrians and the British are building up their navies.

# ITALY ATTACKS LIBYA

**November 1, Tripoli, Libya** Italian marines have landed at Tripoli. Italy has also bombed towns and shelled ports in Libya. Turkey controls Libya, but the Turks have been neglecting their once-powerful empire, which includes countries in the Balkans. These countries may seize the chance to rebel against Turkey while her empire is weak.

# CHINA IS REBORN

**December 29, Peking, China** The Chinese people have ended the Manchu dynasty. The first president of the new Chinese republic intends to modernise China. He has forbidden men to wear pigtails, a hairstyle introduced by the first emperor of the Manchu dynasty in the 1600s.

A citizen of the new China has his pigtail removed.

# NEWS IN BRIEF...

## POPULATION INCREASE

April 8, London, England The British population has increased by almost 11 per cent in ten years. France's population has not changed. Russia's has increased by a third, to 160 million. In recent years the USA has welcomed thousands of immigrants. Many of them are from Eastern Europe and have emigrated to the USA in search of work. The US population has risen from 76 to 92 million.

## ATOMIC THEORY

May, Manchester, England The British physicist Ernest Rutherford has published a scientific paper about atomic theory. In it he describes an atom as a small, heavy nucleus surrounded by electrons. Scientists believe Rutherford's discovery will be of great significance as research continues in this field.

# CURIE WINS AWARD

December 10, Paris, France Marie Curie has been awarded her second Nobel Prize. Mme Curie has extracted pure radium from a rock called pitchblende.

# WHAT THE FASHIONABLE SET IS WEARING

Autumn, London, England Dressmakers and milliners have done good business in this Coronation year. Hats are very tall and topped with feathers. Skirts are long and straight. Blouses have a V-shaped neckline. Gentlemen are equally handsomely dressed. They go to the City in tail coats, striped trousers and top hats. In the country they may wear tweed jackets and plus-fours.

# 1912

# HOME RULE FOR IRELAND

**May 2, London, England** The British government wants Ireland to have its own parliament and run its own affairs. The Liberal government has introduced a Home Rule Bill. Many Protestants living in northern Ireland (Ulster) do not want Home Rule.

# ULSTER UNIONISTS SIGN COVENANT

**October 5, Belfast, Northern Ireland** Two hundred Ulster Unionists, members of a party that opposes Home Rule in Ireland, have signed a Covenant saying they will not recognise a Home Rule parliament. More than 237,000 men and 234,000 women have added their names to the Covenant.

# SECRET TREATY

**March** The Balkan states of Bulgaria and Serbia have signed an alliance with each other. It is thought that Russian diplomats have been secretly involved in bringing the two rival states together.

# GERMANY WITHDRAWS

**July 1, Fez, Morocco** By a treaty signed in Fez, France will in future control Morocco. The German Navy has been asked to leave. In exchange for their withdrawal from Agadir, the Germans will be given 154,000 sq km of French territory in the Congo.

The Ulster Covenant opposes a Home Rule. parliament in Ireland.

## Ulster's
### Solemn League and Covenant.

**B**eing convinced in our consciences that Home Rule would be disastrous to the material well-being of Ulster as well as of the whole of Ireland, subversive of our civil and religious freedom, destructive of our citizenship and perilous to the unity of the Empire, we, whose names are underwritten, men of Ulster, loyal subjects of His Gracious Majesty King George V., humbly relying on the God whom our fathers in days of stress and trial confidently trusted, do hereby pledge ourselves in solemn Covenant throughout this our time of threatened calamity to stand by one another in defending for ourselves and our children our cherished position of equal citizenship in the United Kingdom and in using all means which may be found necessary to defeat the present conspiracy to set up a Home Rule Parliament in Ireland. ¶ And in the event of such a Parliament being forced upon us we further solemnly and mutually pledge ourselves to refuse to recognise its authority. ¶ In sure confidence that God will defend the right we hereto subscribe our names. ¶ And further, we individually declare that we have not already signed this Covenant.

The above was signed by me at _____
"Ulster Day," Saturday, 28th September, 1912.

### God Save the King.

# WOMEN WANT THE VOTE

**March 1, London, England** Today a group of women smashed almost all the shop windows in three of London's smartest streets. They are suffragettes, who demand that women should be allowed to vote for MPs. Their leader, Emmeline Pankhurst, smashed the windows of No. 10 Downing Street, the prime minister's residence. Mrs Pankhurst has been arrested (right).

# WAR FLARES IN BALKANS

**November 30, Sofia, Bulgaria** Romania, Serbia, Montenegro, Bulgaria and Greece have formed the 'Balkan League'. The League is fighting Turkey and its dwindling empire. It has pushed the Turks out of European Turkey, apart from the area around Constantinople. Turkey has governed these provinces very badly and the Turkish government is weak and inefficient. The Great Powers are concerned that the Balkan League will gain too much land influence. For the first time, aircraft are being used to watch over troop movements in the battle zone.

# TITANIC SINKS

**April 14, New York, USA** The ocean liner *Titanic* has hit an iceberg on her first voyage across the Atlantic. There were not enough lifeboats for all the passengers, and more than 1,580 people are feared drowned.

Passengers escape in lifeboats from the sinking *Titanic*. A survivor said that the ship turned gradually on her nose, 'like a duck that goes for a dive.'

# AMERICAN INDIAN IS OLYMPIC HERO

**July 22, Stockholm, Sweden** A record number of competitors have taken part in the Olympic Games. This year's hero is an American Indian named Jim Thorpe (below). He won both the pentathlon (five events) and the decathlon (ten events).

The opening ceremony of the Olympic Games.

# ITALIANS REMAIN IN LIBYA

**October 18, Tripoli, Libya** According to the Treaty of Lausanne, signed today, Italy's occupation of Libya is legal. Turkey is defeated. The Turks are sending their troops to the Balkan provinces, where they are fighting a losing battle with the Balkan League. The Great Powers are anxious to ensure that this war does not spread beyond the Balkans.

# NEWS IN BRIEF...

## NEW US PRESIDENT

**November 5, Washington DC, USA** The Democratic Party has won the US presidential election. Woodrow Wilson succeeds William Taft as president. Wilson said the country needs 'New Freedom' in politics and a strong government.

# NAVY TO MODERNISE

**July 22, London, England** The First Lord of the Admiralty, Winston Churchill, has asked the government for money to improve the fleet. He wants all warships' engines to run on oil rather than coal. Mr Churchill is alarmed at the growing strength of the German Navy.

# DEFENCE AGREEMENT

**July** As a consequence of the crisis in Morocco, Britain and France have made an agreement. It states that, in the event of a major war in Europe, the British fleet will guard the North Sea and the English channel. The French fleet will guard the Mediterranean Sea.

# 1913

| | |
|---|---|
| May 30 | Treaty of London ends Balkan War |
| June 29 | Second Balkan War begins |
| July 9 | Bulgaria defeated at Battle of Bregalnica |
| August 10 | Treaty of Bucharest ends Second Balkan War |
| September 29 | Treaty of Constantinople signed |
| November | Liman von Sanders crisis begins |

# TROUBLE IN THE BALKANS

## YOUNG TURKS DISMISS TREATY

January 23, Constantinople, Turkey The Turkish government has been over-thrown by a political party called the Young Turks. Its members object to a treaty that was signed last month with the Balkan League. The treaty stated that Turkey should give up her lands in Europe.

## NEW TREATY ENDS WAR

May 30, London, England Diplomats from the major European powers have today signed a treaty to end the Balkan War. Austria is concerned that Serbia, a member of the Balkan League, is becoming too powerful. A new state, Albania, is to be created. This will prevent Serbia gaining a coastline on the Adriatic Sea. Serbia has been given lands in Macedonia as compensation.

# WAR STARTS AGAIN

June 29, London, England Bulgaria has invaded Serbia, in a declaration of war. The Greek army is advancing on Serbian positions in the south. Romania and Turkey are concerned that Bulgaria is becoming too strong. Their armies are also advancing on Bulgarian positions. Who knows how this state of affairs will end?

## SUFFRAGETTE KILLED AT RACES

June 14, London, England Thousands of women have attended the funeral of suffragette Emily Davison. She died when she threw herself in front of the King's horse at Epsom races.

# GOVERNMENT PLAYS CAT AND MOUSE

**March 31, London, England** By a new Act of Parliament, suffragettes on hunger strike in prison will be temporarily released. The suffragettes call this the 'Cat and Mouse Act': the cat lets the mouse go, then pounces on it again.

# BRAVE EXPLORERS HONOURED

**February 14, London, England** A memorial service has been held at St Paul's Cathedral for Captain Scott and his companions who died in the Antarctic. Last week a search party found their bodies. They were in a snow-covered tent 17 km (11 miles) from their supply base. The men had died because they had been too weak to reach their supplies.

Captain Scott and his team at the South Pole.

# BALKANS HAVE NEW BOUNDARIES

**August 10, Bucharest, Romania** According to a peace treaty signed today, the Balkan countries have agreed how to divide the lands. Serbia, Romania and Greece have all gained territory, but Bulgaria has gained little. The Balkan Wars nearly resulted in a wider European conflict. The British Foreign Secretary has said, "We are sitting on gunpowder."

# BULGARIA DEFEATED

**July 31, Bulgaria** Serbia has defeated Bulgaria in a decisive battle. Tsar Nicholas of Russia has been trying to agree a peace deal between the two countries, without success. Russia is angry with Bulgaria for going to war.

# RUSSO-GERMAN CRISIS

November, Constantinople, Turkey Russia is angry that a German officer, Otto Liman von Sanders, has been sent to train the Turkish army. Russia suspects that Germany may want to extend its influence in Turkey.

# DRIVE ENDS IN TRAGEDY

April 20, Paris, France Two children and their governess have drowned in a tragic accident. The car they were driving in plunged into a river. The children's mother is the famous dancer, Isadora Duncan.

# NEWS IN BRIEF...

## NO TO CHANNEL TUNNEL

August 5, London, England The British government no longer plans to build a tunnel beneath the English Channel. The government is afraid that it would make England easy to invade.

## BALKAN TREATY SIGNED

September 29, Constantinople, Turkey Bulgaria and Turkey today signed a peace treaty with each other. Both countries have been severely weakened by the recent Balkan Wars. There is a growing sense of concern among other European countries about the extent of German influence in Turkey and Bulgaria.

# WHICH IS THE NUDE?

March 30, Chicago, USA Artist Marcel Duchamp has caused a stir with his painting entitled *Nude Descending a Staircase*.

# SKYSCRAPER CITY

April 24, New York, USA At 422 m (1,384 ft) high, the new Woolworth building is the tallest in the world.

# IRELAND IS ON EDGE

December 4, London, England The situation in Ireland is tense. The Home Rule Bill was passed by the House of Commons in January, but the Lords rejected it. They sympathise with the Ulster Unionists.

## ZEPPELIN DISASTER

October 17, Berlin, Germany The world's largest airship, the Zeppelin *L2*, has exploded in the worst disaster of its kind to date. Twenty-seven passengers have been killed.

# 1914

| | |
|---|---|
| June 28 | Archduke and Duchess shot dead |
| August 4 | Britain joins the war against Austria and Germany |
| August 23 | Battle of Mons begins |
| August 30 | Russians lose Battle of Tannenburg |
| October 14 | Battle of the Marne |
| November 11 | Enormous casualties at Ypres |
| December 25 | British and German troops observe one-day truce |

# MARCHING TO WAR

## ARCHDUKE IS SHOT DEAD

**June 28, Sarajevo, Bosnia-Herzegovina** The Austrian Archduke Franz Ferdinand and his wife have been shot dead. They were visiting the Balkan province of Bosnia-Herzegovina, part of the Austrian Empire. The killer is a Serbian student named Gavrilo Princip.

Archduke Franz Ferdinand and the Duchess Sophie shortly before their assassination.

## SERBIA BLAMED FOR MURDER

**August 4, London, England** The murder in Sarajevo has started a great war. The Austrians are blaming the Serbian government for planning it. Austria has declared war on Serbia, and on Russia because it supports Serbia. France supports Russia. Germany has sided with Austria and declared war on Russia and France. German troops have invaded Belgium. Britain has a treaty with Belgium and has declared war on Germany.

Soldiers are being recruited at offices all over Britain. This one is in Trafalgar Square, London.

## THE BEF LEAVES FOR FRANCE

**August 7, Southampton, England** Crowds lined the streets today to watch the British Expeditionary Force (BEF) leave for France.

# BOTH ARMIES MARCH SOUTH

September 2, France After fierce fighting at Mons in Belgium, the BEF has withdrawn to the south. The men have had very little rest or food, and their new boots are causing blistered and swollen feet. They have marched 320 km (200 miles) in 13 days. The Royal Flying Corps is watching from the air as the Germans march towards Paris.

# BATTLE OF THE MARNE

October 14, Ypres, Flanders German soldiers have been recalled to defend their eastern boundary from Russian attack. The remaining troops have been driven back across the Marne River. They have suffered heavy casualties. The Allied armies have now marched north to Ypres in Flanders. They are digging trenches for protection on the flat plain. The Germans cannot now take Paris, but are trying to reach the port of Calais.

# TRENCH WARFARE

November 11, Ypres, Flanders One side shells its opponent's trenches, then their soldiers advance. The survivors in the trench fire on the advancing soldiers. Shells and rifle-fire cause enormous numbers of casualties. Both sides are exhausted.

# GERMANY COUNTS HER LOSSES

November 15, Ypres, Flanders From a German report: 'We have 134,000 dead and wounded. Most of them are very young men, straight from school or university.'

# BRITISH WIN FALKLANDS BATTLE

December 11, London, England The Royal Navy is celebrating the sinking of four German battleships today. The German Navy was trying to capture the Falkland Islands, which are British owned. But two British battleships surprised them and attacked, with guns blazing.

German and British soldiers meet on friendly terms on Christmas Day.

# CHRISTMAS TRUCE

December 25, Ypres, Flanders Today has been one of goodwill, with no guns fired. Men from both sides walked into 'no man's land' and talked and smoked together. The fighting will start again tomorrow.

# THE EASTERN FRONT

## GERMAN VICTORY OVER RUSSIA

**August 30, Tannenburg, East Prussia** The Russians have two armies in East Prussia. They contain many young recruits and they are not as well trained as the German troops. The Germans outmanoeuvred the Russians at the Battle of Tannenburg. The Germans, led by General von Hindenburg, took 120,000 prisoners. The Russian advance has been halted.

# NEWS IN BRIEF...
# BIG BERTHA

**August 15, Liege, Belgium** The Germans have developed a huge mobile gun. It is known as 'Big Bertha' and is named after the wife of its inventor, Gustav Krupp! The gun is being used to shell Allied troop positions in Liege.

## CLOSE TO PARIS

**September 5, France** The German army is so close to Paris that soldiers can see the Eiffel Tower in the distance.

# RUSSIANS BATTLE FOR POLAND

**November 25, Poland** The Russians are fighting to keep the German army out of Poland. Four days ago they had the Germans surrounded. Suddenly the Germans cut through the Russian lines, taking 16,000 prisoners.

## CASUALTIES OF WAR

**November** More than 80,000 British soldiers have been wounded or killed in the past three months. The French casualties are 50,000. In Britain more than one million men have volunteered for the army.

## CARS ARE BIG BUSINESS

**January 5, Detroit, USA** Henry Ford's car factory is doubling workers' wages to a minimum of $5 a day.

Mr Ford's cars are no longer built one at a time. The parts are put together on an assembly line.

# 1915

| | |
|---|---|
| January 1 | Turks blockade Russia at the Dardanelles |
| April 22 | Poison gas used at Ypres |
| April 25 | Allies land at Gallipoli |
| May 8 | Germans sink *Lusitania* |
| October 12 | Edith Cavell executed |
| December 21 | Serbia defeated by Germany and Bulgaria |
| December 31 | Defeated Allies leave Gallipoli |

# THE GALLIPOLI CAMPAIGN

## DARDANELLES CLOSED TO SHIPPING

January 1, London, England Russia is cut off from her allies. Turkey will not allow any Russian ships through the Dardanelles, Russia's main route to the Mediterranean and Aegean seas.

## DISASTER IN DARDANELLES

March 19, London, England A fleet of Allied battleships has tried to sail through the Dardanelles. The Turks fired on the fleet from both sides of the peninsula. A French battleship exploded and two British battleships hit mines and were sunk.

## SOLDIERS FACE GAS HORROR

April 22, Ypres, Flanders The Germans are using a new weapon, poison gas, which burns the eyes, throat and lungs. Stretcher bearers are carrying victims to the Red Cross tents behind the lines.

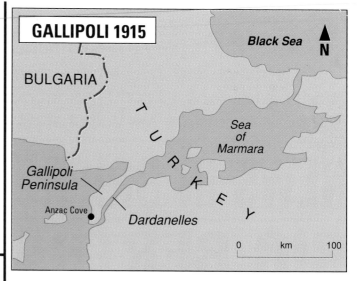

# ALLIES LAND AT GALLIPOLI

April 25, London, England Under Turkish fire, the Allies have landed men on the Gallipoli peninsula at the entrance to the Dardanelles. Hundreds of men have been killed. Hospital ships have taken the wounded to Egypt. The soldiers climbed huge cliffs under fire, then dug trenches for cover. There are too few men left to carry out a proper attack. The troops are from many different countries, including Britain, France, Australia and New Zealand.

*The Landing* by George Lambert (right) shows Anzac troops scaling cliffs at the Dardanelles.

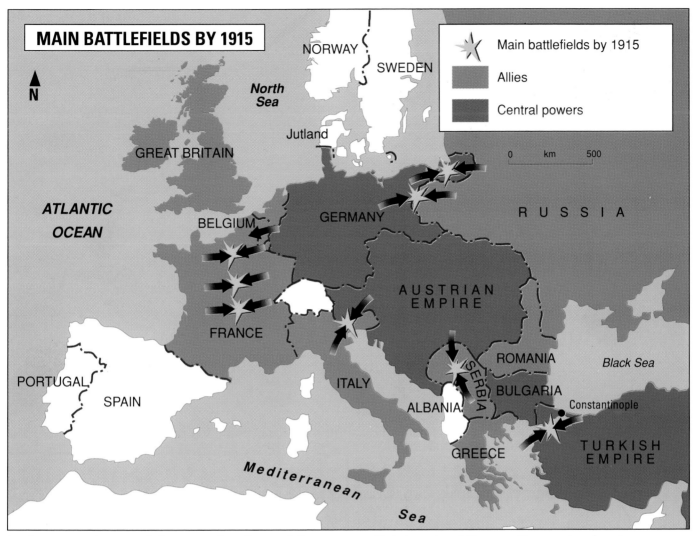

## MAIN BATTLEFIELDS BY 1915

N

NORWAY

SWEDEN

North Sea

Jutland

GREAT BRITAIN

ATLANTIC OCEAN

BELGIUM

GERMANY

R U S S I A

FRANCE

AUSTRIAN EMPIRE

PORTUGAL

SPAIN

ITALY

SERBIA

ROMANIA

BULGARIA

Black Sea

ALBANIA

Constantinople

GREECE

TURKISH EMPIRE

Mediterranean Sea

Main battlefields by 1915

Allies

Central powers

0   km   500

In the second year of the war, the Central Powers are fighting the Allies on five major fronts.

Turkish guns at Gallipoli.

French soldiers in their trenches.

British troop positions at Anzac Cove.

# NO ADVANCE AT GALLIPOLI

**June 25, London, England** The Allies have landed more troops at Gallipoli. The weather is very hot, many men have died of dysentry, and the fighting goes on day and night. The Turks are determined not to surrender the peninsula. If they did, the Allies could take the capital, Constantinople.

# TORPEDO SINKS BRITISH LINER

**May 8, London, England** A German U-boat has torpedoed the British passenger ship, the *Lusitania*. More than 100 Americans were among the 1,200 people who drowned. U-boats have sunk hundreds of merchant ships. The Germans are trying to stop food reaching Britain.

# TROOPS LEAVE GALLIPOLI

**December 31, London, England** The Germans are sending troops to help the Turks. The Allies cannot hope to win; their soldiers are boarding troop ships. The retreat will go on into the New Year. The campaign has left 30,000 dead and 74,000 wounded.

# GERMAN PLANS REVEALED

**July 24, New York, USA** Although the USA and Germany are not at war, German secret agents are spying in America. A US secret service man has uncovered German plans to wreck US ships and factories. Two German officials have been asked to leave the USA.

# NURSE SHOT IN BELGIUM

October 12, Brussels, Belgium Miss Edith Cavell, a British nurse, was shot by the Germans this morning. The Germans discovered that she had helped British soldiers to escape.

# SERBIA IS DEFEATED

December 21, Serbia  The Germans now occupy Poland. The Bulgarians have joined the war on Germany's side and captured Serbia. The Serbs are fleeing.

The Germans executed Edith Cavell for treason.

# NEWS IN BRIEF...

## GERMAN PLANE BROUGHT DOWN

April 1, France A German aircraft has been shot down by a French plane using an ingenious invention. The pilot, Roland Garros, has developed a way of firing a machine gun through the propeller of his aircraft. He added steel plates to the propeller blades, to divert the bullets. Up until now, pilots have relied on taking 'pot-shots' at one another with a revolver or rifle.

# NAVAL ATTACK

January The German First High Fleet has bombarded the British coastal towns of Hartlepool, Whitby and Scarborough. The naval attack has left eighteen civilians dead.

# ZEPPELIN RAID

May 31, London, England A bombing raid on London by German Zeppelin airships has left 28 people dead and 60 injured. The British government fears there could be further raids in the months to come.

# POET DIES AT SEA

April 23, Greece Rupert Brooke, the British poet, died today of blood poisoning. He was 27 years old. Brooke (below) was an officer on a ship sailing for the Dardanelles. He will be buried on the Greek island of Skyros.

# 1916

| February 13 | Women enrol in war jobs |
| May 31 | Battle of Jutland |
| June 5 | Lord Kitchener drowns at sea |
| June 24 | French withstand German siege at Verdun |
| July 1 | Record casualties on the Somme |
| September 15 | Russian success with the Brusilov offensive |

# THE WAR AT SEA

## U-BOATS SINK NEUTRAL SHIPS

**April 18, Washington DC, USA** German U-boats continue to sink the ships of countries that are not at war. Some of these are US ships. Last year Germany apologised to the USA for the sinking of the *Lusitania*.

## WARSHIPS FIGHT FIERCEST BATTLE

**June 1, London, England** A bloody battle involving 259 warships and 100,000 men has been fought in the North Sea off Jutland. British and German fleets bombarded each other with shells, torpedoes and guns. Many ships were sunk and hundreds of sailors killed.

## WOMEN DO WAR WORK

**February 13, London** 400,000 women have joined a new Land Army. 80,000 women have joined the Voluntary Aid Detachment (VAD), working in hospitals and driving ambulances.

# NEWS FROM THE BATTLEFIELDS

## 'THEY SHALL NOT PASS,' SAY FRENCH

**June 24, Verdun, France** The Germans have bombarded French troops with more than two million shells. They want to capture the steel-and-concrete fortresses that ring the town of Verdun. The casualties are appalling.

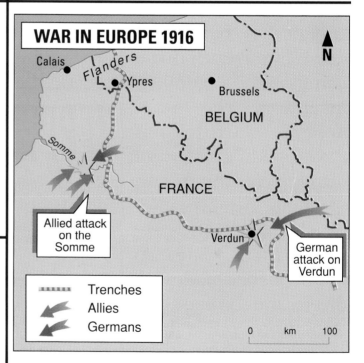

A map showing the major battles of 1916, fought between enemy trenches in Belgium and France.

# WAR MINISTER IS DEAD

**June 5, London, England** The British Secretary for War, Lord Kitchener, has perished at sea. He was sailing to Russia to talk with the Tsar about new battle plans when his cruiser hit a mine and sank. Lord Kitchener's recruiting poster is well known to British people.

# BRITISH ADVANCE IN TANKS

**September 15, France** Today, 18 British armoured tanks crossed the boggy craters and fallen trees of no man's land. From close range they fired on German positions. The crews report that the tanks are dreadfully noisy and stiflingly hot, but that they may change the way the war is fought.

# PORTUGAL ENTERS WAR

**February, Lisbon** Germany has formally declared war on Portugal. This is because the Portuguese government has ordered its navy to seize German ships in its harbours.

# SOMME CASUALTIES

**July 1, France** The British have bombarded the Germans on a front 28 km (17 miles) long to relieve pressure on the French at Verdun. Nearly two million men have died at Verdun and on the Somme.

# EASTER RISING

**May 12, Dublin, Ireland** Troops have had to be recalled from France and Belgium to go to Ireland. Two weeks ago, 1,000 Irish nationalists proclaimed an Irish Republic. After a fierce battle, British troops restored order.

Explorer Ernest Shackleton in arctic gear.

# GREAT EXPLORER IS RESCUED

**August 30, London, England** Two years ago, Ernest Shackleton set out with a team of explorers to cross Antarctica. The team's ship became trapped in pack-ice and drifted for nine months. At last the explorers escaped to a remote island. A relief expedition has now picked up all the men.

# SURPRISE ATTACK SUCCEEDS

**September 15, Eastern Front** On June 4, the Austrian Archduke's birthday party was interrupted by a surprise Russian attack. The Russians advanced on the Austrian army and now occupy 100 km (62 miles) of enemy territory. The attack was co-ordinated by Commander Alexei Brusilov.

# ELECTIONS IN US AND BRITAIN

**December 7, Washington DC, USA** Last month Woodrow Wilson was re-elected president of the USA. In Britain, the new prime minister, David Lloyd George, is determined to bring the war to a speedy finish.

The four allied leaders. Woodrow Wilson is on the right.

# A VIEW FROM THE TRENCHES

**France** "If only the people of England could have seen what I saw yesterday they would not grumble about air raids. I saw motor lorries sunk in the mud over the wheels, also horses with just part of their heads showing above the swamp....

There are men now in the trenches full of water who are nearly dead, they are fast dying of cold, they go sick, see the doctor, go back and try to stick it until they get relieved..."

(Soldier Daniel Sweeney from *Greater Love*, ed. M. Moynihan, W. H. Allen, 1980)

# US TROOPS ENTER MEXICO

June 21, Mexico US troops have entered Mexico in search of a rebel named Pancho Villa (centre, below). He has led raids across the border into North America. The Americans are taking tough action to protect their citizens. They fear that war may break out between the USA and Mexico.

# NEWS IN BRIEF...

## SERBS SALUTE EXTRAORDINARY WOMAN

November 30, Belgrade, Serbia Flora Sandes was nursing in Serbia when the Serbian army fled into Albania last December. She dressed as a man and joined the army. She was seriously wounded fighting the Turks. The Serbs have given her a bravery medal.

# VICTORIA CROSS FOR YOUNG HERO

July 6, London, England Royal Navy sailor Jack Cornwall has been posthumously awarded the VC. He died six weeks ago at the Battle of Jutland. He was only 16 years of age.

# VERDUN RECOVERY

December 18, Verdun, France The French army has retaken the forts of Douaumont and Vaux, capturing 11,000 prisoners.

# MOVIES MAKE MONEY

October 31, Hollywood, USA Hollywood film stars like Mary Pickford (below) now earn up to a million dollars per year.

# 1917

# REVOLUTION IN RUSSIA

## TSAR DEPOSED BY GENERALS

March 15, Petrograd, Russia Russian army generals have told Tsar Nicholas II that he must give up his throne. The Tsar is in charge of the army. The Russian people are sick of the war and blame him for the deaths of two million men in battle. They have asked the government to make peace with Germany. Meanwhile, starving people are rioting all over the country and factory workers are on strike.

## BOLSHEVIKS' BID FOR POWER

October 26, Petrograd, Russia The leader of the Bolshevik Party, Vladimir Lenin, wants to replace the weak government. Lenin's Red Guards seized the Winter Palace, the Russian seat of government, today. The Guards locked the government ministers in a cellar. Lenin is now ready to form a new socialist government.

# GERMAN TELEGRAM TO MEXICO

March 1, London, England The British government has intercepted a telegram from Germany promising support for Mexico if war should break out between Germany and the USA.

# RUSSIA BOWS OUT OF WAR

December 5, Brest-Litovsk, Poland The new Bolshevik government in Russia has signed an armistice with Germany and the other Central Powers. For the Russians, the war is over.

A portrait of the Bolshevik leader, Vladimir Lenin.

## ALLIES FACE HINDENBURG LINE

**March 30, Flanders** From a German report: "Our armies have been digging fortified trenches behind the front line, from Arras to Soissons. This Hindenburg Line is about 50 km (31 miles) long.... In front are many fences of barbed wire. No Allied troops will be able to cross it."

## AMERICA ENTERS THE WAR

**April 6, Washington DC, USA** President Wilson's government has declared war on the Germans. The president said: "The world must be made safe for democracy."

## THE AGONY OF WAR

**August 30, France** One of the worst battles of the war is being fought near the village of Passchendaele. It is raining all the time, and soldiers fight ankle deep in mud. Wounded men drown in shell-holes. The hail of shells and bullets never stops.

## YANKS JOIN UP IN THEIR MILLIONS

**June 5, Washington DC, USA** Recruiting offices opened for twelve hours today to cope with demand. Nearly ten million men have responded to posters like the one below and joined the US army.

## ITALIAN DEFEAT

**November 9, Italy** The Italians have been fighting the Austrians in northeast Italy with some success. Today, however, they were defeated at Caporetto. They have lost a huge area of land, and thousands of men to the German and Austrian armies.

# PLANES BOMB LONDON

June 14, London, England German planes launched a bombing raid on London yesterday. One bomb hit a school, killing many children.

# TURKISH ARMY RETREATS

December 9, Jerusalem Allied forces have taken Jerusalem, and the Turks are in retreat. Commander of the British forces is General Edmund Allenby.

# ENGLAND FACES FOOD SHORTAGES

March 20, London There is only about one month's supply of wheat left in Britain, and there are shortages of other foods too. These have been caused by U-boats sinking British merchant ships.

# WOMEN URGED TO JOIN NAVY

November 29, London, England The Admiralty wants to recruit women into the Navy. The women will be part of the newly formed Women's Royal Naval Service (WRNS).

# NEWS IN BRIEF...

## RED CROSS IS HONOURED

December 10, Stockholm, Sweden This year's Nobel Peace Prize has been awarded to the International Red Cross. Red Cross volunteers are working in appalling conditions on the battle fronts.

## BEF REMEMBERED

August 25, London, England A new decoration, the Mons Star, will be given to all those members of the BEF who fought at Mons and Ypres in 1914.

# GREEK KING DEPOSED

June 29, Greece Greece has entered the war on the side of the Allies. The pro-German king has been deposed.

# KING CHANGES NAME

July 17, London, England King George V has changed the name of the royal house to Windsor. The name was originally Saxe-Coburg-Gotha. The British king has abandoned all his family's German titles. He does not feel that such connections are acceptable now Britain is at war with Germany.

# BIRTH CONTROL ROW

September 30, New York Margaret Sanger has been sent to prison for opening a birth control clinic in the USA.

Mrs Margaret Sanger, pioneer of birth control.

# 1918

| April 10 | German troops advance from Hindenburg Line |
| August 8 | Allies push Germans back |
| October 3 | Arabs and Allenby take Damascus from Turks |
| November 4 | Wilfred Owen dies |
| November 11 | Armistice is signed |
| December 14 | Lloyd George wins British general election |

## GERMANS LAUNCH ATTACK

**April 10, France** Germany's peace treaty with Russia has enabled her to move troops from the Eastern to the Western Front. A week ago, a million German soldiers advanced from the Hindenburg Line towards the River Marne. They bombarded the Allied trenches for five hours. The Allied army is retreating.

Woodrow Wilson has been re-elected as president of the USA. Americans support his decision to enter the war in support of the Allies.

## GERMAN ACE PILOT KILLED

**April 21, France** The Red Baron has been shot down and killed by ground fire. This German airman was famous for flying his distinctive red plane with great skill and courage. He was responsible for shooting down 80 Allied aircraft.

Manfred von Richthofen – the Red Baron.

# ALLIES SUDDENLY GAIN GROUND

**August 8, Amiens, France** Away from the Hindenburg Line, the German troops are not well protected. The Allies are attacking German gun positions and bombing their trenches. US soldiers are pouring into Europe. Hundreds of Germans are surrendering every day.

The French and British armies advance near Amiens.

# TURKS ARE OUT OF THE WAR

**October 3, Damascus** The Turks are defeated. The Allies control Damascus. Arab troops led by Emir Feisal and an Englishman, Lt. Col. T. E. Lawrence, have driven the Turks out of Arabia. They have also arrived at Damascus. The Turks have offered a reward of £20,000 for Lawrence.

A painting of T. E. Lawrence, the Englishman who led attacks on many Turkish troop trains.

# RUSSIAN ROYAL FAMILY MURDERED

**July 16, Siberia** The deposed Tsar of Russia, his wife, daughters and son were shot dead today by members of the Russian security police.

Tsar Nicholas II with his only son, Alexis.

# AIRCRAFT IMPROVING ALL THE TIME

**April 1, London, England** The Royal Flying Corps has been renamed the Royal Air Force (RAF). In 1914, Britain had only 272 aircraft, and the engines were made abroad. Today there are more than 22,000 planes, with British-made engines.

# WAR IS OVER AT LAST

**November 11, Forest of Compiegne, France** At 11 a.m. today, four years of continuous fighting ended. The Allies and the Germans signed an armistice agreeing a ceasefire. The guns are silent at last. The German Kaiser has abdicated and fled to Holland. Germany is now a republic.

Allied and German leaders, pictured here after signing the armistice that ended World War I. The agreement was signed in a railway carriage.

War graves on what was the Western Front, near Arras in France. One of the tasks facing Europe following the war is to erect lasting memorials to the millions of fallen soldiers.

# LLOYD GEORGE WINS ELECTION

**December 14, London, England** David Lloyd George's Coalition Party has won the general election and has 459 seats in Parliament. The prime minister told voters he wanted to make Britain "a land fit for heroes to live in". The main task of the new government will be to give jobs to soldiers returning from the war and to restore the economy.

# ANTI-WAR POET DIES IN FRANCE

**November 4, France** The British poet, Wilfred Owen, has been killed in action in France. He was 25 years old. Many young men have been taught that death in battle is a valiant and noble end. In one of his poems, Owen called this kind of teaching 'the old lie'. His poetry reflects war's stupidity and waste. Owen died just as the war was ending.

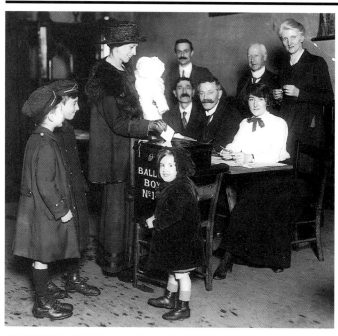

# WOMEN GAIN THE VOTE

**December 28, London, England** Women over the age of 30 have been allowed to vote for the first time in a general election. Suffragettes still want the voting age for women to be 21, as it is for men.

This woman, voting for the first time, has brought her young family with her.

# BITTER END

**November 11, France** An entry from a US army sergeant's diary reads: "Runner in at 10.30 with order to cease firing at 11 a.m. ... 306th Machine-Gun Company on my right lost twelve men at 10.55, when a high explosive landed in their position. At 11.00 sharp the shelling ceased on both sides ... we don't know what to say."

# NEWS IN BRIEF...
## MUSIC BAN

**November 30, New York, USA** During the time that the USA has been at war, the New York Symphony Orchestra has refused to play music by living German composers.

# SECRET ARMY?

**November, France** Around 200,000 African-American soldiers have served in the US army. Black US soldiers are segregated (separated) from white US soldiers. Most of the black soldiers have fought alongside the French army.

# 1919

# PEACE PROPOSALS

## USA SUGGESTS COUNCIL TO PREVENT WAR

**February 14, Paris, France** About three-quarters of the world's population is represented by leaders of 32 states at the Paris Peace Conference. The delegates are working out a treaty which they hope will avoid war in the future. The US president, Woodrow Wilson, has suggested that there should be a council to preserve the peace. It is likely to be called the 'League of Nations'.

# GERMANY MUST PAY

**May 7, Paris, France** The Treaty of Versailles has finally been agreed. President Wilson wants Europeans to forget the war and start afresh. But there is much bitterness in Europe. The treaty states that Germany started the war and says she must pay 'reparations' of about £6,600 million to the Allies.

# GERMANS APPALLED BY TREATY

**May 31, Paris, France** The German Chancellor refuses to sign the peace treaty, and has resigned. The Germans are horrified by the amount they must pay in reparations.

# FLEET SUNK AT SCAPA FLOW

**June 21, Scotland** German prisoners of war have sunk 70 of their own ships moored at a British naval base off the north coast of Scotland. The German admiral said that he was ordered never to surrender his warships.

German sailors arrive on shore after scuttling (sinking) their ship at the naval base, Scapa Flow.

# SILENT SIGNING OF TREATY

June 28, Paris, France Today two German representatives arrived at the Palace of Versailles. They entered the Hall of Mirrors, where the presidents of the USA and France, and the prime ministers of Britain and Italy sat in silence. The Germans signed the peace treaty and left without saying a word. The Treaty of Versailles has placed severe restrictions on Germany. It states that her army must be limited to 100,000 men, with no tanks, no heavy artillery and no poison-gas supplies.

The German delegation (carrying papers) at Versailles.

# EXTREMISM TAKES ROOT

January 15, Berlin Communists Rosa Luxembourg and Karl Liebnecht have been murdered. They led a group called the Sparticists, who tried to start a revolution. Germany is in chaos, and political parties with extreme views are springing up.

# POLAND WINS INDEPENDENCE

June 28, Warsaw, Poland The Treaty of Versailles has granted Poland independence. Poland has also been given a strip of land crossing German territory, which allows her access to the Baltic Sea.

# PROTEST IN CHINA

November 4, Peking The peace treaty has given Japan part of Shantung Province in China. This was once German territory. The decision has been accepted by the Chinese government, but 3,000 students have protested against it in Tiananmen Square.

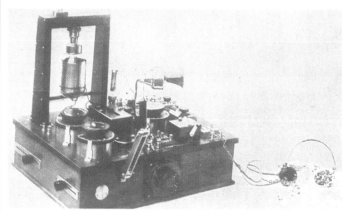

In March 1919, this wireless telephone was used to transmit signals from Ireland to Nova Scotia.

# ITALIAN HERO HOLDS FIUME

September 23, Italy The military leader Gabriele D'Annunzio has occupied Fiume in Yugoslavia with 2,000 men. D'Annunzio has popular support, but not the Italian government's approval.

# FASCISTS GAIN SUPPORT

October 31, Milan, Italy A journalist named Benito Mussolini has founded a new political party called the Fascists. After only seven months, it has a membership of 17,000.

---

# NEWS IN BRIEF...

## DIFFERENT THOUGHTS ON THE WAR

Autumn, France Georges Clemenceau said: "The terrible responsibility which lies at her [Germany's] doors can be seen in the fact that not less than seven million dead lie buried in Europe, while more than twenty million others carry upon them the evidence of wounds and sufferings..."

Captain E. N. Bennett of Britain said: "The fundamental falsehood on which the Versailles Treaty is built is the theory that Germany was solely and entirely responsible for the war. No fair-minded student of the war and its causes can accept this..."

# FIRST WOMAN MP

December 1, London, England Today Lady Nancy Astor took her seat in the House of Commons. She has been elected as MP for Plymouth.

Lady Nancy Astor, MP.

# NEW REPUBLICS

December 30 Since 1910, the former monarchies of Portugal, China, Russia, Austria and Germany have decided to elect leaders instead.

# RELATIVITY IS RIGHT

March 29, London, England The Royal Society of London has confirmed that the Theory of Relativity, formulated by physicist Albert Einstein, is correct.

Albert Einstein, the physicist.

# PEOPLE OF WORLD WAR I

**David Lloyd George, British politician 1863-1945**

Lloyd George entered Parliament as Liberal MP for Caernarvon, North Wales in 1890. From 1908 to 1915 he was chancellor of the exchequer. He was made minister of munitions (military equipment) in 1915, and became prime minister in 1916. Lloyd George was from a poor background and fought for social reform, such as health and unemployment benefits. He was an energetic war leader and attended the Paris Peace Conference.

**Jan Christiaan Smuts, South African leader 1870-1950**

During World War I, Smuts' forces attacked German colonies in East Africa. In 1917 he became a member of the Allied War Cabinet. He helped to create the RAF.

**Vladimir Ilyich Lenin , Russian leader 1870-1924**

Lenin was the leader of the Bolshevik Party in Russia. Following the 1917 revolution, Lenin ordered an armistice between Russia and the Central Powers. He organised a major part of the communist transformation of Russia, seizing land, businesses and property and placing them under government control.

**Woodrow Wilson, US politician 1856-1924**

Wilson was elected US president in 1912 and held this position until 1920. He tried to keep the USA out of World War I. But in 1917, when German U-boats continued to attack US ships, he finally asked the Senate to declare war. In 1919 Wilson was a leading figure at the post-war Paris Peace Conference, and proposed the idea of the League of Nations. He was awarded the 1919 Nobel Peace Prize.

**Kaiser Wilhelm II, German emperor 1859-1941**
Son of the Emperor Frederick and of a daughter of Queen Victoria. His strong character, national pride and personal vanity led other European leaders to regard him as warlike. The Kaiser took Germany to war in 1914, but he was forced to abdicate in 1918.

**Erich von Ludendorff, German general, 1865-1937**
General von Ludendorff took part in the first march into Belgium in 1914. He was transferred to the Eastern Front where he defeated General Samsonov at the Battle of Tannenburg. His military strategies brought about the defeat of the Serbians, and of the Italians at Caporetto. In 1918 Ludendorff planned the last great German offensive. When it failed, he asked the Kaiser to make peace. In October that year, he resigned his post and fled to Sweden.

**Emmeline Pankhurst, suffragette 1858-1928**
Mrs Pankhurst (maiden name, Goulden) was born in Manchester, England, and led the British suffragettes in their struggle to obtain voting rights. She was arrested and imprisoned several times for staging violent protests. During World War I she helped persuade women to go into industry and the armed services. Towards the end of her life, Mrs Pankhurst stood as a Conservative candidate for Parliament.

# GLOSSARY

**abdicate** to give up power

**Allies** In World War I, the Allies were Russia, France, Britain, Belgium and Serbia. They were later joined by 18 other states, including Japan and the USA.

**annexation** the taking over of territory, usually by conquest or military occupation

**Anzac** Australian or New Zealand soldier

**armistice** agreement to stop a war

**Balkans** the mountainous region of south-eastern Europe, between Hungary and Greece

**Bolshevik Party** Russian political party and original Communist Party

**capitalism** an economic system based upon private ownership of business and trade

**Central Powers** In World War I, the Central Powers were Germany, Austria and Turkey

**communist** a follower of communism, a political movement that states a country's wealth and government should be controlled by the people for the benefit of the people

**coup** seizure of power, usually by the armed forces, that results in a change of government

**covenant** a contract or agreement

**delegate** a representative at a conference or business meeting

**dynasty** a family of rulers

**dysentry** an infection of the gut

**Fascist** a supporter of the Italian political movement founded by Benito Mussolini. Fascists encouraged military strength and national pride and were anti-communist.

**fundamental** basic

**Great Powers** Before the outbreak of World War I, the five main powers were Russia, Austria, Germany, Britain and France

**physicist** an expert in physics, the branch of science concerned with the properties of matter and energy

**posthumous** after death

**radium** a radioactive metal

**reparations** financial compensation for war damage

**republic** a government headed by an elected president rather than a king or emperor born to be a ruler

**Sparticists** a political group, formed in Germany in 1916. In 1919 it became the German Communist Party.

**suffragettes** women who campaigned for the vote (suffrage)

# INDEX